BCL- 3rd ed.

# CAMBRIDGE LATIN AMERICAN STUDIES

GENERAL EDITOR

MALCOLM DEAS

ADVISORY COMMITTEE
WERNER BAER   MARVIN BERNSTEIN
RAFAEL SEGOVIA

35

# A SOCIOECONOMIC HISTORY OF ARGENTINA
## 1776–1860

For a list of books in this series please turn to page 303.

# A Socioeconomic History of Argentina, 1776–1860

JONATHAN C. BROWN

CAMBRIDGE UNIVERSITY PRESS

CAMBRIDGE

LONDON   NEW YORK   MELBOURNE

Published by the Syndics of the Cambridge University Press
The Pitt Building, Trumpington Street, Cambridge CB2 1 RP

Bentley House, 200 Euston Road, London NW1 2DB
32 East 57th Street, New York, NY 10022, USA
296 Beaconsfield Parade, Middle Park, Melbourne 3206, Australia

First published 1979

Printed in the United States of America
Typeset by Lexigraphics, Inc., New York, NY
Printed and bound by the Murray Printing Company, Westford, Mass.

*Library of Congress Cataloging in Publication Data*
Brown, Jonathan C., 1942 –
A socioeconomic history of Argentina, 1776–1860.
Includes bibliographical references and index.
1. Argentine Republic – Economic conditions.
2. Argentine Republic – Social conditions. I. Title.
HC175.B77    330.9′82    78–6800
ISBN 0 521 22219 2

For Lynore

# Contents

| | | |
|---|---|---|
| List of tables and figures | | *page* x |
| Preface | | xiii |

Introduction: Argentina in the era of traditional technology

| 1 | Silver and contraband in the colonial Río de la Plata | 9 |
|---|---|---|
| | *Rich in mules and prestige* | 10 |
| | *That refreshing herb liquor* | 14 |
| | *Towns and trade* | 16 |
| | *Of taxes and transport* | 18 |
| | *City of great deprivation* | 20 |
| | *A smuggler's journey* | 23 |
| | *Interest governs everything* | 25 |

| 2 | Buenos Aires in the Golden Age: the viceregal economy | 28 |
|---|---|---|
| | *Golden age of commerce* | 29 |
| | *The inevitable evil* | 31 |
| | *Rivers and cart trails* | 33 |
| | *From hunting to husbandry* | 35 |
| | *Ranching on the East Bank* | 41 |
| | *Hazards of new prosperity* | 46 |

| 3 | Industrial markets for Argentine raw materials | 50 |
|---|---|---|
| | *Tradition-bound industry* | 51 |
| | *Russets and black brogans* | 52 |
| | *Egg yolks and blind horses* | 54 |
| | *Swamp tanyards* | 55 |
| | *Importing "Buenosayres"* | 57 |
| | *Wool's take-off* | 58 |
| | *Mechanizing cheap wool* | 61 |
| | *Transported in grease* | 64 |
| | *Giant soap bars* | 65 |

| 4 | Buenos Aires as outpost of world trade | 69 |
|---|---|---|
| | *Horsecarts over the river bank* | 70 |
| | *Paperwork or protection* | 73 |
| | *Whittling the British share* | 74 |
| | *German flutes to penny whistles* | 77 |
| | *Balance of trade* | 80 |
| | *Attention to endless detail* | 84 |

| | |
|---|---|
| *A dearth of Spanish dollars* | 88 |
| *Making fortunes in a closed port* | 90 |
| *Falling prices — rising trade* | 92 |

| | | |
|---|---|---|
| 5 | Buenos Aires as emporium of regional trade and processing | 97 |
| | *Decks piled high* | 98 |
| | *Hide-roofed freight wagons* | 101 |
| | *Farm wagons to market* | 105 |
| | *Too-awful stench* | 109 |
| | *Disposal of offal* | 112 |
| | *Rainy-day leisure* | 114 |
| | *Creoles of great avidity* | 116 |
| 6 | Expanding the frontiers of production on the pampa | 123 |
| | *Carpet of fine verdure* | 124 |
| | *Production by zone* | 128 |
| | *At their own profit* | 131 |
| | *Fences twenty-four feet high* | 134 |
| | *Early morning risers* | 136 |
| | *From fuel to fleeces* | 138 |
| | *Bone plowing and horse threshing* | 140 |
| | *The common 2 percent* | 142 |
| 7 | Expansion of pastoral society on the pampa | 146 |
| | *No ordinary sight* | 147 |
| | *A great deal of land* | 149 |
| | *The legendary 30 percent* | 152 |
| | *Women and villagers* | 155 |
| | *When the gringos arrived* | 160 |
| | *Ranching in the family way* | 164 |
| | *The social economics of farming* | 168 |
| | *What is to be done?* | 170 |
| 8 | Formation of the Anchorena cattle business | 174 |
| | *A family of commerce* | 176 |
| | *Cattle with good meat* | 179 |
| | *Only God understands* | 184 |
| | *Imported shooting pistols* | 187 |
| | *Without bulls . . .* | 190 |
| | *Patriotism and sacrifice* | 194 |
| 9 | Depression and renaissance of commerce in the Interior provinces | 201 |
| | *Mines filled with rubbish* | 202 |
| | *Scattering about deserters* | 205 |
| | *Rawhide wheel rims* | 208 |
| | *Saladeros and graserías* | 212 |
| | *Wines tolerable but sweet* | 216 |
| | *Hand looms and ponchos* | 221 |

## Contents

Conclusion: the arrival of modern technology 225

*Appendix A:* *Conversion tables* 235
*Appendix B:* *The districts of the province of Buenos Aires and the zones*
*of production, 1838 and 1854* 236

*Notes* 237
*Selected bibliography* 287
*Index* 299

# Tables and figures

## Tables

1　Population growth in the Viceroyalty of the Río de la Plata, 1777−1809　*page* 36
2　British and American imports of Argentine hides, 1826−60　59
3　British and American imports of raw wool from the Río de la Plata, 1827−60　66
4　Foreign shipping entering the port of Buenos Aires, averaged annually by percentage, 1811−60　76
5　Average annual exports of pastoral goods from the port of Buenos Aires, 1811−60　80
6　Buenos Aires' exports as expressed in percentages of total yearly values, 1822−59　81
7　United Kingdom's balance of trade with Argentina, 1849−60　83
8　United States' balance of trade with the Río de la Plata, 1827−60　84
9　The regional river trade of Buenos Aires−Boca del Riachuelo, 1854　100
10　Registration and average size of new craft at Buenos Aires port, 1843−55　101
11　Delivery of overland freight at Buenos Aires, 1829　103
12　Wholesaling in the markets of Buenos Aires, 1828−60　106
13　Influence of drought cycle on Buenos Aires trade, politics, and Indian affairs　128
14　Rural production by zone for one-half year, 1854−5　130
15　Rural expansion in Buenos Aires Province by production zone　132
16　Rural retailing establishments in Buenos Aires Province, 1858　143
17　Ownership and rental of property in Buenos Aires Province, 1854　152
18　Balance sheet of the Estancia de las Palmas, San Pedro, 1846　155
19　Rural occupations in Buenos Aires Province, 1854　156
20　Population in village and countryside in Buenos Aires Province, 1858　156
21　Origin and sex of the rural population of Buenos Aires Province, 1854　157
22　Rural population of Buenos Aires Province by age group, 1854　157
23　Rural occupations among native- and foreign-born in Buenos Aires Province, 1854　163

# Tables and figures

24  Yearly accounting balance of the Obligado farm in Lomas de Zamora, 1866    171
25  Location and extent of the Anchorena family properties, 1830–64    182
26  Ownership of the Anchorena land by family inheritors in Buenos Aires Province, 1864    183
27  Purchase and sale of cattle on Estancias Camarones and Dos Yslas, 1821–31    184
28  Distances between Argentine cities on the principal post roads, 1830    208
29  Percentage of overland traffic between the Interior provinces and Buenos Aires, 1827–49    212
30  River traffic between Buenos Aires and the riverine provinces (expressed as percentages), 1810–60    213
31  Origin of overland freight arriving at Buenos Aires, 1829    220
32  Content and value of the Interior's freight arriving at Buenos Aires, 1836–42    221
33  Population growth of the Argentine provinces, 1809–69    222
34  Indicators of economic growth in Argentina, 1880–1914    230

## Figures

1  Regional trade routes of the colonial Río de la Plata    13
2  Index of real prices of pastoral products in Buenos Aires, 1833–50    93
3  Comparative prices of hides in Buenos Aires and Philadelphia, 1833–50    94
4  Frontier expansion in the province of Buenos Aires, 1797–1864    126
5  Subdivision of landed units in the district of Navarro, 1830–64    162
6  Approximate size and location of the Anchorena estancias in Buenos Aires Province, 1864    175

# Preface

Argentina's historical development is enigmatic. Were this not so, Argentines today would not be puzzled about how a past of much potential became a present of such disillusionment. The natural tendency, therefore, has been to restudy that past and to conclude that it did not contain as much potential as first imagined. In this line of historical writing, authors sometimes trace the present civil unrest directly to the "inequities" and "structural defects" of the nation's historical development. They say that the development of economic and social "dependency" in the nineteenth century formed the historical foundation for the recent confrontation between the military government and youthful revolutionaries. Growth and structure of the economy more than a century ago remains a controversial issue even today.

If the reader seeks in this book a confirmation of Argentina's past socioeconomic discrepancies, he or she may not be satisfied. I attempt here to analyze economic and social changes that occurred more than a century ago. I do not find those transformations to have been entirely negative in their portent. Nor am I able to trace so easily the problems of today's Argentina — particularly the political ones — to the economic and social solutions reached by nineteenth-century Argentines or to the import—export economy of that time. Nevertheless, even if more recent events have determined today's problems in Argentina, my story of nineteenth-century socioeconomic growth may be important for that very reason.

Every author of a historical treatise such as this one is indebted to innumerable patrons. My own debt extends to those who have collected and preserved source materials at the Archivo General de la Nación and the Museo Bartolomé Mitre in Buenos Aires, the Latin American Collection of the University of Texas, the New York City Library, and the Peabody Library of Harvard University. A Fulbright-Hays grant from the Department of Health, Education, and Welfare enabled me to complete a year's research in Buenos Aires. This manuscript is much improved for the encouragement and (constructive) criticism of Lynore Brown, my most prescient editor. She remains the only person who read the entire manuscript before it was sent to the publisher. (Is she, therefore, an accomplice?) Frank and Cynthia Brown and Max and Ethel Gruber encouraged me throughout the researching and writing of this book. Thomas F. McGann and W. W. Rostow offered wise counsel on the earliest and roughest drafts of the first eight chapters. Special thanks goes to Jason Brown who, as an aspiring editor, tore up an early draft of Chapters 1 and 2. They are better for the rewriting. Those who have helped me in Argentina and in the United States are (in alphabetical order): Luis A. Arocena, Carol Dack, Elsa Elías, Karl Graeber, Richard Graham, Donna Guy, Brenda and Garth Hemming, Diana Hernando, Ruth Kibrik, David Landes, Magnus Mörner, Juan Carlos Nicolau, Eduardo Saguier, Alberto Schwartz, Ron Seckinger, Tom Seidel, Susan Socolow, Steve Topik, John Tutino, and Carol Wood-Garces. Jane Tutino and Tom Eisenhower drew the maps, and personnel of the University of California, Santa Barbara, photo lab reproduced the pictures. My thanks to them all. I hope they are not disappointed with the results of their counsel and aid.

JCB

# Introduction: Argentina in the era of traditional technology

The 1860s mark a turning point in the socioeconomic development of the Río de la Plata region and, indeed, of much of Latin America. The railroad and other forms of new technology began to arrive in that decade. Within a half-century, modern modes of transportation and industry transformed economies and societies that had been developing and expanding along essentially traditional lines since the Spaniards first connected America to Europe by wooden sailing ships. Production and social relations in Latin America today bear little outward resemblance to those that existed before the appearance of iron rails and steam locomotives, even though many contemporary patterns were formed centuries earlier. Preindustrial economies were capable of growth despite the lack of modern means of production and power; for there is an important distinction between an expansion in income per capita and the absorption of new technologies. The former can happen under the right circumstances without the latter. Preindustrial societies also can expand, providing greater opportunities to share new wealth yet without disrupting traditional social relationships. Argentina in the late eighteenth and early nineteenth centuries provides the historian with an example of a region engaged in export-led growth with a remarkable degree of social and technological stability.

This study focuses on the twin aspects of Argentina's integration into the world economy − its markets and its production. I maintain that market demand, representing the trade possibilities of the time, was crucial for the type of economic activity that developed in the Río de la Plata. The salient issue in this investigation is the impact of market mechanisms on the methods of production, for the production of goods within a society often determines the possibilities for social expansion.

1

External markets were exceptionally important because the La Plata region had always been a fringe area. Possessing a small native and European population, it served as an economic appendage to other consuming areas. Argentina had spacious prairies in the Litoral, fertile valleys in the Interior, but isolated population centers throughout. (Constant reference will be made in this study to the two principal areas of the Río de la Plata. "The Litoral" refers to those areas of the coast, like the nation of Uruguay and the province of Buenos Aires, and those provinces served by river trade, Entre Ríos, Corrientos, and Santa Fe [the "riverine provinces"]. "The Interior" denotes all provinces served by overland transportation, from Córdoba to the Andes Mountains.) The landlocked market of Potosí in Upper Peru (today Bolivia) provided the original impetus for establishing the colonial economy. Settlements in the Interior supplied cattle, mules, and agricultural products to a mining region rich in silver but poor in arable lands. The second external market, the European trading community, was overseas and more expansive in nature. Toward the close of the colonial epoch, it all but overshadowed the landlocked market, thus heralding the rise of the Buenos Aires port complex and the Litoral's cattle industries. The industrial revolution in Britain and the United States later dominated the overseas market, as technological and concurrent manufacturing innovations necessitated greater quantities of raw materials from abroad. Scrutiny of these processes will explain their demand for pastoral products and their potential meaning for production in the Río de la Plata region. Because demand was translated through international shipping and commodity prices, we cannot ignore these linkages between consumers and suppliers in the world economy of that period.

The system of production on the pampa relates directly to markets. The *estancia* (cattle ranch) of the Litoral was the principal production unit, but the transportation network and processing industries cannot be excluded. They served as functions and corollaries of the whole system of export and provided jobs for a middling social stratum of entrepreneurs and laborers. In the La Plata region, the system consisted of overland freighting by oxcart, coastal and river shipping, the salting factories, the native merchants and warehousemen, and the foreign exporters. The estancia complex was rooted deeply in the soil of the colonial period, yet it displayed great flexibility when confronted in the nineteenth century by changes in market conditions. Clearly, the Argentine cattle ranch had to adapt to survive competitively in the world markets. A salient feature of the industrial revolution was the lower cost of its manufactures because of the application of technology and management to their production. Prices of raw materials such as hides and wool also fell, but cattle and sheep production in the Río de la Plata became more efficient under the pressure of these economic forces. Capital investment, expansion into virgin lands, estate management, marketing, and processing — but not new technology — all contributed to more efficient production.

Like the export trade, the acquisition of landed property in Latin America also has produced much scholarly controversy. Some historians attribute the dominance of large haciendas to a kind of sociopsychological lust for land by a native gentry. Landownership was the magical formula to acquire both social grace and the wealth to support the good life. This study confirms only that, for the cattleman, sound economic reasons existed for settling the virgin prairies with large landholdings. The nature of raising cattle, with the traditional rural technology and meager labor pools of the era, demanded expansive pasturages. Improved management techniques, however, tended to fractionalize large landholdings and to diffuse ownership. Sheep ranching and farming called for production on smaller landed units. Agriculture expanded onto the prairies in order to serve growing domestic markets. A vibrant economy also offers a variety of work and entrepreneurial possibilities, and Buenos Aires as well as most provinces of the region witnessed steady population increases starting from colonial times.

I propose to examine the entire market–production complex, not only through time, but also across oceans and national boundaries. I deal with political questions only cursorily. Social and economic growth in this time and place did not completely transcend politics and international tensions, but the economic plans of Bernardino Rivadavia and Juan Manuel de Rosas had little effect on how the region actually developed. The linkage between industrial demand and the raw materials producer more satisfactorily explains the timing, direction, and change in the socioeconomic history of Argentina in the era of traditional technology.

A socioeconomic study of any country in Latin America

must come to terms with that corpus of ideas known as "dependency theory." This inquiry, therefore, consciously attempts to accomplish three goals: (1) to describe the economic and social evolution of Argentina in the century before the first railroads were built; (2) to test in an empirical manner the historical tenets of dependency theory; and (3) if dependency does not apply, to ascertain which theoretical model corresponds to the Argentine experience. Here is a preview of my findings:

La Plata's society and economy depended upon export markets for their dynamism, yet it would be incorrect to place the region in the "dependency" or "neocolonial" mold of current theorists.[1] Dependent economic growth has come to signify the inequality and conflicts in economic development between the center (the industrial nations) and the periphery (the so-called Third World) of international capitalism. The periphery countries suffer constraints on their domestic development because of the overriding predominance of an export sector providing raw materials for the industrialized nations. In dependency theory, the economic soundness of the neocolonial country rests upon the fluctuating metropolitan demand for one or two export commodities. Independent, powerful, foreign merchants take up residence in the region in order to dominate foreign trade, exacting high prices for imported goods while buying raw materials cheaply. Because commerce is carried on foreign vessels, dependency theorists argue, the raw materials producing region, therefore, supports a consistent deficit in its trade balance with the industrial metropolis. Foreign capitalists make up the deficit by exporting profits back to the metropolis and by gaining control of a variety of local economic assets through foreign investment. The native oligarchy, which cooperates with the foreigner, meanwhile, begins to concentrate local economic enterprise and landownership in its hands. Opportunity thus is closed to many natives and immigrants, who come to form a pool of unskilled workers for the export sector and are forced to endure conditions of insecurity and oppression. Further commercial development of such a dependent economy only intensifies its "underdevelopment," a constant structural weakness of Latin America within the organization of international capitalism.[2] If nothing else, dependency theory deserves credit for identifying the issues of Latin America socioeconomic development.

Research into each phase of the dependency model remains difficult for Argentina, as well as for other Latin American regions, before roughly 1850. Economic and social statistics were kept sporadically — if at all. But research materials do exist. I utilized printed documents, manuscript collections, and travelers' accounts as the basis of two chapters on the colonial economy. For trade and production from the viceregal period to 1860, the extant sources are varied. Customs records, now on deposit at the Archivo General de la Nación (AGN) in Buenos Aires, recorded foreign and local trade at the port. Statistical records and printed matter of the United States and the United Kingdom pertain to their trade in Argentina as well as to the industrial transformation that opened up wider markets for Argentine raw materials. Printed travelers' accounts and document collections at the AGN reveal the marketing and production infrastructure of the region. Existing, if confusing, private account books and business correspondence offer glimpses of the operations of ranching and merchant activities, whereas rural censuses complete the outlines of production and society on the prairies.

In all cases, I caution the reader on the accuracy of the figures quoted from such disparate sources. The celebrated warning of Lord Acton comes to mind: Remember, the numbers we use often come from the village idiot! All figures and tables in this study are intended to demonstrate trends and tendencies. I have striven to make sure that the numbers are reasonably consistent, and have drawn conclusions from them only when their movement is so large as to override any likely inadequacy.

I find the dependency model wanting in important respects and conclude that Argentine history before 1860 more nearly conforms to the "staple theory" of economic growth. Staple theory provides a useful structure with which to analyze regional development where the export of staple products — that is, gold, silver, fur pelts, fish, wheat, sugar, tobacco, timber, coffee, guano, copper, beef, and so forth — carries the entire economy and society. Harold Innis and the Toronto School of economic history conceived and evolved formal staple theory in order to explain the economic and social development of Canada. Other scholars since have applied variations of the staple model to the historical development of the United States and of Africa.[3] Perhaps because staple theory in itself is not ideologically satisfying, it has been used only sparingly to describe the export economies of Latin America.[4] Yet, the importance of the linkages involved in a vigorous export sector has occurred to Argentine historians − especially those who have studied the agrarian expansion beginning in the late nineteenth century. Roberto Cortés Conde and Carlos F. Díaz Alejandro definitively point to the role of staple exports in developing railway building, absorption of new technologies, diversification of exports, population growth, urbanization, and nascent industrial development for all Latin America as well as Argentina. The complementary rather than conflicting relationship between staple exports and industrial expansion has struck Ezequiel Gallo, Guido de Tella, and Manuel Zymelmann. Gallo finds staple theory particularly helpful for its emphasis on the spread effects of staple exports and for its analysis of social development in an export economy.[5]

Briefly, staple theory assumes that the production of raw materials and foodstuffs for export becomes the dynamic sector of the region and thus sets the pace for socioeconomic development. Three situations predetermine the staple setting: first, the existence of a world market for and international trade in certain staple commodities; second, that the region enjoys a comparative advantage, having resources available for exploitation, in producing those staples; and third, that the production function (how the staple is produced) generates discernible characteristics in regional development. Foreign merchant vessels have had easy access to the Río de la Plata estuary since the late sixteenth century, when they first began to exchange slaves and merchandise for contraband silver from Potosí. The appetite of the industrial revolution for raw materials, among them hides and wool, initiated a new era of staple trade at Buenos Aires and, by 1820, native entrepreneurs had begun opening up the fertile grasslands to cattle and sheep raising. Thus, pastoral production, using the native techniques of the day, governed the spread of a thickening veneer of civilization over the pampa. The task of the historian remains to investigate the causal relationship of markets and production to socioeconomic development.

In staple theory, expansion of the export sector stimulates growth within the region's infrastructure and enlargement of entrepreneurial and labor opportunities. Analytically, the spread effects of staple production are classified as backward linkage, forward linkage, and final-demand linkage.[6] In backward linkage, increases in staple production tend to promote investment in the goods and services used in the export sector. Expansion of Argentina's traditional transport system — the mules, oxcarts, riverboats, and freight facilities that collected and distributed staple products — is one example of backward linkage. Forward linkage is that inducement to invest in the processing and marketing of staple goods. Formation of a complex of stockyards, slaughterhouses, marketplaces, and warehouses attests to the strength of the forward linkage in Argentina. Buenos Aires expanded as the marketing and processing center for the entire region, and the Interior provinces, recovering from civil war and from the loss of colonial markets in Potosí, directed their economic activity toward the Atlantic port. Final-demand linkage is defined as the enticement to develop secondary production to meet local consumer demands. The Argentine economy seems to have engendered a broader distribution of income than did the plantation economies of Cuba and Brazil. Considering the population growth and the spread of local production and commerce in domestic consumer goods, one might conclude that the export of staple products from the Río de la Plata did indeed stimulate growth in the domestic market.

Social diversification and opportunities in staple economics also revolve around the export base. The availability of domestic capital and the existence of local entrepreneurs enhances the possibilities of diversification. Some capital, entrepreneurs, and labor may have to be imported into those staple economies that lack one or more of these items. In Argentina before 1860, the technology necessary to exploit the virgin land did not have to be imported; cheap native technology sufficed. Therefore, native businessmen and ranchers, supported by some immigration of labor, were able to expand both staple production and secondary economic activities on the basis of profits that they themselves had made in international trade. In fact, creoles and immigrants — rather than foreigners — dominated marketing and processing at Buenos Aires. Despite formation of a group of wealthy ranchers, expansion of rural production and internal marketing enlarged entrepreneurial opportunity. In addition to the latifundios, landownership actually was fractionalized – not concentrated – and proprietorship was diffused to a broad base of ranchers and farmers. Both in the city and in the country, working conditions seem to have remained more favorable to the individual laborer than has been reckoned.

Prior to 1860, the export sector of the La Plata region did not subvert or constrict the development of the economic infrastructure. On the contrary, diversification and diffusion were characteristic of the staple export economy throughout the colonial and early national periods. Economic and social expansion in this underpopulated corner of the world, in fact, would have been retarded in the absence of a vibrant staple export sector.

# 1

## Silver and contraband in the colonial Rio de la Plata

The economy and society of the Río de la Plata region developed around the two great centers of colonial activity: first, Upper Peru's mining complex at Potosí; and later, the commercial port of Buenos Aires. The market demand of Potosí corresponded to the degree of mining exploitation. Silver production continued throughout the colonial period, and therefore those areas that supplied Potosí with staple produce maintained a corresponding economic growth and social development. Mules came from Córdoba and the Litoral, Paraguay sent native teas and Mendoza, wine and grain. Foreign luxury items and black slaves entered the regional market through Buenos Aires. Towns in between flourished on long-distance hauling and cattle driving, whereas those in closest proximity to Potosí prospered from sales of agricultural products and from the great mule trade.

However, the inelasticity of Upper Peru's landlocked market limited growth in the surrounding regions. Potosí's population and consumption fluctuated according to the output of silver production, as did its demand for goods. Historians often point to an additional hindrance — the prohibitive Spanish regulations and taxes on internal commerce within the American colonies. Actually, royal edicts did not govern colonial economic activity as much as did native methods of producing and transporting staple commodities. Moving goods by oxcart and livestock on foot across the expansive plains was slow and costly.

The rise of a commercial port at Buenos Aires hardly meant the doom of the Potosí trading community. Buenos Aires served as an important (albeit illegal) center for the exportation of Peru's silver and as a port of entry for European luxury items desired in Potosí. Commerce in the form of contraband proceeded throughout the colonial period despite official restrictions. The absence of figures prevents accurate knowledge of the true extent of smuggling, but re-

9

ports and complaints of government officials reveal both the widespread importance of smuggled goods and the economic necessities giving rise to illegal trade. Entrepreneurs and tradesmen of the Interior benefited from the passage of both legal and illegal commerce along the established cart, mule, and river routes. Officialdom's prohibitions on smuggling proved ineffectual in this corner of the Spanish world.

Nevertheless, Buenos Aires was a different type of market than Potosí, international rather than regional. Representing an expanding Atlantic trading community, the *porteño* market (the Buenos Aires port market) therefore proved inherently more flexible. In addition to silver, Buenos Aires gradually became a source of pastoral products scarce in populous Europe. The port admitted the ships of each changing generation of European trading masters, beginning in 1600 with the Portuguese and continuing with the Dutch and British into the 1700s. The fall of one trading nation did not spell the decline of Buenos Aires, for this Spanish-American port offered the staple export that they all wanted and needed for their world trade – Potosí's silver bullion. In a way, the port's early development depended upon and complemented the growth of the Potosí mining complex.

### Rich in mules and prestige

From the mid–sixteenth century to the end of the eighteenth century, Potosí was the silver-mining capital of the world. Its fabulous mountain of high-grade silver ore attracted a transient mining population that, at times, numbered more than 100,000. The largest number of residents consisted of Indian laborers brought to the mines under the rotational work system called the *mita.* By 1700, however, mining operations had drawn a large number of more or less permanent workers comprised of mestizos, Basques, Genoese, and Portuguese. Although most workers camped on the outskirts of the city, Spanish officials, merchants, and clergymen, numbering anywhere from a quarter to a third of the population, inhabited permanent buildings downtown.[1] In this city, Spaniards minted a large but fluctuating part of the world's supply of silver coins for approximately 260 years. Official calculations of tax revenues show that silver production varied from a high of 7.5 million *pesos* (a silver dollar coin; for detailed definition and conversion table, see Appendix A) annually in the 1590s to a low of 1 million in the 1730s. Production returned to nearly 4 million pesos yearly in the late eighteenth century.[2] These figures do not account for the contraband mining of silver ore — perhaps large but certainly unmeasurable.

Without the silver mines, however, no one ever would have established such a city in this Andean wasteland. The entire district lies between 3,360 and 4,760 meters above sea level with few trees or grass, let alone crops, within a radius of 35 kilometers. Provisions for the population and supplies for the mines had to be hauled in over the sierras. Each day, the roads leading to Potosí were choked with mule trains, llamas, Indian pack carriers, and herds of sheep and cattle. Mercury and imported goods came from Lima, potatoes and coca from Lower Peru (today the nation of Peru), vegetables and coarse cloth from elsewhere in Upper Peru, wheat from Chile and Tucumán, mules and cattle from Córdoba, wines from Mendoza and *yerba mate* (a native tea) from Paraguay. High transport costs raised the price of foodstuffs in Potosí to twice the price of victuals anywhere else in the region. In a terrain that forbade wheeled vehicles, mules transported the ninety-kilogram loads of silver and mercury. High mortality rates in the Andean and desert wastes necessitated constant resupply of these pack animals.[3] Still, the static level of the mining production at Potosí placed a ceiling on market activity in the region.

The Potosí market sustained the original settlement of the Interior, supporting groups of Spanish settlers who intended to establish their lifelines to the silver city of Upper Peru. By the close of the sixteenth century, Spaniards in the Río de la Plata already had connected the centers of population and their fertile agricultural environs to the market at Potosí. From Upper Peru, Europeans first descended to settle Santiago del Estero in 1553 and Tucumán twelve years later. Córdoba's foundation in 1573 extended the land route to the edge of the Argentine pampa, whereas the establishment of Salta and Jujuy closer to the highland markets secured the road to Potosí in 1583. Mendoza and San Juan, founded in 1561, tied the Río de la Plata to prior Spanish settlements in Chile. Meanwhile, Spaniards from the Paraguayan settlement at Asunción went down the Paraná River to secure towns at

Corrientes in 1558 and at Santa Fe fifteen years later. Then Paraguayan colonists, after an earlier failure forty years before, finally gained a lasting foothold on the estuary at Buenos Aires in 1580. Settlement of the Río de la Plata had its economic justification in the supply of Potosí. (See Figure 1.)

The first objective was to organize trade over the lengthy transport routes, so that each distant town contributed its produce to Potosí free of interference from intractable Indians. Córdoba lay at the edge of the pampa as a beacon of European civilization between two hostile wastelands. To the north extended the Gran Chaco, home of Indians whom the Spaniards neither conquered nor assimilated. To the south, bands of seminomadic Pampa Indians continued to threaten trade routes, resisting Spanish encroachments into the vast Argentine plains from a line running south of Mendoza to the area directly southwest of Buenos Aires. As long as production for the inelastic market of Upper Peru demanded no further settlement, these Indians were safe from conquest. Spanish authorities, interested primarily in protecting the long commercial lifelines, were content to erect a thin line of poorly garrisoned forts on the Indian frontier.[4]

Befitting its position at the gateway to Potosí, Salta became the foremost commercial town of the Interior. Its principal attraction was the famous mule fair. Each February and March, the fair attracted hundreds of buyers from Peru and equal numbers of sellers of mules, corn, cattle, wines, jerked beef, tallow, and wheat. The chief staple product in this trade was the mule, so necessary for transporting mercury and silver through mountain passes. In support of this annual commercial event, ranches for pasturing cattle and mules dotted the countryside around Salta. At the end of the colonial era, yearly sales of mules varied from 11,000 to 46,000 animals.[5] Commerce at Salta depended on production in Córdoba and Paraguay. Consumer goods from these locales flowed to market through an integrated commercial pipeline of riverboats, oxcarts, and mule trains, which featured numerous customs-collection points and not a little contraband. The extended overland routes united in the same economic complex the faraway localities of Mendoza, at the base of the Andes Mountains, and Buenos Aires, the port to the Atlantic Ocean.

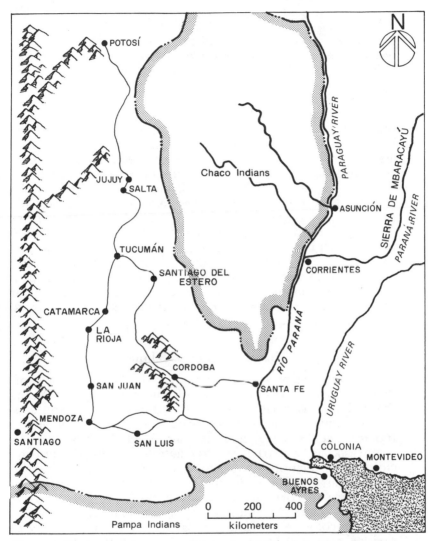

Figure 1. Regional trade routes of the colonial Río de la Plata. Development of extended cart trails between Buenos Aires and the mining region of Potosí was the distinctive feature of the colonial economy. Oxcarts transported silver from the highlands to the port. Carts laden with imported luxury goods and domestic foodstuffs and textiles — as well as mules and cattle — traveled to markets in the Interior. (Map by Tom Eisenhower, based on Archivo General de la Nación, Buenos Aires, Sección Mapoteca, *Esquema del Virreinato del Río de la Plata, 1796.)*

Before the establishment of the viceroyalty in 1776, Córdoba served as the administrative and religious capital of the colonial Río de la Plata. Its 40,000 residents in 1777 made Córdoba the most populous district in the region.[6] Cattle and mule production supported the city's prestige and importance. Spaniards (and Portuguese too) settled on cattle- and mule-breeding estancias on the lush pampa to the east. In the late 1700s, breeders in the Córdoba District alone produced about 8,000 mules a year.[7] By the eighteenth century, livestock production had stretched well out onto the plains leading to Santa Fe, Entre Ríos, and Buenos Aires, but Córdoba remained the trading focus of the livestock industry for the entire pampa area. Córdoba's merchant community flourished, eventually dealing in 30,000 mules and 600,000 pesos worth of commerce annually by 1657.[8] Merchant factors from Córdoba came to Buenos Aires to buy mules and cattle from local breeders and had them driven overland to Córdoba, Tucumán, or Salta, where the herds wintered prior to the next year's fair. In Potosí, livestock brought up to three times the original price per head.[9]

### That refreshing herb liquor

The other great production center in this far-reaching commercial network was located 1,780 kilometers up the Paraná River. Paraguay existed on the very administrative and economic fringe of the Spanish Americas. A group of gentle Indians, the Guaraní, had first attracted the Spaniards to Asunción, and a patriarchal civilization developed featuring close family relationships between the few Europeans and the many Guaranís. The economic base consisted of subsistence agriculture in corn, manioc, sweet potatoes, cotton, rice, sugar cane, tobacco, and later livestock. Having little to export, the colonists in Paraguay participated insignificantly in regional trade until they discovered that a leaf found only on trees growing in Paraguay's rain forests could be used to make a distinctive and flavorful beverage. Yerba mate soon gained favor among the inhabitants of southern South America, and Paraguay became integrated into the regional trading community. Most of the yerba traffic officially flowed through Asunción downriver to Santa Fe, and thence overland to markets either in Chile, Upper Peru, or Lima. Buenos

Aires residents alone consumed approximately 284 tons each year in the mid−eighteenth century.[10] Paraguay's yerba trade boomed from an annual export of 681 metric tons in 1680 to 1,136 in 1756, 2,273 in 1798, and 3,409 before Independence in 1810.[11]

Merchants in Santa Fe and later in the bustling commercial metropolis of Buenos Aires controlled the yerba trade out of Paraguay because they had the necessary commercial contacts to sell the staple successfully in distant markets. Buenos Aires traders spoke for each year's crop before the harvest. Little currency reached Paraguay, because the merchants preferred to pay in kind with goods like knives, scissors, ribbons, taffeta, silk, hats, and coarse native cloth. Yerba exchange took place in the city of Santa Fe, midway downriver between Asunción and Buenos Aires. Merchants then sent the staple overland to markets like Potosí, sometimes selling it there for 300 percent over the original cost at Santa Fe.[12] Profits on yerba sales were not that high, for merchants had to pay freight rates and customs duties all along the trade routes.

The demand for yerba mate throughout the Río de la Plata, impressive as it was, did not compel the transformation of Paraguay's early production methods. The operation remained one of collection, not systematic cultivation. Paraguayan patriarchs in Asunción sent out their Indian retainers to gather yerba in its natural state in the forests of the Sierra de Mbaracayú, 240 to 320 kilometers east of Asunción. These parties roasted leaves and stems on wooden beams laid crosswise over the fire. The residue then was crushed to make *yerba de palos.* This civilian production required many mules and oxen and thousands of men. At least 85 percent of Paraguay's yerba exports was in this common herb tea.[13] Meanwhile, the Indians on the thirty-two Jesuit missions produced the finer *yerba caaminí,* meticulously separating the leaves from the stems before roasting. This product brought twice the price of the common sort. Moreover, the Jesuits cut into the civilian trade from Asunción, because the missions between the Paraná and Uruguay rivers sent yerba directly to Santa Fe without paying taxes at the capital.[14] Yerba collection proved not only a primitive method of production, but a dangerous one as well. Frequent incursions of the legendary *bandeirante* slave hunters from São Paulo, Brazil, had forced temporary abandonment of the

Mbaracayú and the yerba village of Villa Rica in the mid–seventeenth century. Nonetheless, Paraguay's export of yerba reached a value of nearly 300,000 pesos a year in 1790, more than two-thirds the value of all staples exported from this corner of the Spanish-American Empire.[15]

Paraguay's other export products, tobacco, wood, and sugar, did not gain the prominence of yerba in colonial markets. The reason is quite simple — they never benefited from a similar captive market. These products grew elsewhere; yerba did not. Although the tobacco trade became a royal monopoly during the viceroyalty, authorized yearly production of 511 tons never was met. In 1803. for instance, the royal tobacco factory collected only 200 tons from more than 1,500 independent producers.[16] Paraguayan exports simply had too many competitors on regional markets. Peruvian tobaccos supplied Potosí and even sold briskly in Salta. Litoral markets from Buenos Aires to Cordoba received contraband tobaccos from Cuba and Brazil. Likewise, Paraguayan sugar products only supplemented the major sources of colonial sugars from Brazil, Cuba, and Salta.[17] Without the staple of yerba, Paraguay would not have been integrated into the Potosí trading community.

## Towns and trade

Potosí's market stimulus provided the commercial basis for the initial formation of trade routes extending thousands of kilometers across mountains and plains. Tucumán and Santiago del Estero, both midway between the Córdoba producing area and the Salta fairs, were important trading intermediaries in the colonial epoch. Santiago found early prominence as a center of exchange, boasting of some forty plazas for trade. According to a trade summary of 1677, the commodities that passed through Santiago on the way to Potosí included 40,000 head of cattle, 30,000 mules, and 227 tons of yerba.[18] Tucumán eventually supplanted Santiago as the important commercial intermediary. Beginning as a village that produced Indian cloth, in the mid–seventeenth century the city turned to the mule traffic, its merchants buying mules in Córdoba and selling them at the Salta fairs. But the dominant economic concern eventually became oxcarting. Estancias in the area specialized in breeding and breaking oxen for the great cart trains passing between Jujuy, Córdoba, and Buenos Aires. Toward the end of the colonial period, Tucumán's cart-building industry brought in 70,000 pesos annually.[19] Jujuy also depended on the Potosí trade. With its position on the road between Salta and the highland valleys, the town was destined to become the terminus of the overland cart route from Buenos Aires and Córdoba. Teamsters had to transfer their freight to muleback there for the trek up the rocky trails leading to Upper Peru.[20]

The commercial route that formed a great arch from Potosí south to Córdoba turned east to connect with the Paraná River at the commercial settlement of Santa Fe. This river town served as the link between Paraguay's production center and its markets. Paraguay sent its staples downriver in canoes, rafts, boats, and sailing barks. Santa Fe served as the gateway to the Córdoba–Potosí land route as well as to the Mendoza–Chile trail. Either Paraguayan products were transferred there to mule trains and oxcarts for the arduous journey to those markets, or they were sent on to Buenos Aires for consumption. Santa Fe also benefited somewhat from trade originating at Buenos Aires. Not only did porteño merchants ship goods 400 kilometers upriver in exchange for yerba, but they also sent along imported foreign goods for transshipment to Salta and Potosí.[21]

Mendoza was the commercial link between the Río de la Plata and the secondary market at Santiago de Chile. Although *mendocinos* engaged in viticulture as an auxiliary economic activity, commerce remained foremost. In Mendoza, goods from Buenos Aires and Paraguay were transferred from oxcarts to packmules to be conducted across 260 kilometers of Andean passes in week-long jaunts during the South American summer. The return trip might bring Chilean grains and goods from Potosí. Mendoza's wines, like the grape *aguardiente* (brandy) of San Juan, found markets in the other direction at Córdoba and Buenos Aires. But the wines of the Andes foothills only supplemented what those markets lacked in both liquors in their overseas trade with Europe. Andean wines, therefore, encountered the same problem that plagued Paraguayan tobaccos and sugars – lack of a captive market. Overland freighting and original production costs made the wines of the Interior twice as expensive in Buenos Aires as European wines and Brazilian brandy. Mendoza's wine often arrived in poor condition, evaporated a bit from the long overland journey.[22]

On the extensive trade routes between the great market and production areas, travelers found auxiliary services — roadhouses, remounts, forage, and country stores. Farmers along the roads provided teamsters with lambs, pullets, eggs, squash, and watermelons. Persons made a living from ferrying goods across the larger streams, furnishing oxhide tubs and swimming horses for baggage and passengers alike.[23] These services completed the regional trading complex of the colonial era.

## Of taxes and transport

Much has been made about the deleterious effect of Spanish colonial taxes on the production and movement of goods in the Spanish-American colonies. Félix de Azara, a true son of the Enlightenment, seems to have originated the prevalent opinion that Spanish monopolistic practices and mercantilist policies impeded production and supply.[24] Historians have followed his lead by detailing the numerous official decrees on restriction and monopoly. But seldom in this era did economics respond to edicts.

The royal administration as well as municipalities did indeed tax the transport of goods from producer to consumer. In the last quarter of the sixteenth century, the dry customs at Santiago del Estero charged one *real* (one-eighth of a peso) on each cow and mule that passed through town. At a later date, Tucumán charged two and one-half pesos for mules, and as much per *zurrón* (an oxhide bag containing roughly 83 kilograms) of yerba. Asunción, Buenos Aires, and Santa Fe generally taxed goods entering and leaving their jurisdictions. Municipal officials used customs revenues to defend themselves and the commercial system against Indian attack. Moreover, consumers paid an *alcabala,* or royal sales tax, which in Buenos Aires amounted to about six reales per zurrón of yerba.[25] Royal authorities first established the king's customshouse at Córdoba and charged 50 percent ad valorem tax duties on imported goods coming from Buenos Aires. Failing to stop the import of foreign goods and the illegal export of silver through the region, the royal customshouse was removed to Jujuy in 1695.[26]

The entire tax system in the colonial Río de la Plata was

hardly as efficient as we today may suppose. Official reports
are replete with complaints of tax evasion by merchants. In
an expansive and underpopulated region, contraband and tax
evasion were simple matters, and bribery of officials a cus-
tomary practice. High prices in Potosí made it uneconomical
*not* to engage in deception now and then. Concolorcorvo
understood this when he wrote that mule dealers in Salta
deliberately underestimated the size of their herds by 15
percent in order to avoid sales taxes.[27] One can only conclude that the internal customs and sales taxes did raise the
prices that consumers paid for products of the region. Yet
they were not the only cause of high prices.

Expensive overland freighting added much more to consumers' cost. River shipping, oxcarting, and muleteering —
all tradition-bound modes of transportation — had to cover
long distances between producer and consumer. La Plata oxcarts were of the distinctive Spanish medieval model, made
only of wood and rawhide and drawn on two huge wheels by
six oxen. The average oxcart carried up to 150 arrobas (1.7
metric tons) of cargo in a wooden bed covered by a canopy of
hides. The plains offered flat, long passage. Forage for oxen
grew abundantly almost everywhere, and provisions for
teamsters and remounts could be had at post stations along
the way. The great drawback, of course, was the slow speed
and the immense distance to markets. The Buenos
Aires–Jujuy route alone covered approximately 2,340
kilometers of cart trail. Traveling at a rate of 33 kilometers
per day and counting stopovers or transshipments, a caravan
could not cover the distance in less than three months.[28]
Freight rates in the carting industry equaled about 1 peso per
arroba (11.4 kilograms) between Buenos Aires and Jujuy, so
that maximum charges could be as high as 150 pesos per cart.
Mendoza's muleteers charged 5 to 6 pesos per animal, because the load capacity of one mule was only 7 to 8 arrobas,
less than 90 kilograms.[29]

Riverboats plying the trade out of Asunción were small,
twelve to fourteen tons burden at most. They took two
months to pass down the Paraná River to Buenos Aires and
another three months, propelled by sails and oars, to return
upriver. It was said that, because of freight charges and taxes,
imported goods in Asunción cost 30 percent more than in
Buenos Aires. On the downriver trade, for instance, boatmen
charged one peso per arroba of yerba and from two to eight

reales per *vara* (0.8 meter) of lumber.[30] At those rates, river freight charges alone might have constituted 25 percent of the price of yerba and lumber in Buenos Aires.

Evidence exists to indicate that the chief drawback to expansion of the regional trading community was its reliance on native transport technology. In 1972, porteño merchants like Gaspar de Santa Coloma were paying taxes equaling up to 35 pesos per cartload on one-way caravans from Buenos Aires to Jujuy. Their freight bills were four times greater, about 135 pesos per cartload. Wagon charges between Buenos Aires and Mendoza equaled half that amount. Bulkier native goods thus were expensive to sell in distant, overland markets. Freight charges on yerba mate, for instance, might add 60 percent of value to its selling price in Salta and Jujuy. High-value items like imported silk and cotton cloth cost only about 2 percent of value to move inland via oxcart.[31] Costs of carriage aboard the slow-moving native oxcarts certainly were much more prohibitive than the king's taxes. A merchant might evade customs duties – but never freight charges.

The landlocked regional market of Potosí, in which the consuming population rose steadily but not spectacularly, seriously limited socioeconomic growth in its producing area of the Río de la Plata. Sales of mules, cattle, and foodstuffs fluctuated according to mining output at Potosí. Moreover, traditional technology not only limited production in the mines and yerba forests but also encumbered commerce of goods from producer to consumer. Upper Peru's consumption ultimately fell off when mining gave out during the Wars of Independence, and the economic repercussions of the mining decline would be felt in the nineteenth century. But another market, which offered greater economic possibilities, was developing throughout the colonial period. This market was a trading community as expansive as overseas shipping in the Atlantic Ocean. On the estuary of the Río de la Plata, the terminus of international shipping came to be a town called Ciudad de la Santísima Trinidad y Puerto de Santa María de los Buenos Aires.

### City of great deprivation

Many historians share the view that, prior to the establishment of Buenos Aires as capital of the viceroyalty in 1776, the port city was of little account. This view underestimates the extent of contraband. In 1600, Buenos Aires may have been a humble village, but within 150 years it had become one of the greatest commercial centers of Spanish America. Reason: Its geographical-commercial position was strategic. Soon after the city's establishment in 1580, merchants from Córdoba quickly took advantage of the port as the funnel of trade with Brazil, sending cartloads of native textiles down to the estuary for embarkation on a twenty-day journey by boat to the coast of Brazil. Yet, early in the colonial period, Buenos Aires' residents consumed little of the Interior's staple products and few of the imported goods like Portuguese and Castilian cloth.[32] The city's immediate economic importance lay in commercial exchange — illegal exchange at that.

That Buenos Aires should serve as a South American gateway for foreign imports did not fit the empire's mercantilist concepts. Spanish merchants monopolized New World trade at the Iberian port of Seville, where goods were to be embarked yearly via a *flota* of merchant galleons. These great fleets crossed the Atlantic to the Caribbean port of Portobello, scene of the annual Panamanian trade fair. Then goods passed overland via mule train to Panama City and thence by ship down the Pacific coast to Lima. The official system acknowledged only trade via Lima, overland to Potosí, and then down the extended trade route through Salta to Córdoba. Spanish-American gold and silver was to return to Spain along the same route. In this manner, Spanish officials protected the transport of goods and bullion from foreign privateers while taxing it along the way. But the fleet system did not work as effectively as royal officials had conceived. Scarcity and high prices led to smuggling in many areas of Spanish America.[33] At Buenos Aires, access to the sea and distance from the official distribution centers made contraband a more profitable and sensible alternative for meeting the economic needs of the colonists.

Obviously exaggerated reports from the Río de la Plata, for instance, emphasized the need for direct trade through the estuary. Correspondents described Buenos Aires (ca. 1600) as a city of great deprivation. People lacked what they thought were the necessities of life: European clothing, wine, oil, and even arms and ammunition to defend themselves.

What goods did get through the uncertain Lima—Potosí pipeline were generally faulty and sold at prohibitive prices. Spanish woolens, going for 2.5 pesos in Spain, sold at 20 pesos in Buenos Aires.[34] By the same token, porteño correspondents complained that they could hardly pay for Castilian products if their own hides and tallow had to be exported over the Andes Mountains. Price differentials seemed to be on the side of freer trade. An estimated 12,500 pesos of La Plata products — hides, tallow, butter, dried meats, wheat, and native cloth — brought 25,000 pesos elsewhere.[35]

Nevertheless, official trade concessions came begrudgingly and as weak solutions for the economic desires of porteño consumers. After 1617, two vessels were "permitted" to traffic in Brazil and Seville, but they were to be no larger than 300-tons burden (a stricture often ignored) and they were to carry no silver (always violated). Authorities also recognized the right of vessels "in distress" to put in at Buenos Aires for repairs without privilege to trade.[36] Moreover, the crown throughout the colonial era granted slave-trading contracts to foreign companies and merchants. Each small concession led to trade abuses of fantastic proportions in this portion of the empire.

In the end, Spanish officials were powerless to stop contraband. Royal authorities in Buenos Aires occasionally tried to curb the illegal trade, but containment of smuggling along the coastline of the Río de la Plata estuary was difficult. Local Spanish officials often chose an alternative of greater personal profit: to participate wholeheartedly in the illegal trade. Porteño governors freely granted permission to foreign and unlicensed ships to put in at Buenos Aires. Lacking proper import—export figures for clandestine commerce, population growth instead may reveal its importance to this commercial city. For a port officially allowed only minimal trade on two to four permission ships a year, Buenos Aires' growth was spectacular. Its population doubled on an average of once every thirty-one years between 1615 and 1770:[37]

| | |
|---|---|
| 1615 | 1,000 |
| 1639 | 2,070 |
| 1674 | 4,607 |
| 1720 | 8,908 |
| 1750 | 13,840 |
| 1770 | 22,551 |

## A smuggler's journey

Silver was a valuable commodity in European commerce. Spanish specie facilitated the growing commercial exchange between Europe and distant markets in the Levant and the East Indies. As long as Spain's colonies produced the world's largest portion of silver, the Iberian port of Cádiz attracted European ships in large numbers. But direct contraband with New World sources proved the more profitable method of obtaining silver for Portuguese, Dutch, and British shippers. Traders from Portugal became the first in a long succession of foreigners who found a commercial haven at Buenos Aires. Portuguese traders even settled permanently in the city, where they enjoyed considerable influence, intermarrying with families of the king's worthiest town councilors. Their hottest line consisted of African slaves from the Guinea coast. In 1595, the royal grant of the *asiento* (an exclusive contract to sell slaves in the Spanish colonies) aided Portuguese traders in both their legal and illegal dealings. They were to bring only 600 slaves to the Río de la Plata each year in exchange for flour, cloth, jerked beef, hides, and tallow.[38] Smuggling silver, however, consumed much of their effort.

Portuguese smugglers and Spanish officials seemed to have perfected very early their commercial subterfuges. Documents dating from 1599 mention the confiscation of merchandise and black slaves of numerous traders who neglected to secure proper license. These slaves then were sold at public auction by local authorities.[39] As it turned out, the merchants were in collusion with the authorities, and they bought back their confiscated slaves for nominal sums, thus gaining official sanction to sell their human merchandise in the Interior. In the early 1600s, 1,000 slaves entered the Río de la Plata each year under legal and illegal circumstances. These same traders might shroud their illegal exports of silver by buying permits to export wheat, drief beef, or tallow to Brazil. Instead, they often loaded silver for direct delivery to Portugal.[40] In the 1620s, silver specie left this little port of call at an estimated rate of 100,000 pesos each year. Illegal export of bullion tempted even those officials dispatched to this part of the empire to stop such contraband.[41] Although silver and slaves were the principal items of this clandestine commerce, Córdoba and Tucumán merchants participated by sending cartloads of staple products to Buenos Aires for export. Hides, wheat, dried meats, tallow, and domestic woolen and cotton cloth also arrived via oxcarts. For their part, shippers from Brazil and Portugal brought wines, iron ware, sugar, Castilian and Dutch woolens, preserved fish, and quince preserves.[42]

Dutch commerce gained ascendancy at the port of Buenos Aires in the second half of the seventeenth century, and Dutch smugglers turned out to be as adept at the art of clandestine trade as their Portuguese predecessors. Many Dutch ships landed their richest cargoes on the coastline below Buenos Aires before coming to anchor at the port, where customs officials inspected the bulkier and less valuable goods. Nor did these good Protestant merchants neglect to trade with their Jesuit brethren, reputed to have the largest storehouses of silver and gold in the city.[43] The Castilian monarch knew of the contraband commerce at Buenos Aires. In 1672, Carlos II denounced porteño officials who enriched themselves on smuggling while failing to send customs duties to the royal treasury. He was annoyed that Potosí's merchants preferred commodities landed at the Atlantic port, although he admitted that Buenos Aires' imports to the Interior were one-half the price of whatever goods came over the Andes from the official port at Lima.[44] Meanwhile, cattlehides were becoming an increasingly popular staple commodity at Buenos Aires. A royal permission ship arriving at the port in 1656 found that it had to share anchorage with twenty-two Dutch and two British ships that were "laden homewards with Bullshides," as well as with silver plate.[45]

Nothing illustrates more completely the lax attitudes and ingrained evasions that piqued the crown authorities than the commercial venture of Ácarete du Biscay. In 1657, this French priest was a partner in a merchant adventure aboard an official permission ship. After landing a cargo of European goods at Buenos Aires, he traveled inland to sell his goods at Potosí, where his buyers paid him in silver. Du Biscay loaded his specie along with some alpaca wool onto mules for the trip down to Jujuy, where he transferred the cargo to oxdrawn wagons for the four-month journey to Buenos Aires. Back at the port, du Biscay and his associates decided upon private embarkation of the silver — after all, it was illegal to export specie from Buenos Aires even on a permission ship. Having already stowed away hides from the pampa and alpaca wool from the highlands, they took aboard a clandestine shipment of silver just before the vessel raised anchor. Rather than heading for the official port at Cádiz, the vessel put in along the northern Spanish coast at Coruña. A portion of the cargo was transferred to a Dutch ship, and the rest was taken to France. Du Biscay and his associates ultimately declared a profit of 250 percent on the transaction — largely because they had avoided the royal customs officials whenever possible.[46]

## Interest governs everything

Great Britain's rising military and economic power in the eighteenth century gained for British traders a commercial supremacy over the Dutch in the Río de la Plata. The Treaty of Utrecht in 1715, ending the War of Spanish Succession, extended the coveted asiento to the British South Seas Company. With the right to maintain slave-trading posts in several American ports, English merchants in Spanish America could import 4,800 slaves per year in exchange for goods and bullion, paying the Spanish Crown a quarter of all profits.[47] The Buenos Aires station had up to six British commercial agents and a warehouse that supplied slaves for trade to Potosí, Chile, and even Lima. Between 1715 and 1739, 61 asiento ships arrived at Buenos Aires with some 18,400 Africans from Guinea, 3,771 of whom eventually reached the Chilean market.[48] The asiento trade benefited the nascent pastoral industries of Buenos Aires, for more foreign shippers in the estuary began loading hides and tallow to complement their cargoes of silver. Exports from the port increased from 45,000 hides in 1716 to approximately 380,000 in 1733.[49]

The British slave and hide trade did not overstep the treaty agreement so much as did the trade in merchandise. Asiento traders were allowed to import slaves only and not British goods that would compete with Spain's exports. Contraband again was the common practice, and British factors turned to the time-honored custom of conspiring with local authorities. Slave ships always carried merchandise that factors could sell if they shared up to 25 percent of the profits with local officials. For example, South Sea Company factors perfected the ship-in-distress routine. British ships with fake leaks transferred unauthorized freight to warehouses in the port. A "present" for the governor then gained English factors the opportunity to sell the cargoes to local merchants.[50] This sort of illegal trade, eventually reaching about 1 million pounds sterling for all the Americas, cut deeply into official Spanish trade and contributed to war between Spain and Great Britain in 1739.[51] Not without mercantilist justification, therefore, Spain ended the British asiento agreement — yet English contraband persisted in the Río de la Plata.

Smuggling continued across the estuary, not six hours from Buenos Aires by sailing bark, at the Portuguese settlement of Colônia do Sacramento. The Portuguese in Southern Brazil established the settlement in 1680, and Colônia soon became a commercial rival of Buenos Aires. It too was in a position to serve foreign shipping in the estuary as well as river boating in the Paraná River Basin. The Portuguese port tapped the cattle resources of the Uruguayan pampa and the silver caravans proceeding from Córdoba to Buenos Aires. Small boats easily passed from one port to the other with contraband goods.[52] When the South Sea Company lost official sanction in Buenos Aires, British ships simply put in at Colônia to pick up silver and hides. A Spanish military raid on Colônia in 1762 surprised twenty-seven English merchant ships there. The annual value of contraband in the area climbed to approximately 200,000 pounds sterling.[53]

Clandestine trade in colonial Latin America was an aberration of the legal commercial system. Contemporaries and historians alike perceived that economic considerations easily subverted bureaucracy. As the British merchant, J. Campbell, put it so cogently: "It is Interest governs every thing [sic] in the Indies."[54] Smuggling in Buenos Aires was especially rational. The port's economic interest in the Atlantic trading community grew steadily from the beginning of the seventeenth century and developed rapidly in the eighteenth. Buenos Aires drew European shipping like a magnet activated not so much by the metallic but by the commercial qualities of silver from Potosí. Clearly, the economy and society of this colony developed independently of the crown's policies.

By 1776, Buenos Aires already had become the leading

port in Southern South America and entrepôt of the Potosí—Río de la Plata regional economy. The Portuguese presence across the estuary now threatened the Spanish Empire and the established trade in the staple commodity of silver. Bourbon reforms, therefore, made Buenos Aires the capital of the new Viceroyalty of the Río de la Plata — and the pace of socioeconomic growth quickened.

# 2
## Buenos Aires in the Golden Age: the viceregal economy

The evolution of Buenos Aires as center of the staple economy accelerated with its establishment as the viceregal capital in 1776 and as the official Spanish port of call for the entire region. The Bourbon reforms of the last quarter of the eighteenth century enabled the port to capture the Potosí silver trade — amounting officially to 371,000 pesos a year — almost in its entirety. At the same time, the city developed an internal market of its own that gradually drew the domestic production of the hinterlands into its economic sphere. Cattle industries, in particular, responded with growth and sophistication. Increased Spanish and foreign shipping connected the region to expanding European markets for staple raw materials, compelling a major change in cattle production. Early hunting expeditions, which extracted hides and fat from cattle, had begun to deplete the herds of wild stock on the grasslands. Consequently, formal cattle-breeding ranches multiplied in order to control production, and the estancia came to be the chief social and productive unit in the countryside.

The viceroyalty was the true golden era of the region's colonial economy. Markets at Potosí and at Buenos Aires assured the steady growth of production in all settled areas in the Río de la Plata. Paraguay, Córdoba, Mendoza, and other localities prospered on the sales of their products in both places and on the substantial trade that passed between the two economic poles. Still, the integration of the region into the Atlantic trading community was not without its drawbacks. The Napoleonic conflicts, with their shifting European alliances and economic blockades, threw Buenos Aires' trade into confusion. The British invasion of Montevideo and Buenos Aires in 1806 stands out as testament to the commercial tensions of European warfare. The repercussions in Buenos Aires were not only economic, but also political. The Wars of Independence ultimately would destroy Peru's mining economy and leave Buenos Aires as the sole market for La Plata's economy. But a golden age began in 1776.

### Golden age of commerce

The Bourbon reforms that created the viceroyalty finally placed official sanction on the existing economic development of the region. Potosí, Salta, Mendoza, and Asunción, all having previous and often extralegal trade associations with Buenos Aires, now were included in the giant administrative unit of which that port was the capital. Actually, the crown's economic reform was an attempt to control and profit from commerce in the Río de la Plata. Only Spanish ships from Iberian ports or from other colonial ports were to trade at Buenos Aires. The newly established *consulado,* or chamber of merchants, and the customshouse were intended to safeguard Spanish trading interests in the capital. A major portion of the silver and pastoral goods, nevertheless, still found their way into northern European ports. Foreign ships continued to sail up the estuary either as smugglers or legally under wartime measures.

For the first time, Spain was the most important trading partner of its colony of the Río de la Plata. The number of ships proceeding legally from Cádiz and other Spanish ports outnumbered non-Iberian shipping. In 1796, for example, a foreign observer noted that a total of seventy-three Spanish ships arrived in the estuary.[1] Roughly half of Buenos Aires' Iberian trade passed to and from the port of Cádiz, followed by Barcelona, Málaga, and Coruña, yet much of the goods in Spanish ships were merely transshipped from Northern Europe. Merchant vessels proceeding from Cádiz carried at least 60 percent foreign goods in their holds.[2] New England trading ships also began to make their appearance in the Río de la Plata. Engaged in the carrying trade between Northern Europe and the Americas, Yankee shippers dealt in a variety of South American staple goods like Buenos Aires hides, Peruvian barks, and Brazilian sugar.[3] In 1800, forty-three U.S. ships arrived with slaves from Mozambique or with reexported European goods from Boston, New York, and Philadelphia. Yankee skippers also took advantage of the Buenos Aires trade opened by the British invasion of 1806. Within two years, forty U.S. ships put in to the estuary for cargoes of silver, hides, and tallow. North Americans in this early period also began to carry on the trade between Havana and Buenos Aires. For delivery of Cuban tobacco and sugar, they picked up tallow and jerked beef for plantation slaves in the Caribbean.[4]

The few sources on commerce in this era suggest that the viceroyalty experienced not only an expanding commerce but also a favorable balance of trade throughout the remainder of the colonial epoch. Contemporary observers place the value of exports in the 1790s approximately at 5 million pesos and imports at 2.8 million. These traditional estimates may be well below the mark. Recent scholarship indicates that imports at Buenos Aires alone reached as high as 5.3 million pesos in 1790 – a figure that represents only three-quarters of total imports for the La Plata region.[5] Customs revenues on foreign trade perhaps are an indication of the ascent of legal commerce. Before 1777, revenues seldom amounted to more than 20,000 pesos. That figure leaped to an average of nearly 400,000 pesos in the early 1790s and surpassed the 1 million mark by 1804.[6]

Although there is plenty of disagreement about the size of trade, none exists about the fact that Potosí's silver continued to be its single most important article. Available sources list the export value of silver as anywhere from 50 to 80 percent of all freight leaving Buenos Aires and Montevideo.[7] But items listed as *frutos de tierra,* farm and ranching products, soon began to make weighty contributions totaling about one-third of Buenos Aires' exports. Cowhides were the greatest staple commodity in demand by exporters, and Buenos Aires exports increased from 150,000 hides in 1778 to 874,594 in 1796.[8] The Havana trades introduced a new pastoral commodity to the region's production and exports. *Carne salada* (salted and dried beef) from the Río de la Plata, though not exactly tasty, provided a cheap diet for Cuba's expanding slave population. Yearly exports of carne salada to Havana jumped from 158 metric tons in 1787 to 1,785 within ten years.[9] As for imports, textiles from Britain and France as well as Spain continued to dominate as they had during contraband times. Vizcayan iron and general European luxury items also found markets in Buenos Aires. Spanish mercury, which formerly went to Lima, now flowed through this port bound for the mines of Potosí. By 1790, the yearly imports of quicksilver reached 273 metric tons.[10]

The inevitable evil

As trade flourished, so did those merchants who handled commerce at Buenos Aires. At the top of the viceregal structure were the wholesalers, or *comerciantes*. They conducted the import—export trade from the port, controlled most capital resources, and arranged freighting of goods to Interior markets. The porteño merchant class during the viceroyalty numbered about 178. Approximately 20 percent of these, considered large-scale operators, had investments of 50,000 pesos or more in the city's commerce. The largest merchants maintained trade contacts both in Spanish ports such as Cádiz and Bilbao and with commercial agents in Interior localities such as Potosí, Mendoza, or Córdoba. Thus, the merchant might import goods from Spain and direct their distribution through Buenos Aires overland to Potosí for retailing. With their profits, porteño merchants could invest in auxiliary economic activities, like coastal and river shipping, meat-salting plants, or ranching. The comerciantes also made loans to retailers, ranchers, or government officials, usually at an interest rate of 6 percent per annum.[11] Thus, the domestic capital market depended upon the continued expansion of foreign trade.

Below this group of commercial moguls existed an expanding network of warehousemen and retailers. A British observer in 1804 noted that porteño retailers of cloth and imported goods numbered about 600. In addition, some 700 *pulperías* (shops) were located throughout the city for the sale of wines, spirits, candles, salt, bread, kindling, and other consumer items. These retailers — and the street peddlers who competed with them — often were beholden to rich merchants from whom they received wholesale goods on credit. Manufacturing in the same era was at a low technological and market level, but artisan shops expanded to supply local necessities. Many workers in trades such as masonry, carpentry, tailoring, shoemaking, and silversmithing were blacks and mulattoes held in bondage by native-born and immigrant artisans. A numerous body of free laborers also existed, like tanners, lime burners, and woodcutters. Porters were particularly visible in this commercial city, running around the streets unloading merchandise from carts.[12]

Increased legal commerce and relaxed trade restrictions did not resolve all the market conditions giving rise to smug-

gling. Clandestine commerce continued on a smaller scale
because Bourbon reforms neither eliminated high customs
duties, ended certain monopolies, nor permitted *unrestricted*
foreign shipping in the Río de la Plata. Porteños often dealt
directly with foreign ships in the estuary and brought goods
ashore to their warehouses under the cover of darkness.[13]
Contraband was never surreptitious enough to escape the
notice of viceregal officials. Indeed, those very functionaries
charged with suppressing contraband — customs officials,
coast guard officers, and the viceroys themselves — profited
from condoning it.[14] Authorities occasionally did punish
large-scale abuses. A raid on the warehouse at the country
home of Pastor Lezica in 1799 uncovered large amounts of
foreign cotton, linen, wool, and silk that he had exchanged
privately for hides. The merchant was not jailed; he merely
paid a heavy fine of nearly 3,000 pesos to cover the customs
duties he had avoided and the costs of apprehension and
trial.[15] Such smuggling was common enough, and officials
were aware that silver was being exported in much the same
fashion.

Merchants and country folks alike also carried on contraband in tobacco, a commodity whose supply was a royal
monopoly. The countryside of the Banda Oriental served as a
surreptitious clearinghouse for the black tobacco of nearby
Brazil. Constables around Montevideo regularly ap-
prehended persons with Portuguese surnames who delivered
modest amounts of Brazilian tobacco to country stores, estancias, and farms in the area. Clandestine cigar factories
even operated in regular competition with those of the tobacco monopoly.[16] Smuggling was not without its economic
rationale, according to Félix de Azara:

> ... contraband is an inevitable evil, but not everywhere
> is it as prejudicial as we imagine. It is true that the
> Portuguese from [Brazil] introduced much ... tobacco
> and some Indian goods into our countryside of Mon-
> tevideo and into the Guaraní missions. But it is equally
> true that we send them ... almost double the value in
> ponchos, saddles, horses and cattle, because our country
> folk consume few Indian goods in their isolated country
> homes.[17]

The Bourbon reforms allowing greater shipping and silver
exports at Buenos Aires did lop off one head of the monster

Contraband – only to discover that the giant was of the two-headed variety.

## Rivers and cart trails

Owing to its population growth, administrative importance, and commercial wealth, Buenos Aires soon became the largest and most important domestic market in the entire region. Statements about the economic decline of the Interior because of freer trade regulations may be misleading. The existence of an alternate market – besides Potosí – actually served to heighten economic activity in the Interior. Ponchos and cheap native textiles from Tucumán and Santiago del Estero found their biggest markets in the port city, where they were sent via oxcart in bundles of fifty ponchos each. In the highlands, Cochabamba's weaving workshops flourished in the late eighteenth century by dispatching their famous cotton cloth to markets in Salta, Córdoba, and even faraway Buenos Aires. Raw cotton, in turn, came from fields around Tucumán and Lower Peru.[18] Córdoba's leather industries supplied Buenos Aires and other provinces with chamois and suede. Lime for the capital's brick kilns and tanneries came to Buenos Aires from the Paraná River Basin. Oxcarts carried the lime in hide sacks overland to Colonia for transshipment via cutter.[19] Paraguay provided timber for boat- and cart-building in the city, whereas quantities of kindling wood came from the delta of the Paraná River and from arroyos off the Uruguay River. Paraguay also found greater markets in Buenos Aires for its hemp, fruits, vegetables, raw cotton, and its own native textiles.[20] When imports of salt for the growing city proved insufficient, local merchants turned to domestic sources in the salt flats 725 kilometers by cart trail southwest of the port. Because Salinas Grandes lay deep in Indian territory beyond the frontier, salt expeditions of some 100 oxcarts needed military escort and viceregal sanction. Buenos Aires' merchants underwrote the cost of these irregular expeditions, then reaped the profits from the local sales of salt.[21]

The buying power of Buenos Aires' domestic market was increasing yearly. The administration made greater expenditures of viceroyal funds on defense and bureaucratic salaries for the capital than for any other jurisdiction in the region. In

1790, various taxes and fees in Buenos Aires brought in some 2.3 million pesos, yet government expenditures in the capital amounted to more than 3 million pesos. High salaries in Buenos Aires contributed to consumption power, even though distance from the cultivated areas of the Interior meant higher prices for foodstuffs in the capital.[22] Porteños did indeed consume more. Revenues from the sale of tobacco in the port city increased some 20 percent in the five years after 1789.[23] The viceregal capital also consumed the major portion of imported goods. Merchants sold their quality merchandise in the capital and sent unsalable or shoddy goods to the Interior. In 1802, for example, Buenos Aires passed on to the Interior only a third of the 4 million pesos worth of goods it received that year from Europe.[24] No single factor added more to the consumption power of Buenos Aires than its growing population. The number of urban inhabitants climbed from 24,205 to 42,252 in the thirty-three years of the viceroyalty. The annual population growth rate was 1.62 percent. If the Buenos Aires countryside also were included, the yearly population increase would show a rate of 2.92 percent — impressive even by modern standards.[25]

The transport trades, benefiting directly from the commercial development of the port, flourished throughout the Río de la Plata. Legal trade between Buenos Aires and Potosí rose significantly, although Lima served as an alternate outlet for Upper Peru. In 1800, the silver city received 600,000 pesos worth of goods from Buenos Aires and approximately half that amount from Peru.[26] This commerce redounded to the prosperity of trade centers between the two poles of La Plata's economy. Already, in the early 1770s, caravans of twenty carts or more regularly arrived in Buenos Aires with dried fruits, wines, brandies, flour, dried peaches, and passengers from provinces like Mendoza and San Juan. The Chile trades, formerly conducted through Lima, now flowed by way of Buenos Aires, overland to Mendoza, and through the Cordillera to Santiago de Chile. Tucumán and other trading towns participated in the export market of Buenos Aires as the Interior's teamsters transported silver and vicuña wool from Jujuy to Buenos Aires for export overseas. Increased river trade in hides and domestic products gave rise to considerable boat building not only in Buenos Aires but in those river towns like Corrientes and Asunción closer to the sources of timber.[27] Commerce in the Interior expanded substantially during the viceroyalty, as did the collection of taxes. Tax receipts on domestic trade eventually increased some twenty times over those of 1773 — although trade itself expanded at a lesser rate.[28]

Population figures — a much overlooked gauge of the region's economic expansion before the mid—nineteenth century — reveal substantial rates of growth for the Interior provinces. Naturally, the Intendency of Buenos Aires had the largest population. Other areas, especially those crucial if smaller entrepôts on the much-traveled trade routes to Chile and Potosí, also displayed healthy population increases. Most of the Interior, it appears, experienced anything but economic depression as a result of freer trade (see Table 1).

Overseas and local trade assumed such large proportions in the Golden Age that the village of Montevideo (founded in 1726) was used as an auxiliary shipping point. Like the harbor of the capital, Montevideo's anchorage was rather shallow, and its bottom of soft mud occasionally grounded ships larger than 300-tons burden. Circumstances and location confined trade on this side of the estuary primarily to the export of pastoral goods from the estancias of the Banda Oriental. Hides and tallow went to Europe, and salted beef to Havana.[29] Little competition existed between Buenos Aires and Montevideo. The capital remained the center of river shipping, the cart and mule trades, and the distribution of European merchandise. Cutters and sailing barks easily connected the two ports in a twenty-four-hour journey over some 725 kilometers of estuary waters.[30] Foreign ships from Brazil and the United States made Montevideo their chief port, as did French Republican shipping after that nation's revolution. British merchantmen, moreover, headed for the port on the East Bank whenever war closed Buenos Aires to British ships. Montevideo had no direct access to the Interior's cart trade and therefore transshipped foreign goods to Buenos Aires for further distribution.

### From hunting to husbandry

Steady growth of foreign shipping held important implications for production on the grasslands surrounding this outlet

Table 1. *Population growth in the Viceroyalty of the Río de la Plata, 1777–1809*

| Intendency | 1777−8 | 1809 | Annual population growth rate (in percent) |
|---|---|---|---|
| *Buenos Aires* | 37,130 | 92,000 | 2.92 |
| *Córdoba* | | | |
| Córdoba | 40,203 | 60,000 | 1.28 |
| Mendoza | 8,765 | 21,492 | 2.89 |
| San Luis | 6,956 | 16,242 | 2.73 |
| San Juan | 7,690 | 22,220 | 3.43 |
| La Rioja | 9,723 | 12,619 | 0.83 |
| Totals | 73,337 | 132,573 | 1.90 |
| *Salta del Tucumán* | | | |
| Jujuy | 13,619 | 12,278 | −0.33 |
| Salta | 11,565 | 26,270 | 2.64 |
| Tucumán | 20,104 | 35,900 | 1.86 |
| Santiago del Estero | 15,456 | 40,500 | 3.11 |
| Catamarca | 13,315 | 24,300 | 1.93 |
| Totals | 74,059 | 139,248 | 2.02 |

*Source:* Jorge Comandrán Ruiz, *Evolución demográfica argentina durante el período hispánico (1535–1810)* (Buenos Aires, 1969), pp. 80−115. Unfortunately, these figures do not include the population growth of Paraguay and Upper Peru, which were integral parts of the viceroyalty.

to the sea. The principal pastoral products required in overseas markets were hides, tallow, and dried and salted meats. In the seventeenth and early eighteenth centuries, extractive hunting expeditions called *vaquerías* sufficed to meet the erratic demand of smugglers. The vaquería would have been impossible, had not the surrounding grasslands been so conducive to the subsistence of wild cattle. The few horses and cows brought by the Spanish in the sixteenth century multiplied along the coasts of the estuary until wild herds roamed the plains in large − but not unlimited − numbers. On the hoof, the wild bull was worthless. But it was the source of tongue, tallow, and hides, which did have value when processed very simply by the hunting bands. A leading porteño citizen organized a band of hard-riding horsemen from among the country folk of the vicinity. The party rode out to the prairies some distance from Buenos Aires to find suitable herds of cattle, and the hunt began. Several mounted hamstringers chased down the wild bulls to cut their hind tendons with poles sporting a crescent-shaped blade at the business end. Those with lassos then haltered the crippled bulls, while their comrades with knives approached from behind for the kill. When sufficient cattle had been slain, the horsemen returned to flay the hides and cut out the tongues and fat. They collected the hides at a spot suitable for staking them in the sun. A large hunting expedition might last from two to three weeks and produce several thousand hides.[31]

The waste from this system of extractive production, needless to say, was great. The major part of the carcass was left to wild dogs and vultures, and no effort was made to preserve the reproductive capacities of the animals. The arrival of Dutch ships and eventually British slavers, all seeking exports of dried hides, created a real hazard of herd depletion. Numerous vaquerías pushed farther into the frontier regions south of Buenos Aires, until the scarcity of accessible wild cattle alarmed the authorities. Throughout the eighteenth century, the town council issued injunctions and other regulations on cattle slaughtering in order to avoid permanent loss of this resource.[32] By midcentury, the vaquería had passed from the pampa around Buenos Aires, but the technique persisted deeper in the hinterland, where one still found wild cattle. Reports of black and Indian horsemen who still hunted with the crescent-shaped blades date to the end of the colonial period.[33]

Estancias, the formal cattle-breeding ranches, allowed the introduction of better methods of pastoral production — a pressing need in light of the increased commerce in such products. In domesticating their herds, porteños depended on two traditional Hispanic practices: the rodeo and the brand. Town councils traditionally granted both estancia lands and cattle brands to prospective ranchers among its citizens. On the hacienda, the rancher's men gathered the cattle into designated pastures called rodeos. They rounded up the cattle perhaps once a week in order to accustom them to both the cowhand on horseback and to each herd's designated rodeo area. Once branded, stray cattle could be reclaimed by the owner when all cattlemen in the vicinity rounded up their herds on the fenceless range. This type of rudimentary husbandry assured greater reproduction of cattle herds and accessibility to the sources of staple exports.

Yearly slaughter of only a number equal to the increase of the stock guarded against herd depletion.

Labor now became an important consideration, for the cattle owner needed cowhands to watch his herds all year long. The hired man's job was to round up strays, participate in branding and slaughter, break and train the horses, and maintain the wood corrals. Itinerant cowboys supplied most of the labor. The coastal lands along the Banda Oriental west of Montevideo, for instance, drew numerous Paraguayan horsemen seeking permanent and seasonal employment on the estancias.[34] Labor, after all, added value to an otherwise abundant critter − the cow on the hoof. A sun-cured hide brought a higher price in the marketplace than the entire carcass of its former occupant. The task of preparing hides consumed the time of scarce manpower, a valuable commodity in the Litoral. A German Jesuit from Santa Fe explained the drying process:

> [The hides] are carefully fastened to the ground, to be dried, with wooden pegs, under shelter, in a place where the fresh air is admitted; and lest moths should gnaw or strip them of their hairs, for thirteen or, at least eight days, the dust which ingenders these insects must be diligently beaten from them with a stick. This labour, which was often continued for many months, whilst some thousands of them were disposed of, is rated very high by the Spaniards who sell them.[35]

Production responded to improvements in animal domestication, even though colonial ranching could count only on a minimal amount of manpower. The lack of manpower was inevitable in an underpopulated region, but the nature of cattle grazing did not demand extensive handling. Azara claimed that an estancia of some 10,000 head of cattle could assure an increase in the size of the herd by one-third each year. Only one foreman and ten cowhands were needed to run such an operation.[36] The appearance of several ships all at once in the port sometimes led to an excessive slaughtering for quick profit. Cowboys continued to kill the cattle without distinction of age and reproduction, leading a Spanish traveler to fear that this might truly lead to the extinction of cattle on the pampa.[37] His caution proved premature.

Cattle ranching prospered particularly well on the East Bank of the estuary, today the nation of Uruguay. It was an area of numerous streams, with abundant wood for kindling and the construction of corrals. Most of all, no mounted Indians ever found their way across the Paraná and Uruguay rivers, which separated the Banda Oriental from their home on the southern pampa. Ranching and trade originally attracted the Portuguese to the East Bank in 1680, and they soon established numerous estancias around Colônia with Spanish cattle. The Jesuits later organized their famous seven missions on the East Bank, the largest of which was the *vaquería del mar* near Montevideo Bay.[38] In viceregal times, cattle grazing was so well established along the coast that travelers every few leagues saw *ranchos* (huts), corrals, and cowboys on horseback tending large herds of cattle and horses. The largest cattle estates were bounded on the south by the estuary and on each side by riverlets.[39] Montevideo was the principal outlet for hides on the East Bank. Estancias to the west also produced great numbers of hides, which were brought to Buenos Aires on boats out of ports on the Uruguay River.[40] The first meat-salting plants, or *saladeros,* were established on the East Bank, because demand for salted beef to feed slaves in Cuba and Brazil stimulated trade in this commodity. By the 1790s, saladeros also provided barrels of salted meat for the Imperial Army and Navy in Spain. A few estancieros set up salting works on ranches near Montevideo and processed their own stock into salted beef and hides right on the premises.[41]

Whereas the East Bank was the center of colonial ranching, cattle-breeding establishments also spread out on the prairies south of Buenos Aires. The Indian frontier, represented by a porous line of forts, permitted only a limited area of land to be settled. But settled it was! The rural population of these frontier districts swelled rapidly during the viceroyalty — more rapidly, in fact, than did the population of the port itself. Despite the danger of Indian raids, cattle husbandry attracted people to the old frontier districts. Estimates of the population growth in country districts of Buenos Aires yield the following figures:[42]

|  | 1781 | 1798 |
|---|---|---|
| Chascomús | 374 | 1,000 |
| Pilar de los Ranchos | 235 | 800 |
| Monte | 345 | 750 |
| Luján | 464 | 2,000 |
| Salto | 421 | 770 |
| Rojas | 425 | 740 |
| Areco | 85 | 400 |

Meanwhile, the river system provided further avenues for the trade in cattle products. Ranchers up the Paraná and Uruguay rivers regularly sent down to Buenos Aires branded hides — indicating some degree of cattle husbandry upriver — as well as unbranded hides acquired in vaquería. Hides arriving by boat were either offered for sale at large or consigned to hide purveyors who collected shipments for export merchants. Cattle hunts continued in the country of Entre Ríos and Corrientes, where the thickets and brush still harbored numbers of the wild beasts. Residents of Paysandú on the Uruguay River occasionally shipped to Buenos Aires several thousand hides that they had collected on hunting expeditions in the vicinity. Estancieros in Santa Fe and across the Paraná River at Bajada, on the other hand, turned out branded hides in the late 1780s. The majority of hides that they sent to the port were from numerous small ranchers who perhaps also bred mules for the Potosí market. One shipment from Bajada contained 300 hides with brands and another 251 without marks. It appears that ranches upriver were smaller than the grazing estates along the coast, for many estancieros contributed to the hide cargoes from the river provinces.[43]

A sure indication of the value of cattle products was not only the viceregal edicts against excessive slaughter but also the prevalence of cattle rustling and smuggling. Robber bands roamed the hinterlands of the Banda Oriental, stealing domesticated cattle if they found no wild ones to hunt. The hides that rustlers stripped from stolen cattle found their way to export markets at Buenos Aires and into the warehouses of respectable porteño merchants. Rustlers also found profit in running cattle and cattle products from the East Bank into Brazil. Hide stealing became so common around Montevideo that estancieros requested authorities to protect the roads over which they carted their hides for shipment to Buenos Aires.[44]

Appreciation in the commercial value of hides brought about the expansion of cattle production into parts of the pampa as yet unsettled by the mule-breeding estancias that served the Potosí market. The Banda Oriental, well watered, well wooded, and well away from hostile Indians, became the principal region of new cattle breeding. Cattlemen also started to fill in the fontier areas south and southeast of Buenos Aires, and areas accessible to boat landings on the

Paraná River sent hides acquired from both cattle hunts and settled estancias. The pastoral orbit of Buenos Aires expanded progressively before Independence – not only in area but also in cattle-breeding technique.

## Ranching on the East Bank

Nothing better testifies to the significance of the Buenos Aires export market for the region's staple economy than the formation of large, well-ordered units of production to serve that market. Of the important estancias on the East Bank in this epoch, the Estancia de las Vacas was among the largest. The market orientation of its operation is undeniable. The ranch had ties of ownership in the commercial metropolis of Buenos Aires, to which its products were sent. Its location directly across the estuary from the capital made Buenos Aires, rather than Montevideo, the logical market outlet. Moreover, the estancia was operated by the Hermandad de la Santa Caridad, an important lay brotherhood in the capital. Its chief administrator handled the estancia business affairs in Buenos Aires. Organizational ownership undoubtedly made available greater outlays of capital for initial operation. All evidence – numbers of workers and slaves, size of herds and physical properties, and sales of products – indicate that the Estancia de las Vacas was highly capitalized.[45]

Physically, the ranch must have been the pastoral marvel of the time. The Estancia de las Vacas consisted of not less than nine sub-estancias of varying sizes. A *capataz* (foreman) ran each of these for the *mayordomo* (estate manager) and supervised the work of three or four peons in his charge. The main estancia had a capataz and nineteen workers. Each section probably was further broken down into rodeos, sometimes known as *puestas,* in which one cowhand usually tended a specific herd of livestock. A total of twenty huts and eighteen corrals were spread throughout the ranch. The principal estancia had a more imposing physical plant, including seven ranchos, two large sheds, three lime kilns, soap-making equipment, ten oxcarts, a country store, and a chapel. Most sub-estancias were used as livestock pastures. Two were more specialized: One was listed as a *matadero,* slaughtering area, with one corral; and the other, stocked with numerous beasts of burden and several boats, served as a small port. Supplies and products regularly passed from this river landing to Buenos Aires, aboard the vessels of independent boatmen, who returned with goods like sugar, tobacco, clothing, and tools.[46]

The economic function of each person connected with the estancia — whether administrator, manager, foreman, or laborer — defined the social organization of the cattle-grazing estate. At the apex was the estancia owner, in this case, the corporate Hermandad de Santa Caridad. The administrator who represented the brotherhood marketed the pastoral products in Buenos Aires and saw that supplies and money for salaries were sent back to the estancia. The estate manager lived on the ranch itself. He supervised the work on the sub-estancias and accounted in his messages and bookkeeping to the administrator in the city. Under the mayordomo's authority were the numerous foremen. They directed work on the sub-estancias, the boat landing, the slaughter area, and the cart train. Free laborers, called peons, did the physical work on the estancias and were the most numerous.

Labor at the Estancia de las Vacas appeared rather stable. Because much of the work was seasonal, the huge ranch needed only eight foremen and approximately thirty peons all year round. Slaves formed the core of the labor pool. The most experienced cowhands on the ranch, black slaves, were entrusted with positions of responsibility. The senior foreman and three of the other capataces were slave cowboys. They directed the work of the salaried peons and seasonal laborers, who were freemen. Other slaves worked in specialized jobs at the lime kilns and in the storehouses. Female slaves cooked, gardened, and brought up their families. Inventories of the estancia reveal a significant but dwindling number of slaves, because their replacements were expensive. In 1790, twenty-one male and seven female slaves lived and worked on the estate. The listing nine years later amounted to just sixteen persons.[47]

The mayordomo's pay records show that nearly eighty different men might work on the estancia once or twice during the year. Most seasonal workers signed on from small farms and family plots nearby. These country folk used the estancia as a source of cash and goods from Buenos Aires. Even this itinerant labor proved stable over the decade as, year after year, the same seasonal workers signed on for slaughtering and wood cutting. Additional workers were enlisted in

Buenos Aires, from where groups of hired hands occasionally took a boat across the estuary for two months' work on the ranch.

The estate manager assumed the responsibility of paying the salaried laborers in silver pesos or in kind. Capataces hired on at eight pesos (on rare occasions, for as much as twelve pesos) per month. The peons generally made six or seven pesos each a month, and took their pay in both silver and goods such as domestic and foreign clothing, tobacco, and horse equipment. Popular articles among workers were silk kerchiefs, fine linen cloths, hats, ponchos, cotton and woolen goods, shirts, various tobaccos, knives, and bridles. Each item had its monetary equivalent, which was subtracted from the men's pay. Payment in kind also had a profit motive. The general practice of the administration at the Estancia de las Vacas was to buy hats and ponchos at certain prices and distribute them to workers at higher rates, sometimes at twice the cost. The mayordomo then declared the difference as profit on his balance sheets. Along with general store sales to the workmen and to country people living near the Vacas, payment in kind was another way that the estancia returned a profit to its owner.[48]

If the success of the colonial ranch were measured by its productive capacity, then the Estancia de las Vacas earned high marks. It produced a variety of staple products for foreign and domestic markets and provided much of the subsistence for its employees. The greatest economic gain lay in cattle breeding and in sales of hides. In the 1790s, the Estancia de las Vacas dispatched to Buenos Aires a yearly average of 4,000 hides, according to the following account:[49]

|      | *hides sent to Buenos Aires* | *other hide sales* |
|------|------------------------------|--------------------|
| 1795 | 1,632                        |                    |
| 1796 | 4,309                        | 1,331              |
| 1797 | 9,180                        |                    |
| 1798 | 5,351                        | 683                |
| 1799 | 1,007 (6 months only)        |                    |
|      | 21.479                       | 2,014              |

Estancia operations produced cowhides in a variety of ways. In 1790, the number of wild cattle found on the vast properties of the Estancia de las Vacas outnumbered the domesticated herd. As domesticated animals increased over the years, greater numbers of the wild herd were hunted

down for their hides. Domesticated cattle in 1791 amounted
to more than 16,000 head, only one-tenth of which were sold
or slaughtered for meat. Wild cattle, however, numbered
nearly 42,000 head. Almost 10,000 of these were killed for
hides, another 1,000 died in an epidemic, and nearly 500
joined the domesticated herd. The tendency over the years
was to increase the domesticated herd and reduce the wild
cattle.[50] In this manner, the Estancia de las Vacas rapidly
developed its domesticated cattle into a formidable herd. By
the mayordomo's own inventory (figures in head of cattle),
the *ganado de rodeo* multiplied annually by 33 percent:[51]

|      | size of domestic herd |
|------|-----------------------|
| 1794 | 16,239 |
| 1795 | 21,692 |
| 1796 | 28,869 |
| 1797 | 38,492 |
| 1798 | 51,322 |
| 1799 | 68,429 |

Domesticated animals at the Estancia de las Vacas were divided into *partidas* (herds) and kept in rodeos on the sub-
estancias. The entire stock of cattle was divided into seven
different herds, and each sub-estancia and its personnel were
entrusted with certain partidas of livestock. Horses came
next in importance; they were accounted for by type and
function, and the inventory of 1790 at the Vacas shows that
breeding mares numbered more than 2,000. Ninety-two
oxen and 700 burros made up the beasts of burden.[52]

   Livestock raising was not the only productive activity un-
dertaken on the Estancia de las Vacas. Workers cultivated a
surplus amount of wheat, which the estate manager used to
pay the *diezmo* (tithe), to feed estancia employees, and to sell
on the domestic market. The ranch produced 177 fanegas
(241 hectolitres) of wheat in 1791. Besides the usual pastoral
by-products, meat and tallow, the large estate also marketed
wood products. The operation entailed cutting the virgin
shrub of the numerous arroyos on the properties. Kindling
wood, sold by the cartload in Buenos Aires, was the second
largest moneymaker after hides. Fence posts were also sent
to the opposite bank of the Río de la Plata, where lack of
natural wood and modest cattle expansion guaranteed a brisk
market for corral and fence materials. The mayordomo of the
Estancia de las Vacas listed the total sales revenue for the
second six months of 1795 as follows:[53]

| product | quantity | value (in pesos) |
|---|---|---|
| Cattlehides | 912 hides | 1,054 |
| kindling wood | 405.5 cartloads | 710 |
| wheat | 79 fanegas (112 hectolitres) | 355 |
| yanduay posts | 2,280 posts | 285 |
| fresh meat | 256 beasts | 256 |
| tallow | 245 arrobas (2,784 kilograms) | 101 |
| grease, dried meat, mules, and salt | | 83 |
| | | 2,842 |

Total sales, of course, do not show the profit. The accountant-manager had yet to balance out earnings with costs. In the case of the Estancia de las Vacas, expenditures included the money paid out in wages to employees, the cost of merchandise and tools from Buenos Aires, and the cost of the purchase and upkeep of physical properties, oxcarts, and slaves. The mayordomo provided a glimpse of the financial state of his estancia in this rather unorthodox (according to modern accounting procedures) balance sheet (figures in pesos) from July 1 to December 30, 1795:[54]

| expenses | | assets | |
|---|---|---|---|
| received in goods | 2,360 | value of goods left from previous inventory | 792 |
| received in cash | 1,256 | amount of cash left from previous inventory | 200 |
| revenue from goods paid in kind | 233 | amount of goods sold to the peons | 845 |
| value of goods sold for cash | 399 | amount of goods sold for cash | 399 |
| revenue gained on above sales of goods | 119 | salaries and pay of employees and additional expenses of the estate | 1,588 |
| adjustment for error in this account | 13 | expenditures on the slaves | 556 |
| revenues from sales of ranch products | 2,842 | revenues from sales of ranch products | 2,842 |
| | 7,222 | | 7,222 |

The profits revealed by this account are very impressive: 28 percent on items sold to the peons, and 30 percent on goods sold in the general store. Together with the sale of products, the mayordomo of the Estancia de las Vacas could have claimed total gross profits of 3,194 pesos for the last six months of 1795. In other words, gross profits equaled 44 percent of all cash transactions during the same period. After deducting for transport and storage costs at the port, net ranch profits still must have been high. Cattle raising for export through viceregal Buenos Aires was a profitable business. Unfortunately for ranchers and merchants, 1795 was one of the last years of uninterrupted foreign trade for a decade.

### Hazards of new prosperity

Pastoral production on estancias like the Vacas responded to the demand of markets that international commerce had opened to the staple products of the Río de la Plata. Such affiliation was not without its economic frustrations. Buenos Aires also suffered the consequences of membership in the Atlantic trading community — to wit, the disruptions in trade caused by European wars. In fact, the viceregal trade boom did not begin until the conclusion in 1783 of the general wars attending North American independence. Only then did the Bourbon reforms of the 1770s have any impact on commerce at Buenos Aires. The era of peace lasting to 1796 brought prosperity to the Río de la Plata, as an average of sixty ships a year put into the port of Buenos Aires.[55] Then the Napoleonic conflicts upset world trade once again. After years of sipping the finest imported wines, porteños had to settle for domestic substitutes at higher prices.

Spain was allied to France in the early bouts of the European wars and thus found itself at odds with the greatest sea power of the age, Great Britain. This bellicose entanglement produced two effects. First, the British naval blockades against the Spanish mainland reduced that country's trade with its colonies. Exports from Buenos Aires, for instance, fell precipitously after 1796 — from more than 5 million pesos to less than .5 million pesos.[56] Secondly, Spanish-American ports were shut to British merchant vessels, much to the consternation of porteño merchants who had been prospering on trade with Bristol and Liverpool. British shippers caught in the Río de la Plata when hostilities broke out found their merchandise confiscated and themselves incarcerated.[57]

The shifting fortunes of war occasioned Spain to issue a welter of wartime port regulations for the Indies, which in effect opened Buenos Aires and other American harbors to neutral shipping. North American vessels began to call in the Río de la Plata estuary, and Portuguese shipping from Brazil revived. It was not uncommon by 1806 to find more than two dozen Boston and New York ships at anchor in Montevideo Bay, and almost an equal number of Portuguese ships.[58] Spain's republican ally, France, also sent its merchant vessels and privateers into the Río de la Plata — although local officials did become somewhat nervous in 1799 when an armed French corsair and three frigates-of-war from the African coast stopped at Montevideo. Wartime and neutral shipping did not compensate Buenos Aires and Montevideo for the peacetime European trade to which they had become accustomed. Native-born consumers yearned for a return of foreign goods, while production on the hinterland's cattle ranches declined. Had Montevideo's hide mongers collected their usual half-million hides for annual export, their warehouses soon would have been full of rotting hides for lack of ships on which to send them to European tanneries.[59]

Great Britain felt the same pinch of wartime trade disruptions that pained Spain and its empire. The great Atlantic port at Liverpool was in the doldrums, and unmarketable goods piled up in the warehouses of British factories in Manchester and Glasgow. Prices began to rise because raw materials were scarce and world shipping dangerous. Napoleon's European blockade and Thomas Jefferson's embargo denied to British merchants both their sources of raw materials and their sales in Europe and the United States. The Treaty of Tilsit between France and Russia in 1808, for instance, temporarily cut off traditional Russian supplies of tallow for making British candles and soaps. The observation of an eighteenth-century English merchant, that Great Britain had few commercial reasons to wish that Spain lose its colonies (because the British had traded briskly with the empire through Spain and via contraband), no longer held true.[60] After a decade of commercial frustration, the British invasions of 1806 reopened old markets in the Río de la Plata.

Nonetheless, the military expedition from the Cape of Good Hope to Buenos Aires by naval and land forces under Commodore Sir Home Riggs Popham took Great Britain by surprise. It had been Popham's own idea, albeit formulated

on commercial notions, and executed on his own recogni-
zance. British business opinion was ecstatic. BUENOS
AIRES AT THIS MOMENT FORMS A PART OF THE
BRITISH EMPIRE, trumpeted a headline in the London
*Times.*[61] Sir Home wrote to British businessmen that "The
conquest of this place opens an extensive channel for the
manufacturers of Great Britain." Immediately, they fitted out
100 merchant ships for Buenos Aires. The merchantmen had
to settle for the port of Montevideo. Even while Popham was
returning to face a general court martial in London, the porteños expelled his troops from Buenos Aires.[62]

British military and political hegemony in the Río de la
Plata proved to be fleeting, but English commercial
hegemony succeeded in returning. Occupation forces reduced import–export duties in Buenos Aires and Montevideo, and so much foreign merchandise glutted the market
that price levels soon collapsed. Anglo merchants at Montevideo, faced with the awesome sight of 150 sail in the small
bay, found themselves dumping their wares just to get out
from under falling prices.[63] They regained legal commercial
access to Buenos Aires in 1808, when the course of Napoleon's ambitions on the Iberian peninsula threw Spain into
the arms of Great Britain. In the year preceding Buenos
Aires' revolution, British mariners unloaded more than 1
million pounds sterling of cargo both legally and clandes-
tinely at Buenos Aires.[64] The political issue of free international trade in the Río de la Plata was not solved until the
Revolution of 1810. But the region had long since entered
the Atlantic trading community and had enjoyed the wealth
and suffered the vicissitudes that the market proffered. Free
trade itself was to be anticlimactic.

On the eve of the revolution, Buenos Aires already was
well along the road of staple growth, a process that had tied
the region's economy and society irrevocably to world trade.
The port already had been the anchorage of ships from a
variety of nations, and Porteño merchants established themselves as the arbiters of trade throughout the region. Com-
mencing in contraband times and continuing in the viceroyalty, a staple trade in pastoral goods through this port
increased steadily until the cattle industries had passed from
fledgling to junior partner in the city's commerce. Potosí's
silver was still the leading export. The socioeconomic trends

begun in the colonial period were to continue in the nineteenth century: International shipping would increase substantially, the merchant community would broaden, the growth of the Interior would depend more and more on the port, pastoral industries would spread to the virgin prairies, and the Litoral's population growth would outstrip that of the Interior. The nineteenth century held only decline and final exhaustion for the great silver mines of Upper Peru. Even so, the pace of socioeconomic growth intensified in this under-populated part of the world beyond even the possibilities of silver trading. Pastoral raw materials exported from Buenos Aires now would carry the entire region. The reason why La Plata's staple economy refused to decline when the Peruvian mines did is explained in market developments far away in Europe and North America – developments that have come to be known as the industrial revolution.

# 3

# Industrial markets for Argentine raw materials

Someone once compared the industrial revolution to the loss of innocence — that is, once compromised, naiveté can never be regained. Having been the first to be so ravished by take-off and technological change, Britain and the United States remain the classic examples of the process that transforms an agrarian society into an industrial nation within some thirty years. Yet, historians must acknowledge an important corollary: that the industrial revolution of the nineteenth century affected nonmetropolitan nations as well. The release of modern economic forces ultimately had nearly as profound an impact on the bystanders as on the participants. The emergence of Buenos Aires as a major international port serves as a reminder of this peripheral development. The industrial revolution permitted Buenos Aires to shed its colonial dependence on declining levels of silver exports and to capitalize on volume trade in a variety of staple commodities. In the Río de la Plata, the pastoral trade boom and the expansion of a ranching society was every bit a part — albeit a distant part — of the revolution in the world economy.

Argentina's staple economy responded to markets outside South America. A region of abundant land and limited consuming population, the Río de la Plata was a raw materials producer, and world markets for staples underwent unprecedented changes beginning in the early nineteenth century. The story rests with the transformation of the manner in which metropolitan industry produced goods from raw materials. Technological and managerial innovation in industrial production had several effects. It increased the efficiency and scale of certain manufacturing, cheapened the finished product, widened the consuming market, and vastly enlarged the use of raw materials. In turn, industrial demand induced growth in international trade and strengthened the commercial ties between manufacturing countries and regions of raw material production like the La Plata. The industrial revolution had spreading effects that were international in scope. Specifically, developments in the leather and woolen industries of the United Kingdom and of the northeastern United States stimulated imports of Argentine hides and wool and focused the socioeconomic development of the Río de la Plata on the production of these pastoral staples.[1]

## Tradition-bound industry

Wool weaving and leather working were ancient arts of considerable importance, providing goods of variety and necessity. In fact, both the textile industry and the leather industry were leading sectors of manufacture in Britain's eighteenth-century commercial growth. Broadcloth, a finely finished woolen textile, was the principal export commodity; leather was worked by craftsmen into all manner of goods, from shoes and clothing to saddlery and war matériel. Naturally, centuries-old technology governed production in both industries. The lime baths, hand scraping, and bark solutions in the tanning process of 1800 had changed little from techniques used in the fifteenth century. Meanwhile, the putting-out system persisted in the woolen and worsted industries, allowing the wool merchant minimal capital outlays and flexible supplies of workers to man the domestic spinning wheels and hand looms.

Both ancient trades lagged in exploiting the new technology of the nineteenth century. Neither tanning nor wool weaving shared in the 1790 British take-off, which was led by cotton textiles. In spectacular and irreverent fashion, cotton textiles quickly surpassed woolens as Britain's leading export commodity. Comparative trade figures (in pounds sterling) tell a compelling tale:[2]

|                  | *1766*    | *1825*     |
|------------------|-----------|------------|
| woolens exported | 5,559,000 | 6,926,000  |
| cottons exported | 200,000   | 30,795,000 |

To explain this lag, one must seek a reason more basic than the mere tenacity of tradition. Both the leather and woolen trades were dedicated to altering animal materials which, by their very nature, required special handling and defied all but the most complex mechanical processing. Few oxen in the area, even of the same breed and herd, yielded hides of identical quality — not to mention horse- and calfhides, and skins from sheep and the fur-bearing animals! Sheepskins, for example, contained much oil, which had to be forced out of the skin by hydrostatic presses before tanning.[3] Wool had similarly capricious characteristics. The hair was irregular and curly, no strand being the same width throughout. Each fleece was impregnated by a secretion of oil that had to be removed before spinning the strands into yarn. Since ancient times, a thorough soaking in human urine sufficed. In addition, the wool of each clip varied in length and consistency according to where it came from on the animal, so that each fleece had to be separated by hand.[4] Thus the nature of the raw material hampered growth in woolen and leather production.

Production bottlenecks and tradition inhibited the leather industry far more than the woolen trades. Yet the industry did undergo change in the first half of the nineteenth century — change that was perhaps more style than substance, for new technologies were applied very slowly to tanning and leather making.[5] Primarily, the pressure of greater consumption of conventional leather products dictated increased production. The result was rationalization of existing production techniques. A concentration of tanning plants took place to solve problems of insufficient local supplies of hides and barks. Larger tanyards, moreover, facilitated the tardy addition of a few new techniques to age-old processes.

The combined leather industries — tanning, shoe making, and harness making — ranked among the most prominent industries in Britain and the United States because of the wide uses of leather products. In the British Isles, they followed only cotton and wool textiles and possibly iron working in importance. The American boot and shoe industry itself was third in value of production (but first in number of workers), followed by the tanning industry.[6]

### Russets and black brogans

Traditionally, leather provided the materials for a wide variety of goods. Tanned oxhides were thick and long-wearing, ideal for straps, harness leathers, and the soles of shoes. Horse- and cowhides were thinner, used for saddlery, upholstery, and the upper parts of shoes. Craftsmen converted goat- and sheepskins into bookbinding, fancy shoes, and polished or buffed clothing items. Additionally, military equipment, carriages, ship's riggings, pails, bags, hats, and aprons were made of leather. The era's industrial expansion broadened the use of leather products. Leather belts replaced ropes made of cotton scraps in driving the industrial machinery and, consequently, reduced the number of breakdowns. Steam engines had leather couplings, hoses, and sealing devices, and fire engines were equipped with leather hoses and buckets. As continental Europe expanded its rail networks after the 1840s, leather became one of the materials used in upholstering new passenger cars.[7] From the end of the Napoleonic Wars, the British leather industry's growth surpassed the population increase. The population of Great Britain rose by 1.5 percent yearly, and the value of leather production grew annually by 3 percent. The per capita consumption of leather goods thus doubled between 1815 and 1850.[8]

There is no better illustration of the power of consumption than the growth of the boot and shoe trades, an industry with a naturally wide market utilizing about 80 percent of all leather produced in that era.[9] Real technological change did not occur until midcentury. Yet both the American and British footwear trades expanded through rationalization of the hand labor previously found in cottage production. Employers began to organize workers into central shops, placing more emphasis on standardization and style. In this way, they reduced the cost per shoe and increased productivity per worker. The industry concentrated in areas around Boston and in central English towns like Leeds and Leicester, where imported foreign hides and tan barks supported the growing tanning industry. In Massachusetts alone, production of shoes increased steadily − 15 million pairs in 1837 to 34 million in 1855 − while smaller firms in other seaboard states began to close down.[10] Enlarged shops tended to augment the production of each laborer without much technological advance. By the 1840s, foot saws that cut uniform patterns, stripper machines that sized the soles, and leather rollers that pressed sole leathers combined with, but could not replace, the ancient hand tools of shoe making. Statistics of a central shop in Lynn, Massachusetts, prove only modest increases per worker as the factory became larger:[11]

|      | workers | shoe production (in pairs) | pairs per worker |
|------|---------|----------------------------|------------------|
| 1836 | 18      | 18,000                     | 1,000            |
| 1845 | 52      | 58,000                     | 1,115            |
| 1847 | 109     | 122,000                    | 1,119            |

Yankee merchants, meanwhile, began to export shoes, shipping "russets and black brogans" to the West Indies and southern plantation areas and sending boots to markets west of the Mississippi River. British shoe factories tended to be smaller than their American counterparts in Boston. The rise of central shops of a smaller scale in Leeds and Leicester, nevertheless, did facilitate the arrival of the United States' Singer sewing machine in the 1850s. The first real technological innovation in shoe making, mechanical sewing, replaced the slower attachment of soles to upper leathers by hand.[12]

### Egg yolks and blind horses

Despite the demand for leather in the footwear and other industries, tanning operations remained basically decentralized, dispersed, and backward in developing new production methods. British tanners of the era perhaps employed as many as eight workers on one location. American tanneries usually were located in each small town, close to stores of oak bark and bird droppings used in curing the hides from local abbatoirs. A typical Delaware tannery, for instance, processed 1,500 to 2,000 hides a year, employed six workers on seventy-two soaking vats, and ground 22.7 metric tons of bark. For all this, the capital investment was about $20,000. Bankruptcy of such modest operations was not uncommon.[13]

The tanning technology of the day turned a hide into imputrescible leather after six to fifteen months, depending on the skin's thickness. Initial trimming and cleaning prepared the hide for three weeks of soaking in vats of lime wash. Lime loosened the hair so that a worker with a fleshing knife could easily remove it by scraping. Next, the lime residue had to be removed and the hide softened in a solution containing chicken, pigeon, or dog dung. Finally, various and long-term baths in bark powder and water impregnated the hide with tannic acid. After a final drying and pounding, the product had become incorruptible and water-repellant leather. Most shortcuts (like doubling the potency of the lime and tanning solutions) seldom succeeded, for the product invariably emerged imperfectly tanned and in poor condition.[14]

The chief reason for the lag in developing new techniques was the extraordinary dependence of nineteenth-century tanning on a variety of vegetable and animal substances –

and plenty of water. Tanneries were commonly located along streams or close to sources of water used for the various solutions. Because of the uncommonly offensive smells, one usually found tanneries well away from towns. London's tanneries had settled in Bermondsey, where they obtained water from the tidal streams of the Thames.[15] Water shortages, therefore, slowed an already quite lengthy tanning process. Icy winters did the same, because tanning pits generally were located outdoors and without cover. Here was the greatest bottleneck in production, the soaking vats. Big tanneries increased production by adding more pits — three-meter-long wooden boxes sunk into earth and clay — where the hides lay for months in solutions of lime, tannin, or dung.[16]

The problem in using such organic substances in tanning lay in their supply. In the early years of the century, most American tanneries depended on local stocks of fresh hides from the slaughter of meat animals like cows, pigs, or sheep.[17] Neighboring farmers provided these small concerns not only with hides but also with chicken or pigeon dung. Barks for tanning came from lumbering projects or from timbers cleared by farmers for arable land. Black, white, and red oaks yielded the best tannin barks. Larger cities, whose surrounding forests already had been cut, turned to importing bark from other locales and from foreign countries. Still, tanneries needed two to six pounds of bark, ground at their own mills by a blind draft horse, for each pound of processed leather.[18] Even in alum tanning, one large London tannery specializing in goatskins had to import special French eggs each spring, preserving them during the year in lime water so that the yokes could be mixed into the alum solutions. Not until the 1880s did a mineral substance, chromium, replace these organic tanning agents.[19]

### Swamp tanyards

The tanner's extravagant use of vegetable and animal resources to meet the greater demands for leather resulted in the failure of smaller firms and the concentration of the tanning industry closer to external supplies of hides and barks. Larger tanyards ultimately permitted gradual adoption of a limited set of new procedures — but without a wholesale replacement of old substances. U.S. tanneries installed water wheels and steam engines in their bark mills, built sheds to cover the tanning pits, and constructed pumps to fill and drain the vats.[20] British tanners, meanwhile, developed manual hide-splitting machines and the heating of tanning liquors, which somewhat speeded processing. At midcentury, steel presses and rollers gradually replaced manual hammering to smooth and make pliable the finished leather. Foreign barks such as gambia, valonia, and sumac had to be imported to supplant low stocks of domestic British tanning agents. These imports alone equaled one-third of production costs, yet failed to reduce pit time until stronger quebracho and chestnut extracts arrived after 1870.[21]

In both the United States and England, the trend in tanning was toward large-scale operations. The absolute number of tanneries diminished at the same time that production of leather increased. A few labor-saving devices reduced the need for more tannery workers. Newer Midwestern tanneries remained dispersed and dependent on local supplies. Large tanneries, meanwhile, developed around Eastern ports, where foreign and coastwise shipping delivered barks and hides, and exported leather products.[22] New York State, responsible for one-third of all U.S. leather production in 1840, provides an apt example. Early nineteenth-century tanning had focused in the Swamp, a quagmire of small tanyards on Ferry Street in Manhattan. Their owners seldom bought more than fifty hides at one time. By 1859, however, the leading tannery had grown into a 4-million-dollar-a-year business. Later, tanning establishments moved upstate to tap the hemlock forests of the Catskill Mountains, without straying far from sources of imported hides via the Hudson River.[23] Available New York statistics corroborate the major trends toward larger scale, greater production, and labor stability.[24]

|      | tanneries | capital       | laborers |
|------|-----------|---------------|----------|
| 1841 | 1,212     | $ 3.9 million | 5,811    |
| 1855 | 863       | $15.1 million | 5,579    |

In England, where local tanning had been equally as dispersed, the center of the industry gradually moved out of London toward Leeds, Leicester, and Bristol, closer to the port of Liverpool. Most tanyards remained quite small, and produced some twenty leather butts (hides) a week, with a few hundred pounds sterling invested in hides and tanning agents. The average tanner in 1850 employed only sixteen workers. Still, other concerns were larger. Bevington's factory in Bermondsey annually processed 470,000 sheep- and goatskins. The London port facility was becoming increasingly expensive, and land prices had risen so high that most tanneries there could ill afford to expand.[25] The concentration of the industry in north-central England did permit increased size and production. Leeds also became an important site for saddlers, bootmakers, and machine works – all large consumers of leather. Inland waterways connected Leeds to Liverpool, the primary port of call for ships carrying South American barks and hides. As early as the 1820s, England already imported more than 41,000 metric tons of tanning barks a year.[26] Notwithstanding the impressive growth of tanning in both metropolitan countries, British and American tanners continued to use traditional organic tanning and cleaning agents. An eighteenth-century tanner would have been quite at home in a mid-nineteenth-century tannery.

### Importing "Buenosayres"

Europe and North America long had been accustomed to importing foreign hides to supplement insufficient domestic supplies. Population growth throughout the seventeenth century compelled the tillage of English grazing lands, which caused domestic cattle farmers to fall behind the demand for hides and meat. Rising hide prices consequently raised the cost of leather goods. While the amount of leather produced from domestic British hides actually declined, leather from imported hides increased from a volume of 1.8 million kilograms in 1770 to more than 18 million at the close of the Napoleonic Wars.[27] Meanwhile, early nineteenth-century cattle raising in Pennsylvania and New England had begun migrating westward to Ohio and Illinois. When domestic pastoral products became scarce relative to demand, both the United States and Great Britain either lowered or eliminated customs duties on the importation of foreign raw hides. Soon, New England was importing approximately 90 percent of its hide supplies aboard foreign and domestic shipping; and Delaware, at least half its hides.[28]

Tanners in the seaboard states had been accustomed to working with hides from the West Indian and Hispanic dominions. Late eighteenth-century stocks came from

Jamaica, Curaçao, the Azores, and South America. The nineteenth century added New Orleans, Texas, California, Africa, and Calcutta. South America, providing one-third of all imported hides, emerged as the chief source for the coastal states.[29] In fact, the standard terms for imported hides came to be "Spanish," or more specifically, "Riograndes" (from Brazil), "La Guayras" (Venezuela), and "Buenosayres." Tanners in Delaware and New Jersey acquired hides brought on coastal sloops from the nearby ports of Philadelphia and Baltimore.[30] British tanyards also began to use more foreign than domestic hides. Merchants at hide markets offered salted Argentine oxhides alongside German lambskins, East Indian goatskins, and sun-dried African hides. At midcentury, Britain yearly imported more than one-half million hides from the Río de la Plata through the port of Liverpool alone. Argentina likewise dominated hide markets in the major ports of the East Coast, which in 1841 imported the following quantities from Buenos Aires:[31]

|  | *hides* | *sheepskins* |
|---|---|---|
| Boston-Salem | 187,102 | 28,142 |
| New York | 124,479 | 32,163 |
| Philadelphia | 75,596 | 12,730 |
| Baltimore | 21,414 | 3,500 |

The United States, a better consumer of South American hides, took a quarter of its supply from Argentina, a major portion as sun-dried hides. England, meanwhile, preferred salted Argentine hides. Although accepting more hides from within the empire, Britain still reexported La Plata hides to other European ports on British shipping.[32] Throughout the first half of the century, both countries increased their total hide imports — as well as their Argentine imports — three- and fourfold (see Table 2).

### Wool's take-off

While the leather industry experienced a demand-oriented growth with only modest changes in production methods, the woolen trades underwent real innovation. In the 1790s, when the cotton industry was introducing its first spinning machines, British wool continued to be produced by a decentralized putting-out system. Wool staplers delivered raw wool to the rural cottages of their workers. They generally

Table 2. *British and American imports of Argentine hides, 1826–60 (in millions of pounds of dollars)*

| Great Britain | | | United States | |
|---|---|---|---|---|
| Total hide imports (pounds) | Argentine percentage | Years | Total hide imports (dollars) | Argentine percentage |
| 1.4 | n.a. [a] | 1826–30 | 2.0 | 26 |
| 1.7 | n.a. | 1831–35 | 3.6 | 27 |
| 2.0 | n.a. | 1836–40 | 3.0 | 16 |
| 2.8 | n.a. | 1841–45 | 3.4 | 26 |
| 2.7 | n.a. | 1846–50 | 3.5 | 21 |
| 1.9 | 22.0 | 1851–55 | 6.5 | 21 |
| 2.9 | 19.0 | 1856–60 | 10.3 | 19 |

[a] Not available.
Source: British figures to 1850 represent "hides and skins," and those from 1850 to 1860 pertain only to "raw hides." Werner Schlote, *British Overseas Trade from 1700 to the 1930's,* trans. by W. O. Henderson and W. H. Chaloner (Oxford, 1952), p. 142; and Great Britain, Statistical Office, *Annual Statement of the Trade and Navigation of the United Kingdom with Foreign Countries and British Possessions* (London, 1855–62). All American statistics are from U.S. Treasury, "Report of Commerce and Navigation of the United States," in *Executive Documents* of U.S. Senate and House of Representatives, 1827–61.

worked the land during the day and spun wool on hand-operated spinning jennies in the evening. The merchant then carted the thread to the weaver's house to be made into fine broadcloth on the hand loom. The putting-out system featured all the advantages of the division of labor, a flexible work force, and little capitalization — but none of the advantages of speed and low production costs.[33] Woolen production in the newly independent United States was even more simple. Farming families often carded, spun, and wove their own wool. The American woolen industry in the late eighteenth century suffered competition from superior British goods, want of machinery and skilled labor, and lack of a sizable domestic market.[34]

The first breakthrough in the manufacture of woolen goods occurred in England — a direct result of developments in the cotton trades. Wool manufacturers began to apply the spinning and weaving equipment of Lancaster's cotton factories to the more intransigent wool fiber. Before 1820, the awkward machinery merely produced a hairy, weak, and uneven woolen yarn. The earliest improvements in mill-spun yarn, like the false slay, permitted attachment of the fly shuttle to hand looms in order to speed the weaving of the tougher woolen yarn. They were the only improvements possible that did not break the brittle wool threads. Then the "slubbing frame," used in the early 1820s to keep fibers stretched while being converted into woolen thread, allowed the spinning of shorter wool fibres.[35]

Wool's take-off came in the late 1820s, when the industry, at a brisk pace, adopted power machinery perfected in cotton textiles. Manufacturers had begun to attach power mules to water wheels for spinning wool. "Dead" spindles, which increased the thread's strength, and "screw gills," which straightened fibers firmly before they were twisted into yarn, promoted efficient spinning. Cottage weavers suddenly found it impossible to weave on their hand looms all the thread produced by machinery. Thus, several advanced firms added power looms, displacing some hand weaving. Within a decade, the power-driven Jacquard loom arrived and made fancier wool goods and patterned cloth possible.[36] In one center of the new wool industry, West Riding, the use of power looms increased in number from 2,768 in 1836 to 29,539 by midcentury. Even so, the latest power looms were still clumsy and slow, made of wood instead of iron, and powered by waterwheels rather than steam engines.[37] By 1850, breakthrough was imminent in the remaining bottleneck to complete mechanization — combing to remove impurities in the wools and to prepare the fibers for spinning. A tolerably efficient "nip" machine comber finally supplemented handcombing, the last handicraft of the industry. Furthermore, increased productivity would have been impossible had not the chemical industry perfected sodium alkali to replace human urine in cutting the oily coating on wool fleeces.[38]

The American woolen trades and their transfer from the home directly into the factory benefited from the British example. Despite the famous ban on the export of Britain's industrial secrets, U.S. manufacturers were familiar with all the modern British equipment by 1830. British carding rollers were among the first acquisitions for the New England mills, thereby displacing hand carding in the late eighteenth century. Mill owners installed spinning jennies identical to those used in British industry and then rigged multiple-spindle spinning mules to water power. The American card machine made of iron rather than wood improved on the British prototype because it reduced by one-half the need for manpower by eliminating much of the later slubbing process. Wool was delivered directly from the carding rollers to be woven into yarn. Many American manufacturers could assert that their factories were as efficient as British mills.[39] The U.S. woolen industry was now in a position to increase production dramatically. Census figures (in millions of dollars) show a 300 percent increase within twenty years:[40]

|      | capital investment | value of production |
|------|--------------------|---------------------|
| 1840 | 15                 | 20                  |
| 1850 | 32                 | 49                  |
| 1860 | 42                 | 80                  |

## Mechanizing cheap wool

The technological breakthroughs in the woolen industry accomplished what demand did for the leather industry — namely, the concentration of production in manufacturing districts with access to greater supplies of raw materials. The English woolen industry gathered in West Riding, also the home of the leather trades, where abundant water resources and nearby coal supplies for steam power existed. Finally, the Liverpool-Leeds canal system, built in the previous century, connected West Riding to the major British seaport. By mid-century, mechanical innovations had brought each stage of woolen cloth manufacture into the factory. Laborers moved from the countryside to work the woolen mills. Only hand looms in scattered cottages remained in use for the production of fine cloth. The average firm of 1825 might have had thirty-five workers on the premises, with important functions still being performed in the cottages. Fifteen years later, the same factory employed as many as seventy-five workers.[41] The following figures reveal just how rapidly this technological take-off transformed the British woolen industry:[42]

|                   | 1836   | 1855      |
|-------------------|--------|-----------|
| factories         | 415    | 511       |
| horsepower employed | 7,166 | 14,481   |
| spindles          | —      | 1,298,326 |
| power looms       | 2,768  | 38,819    |
| persons employed  | 31,607 | 86,690    |

New textile technology also permitted expansion in the manufacture of cheaper woolen goods as well – and the use of foreign wools of poorer quality and shorter staple like those from the La Plata region. The American wool industry found greater markets for its cheaper, heavier fabrics such as satinets and cassinets (known as "slave cloths"), made of cotton mixed with cheap foreign wools. Both cloths accounted for 38.5 percent of all fabrics produced.[43] The cheapest of the coarse raw wools came from Smyrna (Turkey) and South America. These wools were used commonly in Britain for "horsecloths and collar cloths, and common blankets, and rugs for covering soldiers' beds."[44] Blankets and carpets became the final product of most of the cheapest foreign wools used in Anglo-American woolen manufacture. British blanket factories experienced a slight technological lag until power looms were proficient enough to weave the brittle yarn of short-stapled wools. In the 1840s, the use of a tough cotton warp added strength to the blanket woven on the power loom. Blanket making soon moved from the cottage to the factory and British mill owners turned out blankets in colors and strips for export markets in New Orleans, Mexico, and South America. In the early 1850s, Britain exported nearly 10 million yards of blanketing each year.[45] Yankee blanket factories experienced a similar lag, having to wait for the arrival of the American "burring mechanism," so that the impurities of the cheaper wools could be removed mechanically.[46]

Floor carpets at the beginning of the nineteenth century had been something of a luxury item even in the best homes. All carpets to that time were laboriously produced on hand looms. Yet development of mass markets in Britain and the United States, tariff protection of home industry, and the availability of cheap foreign wools contributed to rapid growth in the carpet industry. In spite of the high importation of British hand-loomed carpeting – (420,000 meters) in 1825 – Yankee entrepreneurs set up over a dozen factories with secondhand cotton machinery in the following decade.

They utilized heavier versions of ordinary hand looms operated by skilled foreign weavers and boy apprentices. The French Jacquard loom put out simple two- and three-colored patterns of cotton and woolen mixtures.[47] With the arrival of the Bigelow power loom, a Yankee contribution to rug making in 1845, daily production per loom jumped from 6 to 21 meters — and the apprentice was displaced. Most U.S. factories before the 1850s had replaced hand looms with power looms.[48] British rug manufacturers, it appears, did not begin to replace their hand looms until well into the 1850s. Hand weavers still produced quality piled carpets, but now in a factory setting. Britain was exporting carpets as well, sending to foreign markets some 1.8 million kilograms of carpeting in 1853.[49]

Technological advances made for greater factory production, lower prices, and increased use of foreign wools. The American carpet industry developed in most seaboard states but grew especially in central Massachusetts. One factory in Lowell increased its yearly production of carpets from 84,000 to over 840,000 meters within twenty years. Its use of raw wools rose from 1,590 to 16,360 kilograms per week. National carpet production, meanwhile, climbed to a value of nearly $5.5 million, but at the same time the retail price of three-ply carpets dropped from $1.23 to 83¢ a yard (.84 meters).[50] Falling prices and increased production of rugs, as in all woolen goods, widened their market appeal considerably. The woolen industry not only met the needs of growing populations, it also distributed its products on a massive scale to lower-income groups and to foreign customers.

The application of technology to woolen manufacture taxed the domestic supplies of raw wool, and both Britain and the United States turned to foreign sources. As early as the 1820s, the larger American mills in the Northeast derived as much as a quarter of their raw wool from abroad. Great Britain, using only 5 percent foreign wools in its industry in 1800, increased that share to 30 percent within a half century.[51] Whereas British and American wool growers improved domestic production, their flocks turned out neither the finer wools like the French Merinos and German Silesians, nor the coarser wools such as those from Turkey and Argentina. Yankee sheepmen responded to the earliest stirrings in the domestic woolen trades with great investment in breeding Merinos. The trend of the 1830s among New England and Middle Atlantic breeders then turned to producing a medium-grade wool with new German Saxonies. Still more wool was needed, and the expansion of the Midwestern sheep farming a decade later coincided with the rise of the Southern Hemisphere's wool producers in Argentina, Cape Colony, Australia, and New Zealand.[52] British sheepbreeding, on the other hand, possessed a long tradition that had deteriorated behind import duties on foreign raw wools. Woolen merchants found that their broadcloths, produced from domestic Southdown wool, had been forced out of European markets by finer Flemish and French goods. British farmers, moreover, began to maintain sheep merely as sources of manure for commercial crops rather than as wool producers.[53]

The need for so much foreign wool in domestic industries justified steady decreases in import duties on raw wool. British customs accorded preferential treatment to the cheaper wools selling at less than one shilling a pound. The government dropped duties from six to one pence per pound in 1825, then to one-half pence four years later, and finally repealed the duty altogether in 1844.[54] U.S. customs duties served to protect American wool breeders, and permitted a freer entry of the cheapest foreign wools such as those from Argentina. Wools valued at less than 8 cents a pound (.4536 kilogram) entered free. Later, free access was extended to all wools at 20 cents or less a pound.[55] The latter tariff revision benefited La Plata wools, whose improvement in quality by this time had raised their traditionally low price.

### Transported in grease

Wool markets in Great Britain and the United States, therefore, opened up to foreign wools, especially to the cheap, coarse wools of South America. In the first half of the nineteenth century, La Plata's raw wool was poor in quality, of short staple, dirty, and full of burrs from native pampa grasses. It brought well under one shilling per pound (.4536 kilogram), whereas the finer German, Spanish, and Australian wools brought roughly two shillings or more. At first, British merchants in Buenos Aires traded for the wool only to get a barter return on the trade of British manufactured goods. Almost nine-tenths of La Plata's wool was shipped in grease (that is, without being washed), so that scouring at the factory reduced the weight by as much as 50 percent.[56] Buenos Aires wool with its vegetable burrs was the nemesis of machine spinning. If they remained among the wool fibers, burrs caused uneven lumps and breaks in the yarn. Moreover, the burrs had to be removed by hand. Not that the wool fiber was the worst of the lot, but its state of importation kept the price of Argentine wool under eight cents a pound. When the manufacturer had it washed, the cost per usable pound was about thirteen cents.[57]

Shipments of wool from the Río de la Plata to Britain increased steadily yet remained only about 5 percent of all wool imports. Britain preferred new wools from the imperial fold — Cape Colony, Australasia, and the British East Indies.[58] The market for Argentine wool in the United States, on the other hand, lacked such competition and even improved greatly in the late 1830s with the invention of Simpson's burr picker, which mechanically removed those perverse pampa burrs for American carpet makers. In fact, Argentine wool was the fastest growing wool import in the United States. It dominated the North American market, often constituting more than half the entire value of all foreign wool imports. The burr picker did not come into general use in Britain until the late 1850s, at which time the import of Argentine wools also began to increase (see Table 3).

### Giant soap bars

Besides hides and wool, the metropolitan industrial countries imported several other Argentine pastoral products destined for industry and agriculture. Britain purchased horsehair for stuffing fine furniture and cushions, and Argentina and Uruguay together came to supply almost two-thirds of Briain's horsehair. The La Plata region became the major source of horns for handles on tools, umbrellas, and utensils, and for the manufacture of combs and buttons. In the 1850s, Britain received over 49,446 metric tons of horns a year from the pampa region.[59] Grease or lard, a product of melted animal fats, came to be another important import because it was universally used for cooking purposes. Animal bones collected from the slaughter of cattle for the export market

Table 3. *British and American imports of raw wool from the Río de la Plata, 1827–60 (in kilograms)*

|           | Great Britain | United States |
|-----------|---------------|---------------|
| 1827–30   | 80,941        | 155,956       |
| 1831–35   | 1,162,806     | 1,320,634     |
| 1836–40   | 2,382,692     | 3,723,130     |
| 1841–45   | 6,153,276     | 17,725,732    |
| 1846–50   | 5,155,498     | 14,614,973    |
| 1851–55   | 7,161,782     | 17,037,834    |
| 1856–60   | 8,131,765     | 18,462,799    |

*Sources:* Archibald Hamilton, "On Wool Supply," *Journal of the Statistical Society of London,* Vol. 33 (Dec. 1870), p. 505; Thomas Southey, *The Rise, Progress and Present State of Colonial Wools* (London, 1848), p. 331; Great Britain, Statistical Office, *Annual Statement of Trade and Navigation of the United Kingdom with Foreign Countries and British Possessions* (London, 1855–62); and U.S. Treasury, "Report of Commerce and Navigation of the United States," in *Executive Documents* of U.S. Senate and House of Representatives, 1828–61.

provided the sodium nitrates for Europe's agricultural fertilizers. As its needs increased, Britain got up to three-quarters of its bone supplies from abroad, and the Río de la Plata contributed 6,357 metric tons a year.[60] The United States, on the other hand, imported few of these pastoral by-products.

Of all the secondary animal goods, tallow was by far the most important. Animal fat was the basic ingredient in the manufacture of candles and soap. Consumer demand — rather than technological breakthrough — increased the use of tallow in manufacturing. Besides adding a few mechanical devices, nineteenth-century candle and soap factories merely rationalized traditional domestic production procedures. Workers in larger candle factories still dipped the quality candles by hand and formed the commoner ones in single mold machines. The latter machine rotated several racks of candle molds, simultaneously filling all the molds through multiple spigots. Workers used racks with 100 candles to a frame, usually dipping one rack of candles as five others were drying. Two men on this apparatus could dip some 21,000 candles in a ten-hour day, and a large factory, mixing hand-dipped with molded candles, turned out some 20 million candles each year.

Such traditional methods, accomplished on a factory scale, likewise sustained the increasing interest in cleanliness among British consumers. Contemporaries estimated that an artisan's family used about 4.5 kilograms of soap per year. Soap making was a relatively simple process, frequently accomplished in the same factory that produced candles. Steam boilers melted tallow together with alkali and lye in large cauldrons until the mass reached the proper consistency. Workers with buckets then poured it into ten-foot-high rectangular molds, each of which produced a 1,360-kilogram slab of soap. Two men armed with cutting wire finally reduced the giant slab into bars three inches on a side for retail sales in shops.[61]

Production of soap and candles called for large amounts of raw tallow, and British manufacturers always had depended heavily upon external sources for their animal fats. Russian tallow, an important import in the eighteenth century, continued its dominance of the British market throughout the nineteenth as well. Argentina was able to capture part of that market when the Napoleonic Wars disrupted trade with the Continent. Tallow prices reached a peak of 81 pence a hundredweight (45.36 kilograms) in 1815, the year of greatest imports from Argentina. The La Plata region thereafter maintained its place on the market, providing 14 percent of British tallow supplies.[62]

Transformations in the tallow, leather, and wool trades typify the nature of increased demand for raw materials in metropolitan industry. First, greater consumer demand goaded increased production in tallow and tanning industries that continued to utilize age-old materials and techniques. Second, technological innovation begot spectacular increases in the production of woolen cloth and carpets. In both cases, the manufacturing unit was enlarged while inefficient small factories closed down. Greater use of raw materials forced more foreign imports to supplement increasingly insufficient local supplies within industrializing countries. Consequently, leather and woolen industries concentrated near ports of entry for raw materials from the La Plata and other regions.

The loss of innocence that was the industrial revolution brought a certain economic worldliness to the Río de la Plata.

Just as colonial trade had tied the port to a global system of commerce, so the nineteenth-century industrial revolution and its quickened rhythm of trade cemented that regional interdependency known as the world economy. Industrialism's "spreading effects" reached across oceans as well as land masses, linking the manufacturer to staple producer. North Atlantic ships carried the requirements of metropolitan industry to Buenos Aires and to a hundred ports throughout the Americas, Africa, and Asia. The pampa, center of expanding cattle ranching, also succumbed to technologial advances in faraway woolen factories, making possible a wholly new pastoral pursuit, sheep raising. Although its silver trade diminished, Buenos Aires was to become an even greater entrepôt of European and American shipping and the growing center of a system that drew staple exports from the entire Río de la Plata region.

# 4

## Buenos Aires as outpost of world trade

Buenos Aires' phenomenal commercial growth was part and parcel of nineteenth-century industrialism, because the city served as the emporium for one of the world's most important regions supplying pastoral raw materials. Port operations remained basic and unimproved. Yet oceanic ships in increasing numbers risked the hazardous journey up the shallow estuary. The export of staples produced on the ranches of the hinterland likewise increased, adding to a commercial prosperity that defied the region's political instability and four foreign blockades of the port. The first half of the nineteenth century also witnessed the usurpation of the import—export trade by non-Spanish — especially British — merchants who had important connections in industrial markets. They assumed the risks of the era's commerce and reaped the profits as well.

It might be an error, however, to view Buenos Aires merely as a commercial submetropolis whose trade was dominated by Great Britain, or even by industrial markets. True, the prosperity of the entire region depended upon the staple trade, and the major proportion of that trade went to industrial nations of the North Atlantic. Yet, important shares of Buenos Aires' exports went to nonindustrial nations as well — Brazil, Cuba, Italy, and Spain. After an initial period of shipping preeminence up to the 1830s, Britain lost its dominance of the carrying trades out of Buenos Aires to the vessels of other nations. Foreign merchants had to depend on a domestic marketing structure controlled by Argentines.

Finally, conventional theory leads one to believe that the balance between industrial consumers and raw material producers in this era tended to favor the industrialist. A region like the Río de la Plata was believed to have imported more from Britain and the United States than it exported, resulting in the drain of specie without adequate exchange. La Plata's legendary trade deficit is suspect: The United States never, and Great Britain not always, had favorable balances with Buenos Aires. Even though prices of pastoral goods declined during the entire period, the staple economy of Argentina increased exports in order to continue profiting from expanding industrial and world demand. Native producers were mastering the art of producing more at less cost — without the aid of new technology. While exports expanded, the domestic market for imports remained relatively stagnant, and at midcentury the staples trade of the Río de la Plata actually produced a surplus. Commercial imperialism in this region had no substantial reality up to 1860.

### Horsecarts over the river bank

By today's shipping standards, the port of Buenos Aires was a miserable place to transfer the freight of international commerce. Ships plying the pastoral trades had to venture 200 miles (nearly 300 kilometers) up to Buenos Aires by tacking back and forth across the dangerous sandbars of the estuary that is the Río de la Plata. If they avoided running aground, Liverpool ships could make the journey in about seventy days, and New York ships joined them in something like eighty days. Later improvements in sailing vessels seem to have cut sailing time to this South American region by about fifteen days.[1] Most oceanic vessels that sailed up to Buenos Aires were small (150- to 300-tons burden) for several reasons. Often the port lacked sufficient freight to fill larger ships. The hide cargo, because of its tendency to putrefy in transit, called for faster, lighter sailing vessels; and passage up the estuary was challenging to large ships. American merchant vessels, which arrived in number toward midcentury, tended to be larger, picking up partial cargoes from many ports on one voyage.[2]

Approaching the outer roads ten kilometers from shore, foreign sailors sighted the two-story, stucco dwellings that formed the city's skyline, punctured occasionally by church spires, stretching out for three kilometers along the banks. Black and mulatto washwomen, the servants and slaves of the finer porteño households, daily lined the shores with their laundry while they scrubbed articles of clothing on the rocks. One visitor asserted that Buenos Aires was not an imposing view.[3] The city, nonetheless, was taking on a cosmopolitan

aspect. Foreign sailors filled the waterfront grog ships, singing foreign sailing songs to fiddle and flute, while Madame
Faunch's Hôtel de Provence catered to ships' officers and
foreign merchants.[4]

From the ship captain's point of view, loading and unloading at Buenos Aires was as unimpressive as the skyline. Shoal
water and unimproved port facilities meant that loading time
in the outer roads could extend from 30 to 150 days.[5] Even
smaller oceanic vessels could not anchor close to shore.
Hence, sailors unloaded freight by hand from the ship's hold
over the gunwales and into sailing lighters, which then carried it across the shoals closer to the shoreline. Each piece of
freight needed additional shipping documentation in the
transfer, adding to a cost often greater than the entire freight
charge from Europe.[6] Mooring in the outer roads, moreover,
could be dangerous. Oceanic vessels as well as the smaller
rivercraft were exposed to violent *pamperos,* cold-front
storms from the southern pampa that swept wind and rain
over the estuary. Rough weather also might overturn a
lighter with all its cargo.[7] Once into the inner roads, passengers and freight were transferred from sailing lighters to
horse-drawn carts, which had been pulled into the water to
serve as mobile piers. The carts, made of Paraguayan timber
with wheels eight feet high, carried the freight over the steep
embankment of mud to the customshouse. As described by
travelers, the whole port presented a scene of bedlam: "The
sand-flat, and water beyond it, was covered with carts . . .
conveying goods to and from the ships in the roads, with
Gauchos riding about with lassos, made of strips of hide
plaited, tied to their horses' girths, to help carts requiring an
extra tug."[8]

Modest harbor improvements added little to freighting efficiency. Stone and earth moles did not extend far enough
into the shallow water to be of use, and, at any rate, rough
waters frequently washed them away. Even the two long,
heavy wharves built in the 1830s did not permit the ships to
be anchored alongside.[9] On the other hand, a pilot system in
which foreign ships picked up Buenos Aires pilots downriver
at Punto del Indio made navigation on the estuary a bit safer.
The pilot company, charging rates according to the vessel's
draft, provided service from Cabo de Santa María, Montevideo, and Ensenada.[10] Lights and buoys also were placed

over dangerous shoals of the estuary. Still, porteño officious-
ness and lethargic protocol rankled and inconvenienced
foreign shippers. They could not begin to discharge freight
until visited by customs and health officials in their sail craft.
Contrary winds might postpone those visits for several
days.[11]

Though not a natural or a convenient port, Buenos Aires
nonetheless remained the principal port of call for the entire
La Plata region. Both Montevideo and Colonia, on the East
Bank in Uruguay, had better harbors and were accessible to
oceanic and river shipping. Yet liberal commercial and customs reforms could not make Montevideo the major port,
for Buenos Aires was the gateway to the important cart and
mule trades of the Interior. Lacking greater productive hinterlands, Montevideo and Colonia merely became ports for
coastal transshipments in the region's unified commercial system dominated by the major entrepôt at Buenos Aires.[12]

*Horsecarts at the Buenos Aires customhouse, 1817.* The continued use of
horsecarts in loading and unloading international cargoes illustrates the
traditional nature of port operations at Buenos Aires. Outriders on horseback had to assist the unwieldy carts up and down the steep river bank. The
customshouse is at right. (Watercolor by E. E. Vidal, 1817.)

## Paperwork or protection

The major political-economic issue of the early nineteenth century was so-called free trade. Shortly after the May 1810 Revolution, patriots in Buenos Aires lowered customs duties and ended Spanish trade restrictions. Soon the outer roads were filled with the masts of British and American ships.[13] Free trade doctrines prompted the early revolutionary governments at Buenos Aires to end the tobacco monopoly, lower export duties on silver and gold specie, and cut ad valorem import taxes by half. Only nominal duties were laid on export items, amounting to no prohibition at all on hides and tallows as well as on specie.[14] The new trade regulation encouraged liberal commercial exchange between the city's merchants and foreign ships of all nationalities.

Actually, the prohibition of foreign vessels from trading at Buenos Aires seldom became the central issue. Rather, politicians and interest groups haggled over the customs rates on imports that might compete against national goods, and over the very control of the port and used customs revenues to fund their own government and armies, whereas the governors of the Interior and riverine provinces resorted to the traditional taxation of overland and river freight.[15] From time to time, political authorities also attempted to promote the domestic economy with outright trade restrictions. The 1824 wheat embargo, which caused much trembling among North American merchants handling the lucrative flour trade, failed to halt wheat imports. But agricultural self-sufficiency was promoted after 1836 by a sliding tariff that automatically raised import rates when local wheat harvests proved sufficient.[16] In addition, the government levied a host of port charges on foreign ships, ranging from twenty-five paper pesos for the visit of the health inspector to a forty-peso levy on ships of nations having no consul in Buenos Aires to make out the ship's roll.[17] With Argentine inflation running high in the 1840s, however, these charges created more paperwork than protection.

Two important revisions of revolutionary free trade regulations came in the 1836 and 1853 customs laws. Both had different sets of political-economic goals. The first appeared frankly protectionist, levying the sliding tariff on flour and placing a 50 percent duty on foreign wines that competed with products from the Interior. Although silver exports were discouraged, practically all other export duties were removed. The law of itself failed to promote internal trade and domestic industries, principally because its instigator, Juan Manuel de Rosas, modified those very trade restrictions five years later.[18] Other Rosas policies maintained the port as a monopoly of the province of which he was governor. He decreed that foreign vessels be prohibited from the river trades and that the Interior's import and export trade pass through Buenos Aires, thus contributing to the province's revenues. Rosas even attempted to levy additional port taxes on foreign vessels first landing at Montevideo.[19] His political efforts merely tried to reinforce existing economic reality: That is, to make Buenos Aires the principal port of the Río de la Plata. Behind the intellectual leadership of Juan Bautista Alberdi, the customs laws written into the Argentine Constitution of 1853 further liberalized trade in the region. Alberdi envisioned a freer trade, a dispersion of porteño commercial hegemony, and a growth of internal commerce. Most import duties were lowered, and port charges eliminated. Whereas foreign shipping gained direct access to ports up the Paraná River, all transit duties on interprovincial overland trade were dropped.[20] Nineteenth-century free trade developments encouraged ships and merchants of all nations to trade freely at Buenos Aires. Apart from taxing imports for revenue purposes, tariff reforms did not create the commercial system at Buenos Aires. Demand from industrial consumers and the production advantages of this pastoral region accomplished that. Restrictive customs laws rarely succeeded in discouraging the import–export syndrome.

### Whittling the British share

Two-masted sailing vessels of foreign registry served as the important link between centers of consumer demand and La Plata's pastoral production in the nineteenth century. The story of foreign shipping in the estuary is one of steady increase in volume and of significant diversification in nationality. Most ships carrying the Latin American trade at the time engaged in port hopping. Only occasionally was a ship fitted out and freighted particularly for commerce at Buenos Aires. Most stopped either at Montevideo or at other South American ports like Rio de Janeiro, Valparaíso, and Callao. In the absence of Argentine oceanic shipping, foreign vessels likewise carried La Plata's products to numerous consumers along the trade routes. Port activities at Buenos Aires increased by 5.3 percent yearly in spite of the region's political unrest and blockades, according to these figures on the annual average arrivals of foreign vessels:[21]

| | |
|---|---|
| 1810s | 107 |
| 1820s | 288 |
| 1830s | 280 |
| 1840s | 452 |
| 1850s | 674 |

British merchantmen dominated the foreign commerce of Buenos Aires early in the century but relinquished much of their hegemony as ships from other consuming nations began to carry on their own trade. At first, ships of British registry handled up to 60 percent of Buenos Aires trade. British vessels, ranging from 115 to 355 tons, arrived at the port principally from Liverpool and Gibraltar, but they also brought goods from the West African coast and Northern Europe. In those days, shipmasters were willing to take all Argentine goods offered because they were confident of being able to unload them somewhere in Europe. In fact, British ships had standing orders to touch England at Falmouth in order to receive orders whether to deliver their pastoral cargoes at Liverpool or on the Continent at Antwerp.[22] In absolute numbers, the combined shipping of other nations soon outstripped British shippers so that their share of the Buenos Aires trade dwindled to something over 20 percent. Spanish and North American tonnages, for instance, challenged and occasionally surpassed that of Great Britain, according to statistics for ship arrivals at Buenos Aires (figures in tons):[23]

| | *1857* | *1860* |
|---|---|---|
| British | 35,159 | 37,696 |
| North American | 42,842 | 39,980 |
| Spanish | 23,214 | 26,065 |
| French | 21,995 | 23,575 |
| Sardinian | 11,468 | 13,984 |
| others | 39,444 | 39,942 |

Great Britain's greatest shipping competitor toward mid-century came to be the United States. Yankee sea captains included Buenos Aires on an itinerary that carried both

European and American goods to Vera Cruz, Rio de Janeiro, California, and China. Havana, particularly, was a haven for American ships proceeding from the Argentine. Buenos Aires became the apex of a trade triangle in which Yankee brigantines from Boston, New York, and Philadelphia exchanged flour and lumber for salted meats bound for Cuban markets.[24] In Havana, the Yankee ships picked up sugar and molasses used in the United States for making rum. The remainder of the cargoes in Argentine hides and wool went to American tanneries and textile factories. By the middle of the nineteenth century, countries on the European continent also had expanded trade with the Río de la Plata on their own national vessels (see Table 4). Judging from the destinations of the ships clearing the port of Buenos Aires from 1849 to 1851, the pastoral products of the region were going to a diversified set of customers:[25]

| destination | ships | tonnage | percent of tonnage |
|---|---|---|---|
| Great Britain | 322 | 71,140 | 22.8 |
| United States | 253 | 67,589 | 21.6 |
| Cuba | 205 | 41,107 | 13.2 |
| The Germanies | 173 | 37,526 | 12.0 |
| Brazil | 207 | 35,320 | 11.3 |
| France | 135 | 28,548 | 9.1 |
| Italy | 75 | 15,622 | 5.0 |
| Spain | 56 | 15,700 | 5.0 |

Table 4. *Foreign shipping entering the port of Buenos Aires, averaged annually by percentage, 1811–60*

| Years | British | American | French | Spanish | Sardinian | Others |
|---|---|---|---|---|---|---|
| 1811–20 | 59.05 | 11.45 | 4.65 | 13.7 | — | 17.75 |
| 1821–30 | 38.8 | 34.95 | 8.9 | — | 4.7 | 12.65 |
| 1831–40 | 24.7 | 24.25 | 7.95 | 2.0 | 10.3 | 31.0 |
| 1841–50 | 20.8 | 14.35 | 7.35 | 11.65 | 10.5 | 50.65 |
| 1851–60 | 25.6 | 13.8 | 12.8 | 17.9 | 8.2 | 21.7 |

*Sources:* Adapted from Juan Carlos Nicolau, "Comercio exterior por el puerto de Buenos Aires: movimiento marítimo (1810–1855)," unpub. ms., Table 2; Clifton B. Kroeber, *The Growth of the Shipping Industry in the Río de la Plata Region, 1794–1860* (Madison, Wis., 1957), p. 127; *Registro Estadístico de Buenos Aires (REBA)*, 1857, vol. 2, p. 68; *REBA*, 1858, vol. 2, p. 81; and *REBA*, 1858, vol. 2, p. 105.

At the time, almost 35 percent of Argentine trade was destined for nonindustrial countries – Cuba, Brazil, Italy, and Spain.

The improvement of communications to Europe further integrated the Río de la Plata into the world economy. Early market information in the form of foreign newspapers and letters arrived at Buenos Aires aboard merchant vessels whose slow speed and lengthy itinerary did not always assure timeliness. In 1824, British post office packets, which had been running between Falmouth and Rio de Janeiro for sixteen years, extended a connecting run to Buenos Aires and Montevideo. Thereafter, foreign merchants in the La Plata easily maintained communication with their agents in Brazil and Britain. The royal government maintained some fourteen sailing vessels on the two routes.[26] Steam packets replaced the sailing vessels in the 1850s, so that passengers and mail traveled from Britain to Buenos Aires via Rio within one month. The Argentine government soon followed suit and operated seven steam packets on routes to Montevideo, Rio, and towns on the Uruguay and Paraná rivers.[27] The main purpose of these native steam lines, a significant technological advance in river transport, was the transportation of mails and passengers – not freight.

### German flutes to penny whistles

The La Plata region, like all Latin America in the early nineteenth century, was an importer of manufactured goods and processed foodstuffs and an exporter of raw materials. Cotton and woolen cloth, because of their manufactured cheapness, dominated that import trade. The initial market in the Río de la Plata was large. But at the same time its growth was limited. The buying market for relatively expensive foreign products was restricted to the wealthier classes and to the population living close to the port of Buenos Aires. Local manufactures and freight costs limited markets for foreign goods in the Interior.[28] At first, the high cost of such goods compared to the lesser remittance that the region earned in sales of pastoral goods aboard saddled Buenos Aires with a serious balance of payments problem. The city imported more than it exported, accounting for the exodus of much silver and gold specie to help pay off the deficit. Nevertheless, as midcentury approached, Buenos Aires' export markets had grown much faster than its own domestic use of foreign imports. While Europe's industry demanded more raw materials, Argentina's population tended to consume about as many foreign goods in 1850 as three decades earlier. The result: Later balance of payments began to favor the Río de la Plata and turn against its European and North American industrial trading partners.

Again, Great Britain monopolized markets in the port of Buenos Aires in the early nineteenth century with all manner of manufactured goods. It was said that most clothes worn by men and women in the streets of the city had been manufactured in the factories of Manchester and Lancashire. In addition, British ironmongery, earthenwares, and cutlery predominated, even among the rural population of the province. The great secret of the early success of Britain was its industrial headstart, which lowered the price of its manufactured articles and somewhat broadened traditional markets for import items in Latin America.[29] Woolens and cottons contributed up to 85 percent of all British imports in 1818 and four decades later still retained approximately 80 percent of British trade at Buenos Aires. This fact explains, in part, why Great Britain's exports to Buenos Aires in the 1850s (averaging a little more than 1 million pounds sterling) had increased only moderately over the figures of the 1820s (a little less than 1 million pounds sterling).[30] The rest of the explanation lies in the fact that other nations had begun to carve out their own market niches in the La Plata region.

The reason Great Britain's dominance fell from 60 percent of all Buenos Aires' imports in 1835 to 45 percent seven years later was the increased non-British shipping that showed up to trade at Buenos Aires. French ships arrived with fine clothing, perfumes, and wines, and Genoa and Cádiz sent out Italian and Spanish wines. From Hamburg and the Baltic came iron goods, gin, and stockings; Portugal sent salt, and Brazil contributed sugar.[31]

Yankee traders, first appearing in South America as the independence movement freed foreign trade in port after port from Rio around Cape Horn to Callao, proved to be Britain's greatest competitors. Early cargoes consisted of assorted American and European goods: as the saying went, "every thing, from a German flute to a penny whistle."[32]

Whereas more than half the American trade had been in foreign products, the pampa droughts of 1820 and 1830 firmly put U.S. flour on the Buenos Aires import market. Soon the principal South America−bound cargo out of the milling cities of Baltimore and Philadelphia came to be flour.[33] Despite the effective 1836 tariff on grain imports at Buenos Aires, U.S. flour continued to supplement local wheat production. Yet, average annual imports of North American flour never quite reached the levels of the early 1830s (figures in hectoliters):[34]

| 1826−30 | 20,104 | 1841−5  | 13,596 |
|---------|--------|---------|--------|
| 1831−5  | 34,270 | 1846−50 |  9,350 |
| 1836−40 |  6,256 | 1851−5  | 25,338 |
|         |        | 1856−60 | 29,934 |

Whereas American textiles could not challenge British clothing goods, U.S. vessels began to carry greater American manufactured goods, provisions, and especially lumber products. So great was Buenos Aires' market for lumber that Yankee skippers sailed delapidated hulls onto the very shoals near the city to be broken up for kindling.[35]

A combination of industrial and nonindustrial trading competitors also began to purchase more of Buenos Aires' export goods than Great Britain. Britain still took greater portions of Argentine tallows, horsehides, and bones. The United States, the Germanies, and France became better customers for Argentine raw wools. Although most salted hides went to the British market, these three countries − and even Spain − usually demanded greater numbers of dried cowhides. France and North America imported most of the sheepskins, whereas all the salted beef produced in Argentina found markets in Cuba and Brazil. With these competing markets, the exports of Buenos Aires increased in nearly every product (see Table 5).

Buenos Aires in this era did not have a typical monocultural export economy, depending on the export of one staple product. The very diversity of products ensured a well-diversified group of customers. Cattlehides dominated trade throughout the entire period, but that item lost its primacy to raw wool as the principal export at the close of the 1850s. In addition, many of the primary exports underwent modest industrial processing accomplished in slaughterhouses and wool-washing houses (see Table 6).

Table 5. *Average annual exports of pastoral goods from the port of Buenos Aires, 1811–60*

|  | 1810s | 1820s | 1830s | 1840s | 1850s |
|---|---|---|---|---|---|
| Cattle hides | 574,460 | 624,101 | 798,564 | 2,303,910 | 1,762,356 |
| Salted meat (tons) | 984 | 1,498 | 9,860 | 21,092 | 19,048 |
| Raw wool (tons) | 150 | 252 | 2,106 | 6,158 | 10,116 |
| Tallow, grease (tons) | 1,294 | 380 | 2,078 | 9,542 | 7,766 |
| Horsehides | 144,898 | 296,889 | 31,903 | 163,022 | 158,220 |
| Sheepskins (doz.) | n.a.[a] | n.a. | 78,002 | 101,047 | 382,922 |
| Nutria skins (doz.) | 9,149 | 14,939 | 107,908 | 28,160 | 7,856 |
| Horsehair (tons) | 108 | 428 | 812 | 1,182 | 1,148 |

[a] Not available.
*Sources:* Averaged only from available statistics. The years 1811 to 1823 from R. A. Humphreys, ed., *British Consular Reports on the Trade and Politics of Latin America*, vol. 63, *1824–1826* (London, 1940), p. 60; 1822, 1825, 1829, and 1837 from Woodbine Parish, *Buenos Ayres and the Rio de la Plata* (London, 1839), p. 354; 1829 from José María Mariluz Urquijo, *Estado e industria, 1810–1862* (Buenos Aires, 1969), p. 67; and Archivo General de la Nación (AGN), Buenos Aires, Colección Biblioteca Nacional, bundle 27, document 18, pp. 154–5; 1836 to 1839 from AGN, Sala 10, 42-10-11, "Aduana. Movimiento Portuario" (1830–42); 1842 from Freeman Hunt, ed., *Merchant's Magazine, and Commercial Review*, vol. 9 (1844), p. 90; 1848 to 1851 from Woodbine Parish, *Buenos Ayres and the Rio de la Plata*, 2d ed. (London, 1852), p. 354; 1857 from *Registro Estadístico de Buenos Aires (REBA)*, 1857, vol. 2, pp. 29–30; and 1859 from *REBA*, 1860, vol. 2, pp. 76–7.

## Balance of trade

Throughout the first half of the nineteenth century, Buenos Aires' exports grew in volume and in value at a greater rate than its imports. Was that increase enough to offset Argentina's original trade deficits? That remains a question much less easy to answer, because customs reports at Buenos Aires seldom calculated trade balances. Even those fragmentary statistics that were reported are suspect as to their real meaning.

Indeed, all porteño trade figures at the time do point to serious and consistent trade deficits. In fact, the only continuous statistics available show that the deficit between 1835 and 1842 was running at more than one-quarter the total value of all trade (imports plus exports). Buenos Aires' customshouse registered 484.1 million paper pesos worth of foreign imports, and only 311.1 million paper pesos worth of Argentine exports for the eight-year period. Even accounting for the inflation of the paper peso — from 1835 to 1840, inflation had reduced its value by three-quarters — the annual trade deficit was running at some 3.7 million gold pesos.[36]

Nevertheless, these statistics of the Buenos Aires customshouse do not represent even the approximate trading picture for the entire region. They only account for what passed through the customshouse of the port city — and it was well known that not everything did. Contraband, the onus of colonial trade, carried over into the early Independence period, when the Argentines tried to teach the first British merchants the fine art of smuggling.[37] Even so, governmental edicts condemning smuggling ceased for the later period, and it is likely that the major merchants, because they were foreigners, actually paid their customs duties.

One must have other reservations about the customshouse figures, for they tend to underestimate real exports. Buenos Aires served as the center of importing, because the distribu-

Table 6. *Buenos Aires' exports as expressed in percentages of total yearly values,* *1822–59*

|  | 1825 | 1837 | 1848 | 1859 |
|---|---|---|---|---|
| Cattlehides | 47.2 | 56.8 | 50.4 | 31.5 |
| Salted meat | 9.4 | 7.1 | 7.7 | 13.7 |
| Raw wool | n.a. [a] | 10.8 | 12.5 | 33.7 |
| Specie | 27.9 | 16.0 | n.a. | n.a. |
| Tallow grease | 0.3 | 5.0 | 22.2 | 9.6 |
| Horsehair | 2.4 | 4.1 | 3.4 | 1.4 |
| Horsehides | 6.1 | 0.8 | 1.1 | 1.6 |
| Nutria skins | n.a. | 2.6 | n.a. | 1.4 |
| Sheepskins | n.a. | 2.6 | 1.3 | 1.4 |

[a] Not available.

Sources: Woodbine Parish, *Buenos Ayres and the Rio de la Plata* (London, 1839), p. 354; Archivo General de la Nación, Buenos Aires, Sala 10, 42-10-11, "Aduana. Movimiento portuario" (1830–42); Woodbine Parish, *Buenos Ayres and the Rio de la Plata*, 2d. ed. (London, 1852), p. 354; and *Registro Estadístico de Buenos Aires*, 1860, vol. 2, pp. 76–7.

tion system focused on the port and its merchant community. But it was not the funnel of *all* pastoral exporting. Quilmes and Ensenada, downriver from Buenos Aires, were alternative outlets used particularly during the blockades. Estancieros along the coast in the South and East often sent goods to Montevideo or to oceanic ships in the river via small coastal sailing craft. One reference exists to a English-born estanciero on the coast who transported bales of wool *directly* to Great Britain.[38] More commonly, riverboats from the riverine provinces transferred produce to oceanic ships at Colonia and Montevideo or elsewhere in the estuary. Producers in Entre Ríos, for instance, resorted to this export channel, especially when blockages hampered the most convenient deposits at Buenos Aires. In the 1850s, foreign ships proceeded directly to river ports on the Uruguay and Paraná rivers, often arriving in ballast after depositing import goods at Buenos Aires.[39] Buenos Aires may have been the largest and most convenient entrepôt of pastoral exports, but it was not the only avenue of export in the region. Porteño customshouse records, therefore, more perfectly reflect imports than exports.

At least one well-placed and interested observer in the 1820s cautioned about the interpretation of customshouse receipts. Woodbine Parish, the British consul general, normally subtracted 30 percent from import values for the duties, port charges, commissions, and warehouse rent on foreign products that were paid to Argentines but which were normally included in the total value of imports. Alternately, Parish added 30 percent to export figures because exporters apparently short-manifested their shipments to avoid even nominal export fees. The difference, still showing a small balance in favor of imports in the 1820s, was more than made up by the limited investment of foreign merchants in Argentine shops and estancias.[40] If one applies the Parish formula to the official trade figures mentioned above for 1835 to 1842, Buenos Aires' trade deficit, in fact, would be converted into a substantial surplus!

Little doubt exists that initial trade balances, at a time before export markets had expanded sufficiently, were unfavorable. But historians have assumed negative balances of trade for the entire period without having reliable and consistent data.[41] British parliamentary figures for 1824 indicate

that Buenos Aires' dominant trading partner exported
803,237 pounds sterling worth of goods to the La Plata, while
importing less than half as much, 388,338 pounds.[42] The
reason for the suspected trade deficit was the very weight of
British products, often three-quarters of all Buenos Aires'
imports. Nevertheless, published British trade figures for the
1850s reveal a trade deficit with Argentina. Between 1849
and 1860, Great Britain's trade deficit averaged 125,000
pounds sterling a year (see Table 7).

In addition, U.S. customshouse figures for American trade
with the Río de la Plata indicate that the balance of trade
consistently favored both Argentina and Uruguay to such an
extent that the amount of the American deficit annually
reached 1.6 million dollars in the early 1850s (see Table 8).
In fact, it was the industrial trading partner, the United
States, that lost silver and gold specie to the raw materials
producer, Argentina, in order to pay for that deficit. In the
decade of 1850, Yankee merchants yearly were sending

Table 7. *United Kingdom's balance of trade with Argentina, 1849–60 (in pounds sterling)*

|      | Imported from Argentina | Exported to Argentina | United Kingdom's balance |
|------|-------------------------|-----------------------|--------------------------|
| 1849 | 1,392,445 | 1,426,812 | +34,373 |
| 1850 | 984,372 | 873,669 | −110,703 |
| 1851 | 1,006,420 | 472,944 | −533,476 |
| 1852 | 998,394 | 875,140 | −123,254 |
| 1853 | 800,366 | 573,911 | −226,455 |
| 1854 | 1,285,186 | 1,300,148 | +14,962 |
| 1855 | 1,052,033 | 769,538 | −282,495 |
| 1856 | 981,193 | 1,042,221 | +61,082 |
| 1857 | 1,573,558 | 1,342,419 | −231,139 |
| 1858 | 1,194,977 | 1,036,204 | +158,773 |
| 1859 | 1,664,092 | 987,743 | −676,349 |
| 1860 | 1,101,428 | 1,820,935 | +719,507 |

*Source:* Adapted from Great Britain, Statistical Office, *Annual Statement of Trade and Navigation of the United Kingdom with Foreign Countries and British Possessions* (London, 1853−61). Figures for 1849−53 are given in official value, and those for 1854−60 in declared value.

Table 8. *United States' balance of trade with the Río de la Plata, 1827–60 (averaged annually in thousands of dollars)*

|  | Imported from | | Exported to | |
|---|---|---|---|---|
|  | Argentina | Uruguay | Argentina | Uruguay |
| 1827−30 | 685 | — | 390 | — |
| 1831−5 | 1,235 | — | 793 | — |
| 1836−40 | 775 | 230 | 327 | 61 |
| 1841−5 | 1,483 | 243 | 469 | 268 |
| 1846−50 | 1,286 | 148 | 486 | 211 |
| 1851−5 | 2,446 | 214 | 899 | 296 |
| 1856−60 | 3,184 | 607 | 1,183 | 711 |

*Source:* Adapted from U.S. Treasury, "Report on Trade and Navigation of the United States," in U.S. House and Senate *Executive Documents* (Washington, D.C., 1828−61).

131,000 dollars in specie to Argentina and getting only 7,000 dollars in return.[43]

### Attention to endless detail

Shortly after 1810, a group of non-Hispanic merchants with connections in North Atlantic markets supplanted those wealthy Spaniards and Creoles who had directed the import−export trade of viceregal Buenos Aires. British merchants predominated, but by no means excluded French, German, and U.S. traders who resided in the Río de la Plata. The basis of their advantage over Argentine merchants was the foreign traders' affiliations with markets abroad and access to superior capital resources for the worldwide movement of goods. Unlike their viceregal counterparts, these foreigners lacked domestic contacts throughout the region and therefore depended on a secondary level of native porteño merchants to handle the merchandising to the backlands. Estancia production became an important investment outlet for native capital. Many colonial commercial families, finding their ties to Spanish markets ruptured after the revolution, put their funds into cattle raising. Still, the absence of capital-intensive production such as mining, and the cheapness of traditional technology in production and transportation, restricted foreign capital to commerce and sheep-breeding estancias. Although foreign merchants manipulated most imports and exports through the port, they themselves did not determine the nature of that trade. They merely responded to conditions in markets for raw materials abroad and to Argentina's advantages in production.

British merchant dominance at Buenos Aires in the early national period reflects the primacy of British trade in the region. The arrival of a British consul general in 1824 with a trade treaty established Britain as the most favored nation. Great Britain was, in fact, the most influential trading partner of the La Plata at the time. By 1818, a total of fifty-five British import–export houses facilitated the trade between Buenos Aires and Europe. British merchants had established their own reading room, which collected the latest commercial news and mails from Europe.[44] Most foreign firms were partnerships, one partner established at Buenos Aires and the other in Britain. Housed in residence-warehouses in downtown Buenos Aires, these foreigners acted as commission agents. They ordered import goods for Argentine wholesalers, and purchased and shipped pastoral goods to mercantile firms back in Britain.[45]

Commercial conditions periodically forced readjustments in the porteño merchant community and ultimately spelled the end of British overextension. Before 1825, twenty-seven merchant houses had to consolidate, face liquidation, or go bankrupt. More fell during the Brazilian blockade after 1826. Beginning in 1835, British merchants slowly relinquished their control of the markets to other foreigners and to native merchants. British firms comprised only one-fifth of all exporters in the 1860s.[46] Later, Buenos Aires' trade came under the authority of influential French, German, and Brazilian exporters and several houses with mixed foreign and native proprietorship. Creole and Spanish traders again flourished when Spanish trade revived. Of the ten largest brokerage houses, handling one-third of all overseas trade in 1850, not one was British.[47]

The U.S. merchant presence in Buenos Aires was never as great or as well organized as that of the Europeans. Only three bonafide U.S. commission houses operated at Buenos Aires in the early 1820s, and thirty years later, there were only five houses. Most U.S. commerce of the era, in fact, was not consigned. Commercial agents traveling on ships under the nomenclature of "supercargoes" generally disposed of cargoes in South American ports as they saw fit.[48]

Foreign traders achieved their supremacy from their contacts abroad, which availed them of international credit and opportunities to purchase goods on consignment. In importing, contacts with manufacturers directly or through European partners offered the foreigner at Buenos Aires the chance to request the consignment of especially salable items. Early British merchants, the Robertsons, bragged of setting looms to work in England to produce exactly the goods they had recommended.[49] Another British trader attempted to corner the large market for ponchos by ordering their manufacture by British factories in popular colors and sizes. Flushed with some success, he later attempted to repeat the formula with the intricately woven rugs of the Pampa Indians – and failed. At least one Manchester cotton manufactuer, Owen & Co., devoted the greater part of its production to the South American trades. It dispatched goods to Buenos Aires through a Liverpool exporter who had a permanent agent in the Río de la Plata.[50] The House of DeForest, an early New York hide importer on the South Street docks, owed much ot its success to the fact that a DeForest relative had been one of the first U.S. merchant adventurers in the La Plata. Additional contacts of these foreign merchants might be in Montevideo or in Rio de Janeiro and Valparaíso, Chile. The largest U.S. counting house, Frazier, Zimmerman, & Co. for example, maintained a warehouse in Montevideo for the transshipment of goods. Many newly established firms in Buenos Aires actively solicited known metropolitan exporters, exaggerating the profit possibilities and advising them as to suitable cargo for La Plata's market.[51]

Despite their management of commerce at Buenos Aires, foreign merchants depended on a far-flung complex of native merchants. Argentines, after all, had inherited domestic commercial expertise and contacts in all parts of the domestic market. The complicated business of the movement of goods from ships, through customs, and to the local warehouses, not to mention their further distribution, necessitated attention to endless detail for which knowledge of local practices and language was indispensable. Foreigners often preferred to sell their goods aboard ship in order to avoid the confusion that followed.[52] Similarly, native merchants took charge of assembling pastoral goods for export. The Anchorenas marketed import goods and purchased hides and tallows for export. The family maintained the necessary connections, for example, to gather hides from some twenty porteño estancieros on an export cargo delivered to Hullet Brothers & Co. of London.[53] Other Argentine merchants actively maintained footholds in foreign trade, especially in the export of pastoral products to minor markets. A prominent local trader still kept up his Rio de Janeiro contacts for exporting salted meats despite having moved into widespread domestic procurement of all export goods.[54]

If Argentines were not actual partners in some export houses, they were at least important subsidiaries. The U.S. brokerage firm of Zimmerman, Frazier & Co. did much business with the Irish-porteño family of Patricio Lynch. Judging from the advertisements in Spanish-language newspapers for export cargoes, foreigners frankly would have been hard pressed to organize export shipments without Argentine intermediaries. Lacking native wholesaling, British and other foreigners had to resort to the *remate público* (public auction) in order to liquidate the shipments of foreign clients.[55] Without doubt, the foreign traders formed the apex of the commercial system of Buenos Aires, but Argentine merchants participated fully in a structure that demanded contributions by both natives and foreigners.

Foreign merchants normally charged commissions of 2.5 percent on consignments handled through their offices. The profits realized from these sales often were put into further mercantile shipments. Nevertheless, much investment did find its way into developing the commercial infrastructure of the region. British merchants were particularly amenable to funding their immigrant countrymen in artisan shops and retail stores. Most foreign tailor shops or linen drapers were located in Buenos Aires, although travelers occasionally encountered European shopkeepers in the Interior.[56] Led by the British, foreigners invested visibly in the pastoral expansion of the age. John Gibson and his brothers were British import merchants who in 1826 shifted their capital into an estancia on Bahía Samborombón. They and their offspring then turned the ranch to sheep breeding. Sheridan, Harrat, and Whitfield, in particular, set up a pastoral operation in the 1820s to breed and sell purebred Merino rams to nascent sheep ranchers throughout the pampa.[57]

Foreign investment had severe limits, however. Domestic

transportation, retailing, processing, ranching, and farming expanded on relatively modest investments by creoles and immigrants. They already knew the traditional technology and management techniques involved, and these were inexpensive. Economic expansion in Argentina, given the markets and resources of the region, justified investments of no grander scale – a lesson foreign investors soon learned. In 1824, a London investment bank, the House of Baring, floated a bond issue for 1 million pounds sterling, backed by the government of Buenos Aires, which had borrowed 600,000 pounds from Baring. The porteños, however, misappropriated the loan for the war against Brazil, and succeeding politicians in Buenos Aires saw little advantage in even paying the interest.[58] Meanwhile, foreigners residing in the port and several porteños attempted to establish an investment bank in Argentina, the Banco de la Provincia de Buenos Aires. They were responding to the European mining mania of 1825. Quickly formed mining enterprises already had foreign engineers attempting to revive old Spanish mines in Potosí and La Rioja. But the Potosí, La Paz, and Peruvian Mining Association and La Famatina Mining Company, both of which had created euphoric expectations among speculators in London, collapsed in the financial crisis of 1826. Soon thereafter, the Banco de la Provincia turned to issuing paper money.[59] At the time, economic opportunities in Argentina were limited to the pastoral pursuits supporting the export trade. This placed a ceiling on foreign investment in the Argentine economy and restricted foreign management to the import–export trade, a few shops, and sheep ranches.

### A dearth of Spanish dollars

The money situation at Buenos Aires – that is, the disappearance of silver and the advent of paper currency – made the foreign export merchant even more indispensable but, at the same time, limited his ability to exploit his commercial ascendency at Buenos Aires. Exports of silver and the collapse of the Potosí mining operations drained the port of its specie reserves in the 1820s. Previously, foreign merchants utilized silver bullion, laboriously hauled about in oxcarts, to pay for their imports of manufactured goods.[60] In its place, the provincial government issued the paper peso. A spiral of inflation, based on the generous emissions of paper money, began immediately. Merchants who accepted remittances in paper currency soon found their profits dwindling at the rate of inflation. Consequently, foreign traders had to take payment in local products such as hides and tallow. They made profits on those sales back in metropolitan markets when and where they could.[61] Moreover, the silver deficiency created the need of international exchange – the Bill or Letter of Credit. "Bills on England in payment for these cargoes [from all parts of the world]," wrote one supercargo, ". . . have been substituted for Spanish dollars, which formerly were indispensable to the prosecution of this trade."[62]

The letter of credit, also known as the trade bill or the bill of exchange, was an international bank draft issued by reputable merchants as convenient payment for trade debts and payable at a specific future date. In those days, letters of credit circulated freely at all levels of trade. A merchant at Buenos Aires might purchase goods from a ship captain with a bill drawn on his partner or on a bigger merchant banker in London. Porteño traders accepted letters of credit on the sales of pastoral goods and used them to pay freight charges in the movement of produce to metropolitan markets. C_<sup>1:</sup>-narily, the bill was payable in British pounds sterling or U.S. dollars at ninety days maturity. He who ultimately paid the bill earned a commission of 2.5 percent. So versatile did these bills become that they often served the holders as money, which the latter in turn could use for their own commercial debts. If the creditor wished, payment could be made on a bill of exchange before maturity – but at a small discount of the face value.[63] A type of letter of credit, called the *libranza,* had been in wide use among Spanish and native porteño merchants since colonial times. Commonly, these credits passed between foreign and local merchants and were accepted by the customshouse in partial payment of customs duties. Foreign exporters collecting cargoes of pastoral goods – if they had no import products to barter – often paid Argentine producers and middlemen with drafts at 1 percent interest and four months maturity.[64] Nineteenth-century international trade and exchange, therefore, was carried forward on credit and not on the cumbersome exchange of silver bullion or inflated paper currency.

Two merchant houses in particular, the House of Baring in London and Brown Brothers & Co. of Baltimore, specialized in covering the international exchange of goods with their financial assets and prestigious names. In faraway ports like Buenos Aires, both houses maintained clients and agents having authority to issue letters of credit payable in most metropolitan ports. The Baring family had made its fortune during the eighteenth century in the European trade, which the Rothschilds came to dominate after the Napoleonic Wars. With a branch in Liverpool, Baring then turned to the American trade and, through their vast credit network, became involved in the worldwide movement of Brazilian coffee, Cuban sugar, U.S. wheat and cotton, and Argentine hides. In Latin America alone, Baring had agents in Havana, Vera Cruz, and Rio de Janeiro. In Buenos Aires, it was represented by German-American merchants with Philadelphia connections, Zimmerman, Frazier & Co. On Baring's account, the porteño brokerage house provided credits for the movement of pastoral goods from Buenos Aires, as well as arranging freight insurance and furnishing international market reports. The London house then collected commissions after the sale of merchandise. Likewise, the American merchant banker, Brown Brothers, honored letters of credit used in the United States to import coffee, copper, sugar, bird fertilizers (*guano*), and hides from South America. The Baltimore firm, through branches in New York and Philadelphia, often retained title to the shipments until import merchants had sold the goods in order to pay up letters of credit drawn on Brown Brothers.[65] Although lack of silver in the Río de la Plata forced merchants to trade for local produce and pastoral goods, the rise of commercial credit demanded traders with international connections.

### Making fortunes in a closed port

Foreign trade through the port of Buenos Aires periodically fell off as a result of four naval blockades by foreign powers within the first forty years of independence. The Spanish Imperial Navy, stationed at Montevideo, maintained a blockade of Buenos Aires from 1811 to 1816, to some extent complicating the lucrative British trade beginning there.[66] In the war over the Banda Oriental, a Brazilian fleet invested

the port in 1827 and 1828. Ten years later, the French block-
aded Buenos Aires simultaneously with Vera Cruz, Mexico,
until 1840. The most effective was the final blockade from
1845 to 1848, when British warships joined a French fleet in
the first year, forcing open the Paraná River to international
shipping. All these blockades had one thing in common —
their general porosity. Far from stopping completely commercial exchange in the estuary, the blockades merely dispersed it and enhanced its speculative nature. In most cases,
commercial capital flowed into pastoral production so that,
once trade resumed officially through the Buenos Aires customshouse, exports reached even greater levels.

Blockade running became an ordinary pastime for many
foreign ships in the Río de la Plata. Whereas British shipmasters refrained out of respect for British foreign policy,
Americans consistently slipped through the barriers to profit
from inflated prices and trading opportunities at Buenos
Aires. At the height of the Brazilian blockade in 1827,
thirty-six Yankee ships and four others slipped through to
trade at Buenos Aires. American merchants even resorted to
timely bribes of the blockading naval authorities in order to
sell their goods at fair prices. "American vessels were weekly
running past, breaking the blockade, and making fortunes for
their owners," observed one traveler, "while scarce an English one made the attempt."[67] Yankee profits annoyed
British merchants at Buenos Aires, who were sitting on their
commercial hands for the duration. Loss of trade also raised
the ire of merchants back in Great Britain. Commercial
interests in Manchester and other industrial towns petitioned
the British foreign office to lift the annoying blockades.[68]
With imports down and prices up in Buenos Aires, speculation in blockade running rose. One Creole merchant actively
sought French cargoes of wine and liquor — during a French
blockade — in order to profit from high prices in the Buenos
Aires plaza.[69]

During blockades, trade also shifted to secondary ports on
the estuary and then was transshipped to Buenos Aires in
smaller coastal vessels. Ships landed below Buenos Aires at
Ensenada, where the lack of customs duties partially made up
for the inconvenience of landing cargoes there. Blockades
diverted Argentine trade to Montevideo and Colonia.
Lighter craft crossed from Buenos Aires with hides and re-

turned with foreign goods.[70] Although freight rates were thus raised by transshipment, higher prices at Buenos Aires easily made up the difference. U.S. shipping especially turned to commerce at Montevideo during the last two blockades. Most pastoral goods that Yankee vessels picked up on the East Bank in the Anglo-French blockade originated from across the river. American vessels carried away no raw wool at all from Montevideo before the blockade, yet picked up more than 450,000 kilograms of wool there in 1849.[71]

Periodic closures of the port also tended to reshuffle the foreign merchant community, turning their profits and capital temporarily into domestic production. As a blockade approached, import—export houses rushed to liquidate their warehouses. Marginal concerns occasionally went bankrupt in the hard times, while stronger firms sought investments in land and cattle as an outlet for their reserves of native currency. Rapid investment of paper money was absolutely necessary, because the blockades at Buenos Aires always quickened inflation. Loss of customs duties forced the porteño government to export silver and print more paper money in order to finance the province's war effort.[72] Far from ruining Buenos Aires trade, port closures actually contributed to the production of pastoral goods for future exports. "In the impossibility of making returns to Europe during the continuance of the [Brazilian] blockade," wrote the British consul general at Buenos Aires, "the greater part of the large amount of foreign property . . . was laid out in cattle-farms, agricultural establishments, saladeros (where the *jerk* beef is made), houses, and a variety of speculations, the general tendency of which was greatly to improve the real resources of the country."[73] Trade continued despite the diplomatic disagreements in the La Plata and resumed in greater measure following each naval blockade.

### Falling prices — rising trade

La Plata exports expanded throughout the entire era, even though prices for pastoral raw materials on the international marketplace gradually declined. Characteristically, the technological and managerial innovations that accompanied the industrial revolution — assuring more efficient production and transportation of goods — lowered the purchase prices of manufactured items.[74] World prices for most raw materials, notwithstanding industry's greater demand for them, also fell gradually from the 1810s through midcentury. Pastoral goods were not immune from these price trends. From their high levels in 1815, prices for hides and tallows fell steadily until they reached fractions of their wartime highs. Wool proved the exception. The dramatic demand of American woolen industries in the 1850s reversed the gradual price decline of Argentine raw wool. In most other cases, increased flow of raw materials into Britain and the United States from production areas like the Río de la Plata actually depressed raw material prices.[75] Plainly, the hinterlands of Buenos Aires continued to produce more pastoral goods.

In like manner, Buenos Aires merchants assembling export cargoes paid less for pastoral items on the domestic market. Available price indexes demonstrate that general prices for almost all Argentine pastoral commodities fell steadily, until by 1850 prices were only 70 percent of what they had been seventeen years earlier (see Figure 2). The lone exceptions were for the sales of wool, because of a dramatic industrial demand in the late 1840s and the 1850s, and of salted meats, which served nonindustrial markets in Cuba and Brazil.[76] Price levels dropped strikingly when blockades temporarily curtailed wholesale exportation. Met-

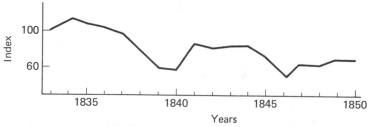

Figure 2. Index of real prices of pastoral products in Buenos Aires, 1833–50. Expanding production of livestock on the pampa and the introduction of the processing industry to Buenos Aires gradually reduced the prices of export products at the port. Only the trade booms that immediately followed the port blockades of 1839 and 1847 momentarily reversed the downward trend. [*Source:* Julio Broide, *La evolución de los precios agropecuarios argentinos en el período 1830–1850* (Buenos Aires, 1951).]

ropolitan markets, too, depended upon untrammeled foreign supplies to maintain low commodity prices. In that regard, U.S. hide markets experienced sharp rises in hide prices as the cessation of normal La Plata hide imports in 1839 caused shortages in hide supplies (see Figure 3). Notably, porteños neither curtailed exports of pastoral products, nor halted the relentless expansion of ranching, nor restricted domestic marketing throughout the entire region.

If economic imperialism is a historical issue, then it must be connected to foreign commercial supremacy at the port of

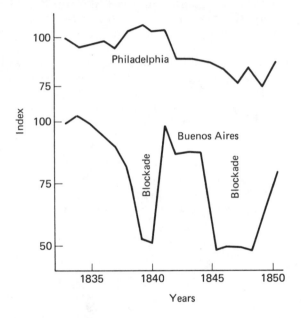

Figure 3. Comparative prices of hides in Buenos Aires and Philadelphia, 1833–50. The fall in wholesale prices of pastoral goods was reflected in metropolitan ports as well. Hide prices in Philadelphia were sensitive to the supply from the Río de la Plata region. In 1839 and 1847, when naval blockades prohibited the exporting of hides from Buenos Aires, the relative scarcity shot prices upward in Philadelphia. Marginal tanners in the United States felt the pinch as their costs for raw materials rose accordingly. [*Sources:* Anne Bezanson, Robert D. Gray, and Miriam Hussey, *Wholesale Prices in Philadelphia, 1784–1861,* 2 vols. (Philadelphia, 1936–7), vol. 2, p. 94; and Julio Broide, *La evolución de los precios agropecuarios argentinos en el período 1830–1850* (Buenos Aires, 1951).]

Buenos Aires. Generally, historians have discounted political intervention as a characteristic of British presence in this era.[77] The reputed British and foreign commercial domination of the import—export sector, however, remains an item of contention. Did foreign merchants, for instance, restrict trade in Argentina to fit the needs of metropolitan industrial economies?

On the contrary, it seems that commerce expanded in a manner quite beneficial to the region right up to 1860. Early British domination of shipping and of importing and exporting had been eroded seriously by midcentury, when a combination of foreign and native merchants combined to erase the early importance in the import—export market that British merchants had enjoyed at Buenos Aires. Admittedly, international mechanisms of supplying foreign markets ensured the place of foreign merchants, but the merchants of no one nationality excluded the others from Buenos Aires. The lack of investment opportunities in traditional transportation and production industries, moreover, prevented foreigners from gaining access to more than just the export-import trade. Even the validity of balance-of-trade deficits, by which the metropolis might drain off the region's wealth, is highly suspect. In fact, the trade balances seem to have been favorable to Argentina. At the time, foreign markets and the staple exports that served them were quite diverse, allowing much flexibility in the growth of local pastoral production. Hides early replaced silver bullion as the leading export and later were replaced by wool. Each shift in staple exports denoted a maturity of pastoral production and of processing in the domestic economy. Buenos Aires maintained and expanded trading relations with nations that could not be termed "industrial" — notably northern Italian states, Spain, Cuba, and Brazil. Production in the Río de la Plata also surmounted possible problems of falling raw material prices. Growth of the export sector, in fact, even overcame temporary setbacks presented by port blockades.

A combination of industrial demand and local production advantages certainly determined the nature of the expanding import—export trade at Buenos Aires more than any conspiracy or competition among foreign merchants residing in the port city. Furthermore, each rise in the amount of export broadened La Plata's economic infrastructure. Metropolitan demand spurred commercial growth in this outpost of international trade. Buenos Aires, in turn, sparked socioeconomic growth of areas upriver to the northwest, of the Interior west to the Andes Mountains, and especially of the prairies to the south. To support growth of the region's staple economy, porteños developed a sophisticated marketing and processing system at the port.

# 5

# Buenos Aires as emporium of regional trade and processing

Exportation of pastoral raw materials could not have proceeded without a concurrent development of Buenos Aires as freight handler to the entire La Plata region. The backward and forward linkages of the staple economy were surprisingly strong. Both the overland wagon routes and the extensive waterways of the Paraná-Uruguay River Basin terminated at the international port, which also furnished wholesale markets and warehouses to gather and store goods prior to delivery to foreign ships. The city also became the center of a cattle processing industry that prepared pastoral products for export. Once sold on the hoof in huge stockyards outside the city, cattle were slaughtered with a minimum of waste in centralized factories. Increased efficiency and rationalization – actually without new technology – marked the development of the entire processing and merchandising system.

Expansion of the export commerce, in turn, provoked development of the domestic market of Buenos Aires – the final-demand linkage of staple exports. Migrants from the Interior provinces and immigrants from Europe seeking employment in the city's economic boom swelled the urban community. A population that nearly doubled every quarter century expanded the domestic market for products from all over the region. Remarkably, a broad complex of Creole and immigrant merchants – not the foreign import-exporter – directed the transport and processing industries at Buenos Aires. Natives arranged, financed, and conducted domestic commerce to river ports and to cities in the Interior. Although stockyards and marketplaces were public domain, Creoles operated a substantial number of warehouses and all the transportation and freight facilities of the region. Natives and immigrant settlers even contributed the capital and management that rationalized the cattle-processing factories and developed the transportation and distribution systems. A staple economy with such widespread linkages also provided much social opportunity.

## Decks piled high

Its location near the delta of the region's two great rivers — the Paraná and the Uruguay — rendered Buenos Aires the leading terminal of river shipping. Expansion in the port's foreign trade stimulated use of wooden sailing vessels for carrying bulk freight from Uruguay, Paraguay, and the riverine provinces of Argentina. Imported canvas sails hoisted on masts of native timbers enabled craft to tack up the shallow rivers against the currents. Two-masted brigantines with square-rigged sails and broad, single-masted smacks carried payloads weighing more than fifty tons. Some craft, like schooners and scows, were shallow-drafted and roomy freight carriers, and others, like the sloop with main and jib sheets, were narrow and sleek. Early British merchants in Corrientes reported piling the decks high with bales of hides for the trip down to Buenos Aires. Approaching the sandbars of the delta, larger craft at times unloaded deck cargoes onto smaller vessels for the journey to port. Most craft proceeded to Buenos Aires or to the Riachuelo, a small river south of the city, to unload regional products and take on return cargoes of European goods. Other vessels put in above the city at Las Conchas, where cartmen transshipped the freight to urban markets.[1] Toward midcentury, riverboats eliminated some transshipment by loading provincial export cargoes directly onto foreign ships in the outer roads of Buenos Aires. Steamboats of foreign make appeared on the rivers in the 1850s but carried little freight. Steam navigation of the era merely facilitated passenger service and commercial correspondence in the region.[2] Traditional sailing vessels of modest size, therefore, bound the territories of the river basin into a regional commercial system whose hub was the port of Buenos Aires.

Of all cargo deposited at Buenos Aires by river shipping, at least a third consisted of export products. Dried hides, horsehair, wool, tallow, sheepskins, and nutria pelts came from small ports serving the grazing areas along the Uruguay and Paraná rivers. River shipping contributed to the boom in foreign trade at Buenos Aires. As oceanic tonnages increased, so did the amount of cargo deposited at Buenos Aires by coastal vessels (figures in tons):[3]

|      | foreign | coastal | coastal as a percent of foreign |
|------|---------|---------|---------------------------------|
| 1837 | 48,354  | 23,626  | 49                              |
| 1858 | 191,376 | 62,933  | 31                              |

Buenos Aires' domestic market, however, provided the chief stimulus for coastal shipping. Foodstuffs like wheat, cheese, yerba, corn, and even watermelons arrived via coastal vessels. Most important was the freight in wood products such as kindling, posts, timber, and charcoal from areas as far away as Paraguay or as near as the delta islands. In 1810, approximately 700 riverboats put in at Buenos Aires, and fifty years later more than 2,000 rivercraft arrived annually. Statistics for Buenos Aires and the Riachuelo River show the following growth of river traffic:[4]

|      | arrivals | departures |
|------|----------|------------|
| 1810 | 664      | 999        |
| 1830 | 1,426    | 2,114      |
| 1860 | 2,558    | 3,877      |

Riverboats utilized alternate ports to avoid the increasing congestion of foreign ships and lighter craft in the channels off Buenos Aires. Boats of five to ten tons delivered domestic cargo at Las Conchas (Tigre), where carts transshipped the produce to market. The number of coastal vessels trading out of the suburban ports of Las Conchas and San Fernando in the 1820s outnumbered Buenos Aires' traffic by three to one – even though freight tonnage was smaller.[5] Boca del Riachuelo, at the mouth of the river immediately south of Buenos Aires, became the most important harbor for domestic boats. Lighter craft regularly transported hides and meats from the slaughter plants along the river directly to foreign vessels mooring before Buenos Aires. River tonnage registered at Boca ultimately outstripped that of Buenos Aires itself, as statistics for 1857 attest:[6]

|                    | vessels | tonnage |
|--------------------|---------|---------|
| Buenos Aires       | 465     | 20,259  |
| Boca del Riachuelo | 1,675   | 34,229  |
| San Fernando       | 1,230   | 8,202   |

Proximity was a major factor in the freight operations of river commerce. Greater numbers of vessels ran between Buenos Aires and the closest river ports. The bulk of traffic proceeded from adjacent areas, Uruguay, Entre Ríos, and Santa Fe. Besides the river ports of Buenos Aires Province itself, domestic shipping also served southern estancieros at boat landings along the Atlantic coast. Boats easily ran the short distances between Buenos Aires and points on the Banda Oriental. They regularly sailed the 250 kilometers across to Montevideo, where vessels drawing less than 3 meters could off-load cargoes onto the promontory in the bay beside the city. Depending on the winds, the trip lasted from twelve to twenty-four hours.[7] Still, more than one-quarter of all river freight entering Buenos Aires originated in Corrientes and Paraguay, both of which, despite their remoteness, formed part of the regional commercial system. The disadvantage of the longer distance to Buenos Aires' markets partially was offset by the fact that larger vessels served the farthest ports (see Table 9).

Ship registries at Buenos Aires reveal the importance of boat building, a domestic industry, in the regional economy of the era. Boatwrights constructed these vessels close to timber sources in Santa Fe, Corrientes, Paraguay, and even on the Banda Oriental. Boats built at Buenos Aires probably came from wood of salvaged ocean vessels or from timbers transported from upriver. Port blockades by foreign warships even fostered the local shipbuilding industry as crews of idled coastal vessels built new boats and refitted old ones. This occurred during the 1847 Anglo-French blockade. La Plata's

Table 9. *The regional river trade of Buenos Aires–Boca del Riachuelo, 1854*

|  | Vessels arriving and departing | Average size (tons) | Tonnage | Percent of total tonnage |
|---|---|---|---|---|
| Province of Buenos Aires | 1,816 | 13 | 22,968 | 15.3 |
| Entre Ríos | 1,042 | 27 | 28,228 | 18.7 |
| Santa Fe | 896 | 32 | 28,771 | 19.1 |
| Corrientes | 877 | 35 | 26,856 | 17.8 |
| Uruguay | 1,229 | 27 | 32,583 | 21.6 |
| Paraguay | 210 | 54 | 11,335 | 7.5 |

*Source: Registro Estadístico de Buenos Aires, 1854, p. 75.*

Table 10. *Registration and average size of new craft at Buenos Aires port, 1843–55*

| | Brigantine (113 tons) | Zumaca (60 tons) | Schooner (40 tons) | Schooner (15 tons) |
|---|---|---|---|---|
| 1843–5 | 15 | 9 | 81 | 23 |
| 1846–50 | 14 | 10 | 78 | 255 |
| 1851–5 | 13 | 14 | 47 | 135 |

*Source:* Archivo General de la Nación, Buenos Aires, Sala 10, 36–8–2, "Marina. Matrículas del cabotaje nacional, libro primero" (1841–5); and Sala 10, 36–9–4, "Matrículas del cabotaje nacional, libro segundo" (1844–57). Average tonnage calculated from statistics found in *Registro Estadístico de Buenos Aires*, 1857, Vol. 2, p. 62. Excluded from the table are 540 sloops of approximately 8 tons burden and 129 whaleboats of 5-tons.

economy developed even though foreign intervention attempted to curtail commercial expansion (see Table 10).

### Hide-roofed freight wagons

In addition to river shipping, Buenos Aires served as freight terminal to the traditional overland trades of carting and muleskinning. Caravans of packmules and oxcarts deposited cargoes for the export and domestic markets at the port and carried imported goods, yerba, and tobaccos back to the cities of the Interior. Yet, the overland trades would not have responded to the expanding markets of Buenos Aires without a shift from road to river traffic.

Overland freighting operated within a strong colonial heritage that changed little in its technology after Independence. The road network consisted of the ruts of heavy bullock carts. It remained basic and unimproved during the entire first half of the nineteenth century. Autumn rains from March to June created huge mudholes and slowed the traffic of carts and mule trains. Overland passages consequently were quite time consuming. A caravan of fifteen carts took a little more than a month to travel from Buenos Aires to Córdoba and journeyed an additional two months to arrive at Salta.[8] Indeed, cart construction had changed little from colonial styles — and from Spanish medieval models. Oxcarts still rumbled along on two giant wheels, six to eight feet high. The freight and passengers inside were protected by sides of reeds and roofs of stretched hides that stood some four meters above the ground. Teams of six oxen were strung out in pairs along lengthy rawhide tongues of the wagons, a procedure that facilitated crossing streams and mudholes.[9] Not a single metal part, only Tucumán timber and rawhide, went into the construction of the oxcarts.

In the early years of Independence, Tucumán teamsters customarily drew up their caravans in the congested colonial markets of Buenos Aires, the Plazas Monserrat and Lorea, to unload their cargoes. Teamsters, oxen, and carts, meanwhile, camped for weeks along the roads outside the city until return cargoes had been arranged or their rigs sold for use in Buenos Aires Province. Wagon trains arrived from Córdoba, Tucumán, Santiago del Estero, Salta, Jujuy, and Catamarca. They bore dried hides, horsehair, raw wool, and sheep- and goatskins for export; and wheat, flour, tanned leathers, timber, blankets, and ponchos for domestic consumption. Mule trains hauled most cargoes from the Andean foothills of San Luis, Mendoza, and San Juan. Packmules also brought pastoral export goods, as well as flour, dried fruits, raisins, figs, and leather bags of muscatel wine and grape brandy. Mule skinners also camped along the roads north of Buenos Aires, unloading their packs and grazing their animals on the river grasses prior to the journey back to the western provinces.[10]

Of the two modes of overland freighting, carts appeared to have been the more efficient, given the generally level terrain between Buenos Aires and the northern provinces. The average wagon train consisted of twenty-two men driving fifteen carts and 120 oxen, and delivering some 24.5 metric tons of freight. In the typical mule train, nine men guided eighty-two packmules and carried nearly 8 tons of cargo. Carts brought much more freight to Buenos Aires than packmules. Because each wagon carried 1.5 tons of freight and the packmule only 91 kilograms, the cargo capacities per teamster ran 25 percent greater than that of the mule skinner (see Table 11).

At first glance, it might appear that the overland transportation industry between Buenos Aires and the Interior did not participate in the port's commercial expansion of the first

Table 11. *Delivery of overland freight at Buenos Aires, 1829*

|  | Number | Total freight (tons) | Cargo per animal (kg.) | Cargo per man (kg.) |
|---|---|---|---|---|
| Cart train | 45 | 1,055 | 205 | 1,129 |
| Mule train | 10 | 78 | 91 | 866 |

*Source:* "Tabla general de las tropas de carretas y arrias venidas del interior en 1829," in Archivo General de la Nación, Buenos Aires, Sala 10, 42–8–5, "Censos" (1813–61).

half of the nineteenth century. The number of cart and mule trains entering the port city from the Interior dropped steadily between 1810 and 1860. In terms of tonnage, the delivery of overland freight totaled more than 3,147 metric tons in 1823 compared to more than 1,800 tons almost four decades later.[11] The following data (in metric tons) support the conclusion that arrivals of overland freight at the port fell off consistently up to 1860:[12]

|  | 1823 | 1828 | 1860 |
|---|---|---|---|
| by mule | 1,179 | 784 | 133 |
| by cart | 1,968 | 1,269 | 131 |
|  | 3,147 | 2,053 | 264 |

Do these statistics support the interpretation so long held by historians that the Interior did not participate in the commercial growth of Buenos Aires? One could cite the very traditionalism and inefficiency of moving long-haul freight via oxcarts and packmules. The other traditional mode of regional transport, river shipping, required less manpower to move more freight. Although boatmen carried three to four tons of freight per man, one cartman transported only 1.25 ton of freight in each trip.[13] Data from Buenos Aires in themselves cannot prove the decline of Interior transport. But overland traffic at the port diminished not only because of the inefficiency of overland freight carrying but also because of the growth of the city. Farmers usurped traditional parking and grazing areas for cultivation. The cattle drives and oxcarts coming from estancias and farms within Buenos Aires province intensified traffic on the roads and in cart terminals of the port. Tucumán wagons also were used to carry goods between the port and the small towns and estan-

*Mule train carrying mendocino wine, 1817.* After oxcarts, packmules formed the second echelon of the overland transport industry in the Interior. This mode of freight carriage had its colonial antecedents in the mule trains that linked the Río de la Plata with the silver-mining regions of the Andes Mountains. The packmule at left has its head wrapped with cloth because it proved a recalcitrant bearer of cargo. (Watercolor by E. E. Vidal, 1817.)

cias on the prairies. In 1827, cart traffic from the ranching areas of Buenos Aires Province already had equaled overland freighting from the Interior.[14]

Commercial congestion in the port city, in fact, only caused the rerouting of overland freight – not its downfall. Caravans from the Interior headed to freight terminals at river ports north of Buenos Aires. Most important of the freight transfer points was Rosario, the small river port in the south of Santa Fe Province. Cart trains traveling over the road from Córdoba deposited their Buenos Aires–bound cargoes in this quiet village. From Rosario, riverboats carried the freight down to Buenos Aires.[15] Despite the inefficiency of overland traffic transport and the congestion of roads and marketplaces at the port, therefore, the Interior trade continued to contribute expansion at Buenos Aires.

## Farm wagons to market

Buenos Aires' regional commerce also inherited from the colonial period a marketing system featuring wholesale marketplaces on the outskirts of the city and numerous warehouses in the business districts. Warehouses catered exclusively to the export business, but markets supported both export processing and the growing urban demand. In the first half-century, the most important domestic wholesale point was North Market (now the Plaza Británica), located on the road to the agricultural district of San Isidro. Farm wagons delivered vegetables, potatoes, peaches, melons, fish, fowl, kindling, and timber products. Crowding in the colonial cart terminals of the Plazas Lorea and Monserrat forced relocation of West Market (circa 1820) further outside the expanding city to the new Plaza Once de Setiembre. Wheat and wool, the leading products bought and sold at West Market, reflected the production of farms and estancias west of Buenos Aires. By far the largest market lay to the south of the city. South Market at Plaza Constitución processed the pastoral products brought to the city by oxcarts and horse-wagons coming from ranches of the southern pampa. Perennially, more hides, skins, tallow, and grease were gathered in South Market than in the other two marketplaces. As sheep ranching shifted to the southern prairies in the 1850s, South Market also began to wholesale twice the wool of the other markets. Toward the end of the 1850s, the municipality founded yet another market, Santa Lucía, also to the south. The new market, although smaller, became an important collection point for hides and wool and alleviated congestion at Plaza Constitución.

The marketplaces of Buenos Aires were focal points of expansion in domestic and export commerce. In the three decades before 1860, the amount of domestic and export products processed in wholesale markets tripled and, in the case of raw wool, increased 175-fold (see Table 12). The market system actually processed only one-quarter of the hides exported from Buenos Aires. The wholesale figures in

Table 12.  *Wholesaling in the markets of Buenos Aires, 1828–60*

|  | 1828 | 1831 | 1854 | 1857 | 1860 |
|---|---|---|---|---|---|
| Hides | 82,188 | 211,424 | 348,064 | 383,083 | 423,996 |
| Tallow (tons) | 177 | 111 | n.a. [a] | 238 | 316 |
| Wool (tons) | 57 | 346 | 6,867 | 5,785 | 12,127 |
| Grains (hl.) | 61,879 | 83,406 | 202,877 | 141,353 | 212,284 |

[a] Not available.

*Source:* "Productos de industria rural registrados en los mercados en el año 1831," in Archivo General de la Nación, Buenos Aires, Sala 10, 42–8–5, "Censos" (1813–61); *Registro Estadístico de Buenos Aires (REBA),* 1854, p. 48; *REBA,* 1857, vol. 2, pp. 50–1; *REBA,* 1858, vol. 1, p. 139; and *REBA,* 1860, vol. 2, pp. 98–100.

Table 12 represent the produce of farmers and estancieros who slaughtered their own cattle. Merchants collecting rural products in wagons passing through the countryside also wholesaled their stocks in the markets. Porteño warehouses and slaughterhouses supplied the bulk of the hide exports. A greater portion of the wool, however, passed through the marketplaces for lack of industrial competition.

Market activity, being heavily agricultural in content, was also highly seasonal. Harvest time on the Argentine prairies lasted from early December through February, and most grains, melons, fruit, and vegetables were marketed in these summer months. Wool sheared in November arrived at market in the summer, an optimal time also for sun drying cattlehides and sheepskins. Firewood, on the other hand, was delivered the year around but sold in greater volume during the winter months of June through August.[16] Judging from market and import statistics, agricultural production to supply the growing city developed considerably. In 1831, for instance, more than a third of the city's flour supply seems to have been imported from the United States. North American ships brought 3,332 metric tons of flour that year, while the local farmers delivered only 5,371 tons of wheat (or 4,027 tons of milled flour) to market. North American flour imports never again reached the 1931 level because native farmers began to produce more. In 1859, pampa farmers delivered to Buenos Aires 13,163 tons of wheat (8,775 tons of four), and coastal vessels deposited an additional 1,135 metric tons of provincial wheat at Boca del Riachuelo.[17]

Wholesale markets should be distinguished from the retail market of the main plaza, la Recova Vieja (today the Plaza de Mayo). Here some 170 small shopkeepers and tailors rented stalls surrounding the main square in order to sell clothing items plus imported and domestic manufactures. In the Central Market, three blocks from the main plaza, housewives and servants shopped daily for beef, fowl, and vegetables.[18] They bought bread from numerous bakeries throughout the city. Peddlers with pushcarts and horsecarts sold beef and other foodstuffs in the streets, as did milk boys who hawked fresh dairy products from horseback. Pulperías, small shops located in both business and residential districts of the city, offered to the public candles, spirits, knives and hardwares, saddlery, and leather goods. Small dry goods stores throughout Buenos Aires provided retail clothing of foreign manufacture, whereas other shops specialized in regional products like ponchos and dried fruit and imported foodstuffs like wine and spaghetti.

The importance of supplying the growing city easily might be overlooked, for the export of pastoral products provided the rationale for expansion of ranching and for much of the city's commercial development. Yet, statistics for 1829 indicate that only one of every fourteen farm carts entering the marketplaces carried export goods. At least 94 percent of the wagons brought products for the domestic market, according to these figures (in wagonloads):[19]

| | |
|---|---|
| foodstuffs | 5,386 |
| woods and lime | 3,232 |
| forage | 2,245 |
| export products | 721 |

Warehouses, or *barracas,* located in the commercial sections of the city, also processed bulk freight destined for export. Warehousemen stored the goods until shipment was arranged, then packed the produce for overseas transport. Most charged 2 percent interest on the transaction, plus storage costs, and maintained accounts with established clienteles of ranchers and merchants. *Barraqueros* also bought produce at the great marketplaces and packed the wool, hides, and sheepskins into bales to fill special orders for the export merchants.

A feature of the colonial economy, warehousing remained a rudimentary business in the first half-century of Independence. Besides hiring several peons for packing and handling, the proprietor needed an ample building near the waterfront or a suburban house near the markets. Most barracas were located on the waterfront for easy deposit of products arriving by coastal vessels. The largest warehouses held up to 80,000 hides and contained bags, rawhide twine, and tools for packing. Hydraulic presses for baling export products reduced the size of bulk cargoes and saved on overseas freight charges. Though specializing in export goods like hides, skins, fur pelts, wool, and tallow, some barraqueros also maintained substantial stocks of flour and wheat bought during harvest season and stored for retail throughout the year.[20]

Merchants dealing in local procurement of pastoral exports, like members of the Anchorena family, utilized several warehouses in the city. On the Anchorena account, a waterfront warehouseman itemized the number of hides received from boatmen and consigned under his client's name. Juan José Cristobal de Anchorena collected dried hides for weeks at a time until he sold them to foreign exporters in lots of 3,000 or more. The barraquero always arranged loading and unloading, inventoried the goods, and presented Anchorena with the bill for handling and storage. The merchant family also employed the services of a warehouseman near South Market. Not yet a rancher himself, Anchorena thus was able to arrange the collection of hides from a number of estancieros on the southern pampa.[21] Warehouses persisted and expanded as an adjunct to the porteño merchandising system throughout the era of commercial florescence that lasted until 1860. The British consul general placed the number of operating barracas at forty-four in 1836, and an English traveler a decade later put the number of "depots and dealers in native produce" at sixty.[22]

The introduction of the railroad in 1857, heralding the modern technological age, began to alter the operation — but not the structure — of marketing rural produce at Buenos Aires. By 1861, nearly half of the cowhides and sheepskins and fully two-thirds of the wheat arrived at West Market in rail cars. Within a decade, North and South markets also became terminals of railroads whose rights-of-way followed the old cart trails to the northern farm area and to the southern ranching district.[23] Buenos Aires' three large marketplaces, therefore, continued to focus domestic supply and some export marketing into the post-1860 technological age.

### Too-awful stench

The *saladero*, Buenos Aires' distinctive abattoir and salting factory, served as the crucial funnel of the entire economic system: Into it flowed the cattle of the pampa and out of it passed the raw materials of international trade. More than other commercial facilities, saladeros applied new management and production techniques in order to serve booming foreign markets. The salting plants brought to bear larger amounts of capital, labor specialization, mass production methods, and greater utilization of the beef carcass. Yet entrepreneurs added no new technological innovations to this processing industry. Despite widespread use of steam vats to extract grease from carcasses, the chief tools continued to be the lasso and knife, wielded by the human hand. Factory processing, nevertheless, permitted the commercial economy both to diversify its exports and to produce them more cheaply.

This industry grew in response to trading opportunities offered by Buenos Aires' varied foreign customers. Industrial nations like Britain and France accepted more than half the saladeros' production in salted hides, tallow, and assorted by-products like hair and bone ash. Salted meat, on the other hand, was destined for use in the plantation-slave economies of Brazil and Cuba. Although European consumers disdained the taste of this gray, salty substance, plantation owners found carne salada boiled into porridge an economical diet for their slaves. As Cuba expanded sugar planting and southern Brazil coffee growing, the number of black plantation workers held in bondage also increased. Brazil already had many slaves in its northeastern sugar economy, but traffickers continued illegal trade in African blacks for the coffee plantations of the South. Cuba acquired slaves from British Jamaica and Africa.[24] This was a growing market ready-made for La Plata's resources and commercial ingenuity.

Meat-salting establishments were not new to the region at the time of the early nineteenth-century trading boom. Several had operated on the East Bank toward the close of the colonial period. Two Englishmen, Robert Staples and John McNeile, set up the first saladero south of Buenos Aires at Ensenada shortly after the 1810 Revolution. Creole entrepreneurs soon realized the opportunities, and saladeros proliferated around the city. By 1825, twenty saladeros had been established in the suburbs of Buenos Aires alone, processing about 70,000 head of cattle a year. In addition, related industries called *graserías* and *mataderos de ovejas* were established around the city, specifically to steam the oils and tallows from carcasses of sheep and horses.[25] One found saladeros north and west of Buenos Aires, but Quilmes and Barracas south of the port became the prime meat-packing districts. After mid-century, thirteen saladeros in Barracas alone were processing nearly 250,000 head of cattle and 90,000 horses a year — for a total sales value of some 4,486,364 gold pesos.[26] Travelers passing on the South Road through Barracas easily noticed the presence of this important industry. "Here the stench was too awful," an English gentleman observed. "There were ditches filled with blood instead of water, actually in all stages of putrefaction; *miles and miles* of fences, three of four feet high and two thick, dividing off the different establishments skirting the road, and forming *corrals,* made entirely of the bones of bullocks' horns."[27]

Initial capital outlays for land, equipment, stock, and labor were relatively high, but certainly not beyond the means or the technological ken of creole entrepreneurs. In 1815, three creoles, Juan Manuel de Rosas, Luis Dorrego, and Juan Nepomuceno Terrero, formed a partnership to buy and operate a saladero in Quilmes. Dorrego acted as the silent partner and financier, putting up half the capital investment. Rosas handled cattle procurement. He had an option to buy estancias on his own and stock them with cattle at company expense. Terrero, a merchant and accountant, arranged the export of saladero products. Provisions were made to plow most profits back into the operation. Dorrego could pull out of the venture with his profits after four years; Terrero and Rosas obligated themselves for six years. Having put down 6,058 pesos (before inflation) for the salting factory with all its livestock, the three partners still owed 3,840 pesos to the original owners. By 1817, however, the company already reported gross sales of nearly 14,500 pesos. They paid off the lien and declared their personal profits at 4,000 pesos each.[28] Such quick and handsome returns made saladero investments worthwhile for both Creole and immigrant businessmen.

The operations of these saladeros are fairly well known, because they became something of a tourist attraction in Buenos Aires — a cause of wonder to every foreigner who sniffed an occasional southern breeze. The salting season lasted from November to March, when cattle were in the best condition and the summer weather was ideal for drying hides and meats. Extensive cattle pens covered acres of land surrounding the salting plants. Standing knee-deep in mud and manure, the animals awaited slaughter for days, without water or food. Finally, a mounted peon lassoed and dragged a beast into the killing area. Another worker on foot hamstrung the animal, then stuck his knife into the spinal cord behind the head, killing the beast instantly. The carcass was placed on a flatbed cart and pulled over rails to the flayers. Their knives quickly removed the hide, which peons covered with shovelsful of salt and stacked. The meat was removed from the bones, cut into long thin strips, and cooled. The strips were stacked between layers of salt, re-stacked and salted again after several days, and finally dried over poles in the sun. Workmen packed the meat, together with grease, in wooden barrels. Fat, bones, and excess flesh were placed in vats and steamed for their tallow and grease extracts. As there were no better methods of cleaning up refuse, herds of pigs shared the discarded entrails with dogs and vultures.[29]

Each new improvement in the salting operations promoted efficiency and reduced the waste in processing cattle through Buenos Aires. In the late 1820s, Antoine Cambaceres, an immigrant French chemist, introduced important assembly-line techniques. He designed cattle chutes in the corrals, a truck and rail system to move carcasses within the sheds, and, most importantly, steam vats to extract the animal fat from bones and flesh. Cambaceres' workers even utilized dried bones as fuel and then packed up the ashes to be exported along with manure from the pens, as fertilizers.[30] Besides the major pastoral items of hides and tallow, saladeros also turned out salted meats and tongues, horsehides, mare's grease, and bones. The average steer now produced a twenty-seven kilogram hide, thirteen kilograms of grease, and fifty-five kilograms of salted meat plus by-products. Although the killing season lasted only five to six months, some workers stayed on all year processing hides, meats, and other products.[31]

With its efficient, capitalized operations, a typical salting factory processed some 200 to 400 cattle per day at the height of the season and required the work of several thousand seasonal laborers. One saladero employed 300 men during peak operations. Porteño salting plants by the 1850s were producing a yearly average of 18,162 metric tons of salted beef for export. Slaughterhouses in ports on the Uruguay and Paraná rivers contributed another 908 tons per year.[32] The saladeros' location in the suburbs of Buenos Aires, close to the port outlet, centralized the processing industry and diminished the estancieros' need to undertake slaughtering and processing on the ranches. Rationalization of cattle processing at Buenos Aires clearly permitted continued expansion of pastoral exports.

### Disposal of offal

Factory demand ultimately enlarged livestock wholesaling at Buenos Aires. In the 1820s, the public corrals of colonial origin remained operating near wholesale markets in and about the city. Here also one found the butchering areas, *mataderos,* which supplied inhabitants with beef and a few merchants with hides for export. Four such mataderos, located to the north and south and even within the populated district itself, existed at the time of Independence. They were soon to be relocated, and again the reason was congestion. The building of more housing expanded the city's limits, while herds of cattle had to compete with farm wagons and overland freight carriers for rights-of-way along the roads to market. By the 1830s, the number of municipal corrals had been reduced to three and, after midcentury, to two. Now the corrals and butchering areas – and their offending odors – were removed well outside the urban center.

The corral–butcher (*abasto*) system, nevertheless, continued to provide beef for city residents by utilizing the same crude, primitive practices.[33] Ranchers who sent in small herds of five to thirty head several times a month paid small fees for the use of municipal corrals. Butchers then purchased the cattle and, with hired peons, slaughtered the animals at the corrals. The ground served as the butcher's block: The carcasses were cut into beef on their own hides. Various meat sellers distributed the meat to stalls in the Central Market or from their horsecarts on the streets of the city. Butchers, meanwhile, saved the hides and tallow for delivery to warehouses. Disposal of offal – heads, entrails, fleshy bones, and blood – presented little problem, as buzzards, dogs, and pigs devoured the last morsels within hours of the day's slaughter.

Urban sprawl and the growth of the export market not only forced relocation of this basic industry of *abasto público,* but also expanded the whole process of cattle wholesaling at Buenos Aires. As cattle grazing spread to the southern pampa, much of the meat-processing industry also shifted south of the city. In 1860, South Corral handled nearly 19,500 head of livestock a month, and North Corral only 2,700 head. Although beef consumption rose with population growth (at the time, the average porteño ate 227 kilos of meat a year), butchers bought only 8 percent of the cattle entering public corrals and stockyards in the 1860s.[34] Estancieros sold greater numbers of cattle to the salting factories.

By the 1830s, the export industry's large demand for cattle occasioned the establishment of huge wholesale outlets, the stockyards. South Stockyard at Quilmes and North Stockyard between Morón and Flores (really in the west) began to market cattle, horses, and sheep in quantity for both saladeros and butchers. The growth of the outlying stockyards eased pressure on the smaller corrals nearer the city. Ranchers sent their cattle to the stockyards to bargain their sale with butchers and representatives of the salting plants. Buenos Aires' merchants who bought cattle in the hinterland also sold these herds at the stockyards. Buyers selected cattle, drove them to pens surrounding their slaughterhouses, and processed the animals into hides, salted meat, and tallow for export. Cattle processing also was seasonal. Spring grasses on the pampa produced the fattest cattle for the summer slaughter season lasting from December to March, when cattle drives numbering 500 head arrived at the stockyards. At the height of the season, as many as 130,000 head of cattle a month were wholesaled through both the public stockyards and the corrals outside Buenos Aires, according to these figures (in head of cattle) for February, 1861:[35]

| use of cattle | stockyards | corrals |
|---|---|---|
| salting factories | 59,852 | 23,839 |
| consumption | 33,521 | 2,343 |
| hides | — | 10,445 |

The trend of the entire half-century was for the cattle-processing industry to move south of Buenos Aires. Once ranching had spread onto the southern pampa, slaughterhouses concentrated to the south at Quilmes and Barracas al Sur for easy access to the cattle-drive routes. Most saladeros and abattoirs operated in this district, and the South Stockyard at Quilmes was by far the largest cattle-wholesale point. Not all cattle processed by saladeros, however, were purchased at the stockyards and corrals. Two-party contracts between the big ranchers and factory owners required direct delivery of herds to the saladeros. Still, the number of cattle wholesaled in all stockyards and corrals — both for local consumption and for export slaughter — increased spectacularly (figures in head of cattle):[36]

| use of cattle | 1830 | 1857 |
|---|---|---|
| salting plants | 185,871 | 325,979 |
| consumption | 71,871 | 150,572 |
| hides | — | 115,897 |

### Rainy-day leisure

Expansion of the commercial and processing economy opened up many entrepreneurial and labor opportunities and attracted European immigrants and provincial migrants who gradually replaced slave labor at Buenos Aires. Slavery for blacks and mulattoes continued from the colonial period into the 1820s. Afro-mestizos still constituted a quarter of the urban population of Buenos Aires, but only half of these remained in bondage. Unlike their brethren on Cuban and Brazilian plantations, Buenos Aires' slaves lived and worked in the city in large numbers. In the 1820s, they still were sold along with property, as in the cases of sixteen slaves who worked in a hat factory or the household servant sold along with the furniture.[37] Slave numbers also diminished following the 1813 law giving freedom to children born to slaves, and as a result of the British campaign to end the slave traffic on the high seas.[38] The black race of Buenos Aires declined because of miscegenation and service in the militias. Consequently, work traditionally accomplished at Buenos Aires by slaves began to go to free, salaried workers.

Neither immigration nor migration were new phenomena at Buenos Aires, for newcomers from abroad and from the Interior provinces always had contributed to population growth at the port. City censuses indicate the continuing arrival of Basques and Galicians from Spain and Italians from

Genoa, along with new surges of Frenchmen and Britishers. In 1822, only 9 percent of the urban population was foreign born. Three decades later, the foreign-born residents constituted fully 34 percent of the urban population. Italians predominated among all immigrant groups, followed by the French, Spanish, and British.[39] In addition, migrants were coming to Buenos Aires from Córdoba, Mendoza, Tucumán, Santiago del Estero, Paraguay, and Uruguay. All these new residents worked at a variety of jobs, from carpenters and cartmen to shopkeepers and shoemakers. Recent research has determined that foreign immigrants especially found opportunities in an artisan industry that was expanding to meet urban demand at Buenos Aires. The number of native artisans also increased, but not as rapidly as the immigrant shopworkers.[40]

Most newly arrived foreigners were either bachelors or married men traveling alone; they were usually between the ages of sixteen and thirty-five years. Married and single women also came, although females made up only one-quarter of all immigration. Europeans arriving at Buenos Aires by ship increased their numbers progressively as the nineteenth century passed the halfway mark, according to these figures on the average annual arrival of passengers at the port:[41]

| | |
|---|---|
| 1823−5 | −283 |
| 1847−9 | 4,161 |
| 1854−7 | 8,644 |
| 1858−61 | 7,196 |

Certainly not all the Britishers at Buenos Aires were export merchants or even worked in foreign commerce. Numbers of Scottish, Welsh, Irish, and English immigrants labored as tailors, masons, upholsterers, painters, blacksmiths, carpenters, grocers, watchmakers, and shopkeepers. Most of the sailors in the river trades probably originated in the Italian seafaring city of Genoa, for names like Repetto, Bruno, Bollo, and Rughi dominated the registry of boat crews. Spanish surnames were hard to find among crewmen, but sailors of Luso-Brazilian extraction like Jose dos Santos or Clemente da Costa also signed on to riverboat crews.[42] Migrants, adept at handling horse and lasso, found jobs among unskilled foreigners manning shovels and vats at the saladeros. *Provincianos* (migrants from other provinces) were suited particularly for ranching and agricultural occupations opening up on the pampa, as were Basques and other Spaniards. Population growth certainly solidified Buenos Aires' position as the chief domestic market in the region. The number of urban inhabitants grew from 55,416 in 1822 to 177,787 in 1869, an annual growth rate of 2.6 percent.[43]

It appears that urban laborers, whether foreign or creole, porteño or provinciano, enjoyed rather favorable terms of employment. Faced with expansion in all sectors of the economy, merchants and processers in the city competed for workers with transporters, boat owners, and ranchers — and everyone keenly rivaled the provincial press-gangs seeking able-bodied men to fight in the civil wars. Such competition seems to have given the laborer a certain amount of freedom, despite municipal laws punishing vagrancy and binding workers to their occupations. Commenting on the lack of labor discipline, a longtime British resident observed that porteño "mechanics" customarily took the day off whenever it rained.[44] An owner of a salting factory even complained to the chief of police that his workers regularly and audaciously insulted him. Processers frequently asked police for permission to work their men on holidays in order to fill waiting foreign ships.[45] These observations do not mean that the police repressed the laboring classes, but suggest that workingmen in Buenos Aires were scarce and had market leverage, including recognized claims to leisure time.

### Creoles of great avidity

Historians often depreciate the role of the Creole (native-born American) in Buenos Aires' commercial structure of the first half-century. Although foreign merchants undoubtedly dominated the import—export trade, the complex merchandising system supporting this commerce undeniably furnished numerous opportunities for local enterprise. British residents at Buenos Aires in the 1820s already had noticed the commercial resurgence among natives — even in exporting. "The Creoles of the country now engage in mercantile pursuits with great avidity," one Englishman commented, "and commerce has spread into so many hands, that money does not roll in [to foreign merchants] quite so fast as formerly."[46] Actually, Creoles operated the entire marketing and transportation system within the Río de la Plata. They collected and processed export products as hide purveyors, river traders, and overland freight carriers. Without exception, Creoles dominated all modes of domestic transportation – oxcarting, mule skinning, and river shipping – including trade to and from the Interior and riverine provinces. Moreover, natives operated the meat-salting factories and warehouses that shunted pastoral products to the import–export merchants. Domestic markets, expanding yearly with the size of the city, belonged almost exclusively to native wholesalers and retailers. Creole commercial success, in fact, enabled natives to generate much of their own operating and investment capital.

Although Britishers headed the community of import–export merchants at Buenos Aires, a combination of French, Italian, Spanish, and Creole merchants collectively outnumbered their Anglo counterparts in the first half of the nineteenth century.[47] Besides, after sojourning in Buenos Aires for many years, some of these foreigners became permanent residents. They married into porteño families and assumed local commercial interests. Local retailers selling tobaccos, foodstuffs, or cloth in shops and general stores, and those who made shoes and wood products, were overwhelmingly Creoles or Italian and Spanish immigrants. Foreign traders formed the apex of the commercial system, but Argentine merchants participated fully in a structure that demanded contributions of both. Foreigners had contacts in industrial markets and dealt with the skippers of international ships in the harbor. If not actual partners or retainers in import–export houses, Creoles served as important subsidiaries. The Anchorena merchant family, for instance, delivered their goods to the British firm of Hullet Brothers & Co., and Patricio Lynch, the Irish porteño, collected pastoral products for the American brokerage firm of Zimmerman, Frazier & Co.[48] Both foreign firms maintained offices in Buenos Aires.

Any list of merchants and river pilots introducing goods from the Paraná River Basin via coastal craft is replete with Spanish and Italian names. Larger merchant companies, Lézica y Compañía, Llavallol e Hijos, Ochoa y Compañía, or Ram y Rubert, handled cargoes from many ports, but the river trades offered splendid opportunities for Italian boatowners and small porteño traders to handle traffic from one and two ports only. Individual small shippers dominated the river trades. Porteños maintained correspondence with commercial agents in the river ports, keeping them informed of market conditions and transportation problems. River pilots delivered most products of domestic consumption — firewood or posts — for sale in the wholesale markets. Export cargoes from upriver, on the other hand, usually were consigned to intermediary Creole merchants in Buenos Aires. Still, the British merchants who were longtime residents of Buenos Aires, and who established commercial and family relations with Creoles, also developed merchant contacts in the riverine provinces. Thomas Gowland and John Temperley handled goods from Entre Ríos.[49]

Concurrent with their control of the river trades, Creoles owned and operated the greater number of each class of river vessel plying those trades. The single inroad of foreign merchants was in possession of whaleboats used in port operations. In 1840–1, half these boats were registered in lots of two to six under English names, and the rest under Spanish surnames. Creoles and immigrant Italians, whether pilots or small merchants, owned the majority of the other classes of riverboats. British and French merchants owned only 10 to 15 percent. Many of these individual owners probably were merchant boatmen from provincial riverports in Santa Fe and Entre Ríos. Boat owners from Montevideo also registered their boats for business at Buenos Aires. Spanish and Creole ownership was common even in the schooner and brigantine classes, where Britishers owned only a fifth of these larger coastal vessels. Only one of every fourteen smacks (vessels of approximately forty tons) was registered under an Anglo name. It was not uncommon for Creoles to purchase boats from foreign owners, or for immigrant Portuguese and Italians, experienced ocean sailors, to own craft made in Brazil and Sardinia.[50] Families and merchant companies owned several boats of all sizes, but individual ownership of river vessels was quite widespread.

A different group of Creoles, almost as numerous, managed overland freight trade from the Interior provinces. Porteño merchants cultivated commercial contacts in certain Interior cities and regularly received consigned cargoes in cart or mule trains. In the 1820s, for instance, a shopkeeper named Juan C. Rosados received numerous shipments of goods from many points within the province of Córdoba but from no other province. As in the river trades, individual petty merchants handled the lion's share of the Interior freight. Nine different consignments of goods from one Interior province, Mendoza, in August, 1833, for instance, might be delivered to as many as nine different Buenos Aires merchants. All accepted either export products or domestic goods exclusively, rarely mixing both types. Shopkeepers specialized in the products of one region and advertised the sale of Mendoza's flour and dried fruit in porteño newspapers.[51] Those traders with contacts in particular provincial cities handled the overland trades either for the retailing of Interior products on the domestic market or for passing along export products to foreign merchants.

Other Creoles specialized in *comercio del campo,* that is, procuring pastoral products from the far-flung hinterland south of Buenos Aires and delivering them to waterfront loading zones. The Anchorenas, for example, collected single shipments of hides from as many as forty different individuals and estancias. The merchant family then arranged the warehousing, weighing, marking, packing, and loading of hide cargoes into carts and harbor craft. Commissions from foreign exporters were 2 percent of the wholesale value.[52] The Larrea brothers, prominent "camp" merchants, maintained a network of agents in the pampa ranching areas of Chascomús, Tandil, Azul, Ranchos, Monte, and Huesos, as well as in the river ports — in all, some twenty-five active agents in the field. From his storeroom in Buenos Aires, the elder Larrea dispatched letters to his agents soliciting produce, explaining market conditions and arranging freight delivery. The agents collected dried hides, tallow, horsehair, wool, and sheepskins from estancieros. Larrea's contacts themselves were either ranchers, ranch foremen, or country storekeepers. Larrea often sent urban goods, like domestic flour, imported spaghetti, and cloth to these agents for retail. He also arranged for the delivery of cattle to the saladeros south of the city. Agents received a commission of 2 percent for buying cattle, forming cattle drives, and delivering them to the South Stockyard.[53] Others engaged in the camp trades as well. Independent freight carriers collected goods in their own oxcarts and delivered them to the marketplaces. Owners of various shops and general stores in Buenos Aires also arranged for delivery of goods from the countryside.[54] Without exception, camp merchants and their agents were Spaniards and Creoles.

With domestic commerce in the hands of so many small merchants, the entire system might appear unwieldy and inefficient, but consolidation of internal merchandising was occurring as the nineteenth century approached midpoint. Many Creole merchant companies had grown impressively. Esteban Rams y Rubert maintained one of the largest shipping networks on the Paraná River out of Santa Fe Province. The Casares y Murrieta family conducted a large coastal shipping business with a warehouse on the river bank at Buenos Aires and seventeen of its own vessels.[55] One regional specialist, José Galarraga, in 1849 was getting a large number of cargoes sent directly from Mendoza and some dispatched from San Luis. At that time, larger Creole merchant houses, run by the Llavallos, Ochoas, and Ocampos — who also had interests in the river trades — handled larger portions of overland freight from the Interior. Even fewer and bigger merchants, it seemed, were involved in dispatching wholesale goods to the provinces. Nevertheless, there remained much room and opportunity for small as well as large merchants in the domestic merchandising system of Argentina.

Creoles — together with immigrant entrepreneurs — likewise dominated the storage facilities and salting factories of Buenos Aires. Foreign merchants occasionally maintained their own warehouses, but natives came to specialize in the storage of goods. More than half the thirty-five warehouses operating in 1836 belonged to merchants with Spanish surnames. Even some foreign warehouse owners like Bunge, Harrat, and Langdon had become immigrant merchants settling in Buenos Aires. Foreigners also were evident among owners of the great salting plants on the outskirts of Buenos Aires. Here again, Frenchmen like Antoine Cambaceres and Francois Baudrix, and Britishers like George Dowdal and Patrick Brown, were resident immigrants. There was still much opportunity for native enterprise. Simón Pereyra, Senillosa y Companía, Santa María Llambí, and Cándido Pizarro all operated important saladeros along the Riachuelo.[56]

Undoubtedly, much capital used to move goods through the emporium of Buenos Aires came from foreign merchants interested in developing the commercial infrastructure of the Río de la Plata. Evidence exists, nevertheless, that the Creoles themselves generated and invested their own liquid funds in regional commerce. They even utilized letters of credit among themselves in payment of commercial debts and to finance collection and distribution of goods.[57] A common Creole investment device was the partnership. Wealthier merchants often financed others in trade between Buenos Aires and the provinces and in supplying the city with lime, sugar, brandy, and rice. Besides dried hides and other exports, Creoles paid for the delivery of yerba and wood for the domestic market at Buenos Aires. Others put up the capital to establish general stores and bakeries in the city. Creole businessmen sometimes provided capital to other traders and saladeristas in order to pay customs duties and taxes. Usually, business associations involved a financier who provided the cash needed for a commercial project and a working party who undertook all the management. Partnerships lasted briefly, usually until the working partner had established himself solidly in a trade or until specific merchandising had been completed. Partners then split the profits within a stipulated period of time. Interest charges on loans between porteños seem high – up to 2 percent per month in 1840. Often, the borrower put up his house as collateral. Partnerships and profit sharing, therefore, was the rational alternative to high interest rates. Creoles not only proved autonomous in the domestic collection and distribution system at Buenos Aires but also financed much of its development with their own capital resources.

No doubt, the extraordinary expansion of trade and the growth of the urban population strained the commercial system that Buenos Aires had inherited from the colonial period. Without technological innovation, economic expansion in the Río de la Plata meant spatial dispersion of marketplaces, port facilities, cattle-processing areas, and freight routes. Economic growth also illustrates two other features of the porteño merchandising system: the concurrent rise of a quantitatively important domestic market and Creole autonomy in the transportation and merchant trades. Fresh influxes of European immigrants and provincial migrants enlarged the labor pool and the consuming population of the city. Although the export market provided the rationale for enlarging the cattle-processing industries, the domestic market proved a capable patron of the overland and river trades and of agricultural pursuits around Buenos Aires.

Moreover, immigrant entrepreneurs and Creole businessmen appear as both catalysts and benefactors in developing the region's economic infrastructure. They managed the transport of all freight on oxcarts and packmules, owned the major portion of the coastal shipping industry, and operated many of the freight warehouses and cattle-processing factories of the city. Indeed, much of the capital for domestic development came from local merchants themselves. The growth of the Río de la Plata's staple economy in the first half of the nineteenth century constituted expansion of a Creole-dominated, traditional marketing system in the region's port city.

Commercial expansion of the export trade and of the domestic market in the nineteenth century had yet another dimension. Porteños, provincianos, and immigrants also were beginning production on virgin prairies of the great southern pampa. The frontier movement that had begun in the vice-regal period now quickened its pace.

# 6

## Expanding the frontiers of production
## on the pampa

The great era of estancia formation and frontier settlement on the Argentine prairies began early in the nineteenth century. Some historians long have concluded that this settlement amounted to the seizure of more and more land by prestige-hungry men pursuing vague Spanish ideals of landed nobility. Successful landowners formed a powerful little coterie, so the argument goes, that conspired to monopolize political and social organization in the La Plata region.[1] Considered purely from the economic standpoint, however, the expansion of the frontier in Buenos Aires Province was surprisingly varied. In the first instance, economic men settled the frontier in order to produce pastoral goods for the expanding market at Buenos Aires. Foreign shipping, the herald of overseas demand, each year increased at the port. Creoles thus pushed the Indians farther south and parceled out large tracts of virgin land for grazing. Given the ranching technology of the day, cattle raising necessarily was an extensive operation, and herds needed much land on which to feed and reproduce. Cattle estancias were huge.

Nevertheless, cattle ranching was hardly the only economic pursuit in the countryside. Expansion of production over the pampa occurred in recognizable belts. Closest to the city, farmers cultivated grains and vegetables and raised dairy animals to supply the growing urban marketplaces. As industrial wool markets opened up overseas, ranchers introduced sheep to grasslands midway between the port and the frontier. In the distant hinterlands, new and large ranches were given over exclusively to cattle grazing. Pastoral expansion encompassed more effective management and production on estancias, for Argentine producers had to compensate for the declining prices of their products all the while. Finally, rural commerce developed apace to support staple production and to link it with the export commerce of Buenos Aires port. The production function of livestock raising resulted in eco-

123

nomic and social development on the pampa that was a good deal more complex than many scholars have imagined.

## Carpet of fine verdure

Because of its proximity to the port, the greatest rural expansion came within the province of Buenos Aires — that is, within the fertile and vacant grasslands that stretch for thousands of kilometers from Santa Fe and the delta of the Paraná River southward to Bahía Blanca and the Negro River (see Figure 4). The pampa is one of the most expansive and exploitable grassland regions of the world. Summers are hot and winters mild. More importantly, rain falls plentifully and evenly throughout the entire year. Only toward the Andes Mountains in the west does precipitation diminish considerably. Before settlement, coarse high grasses and weeds covered the flat prairies, broken here and there by intermittent gullies and arroyos. Spaniards arriving at the end of the sixteenth century found almost no trees on the fertile pampa. Apparently, Indian hunting expeditions and electrical storms had burned off the original trees centuries earlier.

This first ecological change was followed by others soon after the Europeans arrived. Spaniards replanted the famous *ombú* tree from the Andean foothills, and they soon found the soil also hospitable to fruit and hardwood trees. The softwooded ombú had no economic value, but its wide-hanging branches served as summer shade for humans and animals. Along with their livestock, Europeans inadvertently brought seeds of the wild artichoke. This tall, thin weed had spread over much of the prairies north of the Salado River by the mid–eighteenth century. Rats and dogs also found homes on the prairies. They multiplied to become predators to other animals and a threat to agriculture and husbandry in the early nineteenth century.[2]

The domestication of cattle beginning in the late colonial period proved the greatest catalyst for the ecological transformation of the pampa. "A carpet of fine green verdure," as Charles Darwin described it, soon appeared on the prairies in the wake of cattle herds grazing — and spreading manure — over the original coarse grasses.[3] The prairies were made further palatable with seasonal burnings. Manmade fires burned off tall, coarse weeds and "sweetened" the pastures.

As man and livestock spread out into the frontier, native ostriches, antelope, deer, armadillos, and partridges were pushed southward with the Pampa Indians. Vultures and other carrion birds appeared in numbers, as did the carcasses of fallen cattle and horses. Estancieros then declared war on the destructive predators, paying bounties to peons for each dog and puma killed. Prairie dogs (*bizcachas*) and their earthen tunnels destroyed pastures and endangered livestock. Men liquidated whole bizcacha communities by forcing sulphur smoke into their holes with bellows and iron tubes.[4] By 1860, the suzerainty of livestock on the plains was nearly complete.

Despite the pampa's fertility and even rainfall, ranch and farm production in the early nineteenth century was both seasonal and cyclical. Rural production naturally followed the seasons. Estancieros sent most cattle to market on the hoof in the first three months of the year. Lush spring grasses put the most weight on the animals, and the saladeristas of Buenos Aires wanted tallow and meat as well as hides. Wool and dried hides also entered the marketplaces heavily through the summer months. The round of spring sheep shearing began in October, and the summer sun of December through February was ideal for drying fresh hides and sheepskins. Harvests of hay and fodder occurred in December, and wheat ripened in January.[5] Although there was much rainfall in the summertime, the scorching sun soon evaporated it. Arroyos were dry, and the Salado River, nearly unfordable in the winter months, was but a shallow river bed cutting through the prairie in the summer. On the other hand, winter flooding formed lagoons and lakes of standing water, at times stranding livestock on the high ground.[6]

Nature thus dictated two reaons for the initial largeness of individual ranches. First, coarse, unnourishing vegetation supported fewer numbers of livestock until its gradual elimination allowed the succulent, shorter strains of grass to grow through. Second, a good estancia needed enough land for both high and low pastures. Herds grazed the high pastures in the winter when the valleys were flooded and alternately grazed the lowlands when the summer sun scorched grass on the tablelands. Although one square league (thirty-one square kilometers) of good pasturage might support as many as 50,000 sheep in good seasons, it was hardly sufficient to

Figure 4. Frontier expansion in the province of Buenos Aires, 1797–1864.
The expanding export trade of Buenos Aires port stimulated settlement of
virgin prairies in frontier areas. The growing rural population formed cattle
estancias on the frontier, settled in rural villages, and converted older
estancias near the port to sheep walks and cultivated fields. [Map by Jane

support flocks numbering more than 14,000 through years of water shortage.[7] And drought was inevitable. Many of Argentina's civil disorders as well as economic fluctuations correlate closely with periodic lack of rainfall. Because the rural industries were so central to Argentine life in the nineteenth century, drought practically dictated the economic cycle. Dry harvest seasons caused crop failures and thirst and starvation for thousands of head and cattle and sheep. In drought years, many marginal ranchers lost their herds — and their land.[8] Pastoral exports consequently fell off, while Buenos Aires merchants sought greater imports of foodstuffs from abroad. In addition, lightning often set parched grasslands afire, destroying property and livestock. Indian raids on frontier ranches coincided with drought years, for the wild cattle normally hunted by these nomadic horsemen also were desiccated and scattered by the scarcity of water. Indeed, the life balance for the prairie hunters may have been quite delicate, for wild cattle were not very plentiful in Indian territory. Traveling overland from Bahía Blanca to Buenos Aires before estancias had spread very far south, Charles Darwin noted seeing no cattle at all until he approached the frontier estancias along the Salado River.[9]

The greatest drought of the period lasted from 1828 to 1832. Dead livestock were estimated to number in the thousands. Field mice, lacking natural vegetation on the dry plains, destroyed much of the grain harvest of 1833. Flour imports rose to more than 4,177 metric tons in 1830, while stockmen sold weakened cattle at low prices.[10] Indian raids in 1829 provoked a retaliatory campaign led by General Rosas, the businessman-rancher and recently appointed governor. His military successes in 1832—3 created a legend that catapulted Rosas above the political unrest of the period. In 1833, the legislature of Buenos Aires Province offered him a second term as governor. But Rosas refused it until 1835 — long after the destructive drought had ended. Remarkably, large flour imports, Indian raids, and civil unrest coincided closely with the drought cycle throughout the first fifty years of Independence (see Table 13).

Tutino, based on Archivo General de la Nación, Buenos Aires, Sección Mapoteca, *Carta topográfica del territorio de Buenos Ayrés, 1858;* and on the provincial census figures in Ernesto J. A. Maeder, *Evolución demográfica argentina de 1810 a 1869* (Buenos Aires, 1969), pp. 34—5.]

Table 13. *Influence of drought cycle on Buenos Aires trade, politics, and Indian affairs*

| Drought years | Large U.S. flour imports | Indian raids, campaigns | Political unrest |
|---|---|---|---|
| 1817 | | 1816 | |
| 1819–20 | | 1820 | 1820 |
| 1823 | 1824 | 1824 | |
| 1828–31 | 1830–1 | 1830 | 1829–35 |
| 1851 | 1851 | 1852 | 1852 |
| 1859 | 1858 | | 1859 |
| 1861 | | | 1861 |

Floods were as periodic as droughts, but not as devastating. A British sheep rancher recorded floods on his family's estancia near the coast of Bahía Samborombón for 1817, 1834, 1845, and 1857. The flood of 1845 reduced the estancia to almost one-third its normal dry-land size.[11] Locusts too caused havoc among farmers and ranchers. From time to time, swarms of insects descended from the Paraná River over the pampa, destroying vegetation in wide swaths. Yet one foreign inhabitant reported seeing a locust plague only once in a decade.[12] Droughts remained the most common and disruptive threat to the Argentine economy through the nineteenth century.

## Production by zone

Beginning in the late colonial period, the countryside of Buenos Aires Province developed into three productive zones extending outward along lengthening radii from the city. First came an agricultural zone, then a mixed zone of farming and ranching, and finally a ranching zone. These expanding belts of production were the principal mechanism for reducing the original large size of landed units on the pampa. As a rule, land closer to the city tended to be densely populated, intensively utilized, and more valuable. Conversely, frontier land was sparsely populated, less intensively exploited, and cheap. One found a more complex and diversified rural society closer to Buenos Aires rather than farther from the port.

Tillage and dairy farming dominated the *partidos* (rural

districts or counties) in the agricultural zone. For approximately 100 kilometers along the roads leading from the city, landed units were given over to the cultivation of perishable foodstuffs like squashes, peaches, potatoes, turnips, onions, and lettuce for the local market. Agricultural pursuits were very important in the districts nearest to Buenos Aires. In 1855, at least two-thirds of the land in Barrancas del Sur immediately southeast of the port city was enclosed with wire, plant fences, or trenches. The district's agricultural sales on the domestic market equaled 60 percent of its total rural production.[13] Apparently, many *chacras* (farms) were farmed by immigrants, who grew foodstuffs with which they were familiar in Europe. Basque and other foreigners raised pigs, chickens, and dairy cows in the agricultural belt, milking at dawn and delivering eggs, milk, butter, and cheese to Buenos Aires each day by horseback.[14] By 1860, the farming system had become more complex, and intermediary dealers marketed most dairy products for the producers. Within this area, farmers also grew wheat, barley, corn, and alfalfa on farms whose only export produce consisted of wool and goatskins.

Most sheep raising was done in the mixed zone of production, whereas cattle held sway in the extreme hinterland. Cattle were wide-ranging grazers and subsisted over huge areas when the forage was poor. It was logical to start new herds on the cheaper ranges of the frontier areas. On the other hand, sheep ranching benefited from the cattlemen's destruction of the coarser grass. Sheep thrived on the short fine strains of herbs, clovers, and fennel left to sprout after cattle had moved farther out into the frontier grasslands.[15] Finally, cattle could be delivered to market over long distances on the hoof, whereas sheepmen sent their wool and sheepskins to the emporium of Buenos Aires via oxcart.

The farther one traveled into the pampa, the less agriculture one found despite the fertility of the soil. On the frontiers, the lack of manpower to attend the labors of agriculture and the distance from the largest domestic market effectively relegated cultivation to the districts surrounding Buenos Aires.[16] Bullock carts were expensive and slow in carrying perishable foodstuffs to market; thus diffusion of agricultural production was limited. Moreover, cultivation on the outlying estancias was discouraged by landowners.[17] This attitude does not represent a nativist prejudice against cultivation, for landowners closer to the city did mix crops with livestock. With limited access to markets and scarce labor pools, frontier estancieros found little justification for enclosing more land than was necessary for a few small orchards and gardens.

Exceptions existed to this zoned pattern of rural production. Frontier towns had their own belts of agricultural plots to meet limited local demand for perishable foodstuffs and dairy products. Furthermore, many landowners preferred to diversify production wherever possible in order to cushion market changes. Grain in Buenos Aires was grown in many parts of the pampa, and estancieros bred sheep and cattle in all three zones. The major centers of farm, sheep, and cattle production, however, were found in the respective production zones (see Table 14).

The agricultural zone surrounding the port city was, quantitatively, the fastest growing of the production belts on the pampa. More intensively farmed and profitably close to domestic markets, the agricultural belt expanded from eight to thirteen partidos between 1838 and 1854. That meant that five former mixed districts had become more agricultural in production. Each partido in this farming zone had more than 100 persons per square league (thirty-one square kilometers). Many country folk lived in rural villages, served by a well-developed retailing system of country stores. The rest of the inhabitants lived on privately owned or rented farms. Consequently, the agricultural zone supported large numbers

Table 14. *Rural production by zone for one-half year, 1854–5*

|  | Agricultural zone | Mixed zone | Ranching zone |
|---|---|---|---|
| Cattle on the hoof | 29,161 | 44,992 | 201,530 |
| Cattlehides and horsehides | 49,889 | 59,729 | 114,390 |
| Raw wool (kg.) | 78,022 | 199,580 | 16,861 |
| Wheat (hl.) | 23,600 | 13,806 | 21,711 |

*Sources:* Averaged from data found in *Registro estadístico de Buenos Aires* (*REBA*), 1854, Table 14; and *REBA*, 1855, vol. 2, p. 76. Totals represent 12 of 13 agricultural districts, 11 of 13 mixed districts, and 22 of 25 ranching districts.

of foreign immigrants, farmers, artisans, and country merchants.

The zone of mixed production had expanded in area from 14,900 to 26,370 square kilometers in the sixteen years following 1838. This was an area of sheep ranching, but not one that excluded wheat farming and cattle grazing. One found many migrant families from the Interior living in the mixed zone. The largest of the production belts was the one farthest from the metropolis, the ranching zone. Cattle raising was the dominant economic pursuit in the newly founded and huge estancias on the frontier. Ranching districts suffered most from occasional Indian raids and thus had the greatest number of military and militia men. Most workers here seemed to be *peones de campo* (hired hands), yet many women and children lived with them in the countryside. Isolated villages sprang up as intermediate commercial centers. The number of artisans, merchants, foreigners, and provincianos, although smaller than in other zones, was enough to maintain the distribution system for the cattle estancias. Social and spatial expansion of production on the porteño pampa was remarkable both in its complexity and in its character. (See Table 15. Also see Appendix B for the partidos listed within each production zone.)

## At their own profit

The structure of the Argentine unit of production — whether it produced livestock or crops — was much the same in all three production zones. Each chacra and estancia was intensely market oriented, producing goods salable in domestic and export markets at Buenos Aires. Unquestionably, new estancias were established principally to get the proprietor into the money market. Ranchers and frontier merchants erected a collection system that funneled rural products to the commercial emporium of the port. In addition, both estancias and chacras could have been owned by the operator, rented out, or managed for a landlord who resided in the city. It was not unusual that big landowners had both farms and ranches. Every landed unit had a center and a periphery within its spatial organization. Moreover, both the farm and the ranch maintained identical internal social structures, complete with foremen, permanent hired hands, and seasonal workers.

Table 15. *Rural expansion in Buenos Aires Province by production zone*

|  | 1838 | 1854 |
|---|---|---|
| *Agricultural zone* | | |
| Number of districts | 8 | 13 |
| Total population | 20,203 | 64,131 |
| Percent of total rural population | 24.0 | 35.2 |
| Total area in square leagues *a* | 54 | 320 |
| Persons per square league *a* | 319 | 185 |
| *Mixed zone* | | |
| Number of districts | 9 | 13 |
| Total population | 30,482 | 57,568 |
| Percent of total rural population | 36.2 | 31.6 |
| Total area in square leagues *a* | 482 | 852 |
| Persons per square league *a* | 63 | 68 |
| *Ranching zone* | | |
| Number of districts | 18 | 25 |
| Total population | 33,544 | 60,663 |
| Percent of total rural population | 39.8 | 33.2 |
| Total area in square leagues *a* | 2,310 | 4,214 |
| Persons per square league *a* | 15 | 14 |

*a* One square league equals 31 square kilograms.
*Sources:* For 1838, Archivo General de la Nación (AGN), Buenos Aires, Sala 10, 25–6–2. For 1854, *Registro estadístico de Buenos Aires*, 1854, p. 11, and AGN, Sala 10, 42–8–5.

At the center of the estancia property was the head station *(casco),* where the owner built his own residence, at first of adobe and thatch but later of brick. On the frontiers, estancieros often made minifortresses of their houses, with towers for sighting and firing small cannon at Indian marauders. The biggest ranchers lived in the city, and the main residence at the head station either was inhabited by his estate manager (mayordomo) or served as the summer residence of the rancher's family. Within the casco, one also found adobe huts (ranchos) for the family of ranch foremen and for the hired hands. Some houses and bunkhouses contained as many as four rooms. Smaller outbuildings served as kitchens and storage warehouses for hides, tallow, tools, and tack. The casco usually had a large corral for branding and keeping the working horses. Each estancia maintained mules and oxen, a two-wheeled horsecart, and a large oxcart for work and marketing. Sheep ranches had head stations a bit more elaborate, with paddocks, sheep sheds, and processing equipment like boiling vats, shearing tools, and baling presses. Often, a deep trench surrounded the entire head station. Moats not only defended against Indian raiders but protected the breeding stock, garden plots, and rude orchards.[18] The casco was the social as well as physical core of the estancia.

Major pasturage areas within the larger estancia were divided into separate rodeos, each having its select herd of cattle, horses, or sheep. The cowboy responsible for the herd lived with his family in the center of the rodeo (the *puesto,* or post) and maintained a wooden corral nearby. Inside his hut, the *puestero* kept bridles, saddlery lassos, bullock skulls as seats, and hide beds and hammocks. Around the corrals were traces of butchered and fallen animals, attracting hawks and buzzards. The odor was distinctive.[19] Large estancias contained as many as five or six rodeos, each supporting herds of 1,000 head of cattle and 50 horses. Shepherds on sheep ranches lived on the puesto as well and tended up to 2,000 sheep. Depending on the geography of the estancia, a rodeo in itself might have been as large as 1,000 hectares.

The puestero worked permanently in a position of responsibility and trust for the estanciero. His job as cowboy was to ride the limits of his rodeo, return strays to the herd, and drive the cattle into the corrals once a day in order to maintain their sense of the home pasture *(querencia).*[20] Shepherds often tended flocks on a profit-sharing basis. Ranchers acquired much additional labor on a seasonal basis. The *mensuales,* single gauchos who hired on for a month at a time, lived at the head station. They aided especially in branding on all the rodeos of the ranch. Mensuales also parted and cut the herds *(aparte)* prior to sale or slaughter and hunted the wild cattle that strayed from established pastures into the bush.[21] Sheepmen hired additional laborers for a week or two during spring shearing.

The typical chacra shared the structural characteristics of the estancia. Many farms, after all, once had been parts of estancias. The farm, though smaller than a ranch, also had a casco and specific outlying fields within its boundaries. At the head station, one found the ranchos of the farmer, the workers, and their families. Workers' families were allowed to cultivate small vegetable gardens around their huts. Seasonal laborers hired on during shearing and harvest times. The owner provided tools and capital, and he might sponsor a rural merchant in a general store on his property. In addition, outlying plots of the farm were rented to individual families for the cultivation of potatoes and vegetables at their own expense and for their own profit.[22] Many of the chacras actually were too large to continue operation as a single farming unit. Rental of land thus was the landowner's effort to retain his property intact. The pressure of rising land values and farm production forced many a landlord to sell off previously rented or unused plots. Each new unit of production retained the market orientation and the structure common to the porteño estancia throughout the first half of the century.

### Fences twenty-four feet high

The extraordinary expansion of pastoral and agricultural activity on the pampa happened without significant technological change in production. Instead of modern machinery, windmills, wire fencing, and motor power, Argentine producers depended on a variety of well-known, native devices to accomplish rural production in the early nineteenth century. Traditional animate sources, notably the horse and the ox, continued to serve as Argentina's chief mode of power and transportation. Both animals were plentiful and cheap on the grasslands, where their utility is obvious. Gauchos spent the better part of their waking hours on horseback. Horses drew water from primitive wells. Farmers also used the horse, running mares over wheat and corn in order to thresh the grains. Even begging in Buenos Aires was done on horseback.[23] Oxen drew the rude plows that turned up the farmer's earth, hauled rural products to the port in freight wagons, and returned with imported commodities.

Drawing water for sheep and cattle in the oft-parched pastures also depended primarily on native innovation. Cattle holes, dug about two meters deep, served as wells. Early in the century, the principal device for drawing water was the *pelota*, a sewn rawhide bag drawn out of a shallow water hole by a mounted gaucho. Another man, dismounted, had to empty the bag. This simple system was replaced by the *balde sin fondo*. Its virtue lay in a two-rope attachment that permitted one man on horseback to draw and empty water in the same motion. Thus, a single man with a string of horses could water approximately 2,000 head of cattle in eight hours. After midcentury, ranchers were using a variation, the *manga* (sleeve), made of longer-lasting canvas instead of rawhide.[24] The first wind-powered water pumps, imported from the United States, did not begin arriving until the 1870s.

For fencing, estancieros and farmers relied on organic materials of limited supply to enclose parts of their lands. Farmers protected fields and orchards from wandering livestock with fences of native shrubs, cactus, and cattle bones. European travelers, obviously exaggerating, wrote that the fences in Argentina sometimes grew as high as twenty-four feet.[25] On the treeless prairies, wood and plants for corrals had to be hauled to the estancia by oxcart from wooded arroyos along the Paraná River. In lieu of cheaper fencing materials, a ditch measuring twelve feet deep and twenty-five feet wide surrounded several acres of the head station on many estancias.[26] British landowners were the first to use wire fencing. In 1864, a British sheep raiser returned from England with enough wire to enclose his casco and its gardens. Yet barbed wire did not come into general usage until the 1860s.[27] Even then, wire fencing was reinforced with the ditch, an Argentine tradition.

The lack of substantial technological innovation in Argentine pastoral and agricultural pursuits meant continued sensitivity of rural production to the drought cycle. To minimize the tolls of drought, ranchers needed large expanses of land. Scarcity of water and fencing materials also dictated extensive land utilization. Without a reliable water supply, a great deal of land was needed for grazing, and significant pasture improvement was difficult on the open ranges. Cattle breeding especially had to await not only the exportability of fresh beef provided by end-of-the-century advances in refrigerated meat packing, but also the practical separation of breeding stocks in fenced pastures. Argentine ranching in the nineteenth century necessitated production on large landed estates. Traditional technology simply did not permit more efficient use of the land.

Significant technological change came to the Argentine prairies only in the second half of the nineteenth century, when wire fencing, railroads, canals, windmills, and power machinery again transformed the pampa. That does not mean that earlier production could not have been and was not otherwise improved. Indeed, ranchers and farmers in Buenos Aires did perfect a number of management and husbandry practices just short of technological change.

### Early morning risers

Argentina's rural development during the era had another dimension: livestock management. In an era of declining price levels in the Buenos Aires marketplace, estancieros had to increase cattle reproduction and improve wool fleeces to maintain both profits and pastoral expansion. The goal of cattle management, lacking technological innovation, was to augment the size of the herds. Because beefsteak had little export value, the breeding of finer cattle stocks was senseless. Cattlemen depended only on reproduction to produce hides and meats and on lush spring grasses to add weight before the slaughter. Yet profitable herd increase demanded considerable management. Argentine sheepraisers, on the other hand, had to promote the quality of their flocks in order to capitalize on European demand for raw wool. The short, kinky wool of the native sheep was almost worthless, so sheepmen bred imported pureblood rams with selected native ewes to improve their flocks. By midcentury, their mastery of basic ranch management assured porteño ranchers of continued profits and higher yearly exports.

Conditions on the pampa at the beginning of the nineteenth century were not conducive to breeding fine cattle. In 1823, an estanciero imported the first English Shorthorn bull, the famous "Tarquino," but quality meat from Argentine cattle was not yet in demand. Most dairy herds were made up of native cows, although some Shorthorns went into improving the milking stock. In the 1850s, farm owners imported Shorthorn stock for dairy herds in order to set up creameries *(lecherías)* for processing milk, cream, and cheese.[28] Breeding on the open range, at any rate, was difficult. Without practical fencing, purebred animals in time would have been lost among the semiwild native stock. Everyone instead worked with the Longhorn – thin-legged, lanky, thick-hided, and adorned with horns of enormous spread. Having no clover and lucerne, native Longhorns gained little weight roaming over great distances to eat the coarse vegetation. In any case, cattle drives to market often caused the loss of much extra fat gained on spring grass.[29]

Branding, castration, and the rodeo were the major management techniques used to achieve herd domestication and maximum reproduction. Registered brands signified ownership of the bearer in case the animal strayed or was stolen. Police often verified the brands of cattle entering the stockyards and occasionally caught thieves who tried to sell purloined cattle and hides.[30] Branding time on the large estancias occurred all year round. Peons worked the cattle on one rodeo after another until the newborn of all the herds had been branded. Smaller estancias branded once or twice a year. Calves were selectively castrated as they were marked with the branding iron. Breeders saved 20 percent of the best and healthiest of the young bulls and made steers of the most truculent, poorest colored, and fattest.[31]

Above all, profitable production on the cattle estancia called for diligent ranch management. As administrator for a number of Anchorena family properties in the 1820s, Juan Manuel de Rosas wrote up detailed instructions to his mayordomos on the estates. He explained exact procedures for the care of horses, the branding of cattle, and the disposition of animal carcasses. Rosas required that the herds be rounded up daily and counted often to prevent the loss of strays. Dying and diseased animals were killed immediately and skinned, their carcasses being boiled down for fat and tallow. Animals killed for food were to be completely dressed and consumed. Cows in fold or with calf were separated from the herd and carefully attended. Within their first week, newborn calves were to be marked on the ear for identification. Rosas was concerned that boundary markers on the estancias be maintained and that the neighbor's strays be returned immediately. His comments on the diligence and discipline required of ranch foremen is telling:

Capataces must be early risers and not sleepy heads; a foreman who does not get up early is no good at all. The ranch manager must observe that they get up and do their chores. In spring, summer and fall, they should rise a little before dawn in order to have time to wake their men, saddle-up the horses, have their maté, and be ready to leave for the pastures when it gets light.[32]

Rosas' orders to his mayordomos emphasize the economic value of livestock. His instructions sought to increase reproduction and reduce waste, because both represented profit to the rancher.

The greatest efficiency in the ranching industry, however, came when much cattle processing was removed from the estancia proper. At the beginning of the nineteenth century, cattle ranchers prepared most cattle products right on their properties. Besides caring for livestock herds, ranch hands also had to slaughter and prepare the hides and melted tallow. In 1812, one estancia in the district of Monte just south of the Salado River garnered only 12 percent of its sales from livestock marketed on the hoof. Thirty years later, estancieros were sending most of their cattle live to stockyards and saladeros in Buenos Aires. In 1848, a rancher in San Pedro on the Paraná River derived nearly 70 percent of his livestock revenues from cattle drives.[33] No longer did ranch hands prepare the bulk of pastoral products on the premises.

### From fuel to fleeces

Sheep ranchers found greater incentives than did cattle raisers for improving their breeds. Native sheep, known as pampa or creole, grew only to a scrawny size and carried coats of short, tangly hair. When the nineteenth century began, porteños utilized pampa sheep for a quick-roasted dinner or as fuel for the brick kilns. "It is related," wrote a traveler in 1810, "that all the churches are built of bricks burned with the carcasses of sheep."[34] The first order among estancieros who went into sheep ranching in the 1820s was to import French Merino and British Southdown rams. Bred with the best of the native ewes, these rams begot a mixed breed, the mestizo, which sufficed to place Argentine wool on industrial markets. Worthless native sheep then were slaughtered for their tallow and grease. One ranch in particular, owned by Sheridan, Harrat, and Whitfield, specialized in breeding and selling purebred rams to nascent sheep ranchers throughout the pampa. Soon Saxonies and Leicesters also arrived to complement the Merino and Southdown breeds. By the 1850s, advanced ranchers began to experiment with Shropshire, Cheviot, Highland Blackface, Romney Marsh, and Lincoln breeds. Lack of adequate fencing retarded sheep breeding somewhat, because sheepmen had to isolate their quality flocks with trenches and natural enclosures of marshes and arroyos.[35] New sheep breeders then needed to build sheds and paddocks to facilitate flock improvement.

Ranchers did increase the weight of their animals and, more importantly, of wool fleeces. Common pampa fleeces weighed about one kilogram washed, whereas crossbreds later yielded two kilograms of wool each. That meant higher profits. Merino wool brought more than twice the price of mestizo wool and six times that of native creole fleeces.[36] The changeover to long-haired sheep was complete throughout the pampa by the mid-1860s.

In contrast to cattlemen, sheep ranchers utilized a system of profit sharing among the peons. Shepherds *(medieros)* cared for up to 2,000 sheep on a puesto and received one-third of the increase in wool, skins, and tallow. The mediero was allowed the meat of the sheep for himself and his family but provided his own yerba, sugar, biscuit, and salt. He put aside the wool, skin, and tallow for the proprietor. The shepherds drove their flocks into the corral at night, kept them from scattering during storms, and watered them regularly at wells and streams. Instead of brands, sheep were identified by ear marks and nose slits (buttons).[37]

Profit sharing substituted for a practical paddock system, because fencing whole pastures was a luxury. "In lands where a paddock system is impossible the shepherd who tends his flock on a profit share will do his work more thoroughly and conscientiously than a hireling," wrote one Anglo-Argentine sheepman, "and if he earns a large sum of money one year, it is because his employer has made a proportionately larger one."[38] In the mediero system, flock reproduction garnered the profit, sometimes to the detriment of quality breeding. Apparently, some shepherds did not fully utilize breeding rams or systematically segregate rams and ewes. But flocks did increase with proper management. The Gibson flocks near Ajó increased from 6,280 head in 1840 to 32,318 within two decades.[39]

All wool processing was done on the estancia, so that sheepmen too had to employ additional labor during spring shearing from October through December. Men, women, and children earned by piecework — forty pesos per every

100 sheep sheared. Seasonal help also received meals, maté, and shelter from the estanciero during shearing time.[40] First, sheep were washed of dirt in lagoon water before shearing. Most wool was shipped in the grease, because steamed wool washing in village factories was common only toward the end of the century. Steam equipment for boiling down tallow and grease became more common after 1840. Every rural town had a boiling-down factory (grasería) which bought stock or killed on commission for local breeders. At first workers bound fleeces together with jute string. In 1850, the steam and screw baling presses had arrived from Liverpool so that wool could be compressed into 260-kilo bales right on the estancia.[41] Because shearing seldom lasted more than two weeks per estancia, many seasonal workers had the opportunity to work ten sheep estancias or more each spring.

Altogether, diligent herd management, streamlined processing, and effective sheepbreeding added to efficiency in ranching. A host of small husbandry advances allowed porteño ranchers to continue profitable pastoral expansion despite the fall in raw material prices in the Buenos Aires and industrial marketplaces.

### Bone plowing and horse threshing

In many ways, the most surprising expansion came in farming on the pampa. The extent of tillage and cultivation in the early nineteenth century has been underestimated by historians of the pampa. Compared to the voluminous wheat exports at the end of the century, earlier farming was thought to have been neglected. "In the years leading up to 1870," writes one Argentine scholar, "we were almost exclusively cattlemen."[42] Others claim that Argentines practically had forgotten how to sow wheat, and that, at any rate, powerful cattlemen opposed farming and agricultural colonization. Farmers are characterized as economically and politically weak, an insignificant part of early nineteenth-century La Plata society. The scarcity of labor and poor transportation in the era often are cited as deterrents to agricultural production everywhere on the pampa.[43] At base is the tendency of most historians to underrate the size of domestic markets for agricultural produce. The fact that Argentina visibly exported no cash crops in the first half of the nineteenth century does not imply that Argentines engaged in very little farming. Agriculture was important!

Farming in the early nineteenth century technologically differed little from colonial cultivation. Travelers of the late 1700s mentioned finding small chacras around both Montevideo and Buenos Aires that produced wheat, corn, melons, and vegetables. Some were surrounded by cactus fences, and others had peach and fig orchards. Two oxen yoked to a crooked piece of wood sufficed to root up the fertile sod, but weeds also sprouted with the hand-sown seeds. Colonial farmers harvested wheat with hand sickles and threshed by driving horses over the harvest for several hours. A toss into the wind then separated the grain from the chaff.[44]

Until well past midcentury, agriculture in Buenos Aires remained almost as limited and rude. In the 1800s, farmers were doing the same as their colonial counterparts – plowing with a "large bone of an ox" and threshing in corrals with galloping horses. Grains and vegetables were sown in the same fields year after year without crop rotation. There was little use of manure and no large-scale grazing in fields of alfalfa or lucerne. Instead, farmers cut and sold forage in the city for animal bedding and fodder. Grain storage consisted of filling a sewn oxhide with wheat or corn and suspending the bag on poles away from rats.[45]

Despite the continued use of age-old procedures, growth and improvement in agricultural methods did occur. Human effort was still the primary means of cultivating and raising Argentina's agricultural products in the early nineteenth century. Increased farm production – like pastoral production – was, first of all, a matter of greater inputs of manpower. Certainly, the number of laborers in agriculture increased appreciably. By 1854, for instance, at least 10 percent of all rural males either owned or rented farms – not to mention the additonal number of peons and itinerant workers in farming.[46] Yet some qualitative improvements in cultivation also occurred in the period. British and American customs sources show that the export sales of hand tools – shovels, hoes, iron plows – to Buenos Aires had become quite important by midcentury. Hand implements, no doubt, contributed to increased farm production by replacing wood plows and bone hoes.[47] Greater manpower and the limited imports of foreign tools together intensified farm productivity on the pampa to support the expanding domestic market of metropolitan Buenos Aires.

## The common 2 percent

Rural merchandising expanded and diversified with the rural economy. Camp merchants, country stores, oxcarting, and cattle drives were the four vital links between ranches in the countryside and markets in Buenos Aires. The focal point of the rural commercial system came to be the camp merchant, a creole businessman in Buenos Aires who arranged collection and distribution of goods throughout the pampa. Commissions of 2 percent were common in this commerce. The camp merchant also was a source of credit, as he often extended goods on time to his clientele of estancieros and shopkeepers in the *campo* (countryside). In fact, he was accustomed to coordinating the other elements of rural commerce. The camp merchant arranged freight with independent cartmen and organized cattle drives to Buenos Aires stockyards. He sent Brazilian tobacco and sugar, Paraguayan yerba mate, Chilean *sombreros,* and the Interior's ponchos to storekeepers in rural villages.[48]

Taverns and general stores availed as the commercial and social centers of the pampa. Accessible by horseback to the scattered country folk, pulperías (taverns) and *tiendas* (country stores) were natural gathering places under the shade of an ombú tree. Rural inhabitants got their supplies of tobacco, yerba, hardware, and spirits from the pulperías. Instead of paying cash, customers often traded their hides, wool, and other rural produce. The *pulpero* also was a local source of credit in the countryside. Tiendas sold foodstuffs like salt, sugar, flour, corn, and biscuits along with soap, wine, and dry goods. Rural merchants often worked for estancieros, on whose properties the stores were built and who provided the operating capital. At times, the landowners' oxcarts brought in goods from the plazas of Buenos Aires.[49] Otherwise, shopkeepers accepted the services of a camp merchant in Buenos Aires who arranged delivery of dry goods and other merchandise on the oxcarts of independent teamsters.[50] Rural census materials for 1858 indicate the existence of more than 1,100 pulperías and 280 tiendas in the province of Buenos

Aires. At least one saloon or country store served every seventy-five inhabitants (see Table 16).

Freight rumbled back and forth across the prairies aboard oxcarts. Many ranch managers sent loads of wool and hides to their owners in Buenos Aires via estancia carts.[51] Yet, independent cartmen *(troperos)* operated trains of four or five wagons between the port and frontier towns. Bullock carts moved over the prairies very slowly, making only 8 to 18 kilometers a day. From Estancia Camarones, approximately 155 kilometers from Buenos Aires, a wagon train reached the port city in nine days. Consequently, freight rates were rather high, even though camp merchants shopped from among many troperos. From Camarones, the charge was 1.25 gold pesos per *bulto* (weight or cube unknown); from Dolores, 190 kilometers distant, it was 1.5 gold pesos per bulto; and cartage to Azul, 340 kilometers away, was 2.25 gold pesos.[52] High freight costs prohibited transport of bulkier items. Carts easily carried dry goods, tools, and metal goods, but lumber products of size were impractical over the long haul. Oxcarts also delivered rural roods — wool, hides, tallow, grease, horsehair, sheepskins, and fur pelts — collected by commercial agents in the frontier towns.[53] Because cartage was expensive, camp merchants stipulated that the wool be washed of its grit and dirt. Clean wool was lighter, its transport cheaper, and its price higher.[54]

Cattle driving came into prominence when Buenos Aires' stockyards and salting industry removed most cattle processing from the ranches. Estancieros in the city and factory

Table 16. *Rural retailing establishments in Buenos Aires Province, 1858*

|  | Agricultural zone | Mixed zone | Ranching zone |
|---|---|---|---|
| Pulperías | 507 | 394 | 239 |
| Tiendas | 91 | 98 | 95 |
| Number of inhabitants per establishment | 77 | 79 | 68 |

*Source: Registro estadístico de Buenos Aires,* 1858, vol. 1, p. 135. Statistics represent 12 or 13 agricultural districts, 10 of 13 mixed districts, and 17 of 25 ranching districts.

owners arranged contracts specifying direct delivery of herds throughout the slaughter season. Usually, the factory owner sent out five or six peons to help select the cattle and to drive the herd to Buenos Aires. Saladeristas desired that at least two-thirds of the cattle be "fat" steers no less than two and a half years old. The rest of the herd could be made up of cows, but they brought lower prices than the fuller-bodied steers.[55] Cattle in good condition covered up to forty kilometers per day. A large drive sometimes lost 30 to 100 head, especially if the drive averaged only one peon for as many as 100 head of cattle.[56] But more drovers naturally meant higher costs. The value added by labor in one cattle drive from Tandil was 17 percent of the total. With high labor costs, *tropas* (cattle drives) of less than 300 head were discouraged.[57]

Using free-lance cattle drovers, camp merchants arranged tropas from among smaller cattlemen in the countryside. The object was to see that the animals arrived in good condition, that the tropa met with few delays, and that strays were minimized. The scourge of the trail was a band of drovers who lost many animals along the way or who delivered the cattle "quite lean and some part skinny."[58] Therfore, the camp merchants and their agents in the field sought trail bosses (capataces) of confidence and responsibility. As the tropas approached the stockyards, the merchants sent out a guide to meet the trail boss. He arranged the papers for police inspection, and decided which steers were suitable for the butcher and which for the salting factories.[59] In all his business dealings, the camp merchant seems to have served as commercial agent for smaller ranchers − or at least for ranchers who resided in the campo and did not carry on their own business in Buenos Aires like the elite landowners.

The story of the rural economy, therefore, is one of continued expansion of the frontiers of production as well as improvement in ranch and farm management. Yet, productivity in the countryside was approaching a threshold difficult to cross without substantial changes in technology. The absence of well pumping and wire fencing inhibited more intensive land use and the breeding of quality livestock. In addition, ranching and farming on the pampa were highly susceptible to the havoc wrought by periodic droughts. Serious water shortages also affected both politics and society in the Río de la Plata. Rural merchandising, although well organized, had to extend its commercial lines far out onto the prairies while continuing to utilize expensive cattle driving and oxcarting. By 1860, the era of technological change in Argentine livestocking and agriculture already had begun. The first railroads and wire fences were being introduced on a small scale. The addition of windmills. refrigerated meat packing, steam shipping, and harbor construction ultimately would transform production on the pampa once again in the next half-century.

The spread of production onto the frontier greatly influenced the character of rural society. Omission of the social development of the pampa would leave incomplete the account of nineteenth-century economic growth. People and their social opportunities on the pampa — an important but neglected aspect of the economy — were profoundly influenced by the production functions of the staple export economy.

# 7

# Expansion of pastoral society on the pampa

Modern patterns of latifundia in Latin America give rise to extreme social stratification and economic exploitation. Thus the subject of how land is acquired and owned has drawn much scholarly inquiry and controversy. In Argentina, both the formation of large estancias that produced staple exports and the creation of rural society around the export sector are no less controversial.

Many of the elite families of today's Argentina owe their fortunes and status to their ancestors' purchase of public terrain in the nineteenth century. Some historians look upon that original acquisition of land as the sinister act of powerful men. They recognize that the post-Independence estancia was the social, political, and economic core of Argentine life but suspect that the "monopoly" of land ownership by the few had molded pampa society into rigid inequality and immobility. The proprietor's great hunger for land, say some historians, dominated the forces governing land acquisition. The landowner successfully sought to extend his holdings at the same time that he repressed the labor force. Classic "absentee landownership" resulted. The conventional view has it that colonial and early national estancieros kept land for income and for social prestige and avoided the hardships of rural life by living in the city. Even Spanish legal traditions, requiring expensive paperwork and bureaucratic delays, conspired to favor ownership of land for the wealthy few. Meanwhile, rural laborers were repressed harshly, and the monolithic cattle estancia discouraged competing economic activity for farmers, artisans, and tradesmen in pampa villages.[1]

Historians looking for political explanations of land "monopoly" subscribe to the conspiracy school. The idea is that the "dictator," Juan Manuel de Rosas, represented the powerful estanciero class. Rosas was anathema to the development of agriculture − and of the overall economy − in

146

Argentina, they argue. He turned over large chunks of public land to the grazing interests rather than to the more democratic farmers. Rosas' land grants and policies, therefore, created "a system of latifundia from which [Buenos Aires] province has not yet freed itself."[2]

Pampa society, stimulated by diversified rural industries and by extension of the merchandising system, displayed greater complexity in its structure than has been reckoned. Admittedly, landholdings were large, a fact accounted for by the production functions and technology of the day. Yet, for those very same reasons, large landed units were subdivided – not enlarged – as 1860 approached. Landholdings actually were reduced in size and their ownership diffused. The individual family proved to be the most common social unit in the countryside. Ranching and farming themselves turned out to be family projects not only benefiting every branch of the proprietor's clan but also supporting the families of peons who worked on the estates. Although most country folk worked on the land as proprietors and hired workers, porteños, provicianos, and foreigners alike found opportunities in artisanry and rural commerce. Villages mushroomed everywhere to support the estancias and chacras. Pastoral society on the pampa in the first half of the nineteenth century appeared vibrant, booming, and open to economic and social opportunity.

## No ordinary sight

The post-Independence boom in foreign trade made investment in cattle estancias quite profitable for creole businessmen. In the 1810s, many native merchants had been eased out of the export trade by the incursions of the new foreign traders. Old merchant families, therefore, shifted their assets into land and cattle for the first time. Sons of colonial merchant families became some of the new estancieros of the 1820s and 1830s. The Anchorena, Obligado, Alzaga, Lezica, Ramos Mexía, Ugarte, and Inzúe were among the prominent landholders of the 1820s.[3] Most maintained their commercial ties, for ranching was a business endeavor. Members of successful ranching families retained broker houses in order to market products from the family estates. The wealthiest of the landowners lived in Buenos Aires, leaving the daily ranch management in the hands of resident managers and foremen. The social life of the ranchers' families naturally was richer in the city. Economically, too, the estanciero living in town could better facilitate marketing of estancia products. In Buenos Aires, ranchers dealt directly with merchants who collected goods for export and with factory owners who sought timely delivery of fattened steers. Far from being disinterested absentee landlords, Argentine estancieros who lived in Buenos Aires socially and economically linked together the countryside and the city.[4]

Still, rural censuses reveal that the majority of porteño ranchers lived and worked alongside the hired hands in the countryside. Estancieros like Bernardino Rodríguez of Giles, married, with eight children on his ranch, hired five peons to work with him. An even smaller estate was owned by Florencio Díaz, married, with two children, who took on only one hired hand.[5] Despite the visibility of the few wealthy ranchers, the family ranch was by far the most common.

The social eminence of the rich estanciero, nevertheless, was quite evident in Buenos Aires. In the viceregal period, Spanish and Creole merchants dominated the social elite, because they were the wealthiest members of porteño society. Few of the first families owned any grazing property at all in the colonial period.[6] The rancher came into elite status only after Independence, when holding land and raising cattle was especially profitable. Ranch families now took the best houses in the city, educated themselves, and engaged in the social and political affairs of the province. When the prominent estancieros traveled to their rural estates, pedestrians took note, as did one British resident in the early 1830s:

> A [ranching] family going to the country is no ordinary sight; the mules and waggons following with the baggage, and the quantity of out-riders, slaves, and servants, in *ponchos* and little dirty hats, surrounding the carriages containing the ladies and female slaves, appear like a banditti escorting their plunder.[7]

Big landowners in the nineteenth century sought to diversify their rural economic influence and leverage in order to maintain commercial solvency. Occasionally, large estancieros owned pulperías and the carts that supplied these taverns. Ranchers sometimes operated wagon trains for an

entire area and hired a capataz and several peons to deliver
goods back and forth to the city.[8] One such frontier estanciero, José Gerónimo Iraola, had a fleet of three wagons and
ninety-seven oxen that delivered goods between his estancia
and general store in Tandil and a warehouse he owned near
Plaza Once. Iraola also promoted rural artisanry, owning
blacksmith, carpentry, and masonry shops in Tandil. Simón
Pereyra eventually acquired a diversified urban–rural economic network. At death, his legacy included six estancias,
five chacras, a saladero, five quintas, two warehouses, six
urban houses, a toll bridge, and a boat.[9] Pereyra got his first
land from the state for supplying the Rosas expedition in
1832. Family ownership, too, aided in the drive toward
commercial diversification and solvency. The patriarch of the
family, a merchant, might finance the son in ranch management. The son then would send the production of the estancia to his father's warehouse in the city. The son later returned to the city in order to manage the family's diverse
commercial and landed inheritance.[10] Diversification of economic enterprise among wealthy estancieros meant more certain success and solvency.

### A great deal of land

The government participated in the social development of
the hinterland — acquiescing to the large pastoral estate as
the primary mode of expansion. Throughout the nineteenth
century, the policy of the provincial government of Buenos
Aires was to promote settlement of the frontier through the
sale, renting, or granting of land. Superficially at least, land
policy seemed as confusing as national politics. In the 1820s,
the *unitario* government attempted to retain in the state the
ownership of all frontier land. Under Bernardino Rivadavia's
law of emphyteusis, the government distributed new land
with the stipulation that titleholders pay an annual rent. Emphyteusis land was distributed to foreign immigrants as well
as Creoles, and many British, French, and German names
appear on the list of grantees. The liberal laws allowed many
people to acquire vast expanses of vacant territory. Huge
tracts, some amounting to 675 square kilometers, were allot-
ted under the plan. The average grant varied between 150
and 300 square kilometers. Great families acquired huge ex-

panses — the Anchorena alone having gotten more than 864 square kilometers of land under emphyteusis.[11]

Emphyteusis was fiscal in origin. Its proponents hoped that public lands would yield additional funds to a state treasury dominated by customs duties. A contract stipulating annual rental fees was drawn up between the prospective proprietor and the government. Such a fixed rent quickly fell prey to the first inflationary spiral of paper currency in the 1820s. The Rivadavia plan was not intended to promote socialized landholding or to produce a middle class of yeoman farmers.

Rosas allowed emphyteusis to lapse, selling lands to their tenants on easy terms. Some paid in cattle and horses. Furthermore, Rosas made generous grants of land to soldiers who participated in the frontier wars against the Indians and his political enemies. In 1839, for instance, one such series of grants was extended according to the veteran's rank: 186 square kilometers for generals, 155 for colonels, and so on down to soldiers, who received less than 10 square kilometers each. With little capital to stock the land, most soldiers sold their land premiums for ready cash to established merchants and landowners.[12] Civilians also acquired vacant terrain through service to the state. Manuel José Guérrico helped supply Rosas' army expedition against the Indians in 1832. Two years later, he was awarded more than 3,100 square kilometers of land in Lobería.[13]

Land policies may have been confusing, but the trend of landholding was constant. The first estancias to cover the frontier areas tended to be large in size. The original extent of landed units resulted more from the economic realities of pastoral expansion in the early nineteenth century than from deliberate government policy. Even in the last years of the colonial epoch, it was clear that ranchers needed large herds and much land for successful production. In 1797, one hacendado summed up the prospects of profitably breeding cattle in the coming era:

> Whoever has the capital cannot easily decide to raise cattle (which takes all one's time and makes one suffer many inconveniences) unless he begins with the intention of raising a large herd.
> In order to raise a large herd, one needs a great deal of land and many men; because if the land is small and the cattle are many, the countryside becomes sterilized

and calamity comes to the pastures. If the cattle are many and the men are few and of little zeal, the herds then disperse and the owner loses his cattle and his investment.[14]

Disparate sources seem to indicate a rather constant turn-over of land tenure. Although a few families amassed huge tracts of land, those who were able to purchase or rent farms and ranches at one time or another were numerous. Most estancias were held by individuals and families. Seldom in this era did one find ownership by a company or even by a formal partnership except within the family. Land was easily bought and sold and it frequently was rented. Quite often, smaller plots of land were owned by merchants and ranchers and rented out to retainers under formal contract. The An-chorena family, an old merchant clan with colonial begin-nings, owned chacras even before they went into estancias. Juan José Cristobal de Anchorena signed seven-year con-tracts to rent his chacras in San Isidro. The single renter of the two farms paid 500 silver pesos per year in rent. The oxen, carts, tools, buildings, and corrals entrusted to the farmer were owned by Anchorena. The owner also put up 600 pesos with which the renter was to plant fruit trees on the property. Anchorena paid the farm's taxes. The renter thus planted hay and vegetables at his own expense and pro-fit.[15] Rental of property offered those without capital re-sources the opportunity to operate ranches and farms in the era of growing markets.

Landownership in the agricultural zone around Buenos Aires was quite diversified and widespread. Successful por-teño businessmen and estancieros owned country villas and farms in this zone. Lesser urbanites rented out small rural properties for living expenses. Census materials, however, indicate that the smaller units in farming areas were more often owned than rented by the operator. The pattern in ranching areas leaned toward the rental of rural estates. In all, renters and owners made up approximately 28 percent of the adult male population of the countryside (see Table 17).

The spread of estancias, whether rented or owned, "civilized" the frontier and reduced lawlessness in the coun-tryside. Travelers found much political support among estan-cieros for Governor Rosas, the dominant political figure of the era, because his justices of the peace enforced order in

Table 17. *Ownership and rental of property in Buenos Aires Province, 1854 (expressed as percentage of total number of operators)*

|  | Agricultural zone | Mixed zone | Ranching zone |
|---|---|---|---|
| Ownership | 68 | 31 | 41 |
| Rental | 32 | 69 | 59 |

*Source: Registro estadístico de Buenos Aires*, 1854, Table 10. Ten of 13 agricultural districts, 13 of 13 mixed districts, and 22 of 25 ranching districts reporting. One should note that this table does not reflect the percentages of the total amount of land but only the number of properties.

the countryside.[16] Many ranchers may have despised Rosas' controversial political tactics, but they did appreciate the *pax rosensis*.

## The legendary 30 percent

Responding to greater rural production, the value of property began to rise steadily from the turn of the nineteenth century. The basic factor in determining the value of a piece of property was its distance from the market. As a rule, as one drew closer to the marketing center of Buenos Aires, the price of land rose quite rapidly. Land in the agricultural zone, therefore, was worked more intensively than the less valuable lands in the mixed and ranching zones. Even so, as the commercialization of the pampa proceeded, an estancia of fixed size became more and more valuable. The price of one such ranch in the older ranching district of Pergamino, bought at twenty-one gold *centavos* per hectare in 1840, was sold for nearly two gold pesos just sixteen years afterward.[17] Figures (in gold pesos) for the overall rise in land values are taken randomly from the data on Pergamino:[18]

|  | *price per hectare* |
|---|---|
| 1781 | .05 |
| 1800 | .11 |
| 1826 | .30 |
| 1837 | .36 |
| 1850 | 2.00 |
| 1860 | 3.30 |
| 1870 | 6.00 |
| 1879 | 10.25 |

Although land values were rising, there is little evidence of wholesale land speculation. Buying and selling of land for profit did occur, perhaps more after 1850 than before. Yet the theories of some historians that land speculation was widespread may apply more accurately to the end of the century.[19] Instead, land seems to have been acquired for the income of the products that it produced. Rental of land, especially of smaller estancias and chacras, was common. Ranching and farming thus were available to newcomers or to those lacking enough capital to acquire and operate their own property.

Rising land values added to the operating costs and each year drove up the capital costs of ranching. Credit gradually gained importance. Despite the traditional technology and very basic land improvements of the day, estancieros needed a substantial amount of capital to run an estancia. Ranchers had to invest in tools, lumber for corrals and ranchos, bricks, carts, labor, and livestock. If someone bought an established estancia, he usually purchased the improved pastures, orchards, wells, huts, and corrals in addition to the land. Credit between businessmen played a part. A new estanciero might buy cattle on time under an agreement to pay off the balance regularly within a year. It was often imperative to be backed financially by one's family or by a merchant in Buenos Aires. Prudencio de Rosas, the governor's brother, enjoyed considerably more political and financial contacts than the ordinary rancher. Thus he was able to purchase many leagues of land on the frontier with the financial backing of a prominent porteño merchant.[20] However, investment ceilings had not yet risen so high as to restrict farming and ranching to only the most wealthy.

A look at one estancia account book reveals that family finances were the first source of estancia capital and that outside monies merely supplemented family investment. In 1844, Antonio Soler assumed management of the Estancia de las Palmas in San Pedro, which belonged jointly to an aunt and a sister in Buenos Aires.[21] Soler hired one foreman, a peon, a horsebreaker, and a carrier *(changador)* full time to work the estancia. He acquired part-time laborers during branding and special slaughtering times. Seasonal help earned up to seventy gold centavos a day plus meals. In 1846, the peons branded about 2,000 head of cattle and cut out another 1,600 head for market. Soler's herd thus must have numbered approximately 5,000 head of cattle. The estancia had no sheep, for he had sold the flock for operating capital when he took over the ranch. Among Soler's expenses was a monthly subsidy *(asignación)* of sixty-two gold pesos that he sent his sister and aunt. It is not clear if Soler was buying them out or if he continued payments after the extant accounts end in 1847. But the estancia did help support other members of the Soler family.

In the first difficult year of investment, Soler and his family contributed nearly two-thirds of the operating expenses. For the remainder, he acquired a bank loan of 840 gold pesos, enough cash to purchase 400 head of cattle. The loan supplemented family finances before the estancia earned revenues from livestock sales. Soler used the capital to repair corrals and buildings and to pay peons for rounding up and branding the cattle. In that formative year, Soler earned money by selling hides and kindling wood that grew on his property along the Paraná River. Nevertheless, he easily paid off the bank credit in five installments − paying 2 percent monthly interest on the principal − within just one and a half years.

If investment costs were getting higher, estancieros continued to gain worthwhile profits from their capital. Profit seemed almost immediate and tended to follow the reproduction rate of domesticated cattle herds. Within a short period of three years, estancieros reported annual profits on investments of 30 percent. An early British sheep raiser even wrote of making a profit of 110 percent within one and a half years of purchase, principally from the slaughter of the inferior cattle and sheep bought with the land.[22]

The Soler and other estancia account books reveal that normal profit margins in ranching and farming may not have been as high as the legendary 30 percent. Soler's ranch income came from the sale of yearlings to the abasto público (meat provisioners) and steers to the saladeros. Livestock sales comprised 70 percent of Soler's ranch revenues. An additional 13 percent was derived from the sale of hides taken from cattle killed for ranch consumption and from those dying of disease and poor castration. The income side of the estancia's ledger shows that revenues from ranch products actually amounted to 20 percent of expenses (see Table 18). Twenty percent, however, is a healthy margin.

Table 18. *Balance sheet of the Estancia de las Palmas, San Pedro, 1846 (in pesos)*

| Expenses (deve) | | Income (cargo) | |
|---|---|---|---|
| Subsidies to family | 18,600 | Sale of cattle | 27,347 |
| Wages to permanent help | 5,938 | Sale of hides | 5,115 |
| Wages to seasonal help | 5,053 | Sale of wood | 3,751 |
| Miscellaneous | 2,892 | Miscellaneous | 3,231 |
| Total | 32,483 | Total | 39,444 |

*Source:* Museo Bartolome Mitre, Buenos Aires, A1 C44 C71, no. 11, Miguel Estanislao Soler, "Papeles referentes a la administración de la estancia 'Las Palmas' " (1844–52). The figures are given in the original paper pesos. In 1846, the paper peso was worth 3.5 gold centavos.

## Women and villagers

Pampa society was the fastest growing social entity in the Río de la Plata. Rural population increases even outstripped urban growth in Buenos Aires. While the total of city residents yearly increased by 2.2 percent between 1820 and 1860, the population growth rate in the countryside reached 3.1 percent. In 1822, Buenos Aires Province had 63,230 rural inhabitants and, in 1855, 148,000.[23] The statistics are indicative of the vitality of rural life in the early nineteenth century but not of the character of its developing pastoral society. Farm and ranch production not only gave rural society its dynamism but also fostered social development of amazing diversity and breadth.

A statistical breakdown of rural occupations in 1854 shows rather surprising diversity. Those who worked directly on the land, whether owner, renter, or peon, made up 65 percent of the country folk. Yet, others found employ as merchants, artisans, and military men. A few existed without fixed occupation (see Table 19).

Growth of villages on the prairies is also clear evidence that rural production in this area fostered and supported secondary artisans, transportation, and merchandising occupations. Within a century of the founding of the viceroyalty in 1776, fifty new *pueblos* (rural towns) were established in the countryside of Buenos Aires Province.[24] A rather large percentage of rural folk came to live in these towns. The agricul-

Table 19. *Rural occupations in Buenos Aires Province, 1854 (as percentage of the total adult male population)*

|  | Agricultural zone | Mixed zone | Ranching zone |
|---|---|---|---|
| Ranch owners | 9.4 | 7.1 | 8.5 |
| Ranch renters | 4.3 | 12.0 | 13.0 |
| Farm owners | 8.5 | 2.6 | 3.4 |
| Farm renters | 4.1 | 9.7 | 3.9 |
| Peons | 26.5 | 43.2 | 42.6 |
| Merchants and workers | 9.1 | 6.2 | 7.3 |
| Artisans | 6.6 | 3.4 | 2.7 |
| Military | 0.9 | 0.4 | 2.8 |
| Other | 24.0 | 14.6 | 11.0 |
| Without occupation | 6.6 | 0.8 | 4.8 |
| Total | 100 | 100 | 100 |

*Source: Registro estadístico de Buenos Aires,* 1854, Table 10. Ten of 13 agricultural districts, 13 of 13 mixed districts, and 22 of 25 ranching districts reporting.

tural zone, especially, supported a more complex social system. Yet, even in frontier areas, artisan and merchant trades mutually depended on estancia production (see Table 20). The nature of raising cattle in the early national period did not impede town building on the pampa. Estancias actually relied on villagers to transport and market ranch products and to provide seasonal labor.

Table 20. *Population in village and countryside in Buenos Aires Province, 1858 (as percentages of total rural population)*

|  | Agricultural zone | Mixed zone | Ranching zone |
|---|---|---|---|
| Village | 47.4 | 34.5 | 35.8 |
| Countryside | 52.6 | 65.5 | 64.2 |
| Total | 100 | 100 | 100 |

*Source: Registro estadístico de Buenos Aires,* 1858, vol. 1, p. 135. Nine of 13 agricultural districts, 8 of 13 mixed districts, and 10 of 25 ranching districts reporting.

Women, backbone of the rural family, were present everywhere on the pampa. Many women were married, others were common wives, and a few were foreigners. Males outnumbered females, but households headed by widows with children were not unusual. Rural censuses even listed a few estancias and chacras in women's names.[25] Breakdown of the population by both sex and origin reveals the predominance of porteño men and women in the pampa settlements. Yet almost 15 percent of the rural population consisted of provincial migrants. Their presence was evenly distributed throughout the production zones. Foreigners seem to have settled predominantly in the agricultural districts around Buenos Aires. Women are present everywhere in slightly smaller numbers than men (see Table 21). Nor were children absent from the countryside. Census figures reveal that nearly 38 percent of the rural population in 1854 was under fourteen years of age — not yet bona fide members of the work force (see Table 22).

In terms of extension, the most recently settled rural estates on the frontier were the largest of the pampa's landed

Table 21. *Origin and sex of the rural population of Buenos Aires Province, 1854 (as percentages of the total)*

|       | Porteño | Provinciano | Foreign | Total |
|-------|---------|-------------|---------|-------|
| Men   | 39.8    | 9.0         | 7.6     | 56.4  |
| Women | 34.8    | 5.9         | 2.9     | 43.6  |
| Total | 74.6    | 14.9        | 10.5    | 100   |

*Source: Registro estadístico de Buenos Aires, 1854, Table 9.*

Table 22. *Rural population of Buenos Aires Province by age group, 1854 (as percentage of total population)*

| Years old | Percent |
|-----------|---------|
| 0 to 14   | 37.6    |
| 14 to 30  | 31.9    |
| 30 to 60  | 25.8    |
| over 60   | 4.7     |

*Source: Registro estadístico de Buenos Aires, 1854, Table 9.*

units. In 1840, the Anchorena family's new ranch in Mar Chiquita on the Atlantic coast 325 kilometers from Buenos Aires equalled more than 1,550 square kilometers. After mid-century, the norm on the frontier seems to have been the 300- to 500-square kilometer ranch. By 1864, the original Anchorena property had been broken up into five smaller estancias, controlled by various branches of the family. Circa 1860, newer estancias established further south seem smaller than earlier frontier ranches. They now went in lots of 90 to 300 square kilometers. Landed units close to Buenos Aires were comparatively smaller – many measured in varas (nearly 1 meter) rather than in leagues. Riding north on the road through San Isidro, the traveler passed as many as fifteen farm properties on each side of the road within a league's ride. These farms were owned in long narrow strips measuring up to 675 hectares. Some large properties did exist within an 85-kilometer radius of Buenos Aires in 1864, but it is likely that these few actually were broken up into rental land by the owner and worked in smaller plots – not as single large entities so close to the city.[26]

Big estates clearly dominated the ranching districts, where as much as 15 percent of the population might live and work on large ranches. From the sparse census data of only eight ranching districts, one counts a total of thirty-eight big estates having populations greater than twenty persons. In these districts, one of every ten persons owed their livelihoods to working and living on estates owned by wealthy estancieros.[27] Even in the ranching areas, the family-sized unit of five or six persons living together independently in a small estancia, chacra, pulpería, subsistence plot, or rural village is quite revealing of country life on the pampa. The average size of the population units in eight ranching districts was just 10.6 persons per unit. Large estancias dominated the distant frontier areas socially and economically. In 1838, 20 percent of the population of Azul lived and worked on just two ranches – owned by the Anchorenas and Governor Rosas. The Anchorena estate supported 600 peons and families. The rest of the residents of Azul, which bordered Indian territory 340 kilometers from Buenos Aires, lived independently in chacras, pulperías, or subsistence plots in family groups of three to eight persons.[28]

Nevertheless, this figure for Azul fails to dispel the conclusion that the independent family was the most common social unit in the countryside. In many districts, the 1838 rural census listed inhabitants according to the occupation of independent heads of household. Clearly, the family predominated in the agricultural district of Las Conchas (Tigre), which averaged only 4.8 persons per unit. Mixed and ranching zones had higher numbers per unit because estancias listed hired workers and their families as unit members. Monsalvo, for example, averaged 8.2 persons per unit. Even so, ranching areas like Cañuelas and mixed districts such as Ranchos maintained smaller units, numbering 6.7 persons. The small, independent family unit still obtained, even in recently settled areas of the pampa.

In the mixed zone, the size and social importance of large estancias were not as dominant as in the ranching areas. Navarro District in 1838, for example, had a total of twelve landed units with more than twenty inhabitants, but only 9 percent of the population lived on such estates. One in fourteen country persons of Ranchos lived within large estates. At the other extreme, the district of Las Conchas in the agricultural zone had no big estancias. Flores, not more than twenty-eight kilometers from downtown Buenos Aires, had only three estancias having more than thirty residents. Only one of every sixteen persons lived in social units larger than twenty inhabitants. In Quilmes, only 5 percent of the inhabitants lived in larger population units.[29]

Landownership in Buenos Aires Province during the era of rural expansion was diffused rather than concentrated. Large cattle ranches were subdivided numerous times between 1810 and 1860 as the value of the land and its production steadily rose. Older cattle estancias became numbers of smaller sheep ranches, and the latter were divided further into yet smaller dairy and vegetable farms. Each step in the process intensified land use and rural production on the pampa. It was on the frontier that terrain was still held in giant-sized tracts and worked as huge production units. Land closer to the expanding markets of Buenos Aires underwent subdivision and the units of production became smaller. Commercialization was sweeping the pampa!

Nowhere is the general reduction of the size of landholdings more evident than in maps depicting rural properties of the nineteenth century. The district of Navarro, lying ninety-five kilometers south of Buenos Aires, serves as an example. With the Salado River as its southern boundary, the district had been settled as a cattle-grazing area during the colonial period. Navarro was located in the zone of mixed production up to 1860. Having 100 persons per square league (31 square kilometers) in 1869, the partido then qualified for agricultural status.

In 1830, as few as twenty-two different landowners controlled all the property in the district. The largest estate, measuring some 620 square kilometers, belonged to the Almeyra clan. Two decades later, the vast holding had been divided among seven Almeyra heirs. Subdivision and sales also occurred to other large Navarro properties as well. Thirty landowners came to possess rural terrain within the district by 1855, and thereafter subdivisions was especially rapid. Within ten years, the number of owners listed on the property map totaled nearly 100. Much of the original Almeyra estancia now had passed entirely from family possession. The property originally belonging to that one family three decades earlier now belonged to nearly 30 different landowners! (See Figure 5.)

## When the gringos arrived

Throughout the early nineteenth century, commercial expansion into the countryside offered much economic and social opportunity for newcomers. By 1860, a quarter of the population of the pampa had been born outside the province, either in the Interior or in Europe. Work was plentiful and land was still cheap. Immigrants with their families could engage in farming with small capital outlays. While natives handled the cattle work, industrious immigrants found jobs in sheepherding and ditch digging. Some eventually acquired land with their savings. It was not uncommon for poor immigrant men to make 100 pounds sterling a year each in making ditches alone.[30] "When the 'gringo' arrived," a Creole reminisced sometime later, ". . . they came to the estancias as men of pure blood; they came to cultivate the vegetable gardens, to install a windmill, as fence builders, or simply as blacksmiths or carpenters. And they came with their families, and with children of marriages made in Argentina. . . ."[31]

Most immigrants in the rural areas worked as hired hands, artisans, and petty merchants. Significantly, enterprising foreigners were not excluded from ranching and farming — where one-fourth of all foreigners found economic opportunity as renters and owners (see Table 23).

Controversy has arisen about the relative plight of the rural worker in this era of rural economic growth. Though composing as much as 35 percent of the rural male population, the labor pool was always insufficient throughout the entire first fifty years of Independence. Many historians have stated that the result of scarce labor was suppression of the rural peon. For example, they allude to the rural laws dictating that all persons without land on which to subsist were to be classified as servants and that they must have work papers (*papeletas*) from their bosses.[32] At base is the belief that the rural peon needed strict discipline — even "civilizing." However, the whole concept of the gaucho as a happy-go-lucky vagabond singing, playing the guitar, drinking, shunning work, and fighting the police across the fenceless prairies may be a literary invention of the following generation.[33]

Nevertheless, there were harsh rural labor laws that occasionally were enforced. Peons did have trouble moving freely about the countryside without militia licenses and police passports, as ranchers discovered in sending peons on errands.[34] By the Law of 1823, labor in the countryside was supposed to conform to the following conditions:

1. The formal work contract was to be authorized by the rural constable.

2. The peon must have a note of good behavior and a release from his previous boss.

3. The employer must give his worker a pass (papeleta).

4. Without the pass, the peon will be considered a vagabond and forced into public work or the armed services.[35] The strict letter of this law may express the desperation of the landowners — not the workers. Labor statutes attempted to protect employers from the natural advantages of workers in short supply. Such de jure regulations of labor meant that rural workers, like their urban brethren, had the advantage of employment on their side. Estancieros — influential among lawmakers at least — hoped formal law might redress the imbalance somewhat.

In general, farmers and smaller ranchers relied on the im-

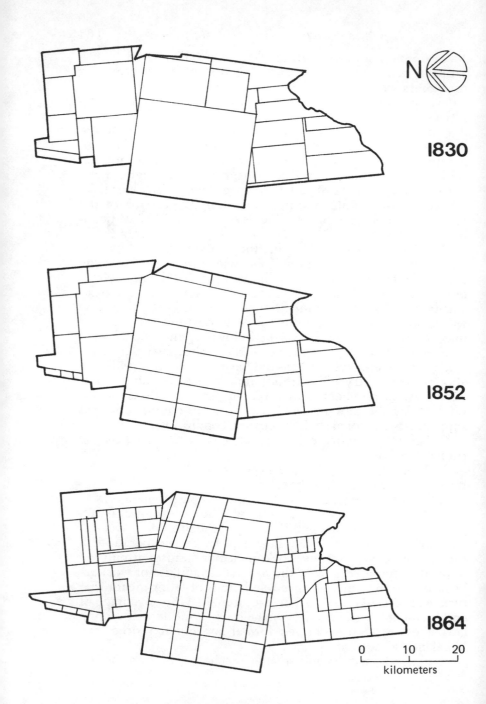

N

1830

1852

1864

0   10   20
kilometers

Table 23. *Rural occupations among native- and foreign-born in Buenos Aires Province, 1854 (expressed as percentages)*

|  | Natives | Foreigners |
|---|---|---|
| Ranch owner | 8.9 | 4.0 |
| Ranch renter | 10.2 | 8.0 |
| Farm owner | 4.5 | 6.4 |
| Farm renter | 5.9 | 6.2 |
| Peon | 39.9 | 20.7 |
| Merchant and worker | 6.0 | 18.5 |
| Artisans | 2.6 | 15.4 |
| Other | 22.0 | 20.8 |
| Total | 100 | 100 |

*Source: Registro estadístico de Buenos Aires,* 1854, Table 10. Ten of 13 agricultural districts, 13 of 13 mixed districts, and 22 of 25 ranching districts reporting.

mediate family first and hired seasonal labor for the extra work. Slaves still were evident in rural production in the early national period. Yet, even in the colonial period, ranchers used more hired help than servile labor. In 1873, a Matanza estanciero, Santiago Villamayor, worked his property with three sons and seven peons. His only slave was an eighteen-year-old woman.[36] The racial heirs of colonial slaves, mulattoes, and blacks remained on the estancias in substantial numbers as free, salaried workers. Although most peons were white workers by 1838, estancieros like Hermenegildo San Martín of Baradero still employed thirty-one *pardos* and *morenos* (of mixed racial heritage), only fifteen whites, and one foreigner.[37]

Permanent estancia labor, as opposed to seasonal labor, actually may have been quite stable. Satisfactory work relationships between peon and estanciero often passed from one generation to the next. As a youthful scion of an estancia

Figure 5. Subdivision of landed units in the district of Navarro, 1830–64. As rural production became more intensive, landholdings in Buenos Aires Province increased in number and decreased in size. Twenty-two landowners in 1830 controlled all the property in Navarro District. Thirty-four years later, the number of proprietors had increased to nearly 100. (Map by Tom Eisenhower, based on *Registros gráficos de los terrenos de propiedad pública y particular de la Provincia de Buenos Aires,* 1830, 1852, 1860.)

family, Isaías de Elía remembers cavorting with the grand-
children of peons who had worked for his forbears in the
1820s. Families lived on the puestas, and peons' children
sometimes grew up to work on the same ranches. Big estancieros counted on a stable number of workers on their rural
properties. The biggest ranchers transferred peons from one
estancia to another with assurance of their dependability and
loyalty.[38] Formal labor contracts not only bound workers to a
certain period of service but also committed the employer to
specific wage payments. A sample contract for 1849 typifies
the dual responsibilities:

> I *Pedro Lazala* am obliged to serve *Don Jorge Sanders* for
> the term of six months and I *Sanders* am obliged to
> satisfy said service with the salary of *200 pesos per month.*
> . . .[39]

No reliable wage series exists for this period. But scattered
data, corrected for inflation, shows a rise in the wages of rural
workers throughout the nineteenth century. In addition to
his salary, the peon received basic rations and housing for his
family (figures in gold pesos):[40]

|      | salary per month |
|------|------------------|
| 1804 | 7.5              |
| 1849 | 10               |
| 1854 | 10               |
| 1864 | 12               |
| 1904 | 15               |

In the ninteenth century, actual labor conditions in the countryside might have been more personal and satisfying to the
worker than the harsh laws suggest.

### Ranching in the family way

A brief case history of the Estancia Rincón de Obligado in the
district of San Pedro illustrates the family business arrange-
ments that generated expansion of rural production in the
1850s and 1860s. The disjointed account books that a family
member, Pastor Obligado, used to keep track of his part in
the venture partially describe the ranching operations.[41] San
Pedro was located within the mixed zone of production in
that part of the province bounded by the Paraná River
northwest of Buenos Aires. The property appears to have
been in the Obligado family at least since 1830, but the clan

*Gaucho tending a herd of horses, 1858.* A traditional rural type, the *gaucho* wore a *poncho* and *chiripás* (cloth pants) and used a lasso, knife, and *bolas* (balls) in his work. His boots, made of soft coltskin, were open at the tip so that he could place his large toe in the stirrup. The *rancho* (hut) where he lived with his family appears at left. His horse had short legs, a thick body and neck, and a prominent Roman nose rather than the romanticized head depicted here. (Oil painting by John Frederick Herring, ca. 1858.)

had owned land elsewhere in the province since colonial days. By the mid–nineteenth century, the family's economic base had grown to include a chacra in Lomas de Zamora and various real estate properties in the city of Buenos Aires. The very diversity of economic assets supported several branches of the family.

The Estancia Rincón de Obligado passed into the possession of various family members after the death of the elder Obligado in the late 1840s. Several male relatives formed a *sociedad,* a company for combining their capital resources, in order to run the estancia. Brothers Pastor and Plácido Obligado joined a brother-in-law, Lorenzo Gómez, and a cousin, Tomás Obligado. It seems that Tomás. assisted by Lorenzo, was to manage the property. They took their families to live in San Pedro. Pastor and Plácido remained in Buenos Aires, acting as bankers and brokers for the estancia, and it was in the capital that Pastor served as provincial governor in the 1850s. Pastor brought provisions and arranged carriage to the estancia with a Sardinian-born cartman. The freight carrier made the round trip between the estancia and Buenos Aires in about ten days. Pastor, the senior member of the sociedad, maintained a bank deposit account in order to keep the estancia's operating funds and sales receipts. The account yielded the depositors quarterly interest at 2 percent. From time to time, Pastor sent money to Tomás on the estancia to pay expenses. He also honored various notes that Tomás gave to his creditors as reimbursements and to workers as paychecks.

The first two years were a time of much investment and few sales. Before the cattle season beginning in December 1850, Pastor borrowed funds from various family members in order to keep the company solvent. He paid each of his minifinanciers a dividend of 1.5 percent monthly on their short-term loans. When ranch manager Tomás sold the first tropas of cattle on the hoof, Pastor used the assets to repay these loans. Later, Pastor himself was able to lend money to other family members, receiving about the same monthly dividends. Profits from sales of wood and cattle allowed the sociedad to pay the family matriarch, the Widow Obligado, a yearly rental fee of 195 gold pesos for her share of the property. When the widow died, Pastor and his brother subsequently paid the annual rent to the estate *(testamento),* perhaps to be divided among younger family members.

Between 1852 and 1857, the family sociedad prospered on the sale of cattle and horses to the saladeros of Buenos Aires. Then, Pastor announced in his account book that "Tomás died on June 18, 1857 at 12 o'clock at night in San Pedro." After the cousin's death, the sociedad was liquidated. Livestock were sold in order to settle the estate, and Pastor arranged the complicated legal paperwork for reforming the society. The widow and children of Tomás received his share of the liquidation.

Pastor himself drew up a personal balance sheet of his cash investments in the estancia's operations. From 1849 onward, Pastor had invested 1,375 gold pesos in the operation of the estancia and had begun drawing his share of the profits by January 1855. Within two years before Tomás' death, Pastor had received a total of 1,917 pesos as his share of the proceeds. Averaged over the eight-year period of investment, the return on his original investment had been 17.5 percent per annum. This amounted to only half the legendary 30 percent of profit, yet was a respectable return on an eight-year cash investment in rural production.

Despite the liquidation, the estancia did not pass from the possession of the Obligado family. Pastor and his brother, Plácido, formed a new working partnership in 1858. Plácido then added another 3,514-peso investment and Pastor contributed 9,783 pesos, until the total capital value of the Estancio Rincón de Obligado reached 16,054 gold pesos. Almost immediately, the brothers set about upgrading the sheep stock on an estancia that had always depended upon a mix of cattle and sheep. Their first purchases included 270 kilograms of wire amd more than 1,200 wooden posts to construct modern fencing. They improved both their cattle and sheep by buying up stock from neighboring estancieros. The brothers entrusted Mayordomo Eugenio with the administration of the estancia. It is uncertain whether he was a family member or an outsider, but Eugenio, unlike Tomás earlier, was not an associate. Plácido traveled to the estancia during branding and shearing times to oversee the work. The family partnership continued to sell cattle to the saladeros, but continuing investment in fencing attests to the brothers' heightened interest in sheep raising. By 1863, the estancia produced 854 arrobas (9.7 metric tons) of sheep's wool, of which 80 percent consisted of medium-grade mestizo wool and the rest of creole wool. The brothers used the mediero system of profit sharing among their shepherds. In 1864, Irish shepherds headed by Miguel Brenen earned a total of 1,055 gold pesos, approximately one-third of the sales volume of wool and sheepskins. Apparently, Eugenio continued management of the cattle herd. He paid a number of permanent cowboys and was given money to hire itinerant cowhands for branding and roundup. By 1864, the estancia annually produced about 3,042 gold pesos worth of sheep products and another 3,917 gold pesos in cattle sales.

The inventory of livestock on the Estancia Rincón de Obligado remained stable between 1857 and 1863. Stability in the number of sheep, however, belies the importance of improvements in the flock's quality through selective breeding. Clearly, estancia profits each year came from selling off the increase in herds:

|        | 1857  | 1863  |
|--------|-------|-------|
| cattle | 2,090 | 2,119 |
| horses | 655   | 559   |
| sheep  | 1,545 | 1,593 |

(The Obligados bought more sheep shortly after the 1863 inventory.) Maintenance of these livestock, however, appeared to have been done on less and less land. Provincial maps show that the Obligado property had been reduced from 310 square kilometers in 1852 to 124 in 1864. Even then, land economics in an area just 72 kilometers from Buenos Aires occasioned the Obligados, in 1864, to rent to farmers two parcels, each measuring more than 15 square kilometers.

For several years, the brothers did not withdraw cash dividends from estancia revenues. Then, starting in 1862, Pastor and Plácido took out a total of 7,600 gold pesos within just two years. Averaged over the six-year period, the withdrawals equaled approximately 7 percent of the estancia's total capital value − and 20 percent of their cash investments six years earlier.

### The social economics of farming

The Obligado family further diversified their total economic interests by developing a smaller piece of property they owned in the agricultural district of Lomas de Zamora, forty kilometers southeast of Buenos Aires. The Chacra San Francisco was operated by Pastor and a younger brother, Manuel.[42] Manuel managed the establishment at first by spending much time there and later by traveling weekly on the newly founded Southern Railroad. The brothers owed rent to their mother. Each December, Manuel paid her a yearly fee for her share of the family property. Although this farm also produced sheep products, its chief development came as a result of producing for the domestic market.

Rather large for a farm, the property measured 465 hectares and had at least 2,500 meters of wire fences. A peach orchard occupied one fenced hectare, and nearly half the estate was sown with alfalfa. Each year, Manuel expanded the alfalfa sowings because of the good sales of forage in the Buenos Aires market. The chacra's head station was dominated by Obligado's house of five rooms and a stock shed. This was a livestock farm. The Obligados maintained flocks of sheep and goats and a herd of milk cows. The accounts mention no other commercial crop but alfalfa. But parcels of the larger chacra were rented out to four different families, who presumably cultivated grains and vegetables. The Obligados further diversified their farm income by building a store. They set up a trusted dependent in business as a rural grocer.

Coming under Manuel's management in 1864, the chacra at first earned little revenue. Initial heavy instruments were made to improve the property by sowing alfalfa, constructing buildings, putting in wire fences, and planting orchards. Capital improvements on the farm continued to be the largest ongoing expense of its operation. The other was labor. Manuel hired at least four full-time peons to tend the flocks and milk cows. In addition, he took on some sixteeen day workers for the October shearing and another fifteen itinerants in December to cut and market the alfalfa crop. Shearers received pay by piecework, the women getting 1.4 gold pesos each per 100 sheep sheared; the men, 1.6. The Obligados regularly sheared up to 2,000 sheep on the farm. Alfalfa harvesters and other day workers got 1 to 1.5 pesos per day. During the year, workers in the construction trades — bricklayers, housebuilders, painters, tree planters, and fence builders — all received pay for their work on the chacra.

Obligado's permanent workers made 12 gold pesos per month, plus room and rations for their families Some did not accept their complete pay each month but preferred to have the back pay mount up as a savings device. When they quit,

Obligado paid them a large lump sum. A Paraguayan laborer, for example, took only two-thirds of his salary each month. After working for the Obligados for five years, he received total back pay of 168 gold pesos just before leaving. One Solano, whose son occasionally was paid for odd jobs around the chacra, took only half his pay each month. Obviously, rural wages and benefits in the 1860s were sufficiently above family subsistence levels so that workers could regularly save part of their wages — with the trusted assistance of their employers.

The chacra seems to have produced profits of about 20 percent over yearly expenses. The major money earners came in sales of forage and sheepswool, and live sheep and goats sold to butchers brought other revenues. Sales of fresh milk and butter produced steady weekly income. Wool and forage sales, on the other hand, were highly seasonal. Income from the four renters, of course, was an additional major source of chacra income (see Table 24). Based upon the pay and rental records appearing in the account book, it is estimated that the Chacra San Francisco supported approximately thirty persons — including the wives and children of four renters, four peons, and the grocer. Itinerant workers finding seasonal work at the farm numbered approximately forty.

## What is to be done?

Expansion of pastoral activity onto the southern pampa begot the inevitable clash with its erstwhile masters, the nomadic Indians. Each year between Independence and the end of the century, new lands were opened to cattle grazing and new towns were built on the prairies as testaments to the export-oriented and expanding economy of the hinterland. The Indians found themselves banished further south and separated from the settled areas by fortified garrisons. The frontier pushed relentlessly southward.

Pre-Columbian Indians of the pampa region were seminomadic hunters and gatherers. They wandered on foot and hunted the meat of native prairie animals like the *guanaco* (prairie alpaca), rhea, deer, and otter. Lacking sedentary work habits, a centralized political structure, and metallic wealth, the Pampa Indians attracted little interest among sixteenth-

Table 24. *Yearly accounting balance of the Obligado farm in Lomas de Zamora, 1866 (in paper pesos)*

| Expenses | | | Income | | |
|---|---|---|---|---|---|
| Capital improvements | | 30,563 | Family-borrowed capital for country store | | 26,593 |
| Regular farm labor | | 16,200 | Sales of farm products | | 52,373 |
| Seasonal farm labor | | 16,490 | forage | 24,076 | |
| Oct. shearing | 1,023 | | milk | 9,245 | |
| Dec. alfalfa | 10,042 | | wool | 17,338 | |
| Other | 5,425 | | butter | 1,349 | |
| | | | cowhides | 365 | |
| Support of house | | 10,207 | Sales of livestock | | 15,955 |
| Rent to Widow Obligado | | 6,000 | sheep | 10,075 | |
| | | | goats | 4,880 | |
| Support of livestock | | 3,414 | Rent of four plots | | 15,000 |
| | | | Grazing rights | | 1,656 |
| Miscellaneous | | 13,274 | Miscellaneous | | 2,640 |
| Total expenses | | 96,148 | Total income | | 113,217 |

*Source:* Archivo General de la Nación, Buenos Aires, Colección Biblioteca Nacional 739, "Libro diario de la chacra San Francisco" (1864–70). The paper peso was worth four gold centavos in 1866.

century Spanish conquerors. But Spaniards did introduce the horse to the grasslands, and during the seventeenth century the entire lifestyle and culture of the Pampa Indians changed. Horses facilitated hunting and raiding, and livestock became the materials of subsistence. Indians organized trade with colonial Buenos Aires around plaited reins, bridles, lassos, *bolas* (rawhide-bound balls), saddles, and other equestrian gear fashioned from rawhide. Pampa Indian bands also sustained a lively commerce in cattle and horses with Chile's Araucanian Indians through the southern passes of the Andes Mountains. Then Chile's Indian wars forced many Araucanian tribes into Patagonia and the southern pampa. These warlike Indians truly became formidable enemies of European civilization in the Río de la Plata. Ranches of Buenos Aires and the Interior attracted Indian raiding parties seeking cattle and ponies. Colonial authorities responded with punitive expeditions and a line of forts, which by 1800 contained the Indians beyond the Salado River.[43]

Skirmishes between white settlers and Indians intensified throughout the nineteenth century. Europeans constantly expanded the frontier and established new forts way beyond the Salado River. Frontier estancias resembled military outposts. Cowboys were armed as Indian fighters, and every estancia head station became a fort with moat, cannon, and lookout towers. Porteño officials outfitted two expeditions when Indian raids became particularly severe during the droughts of 1820 and 1824. The greatest punitive expedition of the era followed the severe drought of 1828–30. General Rosas led troops as far south as the Colorado River and established a frontier post at Bahía Blanca. Rosas signed a pact with several Indian chiefs, promising regular rations of horses, cattle, yerba, sugar, and tobacco. Thereafter, Indian raids occurred when militiamen were distracted elsewhere – during the 1838 port blockade and after Governor Rosas was deposed early in 1852.

Fighting on the frontier at times was quite savage. Indians drove off cattle and horses, killed ranch hands, and even carried off women and children. Troopers and gauchos responded by killing Indian men, women, and children, and occasionally raiding even the camps of peaceful Indians. "This [slaughter of Indian men] is a dark picture," Darwin observed, "but how much more shocking is the unquestion-

*Indian village at Bahía Blanca, 1831.* Expansion of cattle raising on the Argentine pampa reduced the traditional hunting territory of these nomadic Pampa Indians. Note the Indian weapons of bolas and lances, the hide *toldos* (tepees), and the prominent horse culture of the Indians. (Watercolor by Carlos Enrique Pellegrini, ca. 1831.)

able fact, that all the women who appear above twenty years old are massacred in cold blood! When I exclaimed that this appeared rather inhuman, [the gaucho] . . . answered, 'Why, what can be done? they breed so!' "[44]

The maturing pastoral society — and modern technology — eventually resolved this cultural clash on the pampa. In 1878—9, General Julio A. Roca's troops and their modern repeating rifles carried out a one-sided "Desert Campaign" against warriors armed with lances and bolas. The reduction of the Indians, with their culture so alien to the expanding staple economy, was inexorable.

# 8

## Formation of the Anchorena cattle business

If the acquisition of land and livestock adequately measured success in the staple economy of Argentina, then the Anchorenas counted among the first families of the pampa. An old merchant clan, the Anchorenas initially put capital into ranch land in 1818, and they gradually extended their landholdings into the expanding frontiers until, a half-century later, the family had come to own nearly 9,582 square kilometers of land in Buenos Aires Province (see Figure 6). Throughout this era of traditional technology, the Anchorenas never fractionalized their landed acquisitions outside the family. Their ranches and cattle-raising operations successfully withstood the vagaries of drought, the interruptions of trade, and the economic pressures to subdivide. Together, three brothers controlled twenty-three different properties, hundreds of ranch workers, and thousands of head of cattle. They managed all their estates as one production unit, a true Latin American latifundio. The secret of the family's pastoral success lay in its wise and continuous shift of commercial capital into cattle operations. Profits in export-connected commerce afforded the Anchorenas the necessary investment funds to expand their landholdings and to create huge herds of livestock.

The Anchorenas became economically successful because they had participated in three prosperous sectors of the staple economy: foreign trade, river commerce, and cattle production. All these business endeavors converged. Their interest in foreign trade occasioned the Anchorenas to shift their assets into marshaling export goods in the river trades. Windfall profits in regional river commerce then enabled the erstwhile commercial clan to acquire land on the frontiers. Eventually, the family produced cattle and cattle products to exploit foreign markets even further. Their skillful management of the cattle estates ensured the Anchorenas longevity in the economic and social hierarchy of Argentina. The forma-

174

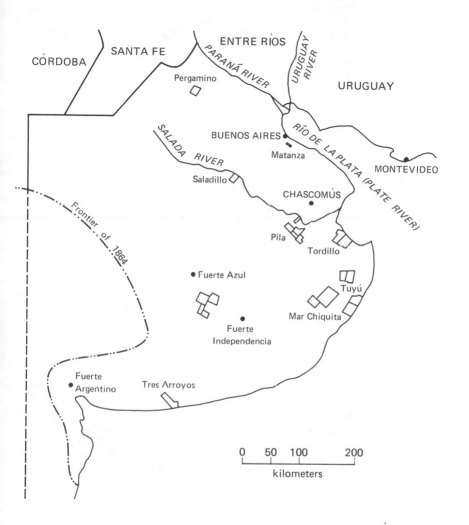

Figure 6. Approximate size and location of the Anchorena estancias in Buenos Aires Province, 1864. The Anchorenas became the first family of Argentine landowners during the era of frontier settlement. By 1864, family members controlled 9,582 square kilometers of prime grazing land, thousands of head of cattle and horses, and hundreds of workers. They operated twenty-three different properties throughout the province in a latifundio that produced pastoral goods for foreign and domestic markets. (Map by author, based on *Registro gráfico de los terrenos de propiedad pública y particular de la Provincia de Buenos Aires,* 1864.)

tion of the Anchorena cattle empire, therefore, provides an important example of the business possibilities that staple economic expansion throughout the region made available to local entrepreneurs.

## A family of commerce

Juan Esteban de Anchorena, the colonial patriarch of the family, immigrated from Pamplona, Spain, to Buenos Aires in 1765. He began a small tobacco and spirits shop (pulpería) in the port city. Soon after Buenos Aires became a viceregal capital in 1776, he expanded his trade into imported dry goods and established a modest commerce with merchants in Tucumán. Eventually, Anchorena developed commercial contacts in Potosí and Chile. Despite his dramatic rise from pulpero to importer, Juan Estaben was not among the richest and most prestigious of the porteño merchants during the viceroyalty.[1] Yet he was able to bequeath his commercial acumen and capital to three ambitious sons, Juan José Cristóbal, Tomás Manuel, and Mariano Nicolás. Following the Revolution in 1810, new economic opportunities permitted them to expand their father's business legacy. Having inherited the commercial wealth of the colonial era, Juan Esteban's sons were not unlike other influential porteño merchants of the early nineteenth century. They participated in the May 1810 Revolution as minor figures. The merchant class of Buenos Aires commonly intermarried in order to interlock their business partnerships, and the Anchorena men married well. Juan José de Anchorena, the eldest, married into the Lezica family, greatest of the colonial merchant clans. The youngest son, Nicolás, married into another commercial family, the Aranas.[2] As the oldest son, Juan José eventually took over his father's commerce. He had traveled to Spain twice before the revolution in order to establish contacts for the Buenos Aires import business. His younger brothers, Tomás and Nicolás, took law degrees at the University of Córdoba.[3]

In politics, the Anchorenas became influential advisers but never leaders. Identified with the conservatives of the era, their politics served to protect their economic privileges. In 1810, for instance, when the first British traders encroached on the import trade of established porteño merchants, Juan José championed the idea of protectionism. He changed his mind within the decade. Having participated in British trade himself, Juan José published an apology for free trade in 1818. He maintained that the greater import of foreign goods would benefit the consumer, who would consequently pay lower prices for quality goods. Free trade would also benefit cattle ranchers, because they would be able more easily to export their pastoral products abroad.[4] Subsequently, Juan José as well as Tomás and Nicolás were perennial members of the province's legislature. As it happened, Tomás became the politician in the family. While on business in the Interior, Tomás Manuel was active in patriot politics and served as one of the porteño representatives at the 1816 Constitutional Congress of Tucumán, the event that Argentines count as the birth of their nation. He later served as minister of the hacienda (treasury) in the administration of President Vicente López in 1827.[5]

But the recognized business head was Juan José, and he directed the entire business activities of the family until his death in 1832. Registered as a comerciante (wholesaler), Juan José maintained an *almacén* (shop) at Calle del Perú 63 in the commercial district of Buenos Aires.[6] In 1813, he sent Tomás to the Interior to reestablish commercial ties that were being disrupted in the Wars of Independence. Meanwhile, Nicolás traveled to Chile, Rio de Janeiro, and London and did not return to Buenos Aires until 1822, after nearly seven years abroad. It is clear that Juan José engaged in both foreign and domestic commerce. In 1821, he formed a partnership with five other Creoles and the British importers, Steward and Call, to import tobacco from Brazil. He and two other porteño merchants also had combined with Thomas Fair to import cloth from England. Besides foreign trade, Juan José and his brothers had an active hand in promoting British capital investments in the nation's infrastructure − an effort that ultimately failed. Both Juan José and Nicolás appeared as shareholders in the Famatina Mining Company in 1824.[7] Although he speculated in the import trade and used his brothers in an attempt to resurrect the overland trade to the Interior, Juan José ultimately developed the Santa Fe river trades as the main business venture of the family.

From the entrepôt of Buenos Aires, Juan José conducted a river trade that sent imported goods upriver and collected products for export in both Buenos Aires and Montevideo. His business agents included Marcelino Carranza in Buenos Aires, Francisco Antonio de la Torre in Entre Ríos, Francisco Alzogaray in Santa Fe, and his brother Tomás in Montevideo. The family's wealth grew as hide exports expanded around 1820. In the few years from 1816 to 1819, Juan José had gathered a total of 45,000 hides, which he sold to British exporters or other merchant middlemen. To a porteño hide purveyor that kind of trade was worth more than 100,000 silver pesos. Anchorena obtained the hides both from these river merchants and from estancieros in Buenos Aires Province.[8] He carried on a 50,000-pesos-a-year trade with a single agent, Francisco Alzogaray. From Santa Fe, Alzogaray sent hides, tallow, yerba, and other Interior products down to Juan José in Buenos Aires. Anchorena dispatched imported goods upriver to his partner in Santa Fe, whence they may have been forwarded to Córdoba and the Interior. The profits are difficult to ascertain from extant accounts, but they must have been substantial.[9]

Meanwhile Tomás Manuel de Anchorena coordinated the family's commercial interests in Montevideo. Directed by his elder brother in Buenos Aires, Tomás took charge of finding Uruguayan warehouses for pastoral goods awaiting export aboard foreign merchant vessels. Tomás also marketed Paraguayan yerba and Argentine ponchos in the urban marketplace of Montevideo. The accounts that Juan José kept with Tomás for the years 1820 to 1823 show that the brothers took in cash receipts that surpassed expenses by more than 39 percent.[10] The entire river commerce of the brothers Anchorena generated substantial amounts of capital.

Profits from their varied commercial ventures of the 1810s and 1820s enabled the Anchorenas to capitalize the rapid development of their rural properties. In 1824 and 1825, they invested 32,699 silver pesos in land, labor, and cattle — enough to begin operations on three large estancias, Camarones, Achiras, and Averías. From January 1826 to March 1827, the family put another 69,286 silver pesos into rural production.[11] Juan José died in 1832, and Nicolás inherited the bulk of the commercial and ranching operations. He seems to have concentrated the entire family inheritance on cattle raising. The commercial almanac of 1836 did not list Nicolás among the city's merchants.[12] But it had been a far-sighted merchant, Juan José de Anchorena, who had actively begun to shift the family's capital into the grazing industry more than a decade before his death.

## Cattle with good meat

It took capital to buy land and cattle — even in the days when relatively uninhabited land *(tierras baldías)* was abundant and the cattle were lanky longhorns. The Anchorenas had the capital. But successful ranching also required a basic knowledge of and experience in land and livestock management. When Juan José decided to branch out into the new field of cattle raising, he acquired the services of an expert, Juan Manuel de Rosas. Rosas, who had made a small fortune in the meat-salting industry, was already a rancher. He maintained his own extensive properties, close to 650 square kilometers, near the rural village of Monte. He raised cattle and horses on Estancias Cerrillos and San Martín, which he owned with his old business associate, Juan Nepomuceno Terrero.[13] More importantly, the Anchorenas could trust Rosas because he was a blood relative, a cousin through his mother. Rosas thus became the "populator, fomenter, and administrator" of the Anchorena ranches from 1818 until his active military and political career blossomed in 1829.[14]

Rosas' first job was to advise and aid the Anchorenas in purchasing land and cattle. Having the power of attorney for the Anchorenas, Rosas purchased land in their name.[15] If they bought an established estancia, the laborers and slaves as well as the cattle went with the land. Estancia boundaries were particularly important to Administrator Rosas. Shortly after purchase, he made certain that the rural judges recorded the exact boundaries of the new Anchorena estates.[16] Even after he left their employ, Rosas helped his cousins acquire land. As an Indian fighter in 1833, General Rosas advised both his partner Terrero and Nicolás to buy up war premiums. In this manner, individual soldiers were able to redeem for cash the "Billetes de Banco" they received as pay from army paymasters.[17] Anchorena got government premiums worth from 26 to 130 pesos fuertes each, and apparently used these premiums to purchase public land on the frontier.

Between 1818 and 1830, while Juan José engaged in the

hide and yerba trade out of Santa Fe, he invested his commercial profits in seven properties comprising 3,400 square kilometers. Most of that land he bought from previous owners, like the Estancia Dos Yslas, which he purchased from Lorenzo López in 1821.[18] Juan José acquired the lease of other properties through declaration of "tierras baldías" under Rivadavia's program of emphyteusis. Eventually, Rosas as governor would sell these state properties to the renters. Thus, Nicolás and Tomás Anchorena were able to add to their private domain approximately 864 square kilometers of land they had leased under emphyteusis.[19] The Anchorena land purchases continued throughout the first half of the century. Nicolás also bought land for members of his family. In 1837, he purchased 1,814 square kilometers of land in Pergamino, called Fortezuelas (little forts), for his son-in-law, Estanislao Peña. Apparently Peña owned the huts, corrals, and cattle. He continued the partnership of Fortezuelas with Anchorena's widow after Nicolás died in 1856.[20]

All the Anchorena ranches appeared to be located on prime ranch land with plenty of water resources. In fact, the pastures were named for *lagunas* and *lagos,* depressions filled with standing water. Both owners and workers referred to cattle herds at Sartén, Los Toldos, or Sermón — all names given to lagoons on the estancias. On inspecting the new ranch of Camarones, north of the Salado River, Capataz Juan Benito Sosa commented that pastures and wells were in good shape and that the "cattle carried good meat."[21]

When Nicolás died in 1856, the Anchorenas were the largest landholders in Argentina. He left an inheritance valued at more than 7 million pesos fuertes. His heirs controlled some 9,582 square kilometers of land in the province alone (see Tables 25 and 26). The heirs of Nicolás came to be the richest branch of the Anchorena family. His son, Juan Nepomuceno Anchorena (1829–95), eventually owned 8,000 square kilometers of land in the territories of Patagonia, 648 in Córdoba, and 2,970 in Buenos Aires. His livestock were said to have numbered a half-million head of

*Cattle rancher, Buenos Aires Province, 1839.* This cattleman is dressed in a traditional but smart outfit for a visit to his estancia. In the city, where the *estanciero* lived and carried out essential business, he dressed in more Europeanized breeches and boots. (Lithograph by Adolphe D'Hastrel, 1839.)

Table 25. *Location and extent of the Anchorena family properties, 1830–64 (in square kilometers)*

| Location | 1830 | 1852 | 1864 |
|---|---|---|---|
| Matanza | 22 | 22 | 22 |
| Pila | 1,571 | 1,639 | 2,754 |
| Pergamino | | 1,814 | 1,814 |
| Saladillo | | 176 | 176 |
| Tordillo | | 797 | 1,015 |
| Tuyú | 510 | 521 | 1,077 |
| Mar Chiquita | 1,296 | 1,361 | 1,466 |
| Azul | | | 880 |
| Tres Arroyos | | | 378 |
| Total extent | 3,399 | 6,330 | 9,582 |
| Total properties | 8 | 13 | 24 |

*Sources:* Calculations based on Archivo General de la Nación, Buenos Aires, Sección Mapoteca, "Registro gráfico de los terrenos de propriedad pública y particular de la Provincia de Buenos Aires" (1830); "Registro gráfico . . ." (1852); and "Registro gráfico . . ." (1864).

cattle.[22] In large measure, Juan Nepomuceno could credit his wealth and power in the late nineteenth century to the land and cattle investments made by his uncle, Juan José, and his father nearly three-quarters of a century earlier.

As they purchased land, the Anchorenas also had to stock their new ranches with cattle and horses. Their superior sources of commercial capital enabled them to buy persistently, in large numbers, and from a variety of sources. For the most part, the Anchorenas bought up established ranches. The previous owners – the real pioneers of the pampa – obviously had lacked the capital resources to properly stock the property. Therefore, the Anchorenas added new stock to the existing herds on these estancias. Between June 1821 and July 1822, Juan José purchased more than 500 head of cattle, 400 sheep, and numerous mares for his first estate in Matanza. Although the ranch delivered livestock to the salting plants as early as 1822, Capataz Sosa continued to buy cattle, horses, and sheep from ranches in the vicinity.[23] The Anchorenas frequently bought livestock on time. In 1826, Juan José purchased cattle for a total of 3,900 pesos

Table 26. *Ownership of the Anchorena land by family inheritors in Buenos Aires Province, 1864 (in square kilometers)*

| Inheritor | Land owned |
|---|---|
| Nicolás Anchorena | 262 |
| Estate of [Juan José?] | 108 |
| Heirs of Tomás Manuel Anchorena | 1,015 |
| Mercedes Anchorena de Aguirre | 356 |
| Pedro Anchorena | 532 |
| Anchorena and Juan S. Boado | 378 |
| Nicolás and Juan Anchorena | 3,040 |
| Anchorena and Peña | 1,814 |
| Tomás S. de Anchorena | 332 |
| Fabián Gómez y Anchorena | 875 |
| Rosa Anchorena y Ybáñez | 694 |
| Other | 176 |
| Total | 9,582 |

*Sources:* Calculations based on Archivo General de la Nación, Buenos Aires, Sección Mapoteca, "Registro gráfico de los terrenos de propiedad pública y particular de la Provincia de Buenos Aires" (1830); "Registro gráfico . . ." (1852); and "Registro gráfico . . ." (1864).

fuertes, to be paid over a seven-year period at 6 percent per annum. If Anchorena bought an entire herd, he also acquired rights to the former owner's brand. In 1830, Juan José purchased 999 cows, 123 bulls and steers, 397 calves, and 453 horses, plus the *acción a la marca* (use of the brand).[24]

As administrator, Rosas often possessed the authority and power of attorney to make cattle purchases for his cousins' estates. In 1825, Rosas bought calves, bulls, and cows from neighboring estancieros. Cows especially were important in building the herds, and Rosas bought them in large lots.[25] In one transfer of cattle, the administrator made out a receipt for 500 breeding cows *(vacas de vientre)* and 500 suckling calves *(crías al pie)* to the mayordomo of a neighboring estancia. The former owner, Juan Antonio Capdevila, ultimately presented the receipt to Nicolás Anchorena in Buenos Aires for payment.[26] In 1828, Rosas traveled to Santa Fe to purchase still more cattle. He paid for them with notes drawn on

Anchorena's commercial agents in Rosario and Santa Fe. Using the libranza, or money order, Rosas was able to make purchases totaling 300 to 600 pesos without having to carry a load of silver coins.[27]

The Anchorenas continued to build their herds throughout the 1820s. Their access to commercial capital meant that cattle purchases, representing a great expense, could far outstrip cattle sales. The account books for two principal estates, Camarones and Dos Yslas, reveal that incessant cattle purchases added to the rapid increase in the herds. Juan José's substantial capital assets even enabled him to buy livestock in 1828, when the Brazilian blockade of Buenos Aires port prevented any sale at all of export-bound cattle (see Table 27).

## Only God understands

The Anchorenas and Rosas managed this vast latifundio from the city of Buenos Aires, with an administrative system based on a management hierarchy and effective communication. Apparently, Administrator Rosas assumed the responsibility

Table 27. *Purchase and sale of cattle on Estancias Camarones and Dos Yslas, 1821–31 (in head of cattle)*

| Number bought | Year | Number sold |
|---:|:---:|:---:|
| | 1821 | 260 |
| 2,500 | 1822 | 1,429 |
| 1,860 | 1823 | 1,644 |
| — | 1824 | 786 |
| 1,000 | 1825 | 467 |
| 4,507 | 1826 | 756 |
| 2,678 | 1827 | 645 |
| 2,801 | 1828 | — |
| 150 | 1829 | 3,357 |
| 2,373 | 1830 | 2,788 |
| — | 1831 | 914 |
| Totals 17,869 | | 13,046 |

*Source:* Archivo General de la Nación, Buenos Aires, Sala 7, 4–1–7, "Libro de cuentas de Juan José de Anchorena." The accounts for 1831 terminate on 9 April.

for organizing communications between the city and the various estates. Horsemen delivered letters back and forth quite rapidly. Rosas was able to write instructions to his mayordomo on estancias some seventy-five kilometers away and receive a reply in writing within two days.[28] Rosas corresponded regularly and in great detail with the chief mayordomo in the field, Manuel Morillo, and also with the foremen. His notes were filled with questions on the composition of the herds and the condition of the corrals. The authenticity of the communication system seemed to have been no problem, for Rosas' notes bore his signature and were sealed by red wax imprinted with the initials JMR.[29]

The messengers passing between Buenos Aires and the estancias were among the most trusted of Anchorena's workers. With a packet of correspondence, the messenger often carried letters for workers that had arrived from the Interior at Anchorena's downtown shop. Often, Rosas and Nicolás would send trustworthy horsemen to Mayordomo Morillo with as much as 1,500 pesos fuertes for petty expenses at the estates.[30] If the horseman carried bags of money, Nicolás dispatched an accompanying letter. The note verified the amount of money entrusted to the messenger and gave the denominations of the bills.[31] In the early days of the ranching business, Rosas frequently traveled to the various estancias and personally directed the branding and other labor. He wrote about these trips to his cousin, Juan José, and offered him tips on estate management such as how to handle cattle sales to meat-salting plants.[32]

For latifundio communications to work well, the foremen on the estancias had to know how to read and write — though they often fell short of Rosas' expectations. The administrator constantly exhorted Mayordomo Morillo to improve his handwriting. Rosas detested receiving letters "that only God [was] capable of understanding."[33] For his part, Morillo wrote of the latest news on the state of the livestock, how many heads were branded, the size of herds on various rodeos, and personnel problems. Foremen like Capataz José Manuel Saavedra at Estancia Del Tala were literate — even though their spelling was somewhat liberal and their handwriting shaky.[34]

Literacy among the foremen meant that either Rosas or Nicolás from Buenos Aires easily coordinated cattles sales throughout the latifundio. They merely handed a sealed order to the purchaser. The buyer's foremen rode out to the Anchorena estate and delivered the order to a mayordomo or capataz. The signed and sealed note instructed ranch workers to cut out a number of cattle or horses. The buyer's capataz then signed the note as a receipt. Rosas' foremen ultimately returned the original order/receipt to Rosas so that he could make the appropriate entry on his books.[35]

When Nicolás de Anchorena gradually assumed control of the estancias in 1828, he set out to streamline the administration. Nicolás managed the vast latifundio from his shop in Buenos Aires or from the Anchorena quinta (country house) north of the city in San Ysidro. Together with servants and three ranch peons to look after carriages and horses, Nicolás was accustomed to moving his family to the quinta for the hot summer months.[36] Previously, Rosas had managed all the landholdings as one large system. Nicolás now arranged the Anchorena properties into formal, well-defined units. He divided his land immediately north of the Salado River into two administrative parts. Then he promoted a trusted foreman, Juan Arista, to the position of mayordomo of half the estates – Averías, Achiras, and Villanueva. He retained the longtime mayordomo, Juan Morillo, as steward of the Estancias Camarones, Chapalafquén, Los Toldos, and Ynofales. He then combined two and three rodeos into one estancia and formalized the nomenclature. He referred to the head station (casco) at Los Toldos as the "puesto principal de la estancia de los Toldos."[37]

Nicolás also assumed greater control over personal and financial matters. He hired a new foreman for Estancia Ynofales. Rosas met the capataz only after getting a letter of introduction from Mayordomo Morillo. Even though he gave out instructions directly to the foremen, Nicolás was careful to inform Rosas, and he often solicited the advice of his administrator.[38] Mayordomos and foremen still addressed their correspondence to Juan José, perhaps out of respect for his position as head of the family. But clearly Nicolás was in charge of ranch affairs.

Ultimately, the growing size of the operations dictated establishment of a more efficient disbursement of operational funds to the mayordomos in the countryside. Nicolás and Juan José eventually secured the services of two financial agents in Chascomús, just twenty-five kilometers from the principal estate at Camarones. Anchorena set up expense accounts with two rural bankers, Felipe Lagasta y Quinteros and Pasqual Galy. The new mayordomo at Averías, Juan Arista, drew money from Galy for pay and expenses, whereas Mayordomo Morillo at Camarones drew up to 300 pesos fuertes in paper currency at a time from Quinteros. Morillo signed receipts for the money, and Quinteros' assistant then presented the receipts to Anchorena in Buenos Aires for repayment. Quinteros' commissions for his services are not known, but the arrangement reduced some of the uncertainties and delays of sending cash over long distances.[39]

Nicolás' rise to complete control of the latifundio was gradual. Part of his transfer involved tutorship in estancia affairs by Administrator Rosas and in financial affairs by Juan José. Meanwhile, Nicolás added formal command and control structure to an estate system that had grown immensely since its inception a decade earlier. In January 1831, Rosas was engaged fully in his military and political career, and Juan José died the following year. Thus, late in 1832, Nicolás de Anchorena took over sole management of one of the wealthiest latifundos in Latin America.

### Imported shooting pistols

Labor scarcity proved to be a universal problem throughout the first half-century of rural expansion in Buenos Aires Province. As the most prominent of the landowning families, the Anchorenas also felt the labor pinch. Civil and diplomatic disorders, like the Uruguayan War in 1827, caused prospective workers to be impressed into military service. In that year, the foreman of the Anchorena estate in Matanza, closest to the urban market, complained of not having enough peons to harvest the wheat and barley.[40] Similarly, the mayordomo at Camarones had difficulty securing laborers during the drought of 1830. Workers were in great demand when cattle raisers needed to move their herds from dried pastures.[41]

In the first flush of expansion, the Anchorenas acquired slaves from the Interior in order to supplement their free labor force. Rosas bought nine slaves for Estancia Dos Yslas and another six for Estancia Camarones in 1822 and 1823.[42]

Administrator Rosas himself had purchased slaves to offset labor shortages on his own ranches. Fourteen adult male slaves worked on his Estancia San Martin and another seventeen slaves labored at Estancia Cerrillos. Most slaves were in their twenties; only four were older than forty years of age. Seven blacks had been born in either Mozambique, Angola, or the Congo. The native-born slaves all came from the Interior provinces, purchased by Rosas in Santa Fe and Córdoba. All slaves had had at least one previous owner, but now, in addition to their given names, nearly all assumed Rosas' last name as well. Only two slaves were married.[43]

Slavery's gradual demise forced a complete conversion to free, salaried workers all over the pampa. The nature of cattle operations excluded most European immigrants; only Creoles handy with a horse and a lasso sufficed. In an expanding pampa cattle economy, estancieros like the Anchorenas recruited Creole migrants from the Interior provinces. Rosas actively sought provincianos for his labor gangs. Unlike native porteños, they were not subject to military duty. Mayordomos were to remind local militia officers that Rosas' peons were either provincianos, foremen of estancias and puestos, or temporary laborers from another estancia. All these categories of men were exempted from the draft.[44]

It is difficult to ascertain how many men worked for the Anchorenas on all their estates. Census reports for 1838 suggest that the number may have been quite high. Nicolás' estate of 270 square kilometers in the Monsalvo district, Estancia Dos Yslas, supported 35 persons, including peons and their families. But the new 1,350-square-kilometer estate at Azul contained a total of 410 persons.[45] No other available documentation exists to support these figures. Clearly, the size of the Anchorena latifundio supported a great many dependents and offered Nicolás flexibility and efficiency in personnel management.

Anchorena's peons, like those of other estancieros, were required to verify their employment in the countryside. According to the 1823 rural labor code, free workers had to carry identification papers called papelitas. Administrator Rosas warned his foremen to assure that the peons carry their registration papers at all times, especially on the estancias close to frontier militia posts where vagrants were liable to impressment. Slaves did not have to bear any documents.

Rosas urged his mayordomos to aid government commissioners whose task it was to eliminate vagrants and deserters in the countryside of Buenos Aires Province.[46] Affiliation with a large rancher probably eased the peon's mobility in the countryside. Presumably, travel might have been more difficult for those who were not ranch hands but specialized in wandering from one ranch to another constructing corrals or digging wells.[47] Because foreigners took up these ranch-support jobs — and they were exempt from the militia anyway — it is likely that enforcement of vagrancy codes discriminated against the jobless creole.

Loyalty and literacy were rewarded in ranch administration, and foremen with these attributes became especially reliable dependents of the Anchorenas. When Juan José first went into land, he hired those who previously had worked for him. Juan Benito Sosa had assisted Anchorena in river commerce in the 1810s. He became the foreman of the Hacienda de la Amistad, Juan José's first land purchase.[48] As mayordomo of the principal Anchorena estancia of Camarones, Manuel Morillo enjoyed greater perogatives than other foremen. He had his own account with Juan José and could write his boss requesting such luxury items as a brace of imported shooting pistols.[49] By the 1850s, Morillo had acquired his own land. Though they were privileged, Anchorena's foremen were also required to observe rigid standards. Administrator Rosas prohibited drunkenness, gambling, and scandal of any sort on the estates. Those foremen who undermined morale and discipline suffered reprimand. Rosas once castigated a capataz who provoked disorder by taking advantage of a peon's wife.[50] Foremen were expected to earn their privileges and higher pay with exemplary behavior.

Most of Anchorena's workers seemed relatively stable, working on his estates for at least one year. Peons usually began at twelve pesos a month. After a period of dependable work, their pay rose to fourteen pesos. Foremen ordinarily earned almost twice as much, or twenty-five pesos.[51] If the peon hired on for a brief time, he often received a *libranza* (money order), which he could exchange for cash with the Anchorenas in Buenos Aires. Juan José and Nicolás usually supplemented the pay of their peons with certain rationed goods from the city, which they dispatched to the estates aboard oxcart transport.[52] Workers expected rations of tobacco, paper, yerba, salt, flour, and ponchos. They received these rations in addition to food and shelter.

Late pay appeared to be something of a problem for Anchorena's workers in the 1820s. The administration always seemed to owe the men back wages. Mayordomo Morillo often paid workers in sums of four to thirty pesos at a time. Occasionally, Rosas himself brought the payroll during his early inspection trips of the ranches.[53] When Juan José contracted the services of rural bankers in 1831, much of the irregularity of pay seems to have decreased. Thereafter, Mayordomo Morillo drew cash as needed at Chascomús.

The Anchorenas also relied on a floating rural population of day workers for seasonal and special jobs. At roundup time, the mayordomos contracted independent capataces with four or five peons to work on the estates for about two weeks at forty centavos a day plus food and yerba, or seventy centavos without rations.[54] Hired help performed traditional jobs such as driving cattle or branding calves. Masons and other skilled workers also appeared to be in great demand for work on the Anchorena latifundio. Mayordomo Morillo once hired a foreign brickmaker named Gilgen and three assistants to fire 80,000 bricks for 416 pesos fuertes. But Gilgen required Morillo first to pay off a debt of 390 pesos that the brickmaker had acquired in Dolores.[55] Morillo hired another foreigner, the carpenter Jaime Easton, to construct corrals. Day workers could expect either to be paid in cash or receive letters of credit. In the latter case, they redeemed the manager's libranza for cash from Juan José or Nicolás in Buenos Aires.[56]

### Without bulls . . .

The reproductive capacities of livestock garnered estate profits in this era of commercial and pastoral growth in Buenos Aires Province. The Anchorenas always attempted to maximize propagation of their herds. Rosas' letters instructed his mayordomos repeatedly and in detail on the care of livestock. When the death rate of calves increased at Estancia del Tala, he reminded the mayordomo to put the cows and young calves into corrals for protection.[57] Administrator Rosas was zealous in protecting the expanding herds. When military authorities appropriated 120 cows from Estancia Dos Yslas in 1824, Rosas protested vigorously. He did not contest the government's right to take livestock in order to supply the garrison, paying the estanciero later. But Rosas did resent the fact that militia commandants took cows, because cows were essential to the propagation of the herds.[58] All the herds consisted of a disproportionate number of cows. Administrator Rosas instructed that 3 to 10 bulls be maintained in every rodeo of 1,200 animals. A topic of particular concern to Rosas was how the bulls were taking to the cows. After all, he wrote to his mayordomos with his usual sardonic condescension, "cows without bulls will not produce calves."[59]

As the herds propagated on the unfenced prairies, branding took on an increasingly important role in livestock management. Cattle and horses easily strayed off their rodeos and onto the neighborhood's property. A cattleman might reclaim his animals from the neighbor through identification of his brand.[60] Rosas, therefore, demanded careful branding procedures so that the Anchorena brands and his own brands appeared distinctly on each animal's flank. Calves were branded before they were a year old. Roundups for branding and castrating therefore occurred at least once a year on each rodeo.[61] No blacksmith could forge a branding iron without a permit from the police. Rural authorities then registered the distinctive brands of the surrounding estancieros. Big-time ranchers like the Anchorenas and Rosas needed many brands to account for the numerous herds on their several estates. In 1830, the Anchorenas had registered several in the name of his business partner, Juan Nepomuceno Terrero. Many Rosas brands were variations of the letter A and undoubtedly appeared on Anchorena cattle administered by Rosas.[62]

One cannot determine with certainty the exact number of cattle on the Anchorena estates, because the family's estancia papers lack an annual inventory. Apparently, Administrator Rosas knew the size of all the herds. He often stressed the mere counting of the herds as a simple device to keep track of the livestock. Rosas scolded his mayordomos and foremen for poor counting procedures and instructed them to maintain lists of the numbers of cattle bearing each of the Anchorena brands. Careful records of branded cattle on each estancia enabled Rosas to report the theft of cattle to authorities, especially in the 1820s, when Indians periodically made off with small numbers of livestock.[63] The only surviving documental sources on herd size are the scattered reports of foremen and contracts of cattle sales to the salting factories. Without much assurance, then, one may estimate that four of the principal Anchorena estancias — Laguna Dulce, Del Tala, Camarones, and Arroyo Grande — together contained approximately 50,000 head of cattle in the mid-1830s. Two decades later, Nicolás informed a Chilean visitor that this same nucleus of ranches had 100,000 animals.[64] Including their nine other estates, the Anchorenas easily could have owned a quarter-million head of livestock.

Like other estancias, the Anchorena properties and livestock were prey to the raids and depredations of Indians. In 1822, Rosas protested to the provincial government that bands of Indians were stealing branded cattle from properties near the frontier. Three years later the administrator claimed that Indian raiders had killed eleven men and made off with 4,000 head of cattle at Estancia del Tala.[65] The incident appears to be the most serious that occurred in the period, for as late as 1830, a number of friendly Indians still resided in their *toldos* (Indian huts) on the Estancia Averías. They were responsible for some robbery of cattle during the drought of that year, but the Indians quickly repaid the damages. As Mayordomo Juan Arista wrote, these peaceful Indians feared that the whites otherwise might erect a fort among their toldos. Ranch managers were authorized to discipline disruptive Indians and to notify militia commandants about armed Indians.[66] Marauding Indians actually presented only a minor threat to Anchorena's livestock in the first half of the nineteenth century. The dangers of drought proved the major hindrance to production.

Drought always threatened the small cattle breeder with uncertainty and possible disaster. Water holes and wells dried up, and pastures became parched. Weakened by both thirst and undernourishment, livestock died in large numbers during lengthy dry spells. Landowners with greater land and capital resources found drought disturbing but seldom disastrous. The great drought that began late in 1829 and lasted until early 1832 caused much dislocation to pastoral production throughout the pampa, and the Anchorena latifundio did not escape the consequences. Irregular rainfall had rendered many pastures useless for several months of the year. Foremen had to make frequent inspections of the puestos to see if the water in lagoons and water holes was still "good and sweet."[67] Yet the Anchorena cattle estates survived the great drought by virtue of their combined size and natural resources.

Lack of rain proved as debilitating to Anchorena livestock as to those of other estancieros. The decay of grass and forage produced stunted calves and thin steers. Mayordomo Morillo reported that cows were aborting their calves.[68] Nicolás was reduced to urging his foremen to put more cows into the cattle drives sold to the saladeros because many would not survive the drought. Anchorena sought to escape the worst effects of the drought by marketing the steers as soon as possible.[69] But working the cattle required sound horses, and horses too suffered from drought. At one point, Mayordomo Morillo reported that the horses of one estancia had become so weakened by poor pastures that they were unable to work. Horses were dying at Estancia Averías as early as 1830. The Anchorenas were also losing cattle. Nicolás admitted that 2,000 head had died on the Estancias Averías and Achiras.[70] Ultimately, these two estancias were abandoned for the duration of the drought.

As owners of great landed expanses, the Anchorenas still had good pastures even during the long drought. Nicolás claimed that his newer estancia at Arroyo Grande would support up to 50,000 head of cattle — although that number seems exaggerated. He therefore ordered his men to move livestock from other ranches to Arroyo Grande. In particular, Anchorena sent young steers southward. When the waterholes on one rodeo at Estancia Camarones dried up in 1832, Mayordomo Morillo evacuated the cattle to another Anchorena estancia.[71] That was a recourse smaller estancieros could not contemplate. As early as 1830, Nicolás ordered the removal of all livestock from Estancias Achiras and Averías. He assigned one capataz, Juan Décima, and seven peons to relocate up to 2,500 animals to better grazing areas.[72]

However, the removal of cattle from certain estancias did not proceed without complications. Peons sometimes had difficulty rounding up desperate animals that had scattered in search of water and grass. Labor also was a problem during dry spells. Nicolás might have been able to move huge herds from one property to another, but he required extra men to drive hungry and thirsty animals over long distances, and because of this higher demand during droughts, peons often commanded higher pay.[73]

Cattle transfers within Anchorena's estates — a form of transhumance, of course — continued until 1832. By that year, Estancia Achiras had been abandoned except for dying animals, and the lagoons at Puesto Villanueva had dried up completely.[74] But their control of numerous other pastures assured the Anchorenas that their cattle operations would survive the great drought. In the 1830s and 1840s, Nicolás continued to expand the family latifundio and to develop new herds on estancias nearer the receding frontier.

### Patriotism and sacrifice

Support of large and small estates on the pampa required constant supply of tools, foodstuffs, clothing, and modest luxuries from the commercial city of Buenos Aires. Many large estancieros established pulperías (general stores) in the countryside to support their ranch hands and the residents of the area. But the successful pulpería needed customers. Earlier, an Anchorena dependent, Juan Benito Sosa, had to shut down the general store on the Hacienda de la Amistad for lack of customers.[75]

On the ranches, the capataces and mayordomos depended upon supplies from the city. Up to 1830, Nicolás and Juan José sent most ranch supplies to the estancias aboard oxcarts. They dispatched items like knives, nails, barrels for grease, boxes for tallow, pots, pans, bags for drawing water, salt, paper, tobacco, and yerba.[76] Carts moved very slowly over the prairies. Simply to travel from one Anchorena estate to another with a load of supplies, the cartmaster needed to pass by way of river fords and established wagon trails. One such cart train left Rosas' ranch of Cerrillos on the near side of the Salado River and arrived at Camarones on the far side of the river eight days later. The cart train finally reached Estancia Del Tala on the frontier in eleven days. Some of the cargo had been damaged along the way. River crossings especially soaked dry goods and tobacco.[77]

By 1839, the region around Estancia Camarones had become populated enough to warrant the establishment by

Nicolás of a general store on his property, and he loaned brothers Vicente and Francisco Letamendi 1,000 pesos fuertes to run the pulpería there. According to the business contract, the new store was not to sell liquors and wines or to encourage gambling. Nor were the Letamendis to advance money to peons without the mayordomo's consent. The three parties to the formal contract claimed equal shares of the profits and liquidations. Letamendis' contact in the city was to be merchant Francisco Bosch. Bosch provided their supplies for over-the-counter-sales, and he also was to receive any raw products – wool, hides, or tallow – that the Letamendis might accumulate in barter sales.[78] Most pulperías were more than rural general stores; they served also as collection points for the products of small ranchers and merchants in the area. The Anchorena-Letamendi pulpería was different. Nicolás maintained his own marketing system for both cattle and estancia goods, whereas Letamendis' pulpería merely served as a retailer of dry goods and hardware on the Anchorena latifundio.

By midcentury, however, Vicente Letamendi had contracted the services of another commercial agent in Buenos Aires, the camp merchant Larrea. Letamendi received his first shipment of clothes, cloth, and ironware from Larrea in November 1848.[79] Letamendi apparently wrote back to Larrea as much as once a week with small orders. The merchant then shipped the requested items on carts that passed near Estancia Camarones. Certain cartmen apparently maintained a Dolores–Buenos Aires run, by which Larrea always sent goods to Letamendi at the Camarones general store. The camp merchant in Buenos Aires paid half the freight charge when he dispatched the goods. Letamendi paid teamsters the remaining fees on receipt of the cargo.[80]

Merchant Larrea had hoped that Letamendi would become another of his rural agents for the collection of pastoral products for export. When he solicited Letamendi's business, Larrea offered the pulpero a fifty–fifty partnership in the roundup of cattle for the saladeros. The camp merchant wanted Letamendi to buy cattle with letters of credit payable by Larrea in eight to ten days' time. Larrea's correspondence also concerned price information on goods he especially wanted from the campo (countryside), and he always stressed quality control. Larrea requested clean hides and washed wool, because they fetched higher prices. "Washed wool, both creole and mixed, is in demand," Larrea wrote to Letamendi. "I have sold what I received from Azul washed and packed at 33 pesos [1.65 gold pesos] per arroba [11.4 kilograms]."[81] The camp merchant kept all his field agents abreast of foreign news that might affect the market prices of export goods in Buenos Aires. He informed the pulpero in December 1848 that the coming year would be good for exports because the French fleet had just lifted its blockade of Buenos Aires, and German demand for hides was on the rise.[82]

There is no indication that the cattle-buying partnership ever was consummated or that Letamendi sent the camp merchant hides and wool in quantity. Larrea kept requesting more pastoral products in the carretas passing through Camarones.[83] The merchant maintained a separate account for each of his agents in the field. When he sold sheepskins dispatched from the Dolores area by Letamendi, Larrea entered the credit on the pulpero's account. When he dispatched supplies to Letamendi's store, Larrea charged the account. His letters show that Letamendi's debt climbed to 663 pesos fuertes, despite payments of libranzas from both Letamendi and Anchorena.[84] It seems clear that the Camerones pulpero got more supplies from Larrea than he returned in the form of pastoral products. Nicolás thereby had streamlined the management of his latifundio further by entrusting ranch supply to Letamendi. Thereafter, Anchorena personally concentrated on selling cattle to processors in Buenos Aires.

Anchorena's estates, like those of other Argentine estancieros, specialized in the sale of cattle and cattle products at the international emporium of Buenos Aires. The family made the bulk of its profits from selling livestock on-the-hoof directly to salting factories in the port city. Various estancias also produced dried hides and tallow, which were sold to warehousemen and exporters. Even the abasto of Buenos Aires, which provided fresh beef for city residents, became an early outlet for Anchorena cattle production. Estancia Laguna Dulce produced a herd of nearly 300 head of cattle in 1831 for the mataderos' supply. They were sold to middlemen who took charge of the cattle drive and subsequent sale at the Western Stockyards outside Buenos Aires.[85] Compared to the salting factories, the abasto proved a small market for Anchorena cattle. Yet, the Anchorenas also prospered from early livestock sales to frontier militia garrisons.

Sales of livestock to the government provided the Anchorenas an initial and substantial amount of income from their new estates. Throughout the 1820s and 1830s, provincial military authorities purchased horses to give to Indians south of the frontier. Ranchers like the Anchorenas thus profited from sales of their old mares. Mares were never used as saddle horses and had lost their value when they no longer produced foals. Anchorena's mayordomos sent 50 to 200 horses to the frontier as tribute for the Indians in the 1820s.[86] Other estancieros also sold provisions to the government. They received recompense for delivering kindling wood, oxen, tobacco, yerba, tallow, cattle, and horses to the garrisons.[87] Anchorena especially sold cattle. Customarily, an army officer arrived at the ranch, and militiamen aided in the roundup. Anchorena peons then accompanied the cattle for the first twenty-five kilometers of the drive. Nicolás' instructions for the roundup and cattle drive were explicit. He wanted to avoid complaints by the government (at least while Rosas was governor) that livestock sold to the garrisons were not those specified in the contract.[88]

Nicolás claimed that he had delivered some 20,800 head of cattle to the troops during the Indian campaign that his cousin conducted in 1831–2. In fact, General Rosas had formed one of his divisions on Anchorena property at Laguna del Sartén.[89] Rosas turned out to be as exacting a commander as he had been a ranch administrator. His orders for remounts were precise about the sex, condition, color, and training of the horses, and he also specified the trail and stopovers that the peons bringing the horses were to make enroute to the frontier.[90]

Nicolás continued the profitable supply of the provincial militia after Rosas again became governor of the province in 1835. Perhaps the Anchorenas came to enjoy special privilege in military supply, for it appears that Nicolás' vast estates provided more cattle and horses for the militia posts than those of all other estancieros. In 1835, Anchorena was delivering approximately 800 head of cattle a month to the garrisons. He divided the task among three principal ranches. Cowhands drove cattle from Estancia Arroyo Grande in the period from August through October, from Camarones in November through March, and from Del Tala in April through July. The following year found Anchorena selling approximately 10,000 head of cattle to the garrisons at Fuerte Argentino, Fuerte Independencia, and Fuerte Azul.[91] Despite his apparent privilege, Nicolás could not always count on timely payment by Governor Rosas' treasury. Anchorena claimed that he provided as many cattle to militia troops as all the other estancieros combined, and he was quick to exaggerate his "patriotism" and "sacrifice" whenever the government fell behind in payment.[92]

Toward midcentury, Anchorena's ranch operations settled into the profitable routine of producing livestock for the saladeros around Buenos Aires. Because he contracted directly with the factory owner for timely delivery of cattle herds, Anchorena seldom sold herds publicly at the stockyards. The contract between saladerista and estanciero often stipulated that the factory owner had exclusive rights to all marketable steers and "fat" cows of one particular estancia.[93] Anchorena provided the cattle evenly throughout the slaughtering season from December through April. For instance, Nicolás might deliver a tropa of 250 head of cattle to a particular salting factory every seven days. Normally, the contracts enabled Nicolás to produce cattle from several estancias in order to fill the order.[94] Factory processors also purchased horses from Anchorena. Contracts asked for mares and geldings sometimes numbering 6,000 head. Presumably, the salderista processed the hides and steamed the carcasses for a fine oil called mare's grease.[95]

The buyer always reserved the right to send his peons on horseback to the Anchorena estate to help form the cattle drives. His foremen and Anchorena's capataz together were to pick out the two-year-old steers. Cows were over four years old when sold, beyond the age of bearing healthy calves. Nicolás usually contracted to add one cow for each two or three steers, but at three-fourths the price of the heavier steers. Occasionally, the foreman who represented the saladerista refused to purchase the steers because they were too skinny.[96] Anchorena assumed the expense of cattle lost along the trail, but the buyer reimbursed him at the rate of four centavos per head when the cattle arrived at the factory's corrals. The factory owner usually paid Anchorena with letters of credit payable after he had processed the cattle. Nicolás redeemed these libranzas at face value in thirty days.[97]

The Anchorena estates also earned secondary revenues from the sale of processed goods. Dried hides, cases of tallow, and barrels of grease were collected and sent to the city aboard oxcarts. Cows yielded most of the hides produced on the estancia. Steers sold on-the-hoof because of their greater weight, but cows were kept until they no longer produced foals. Peons then slaughtered these older cows for ranch consumption and staked the hides to dry in the sun. A typical cartload of dried hides from the anchorena estates might consist of 560 cowhides and only 30 steerhides.[98] Cart manifests of ranch goods also included horsehair, sheepskins, tallow, and grease. On the frontier, the Estancia del Tala also produced bags of ostrich feathers.[99]

Mayordomo Morillo periodically collected the goods at his head station in Estancia Camarones. He kept a record of the puestos, whence came the different types of goods. When he had collected enough products, Morillo then dispatched the goods to Anchorena's contracted warehouseman, Ciriaco Baranda, aboard carts of independent teamsters.[100] For one such delivery to Buenos Aires, Nicolás paid cartman Videla some ninety-eight pesos fuertes for four cartloads containing 378 hides and nine bultos of tallow and grease. Most of these processed goods arrived by oxcart. In one case, however, Nicolás employed the services of boatmen to deliver tallow, grease, horns, and cattle- and horsehides from the Salado River.[101]

Juan José and Nicolás arranged the sale of these processed pastoral goods to exporters through the auspices of a longtime business associate, Juan Nepomuceno Terrero. On a commission of 1 percent, Terrero sold horsehair, tallow, grease, and hides to several different buyers. In 1831, his sales of Anchorena ranch products brought in some 1,551 pesos fuertes.[102] Warehouseman Baranda then provided carts and peons to deliver Anchorena's goods from his warehouse to the waterfront for shipment. He charged the Anchorena account for storage, cartage, and handling.[103]

The sale of processed pastoral goods was essentially a byproduct of cattle production but no less an aspect of the efficient operation of a large export-oriented Argentine

ranch in the era of traditional technology. Because the Anchorenas had large herds of cattle, they enjoyed the advantage of dealing directly with factory owners, export merchants, and government buyers. Convenience of delivery and
timely payment thus were assured. Small ranchers had to sell
their ranch products to middlemen and drive their livestock
to the public stockyards for sale. The size of the Anchorena
cattle operations, on the other hand, afforded the family enterprise all the advantages of the economies of scale.

Although the Anchorena family came to be the most efficient and prosperous of the Argentine estancieros of the
period, they hardly represent the entire panorama of social
and economic expansion onto the Argentine pampa. For
every great landowner of lesser stature than the Anchorenas,
there existed hundreds of other proprietors and renters possessing fewer advantages of access to commercial capital and
managerial talent who, nevertheless, were to contribute their
production to the growing staple trade of Buenos Aires. Only
a handful of landowners, like the Anchorenas, expanded the
size of their landholdings appreciably in an era when landed
properties actually were being fractionalized and ownership
spread among a broader spectrum of the rural population.
Yet, expansion of the Anchorena latifundio was part and
parcel of the commercial revolution at Buenos Aires. The
rising influence of the marketing system at the port, focusing
on the meat-salting plants, removed cattle processing from
the estancia to a sector that collected, slaughtered, and
dressed livestock from all over the pampa. During the first
half of the century, the estancieros were able to concentrate
exclusively on cattle husbandry and herd reproduction on
ranches farther removed from the city. Unlike many other
proprietors of the period, the Anchorenas appear to have
shunned sheep raising and agricultural production at least
until the second half of the century. The only way that their
estates served a growing domestic market was in the provision of livestock to the frontier militia posts. Still, the family
came to be the first among a small coterie of prominent
Argentine landowners whose economic, social, and political
interests would dominate Argentine life from the nineteenth
century onward.

# 9

## Depression and renaissance of commerce in the Interior provinces

The economic florescence of the province of Buenos Aires was not reproduced in equal measure in the Interior provinces. No sooner was Independence from Spanish colonial rule achieved than provincial military chieftains fell out among themselves, and the conflicts often halted commerce and scattered cattle herds and rural residents alike. In the decade of 1810−20, the colonial cart trades between Buenos Aires and the Interior nearly stopped, and river commerce in the Paraná River Basin as far as Paraguay was interrupted. Meanwhile, Potosí's mines declined rapidly after two and one-half centuries of yielding the richest silver ores in the world. No longer could the towns and provinces of the Interior depend on the prosperous carrying trades between Potosí and Buenos Aires. The economic life of the Interior in 1820 seemed depressed beyond remedy.

Historians often make theoretical points off the depression of the Interior in a period when the economy of the Litoral was expanding. Most speculate that the import of cheap European industrial goods displaced the Interior's domestic production, thus exacerbating a process already begun by the decline of Potosí and the disruption of civil wars. The resultant economic dislocation only reversed itself whenever the domestic market was closed to foreign trade by blockades of the port of Buenos Aires. A case in point is the native textile industry of the Interior − which allegedly succumbed because cheap Lancashire textiles dominated clothing markets everywhere in the La Plata region.[1] Dependency practitioners carry the argument to its theoretical conclusion: that the provinces of the Interior fell into "neo-colonial relations" with Buenos Aires in what amounted to an impoverishment of the Interior for the sake of the port's expansion. Indeed, dependency theory also states that the Interior should have flourished whenever foreign trade di-

202 A socioeconomic history of Argentina

minished on the domestic markets (i.e., during the blockades of Buenos Aires port).[2]

It may be historically improper to overemphasize the "depression" of the Interior, because commerce and production in the hinterland of Argentina did recover, beginning in the early 1830s, on the strength of the very export market at Buenos Aires that some historians say "impoverished" the Interior. Contrary to the dependency arguments, growth of the staples trade at the port opened up alternative markets for the production capacity of the Interior that so long had served the Potosí market. The linkage of traditional transport extended into the Interior, often with insufficient strength to make the economic recovery of the hinterland match the growth of the Buenos Aires economy; yet the export trade and the domestic market that it created did influence the Interior. Consider the extraordinary expansion of the pastoral production and commerce in the riverine provinces of Santa Fe, Entre Ríos, and Corrientes; or the fact that the native textile industry of Córdoba, Santiago del Estero, and Catamarca continued to market their ponchos in Buenos Aires and Montevideo; or the fact that the Interior provinces did not flourish but actually suffered whenever Buenos Aires port was closed. In a real sense, these provinces closer to Buenos Aires participated fully in the staples growth of the era, while those farthest from the port suffered most from the closure of Potosí and the impracticality of long-distance hauling of bulk commodities by oxcart. Where there existed genuine depression and economic decline in the period — as there was deep in the Interior at Jujuy, Salta, and perhaps Catamarca and La Rioja — the cause was not the export commerce per se but the fact that the traditional technology of the day prevented those provinces from participating in the staple trade at all.

## Mines filled with rubbish

Without doubt, cases existed of foreign goods driving domestic products off the region's leading domestic marketplace at Buenos Aires. Imports of Italian, French, and Spanish wine practically ended the appearance of Mendoza's wine on dinner tables in Buenos Aires, and nearly all the sugar and tobacco that porteños consumed from Cuba and Brazil.[3]

Foreign sugar and wine even found their way from the port to distant Salta in 1825 — even though that province later would have its own sugar and wine industry. And in the French blockade of 1839, salteño growers again shipped their tobacco down to Buenos Aires.[4] Flour and tobacco from the United States were retailed up the Paraná River as far as Corrientes, Spanish and Italian wine was sent to Entre Ríos, and foreign tobacco reached Mendoza. Domestic brandy from Mendoza — a favorite of the *clases populares* (popular, or lower, classes) — made a comeback on the Buenos Aires marketplace, although the resurgence of Cuyo wines never occurred in any significant proportion.[5] Politicians and merchants of the Interior, nevertheless, favored commercial exchanges and became alarmed whenever trade to Buenos Aires diminished, as it actually did during blockades of the port. One Tucumán correspondent noted that the 1839 French blockade of Buenos Aires "has given death to our industry and commerce. . . ."[6] The reason was that the Interior had survived two decades of civil disturbances and was becoming more integrated into the import and export markets centering on Buenos Aires.

The Argentines fought their Wars of Independence in the Interior, so that the conflicts affected the economic life of the provinces to a greater extent than that of Buenos Aires. Military activity not only cut off communications to Potosí, but also ended ore production in mines that had been in a process of technological decline since the late eighteenth century. The town of Potosí endured four military invasions. In 1811, the retreating patriot army sacked the treasury of 6 million silver pesos, and another Argentine army returned and threatened to detonate the buildings in the center of Potosí with dynamite. The threat never was consummated.[7] Fighting in the North disrupted commerce between Argentina and Potosí. Even Jujuy and Salta were temporarily lost to porteño trade in 1815, when the advancing Spanish army forced patriot merchants to flee with their merchandise to Tucumán.[8]

The revolutionary conflicts between patriot and Spanish forces halted nearly all trade in the northern provinces. In 1816 and 1817, no freight at all arrived at Buenos Aires from the North.[9] Regional businessmen abandoned their posthouses on the cart trails between Tucumán and Salta, while horse raisers in the area lost their herds to competing armies.

Ironically, cattlemen in Tucumán benefited both from the new hide trade at Buenos Aires and from the supply of armies in Upper Peru. Estancieros north of Tucumán, however, were unable to capitalize on rising prices for cattle and horses. One rancher whose property bordered the cart road leading to Salta in 1825 had only 8 cows remaining from the herd of 3,000 despoiled by soldiers.[10]

Potosí's mining industry did not survive the Wars of Independence because the silver content of the ore had been declining steadily since the end of the previous century. In fact, the Spanish crown in 1792 commissioned several German mining experts to seek improvements in the 200-year-old patio process of mercury−silver amalgamation. Their visit to Potosí failed to reverse the trend of sagging production. While the Germans complained of the backwardness of local mine owners, the miners themselves claimed that the Germans' proposals only increased costs without boosting silver production.[11] Apparently, foreign technological know-how was not the panacea, for British experts in 1825 also failed to revive the mines. A British engineer reported that, after fifteen years of revolutionary war in Upper Peru, the mines of Potosí had declined in number from the forty that had operated in 1803 to just fifteen. Those remaining mine shafts, filled with rubbish and water, were hopelessly dilapidated.[12] Potosí had relinquished its centuries-old rank as the premier silver-mining region in the world.

Closure of the Potosí market was felt all along the old commercial routes between Potosí and Buenos Aires. As the former center of the colonial mule fairs, Salta had difficulty adjusting to its new position at the end of the Buenos Aires lifeline rather than at the center of trade between the Río de la Plata and Upper Peru. The impact of Potosí's closing reached Tucumán and Córdoba, where estancieros who once prospered on the mule trades found that the value of their land in 1826 had dropped by 85 percent.[13] In Entre Ríos, estates that prospered on colonial mule and cattle drives to Salta and Potosí began to reorient their production toward the Atlantic. Prospects appeared good in 1810 because Buenos Aires' markets for pastoral exports were expanding. Large estates already had numerous gaucho cowboys who rode herd on thousands of head of cattle, horses, and mules.[14]

### Scattering about deserters

While the Wars of Independence disrupted trade in the northern provinces of Argentina, civil wars broke out to wreak further havoc on those provinces hithertofore immune from the revolutionary disturbances. The countryside of the Banda Oriental, once dotted with thriving colonial cattle ranches, was deserted in 1827, and the country villages lay in decay.[15] A decade before, the gaucho army of Gervasio Artigas fought Spanish, porteño, and Luso-Brazilian troops for the right to rule Montevideo. His forces controlled the province of Entre Ríos and Corrientes and, in the process, disrupted ranching and sent cattle and horses into the wilds. When the followers of Artigas took over the river port of Corrientes, they effectively intercepted trade on the Paraná River between Paraguay and Buenos Aires.[16]

Armed bands led by provincial caudillos occasionally interrupted production and trade from Santa Fe west to the Andean foothills. Rebel chieftains in 1820 easily stopped mule and cart trains on the trails between Mendoza and Córdoba, as many postmen and their families fled the posthouses. Even the Andean passes, through which mendocinos sent yerba mate to Chile and received East Indian and Chinese wares, were infested with robber bands. The decline of Catamarca's exports of raw cotton to tucumano and *cordobes* weavers corresponded not to the import of foreign textiles at Buenos Aires but to the political instability of the 1820s.[17] Of this era, an English traveler later wrote:[18]

> The country people, by the duration of a system of robbery and pillage, had become demoralized; and the passage across the plain would consequently be interrupted, laborious, and perilous. ... In one place was Ramirez, with the troops of Entre Ríos, or, as they are termed in abhorrence, the Mounteneros [*sic*]; in another was Carrera, with the troops of no place at all, but with all the vagabonds who preferred a life of rapine to any other. Here the troops of Mendoza and San Juan; further on, those of San Luis; further on, those of Buenos Aires; all in pursuit, or affecting to be so, of Ramirez and Carrera; all exhausting the resources of the road; all scattering about deserters and assassins; in short − tantara rara roques all.

Indian raiders often took advantage of the general insecurity in the countryside, endangering not only ranchers on frontiers of Buenos Aires but also travelers and producers in the provinces. In 1849, country folk abandoned estancias in Córdoba Province because of Indian raids. Oxcart caravans and stagecoaches were especially vulnerable, because the squeaking of ungreased hubs on cart wheels and the clouds of dust kicked up by swift horse-drawn coaches especially attracted Indian harassment. At night, travelers slept in fortified posthouses, which often retained surrounding moats as a protection from raids of the Chaco and Pampa Indians. Yet pulperías continued to trade ponchos, brandy, and other domestic products to peaceful Indians in exchange for exotic export items like tiger skins and ostrich feathers.[19] Indian and gaucho belligerence may have interrupted trade in the Interior, but they did not sever the commercial links to the export market at Buenos Aires.

Provincial customs policies — a vestige of the colonial administration — became yet another weapon in the civil wars among the provinces. Following the Revolution of 1810, successive governments at Buenos Aires retained the profitable receipts of that port's customshouse, and the provincial governments resorted to raising their own customshouses and to collecting taxes on trade items that passed across provincial borders on muleback or in oxcarts. The principal tax levied in Tucumán and other provinces was the colonial *alcabala,* which taxed incoming goods at the rate of 4 to 16 percent ad valorem. In addition, importing merchants had to pay excise, transit, and special taxes, while in wartime, provincial governments charged an extra duty, the *extraordinario de guerra,* in order to support local militia troops.[20] The customs wars almost reduced each province to a separate trading entity unto itself, and provincial politicians were powerless to rectify the trend.

Interprovincial customs duties combined with civil disturbances to inhibit trade in the Interior, even though neither was able to halt commercial exchange completely. Corrientes in 1830 prohibited all importing of wine and brandy from other provinces. Córdoba briefly participated in the customs wars and charged duties of up to 58 percent ad valorem on goods coming from other provinces; cordobes merchants had to pay 25 percent on the value of Mendozan wines and 50 percent on Catamarcan tobacco.[21] During the revolutionary era, Buenos Aires customs officials regularly collected heavy alcabala and entry taxes on items like Paraguayan tea and Mendozan wine and brandy. Merchants might pay up to 2,600 silver pesos on the departure for the provinces of a tropa of 62 packmules, or 308 pesos on an overland shipment of 3.4 metric tons of yerba.[22] Later, Buenos Aires retained a 4 percent ad valorem duty on all articles from other provinces, except that yerba maté and tobacco from Paraguay, Corrientes, and Misiones paid 10 percent, and brandy paid 6 percent.[23] Because the populace consumed many of these items in large quantities, the higher duties in Buenos Aires as well as in the Interior were designed to gain public revenues for provincial coffers.

Generally, the provinces taxed export goods to a lesser extent, thus encouraging the participation of Interior merchants in the staple economy. Port authorities at Buenos Aires merely made nominal charges on export goods arriving by riverboat. In the first six months of 1838, boat pilots paid only about 1 percent of their cargo's value in port taxes. Early in the nineteenth century, each province taxed the export of its own produce bound for Buenos Aires. Mendocino customs agents in 1816 taxed wine, and the Paraguayan treasury in Asunción taxed the export of tobacco.[24]

Multiple customs duties often raised the prices to consumers of even the necessities of life. Consequently, contraband in the overland and river trades developed, apparently on an extensive scale. Politicians in the riverine provinces, as elsewhere, desired protection of their native industries from foreign competition – yet they also argued with Governor Rosas at Buenos Aires to allow merchant ships to navigate the Paraná and Uruguay rivers. Rosas wanted all foreign vessels to stop at the Buenos Aires port, a policy that did not prevent a few French ships from reaching river ports in Entre Ríos, from where they transported salted hides for direct shipment to Le Havre.[25] After the fall of the Rosas government at Buenos Aires, provincial politicians agreed in the Acuerdo de San Nicolás of 1852 to eliminate all provincial customs duties. Thereafter, customshouses in the Interior closed down, and trade continued unfettered by costs over and above the expense of traditional transport. Ultimate reduction of internal customs further integrated the economy of the Interior with the staple export economy of Buenos Aires.

### Rawhide wheel rims

Given the rude technology of the day, the relative ease of travel overcame the immense distances and did permit the Interior's integration into a staple export economy. Freight transporters encountered mountains only between Jujuy and Potosí or between Mendoza and Chile. Over the rest of the region, packmules and carts traveled easily, if slowly, accounting for the Interior's incorporation into the porteño economic orbit (see Table 28). Nevertheless, oxcarting was a tradition-bound operation. Each wagon required three drivers, the chief of whom operated the thirty-foot bamboo prod suspended from the roof of the cart horizontally over the oxen. The second driver with a short goad rode on the yoke of the second pair of oxen, and the third traveled on horseback alongside the team. Each cart carried from 1.5 to 1.7 metric tons of produce to Buenos Aires, plus enough water in large earthen jars to sustain animals and crew over the dry areas of the road.[26]

Yet the very antiquity of traditional freight carrying reduced the effectiveness of Buenos Aires as a market for many of the Interior's products. Freight rates from Tucumán ranged from 200 to 229 silver pesos per oxcart. The carts, which cost about 50 pesos newly constructed, left Salta and Tucumán in April to May, when the water levels of the rivers began to fall. Teamsters avoided the dry months from July through October for lack of water and forage along the trails.[27] One expected the round trip to last up to twelve

Table 28. *Distances between Argentine cities on the principal post roads, 1830 (in kilometers)*

| Northern cart trail | | Western cart trail | |
|---|---|---|---|
| Buenos Aires–Córdoba | 975 | Buenos Aires–Esquina de Medrano, Córdoba | 745 |
| Córdoba–Santiago del Estero | 629 | Esquina–San Luis | 496 |
| Santiago–Tucumán | 223 | San Luis–Mendoza | 390 |
| Tucumán–Salta | 401 | Total | 1,632 |
| Salta–Jujuy | 100 | | |
| Total | 2,328 | | |

*Source: Almanaque político y de comercio de la Ciudad de Buenos Aires, 1830,* ed. by J. J. Blondel (Buenos Aires, 1830).

months. Oxcart caravans traveled from seventeen to thirty-three kilometers a day and covered the distance between Mendoza and Rosario, for example, in thirty-five to forty-five days. Breakdowns and lack of oxen along the route often extended a trip from Tucumán to Buenos Aires to three months. Once the cart train reached the port city, teamsters waited several months to secure a return cargo and paid local estancieros and farmers for grazing their oxen in the meanwhile.[28] Understandably, the costs of overland transport prohibited trade in certain commodities over long distances. Merchants in Tucumán, for example, could not profitably market tallow in Buenos Aires.[29]

Only the horse and the *galera,* a horse-drawn passenger coach, offered the traveler — but not bulk freight — a rapid passage between the cities of the Interior. Five galloping horses pulled the galera over the distance between Buenos Aires and Mendoza in fourteen days, the drivers stopping for fresh remounts at posthouses along the trail. Like the carts, these carriages were made entirely of wood and rawhide, and carriage makers wrapped the wheel rims in rawhide to protect the wooden wheels from wear.[30] Even the mounted mail courier — despite the hard riding and the change of ten to twelve horses a day — could not travel the distance between Buenos Aires and Mendoza in less than twelve days.[31] Passage of passengers and mail through the provinces was less cumbersome and costly than the movement of freight.

Cumbersome it may have been, but the traditional transport system promoted employment and essential services along the well-traveled freight routes. Owners of posthouses maintained grazing areas and water wells along the way so that draft animals easily found food when freight trains stopped at midday and at night. They often raised cattle and herded the replacement horses and oxen so essential to travel in the Interior. Farmers cultivated the fields surrounding each small village on the cart routes in order to provide for travelers and for the local populace, whereas blacksmiths in Córdoba and Tucumán made horseshoes for the mules and horses proceeding from the pampa onto the rocky trails leading to Salta.[32]

Helpful souls often suggested improving Interior communications by establishing additional roadhouses and spare oxen on the trails from Buenos Aires to Jujuy. But provincial rivalries prevented even the basic improvement and mainte-

*Cart train crossing the pampa, 1858.* Despite its increased use on the pampa and in the Interior, oxcarting remained unchanged from the colonial transport industry. Most carts constructed in Tucumán held approximately 1.5 metric tons of cargo. Its slow rate of speed (seventeen to thirty-three

nance of existing freight facilities. If one province put public monies into repairing cart trails and building wells at the posthouses, neighboring provinces often refused to reciprocate for the common weal.[33] Improvement of the Interior's freight routes required the type of interprovincial cooperation that was not forthcoming in the era of Argentine civil wars. Nevertheless, the Interior's generally level terrain permitted greater integration of hinterland and port in Argentina than was the case in any other Latin American country of the first half of the nineteenth century.[34] Despite their drawbacks, the oxen and packmules effectively bound the Interior provinces — each to a greater or lesser degree — to the growing staple economy of Buenos Aires (see Table 29).

Besides Buenos Aires itself, the riverine provinces enjoyed the greatest commercial prosperity in the region because traditional boat transport on the waterways of the

kilometers per day) notwithstanding, the oxcart effectively tied the economies of the Interior provinces to the staple export economy of Buenos Aires. (Watercolor by Leon Pallière, ca. 1858.)

Paraná River Basin proved more efficient for freight hauling than the oxcart. Even so, sailing upriver was laborious. A shallow-draft riverboat, sailing against the current, might travel the 1,780 kilometers of waterway between Buenos Aires and Asunción in about three months. The return trip was much briefer; Paraguayan riverboats heading out from Asuncion could reach Santa Fe within nine days and Buenos Aires in about twenty-one days. On a large boat of about three meters draft, the pilot carried up to fifty metric tons of yerba maté and other freight. Half the cargo was stowed below the deck and the other half was piled above deck and covered by a roof of sewn cowhides. If the boat went aground on one of the numerous sandbars, the Paraguayan sailors easily lightened the craft by removing the deck cargo.[35]

Occasionally, the presence of foreign warships interrupted the river trades. Porteño merchants, accustomed to sending tobacco, sugar, and paper to Corrientes and to investing the

Table 29. *Percentage of overland traffic between the Interior provinces and Buenos Aires, 1827–49 (in percent)*

|                     | 1827 | 1833 | 1849 |
|---------------------|------|------|------|
| *North*             |      |      |      |
| Córdoba             | 41.1 | 20.2 | 51.0 |
| Tucumán             | 16.2 | 9.0  | 14.0 |
| Santiago del Estero | 1.5  | 10.1 | 7.0  |
| Catamarca           | 1.5  | 4.5  | 4.7  |
| La Rioja            | —    | —    | —    |
| Salta–Jujuy         | 2.9  | 12.3 | 4.7  |
| *West*              |      |      |      |
| Mendoza             | 25.0 | 31.5 | 16.3 |
| San Luis            | 1.5  | 3.4  | 2.3  |
| San Juan            | 7.3  | 9.0  | —    |

*Sources:* Archivo General de la Nación, Buenos Aires, Sala 10, 37–2–17, "Hacienda-Aduana, entradas y salidas marítimas y terrestres, tomas de razón" (1826–8); Sala 10, 27–2–25, "Aduana, Hacienda, entrada y salida martíma y terrestre, tomas de razón" (1832–3); and Sala 10, 37–2–26, "Aduana, Hacienda, entradas martímas y terrestres" (1848–9). The figures represent the number of arrivals and departures, except for 1827, for which only arrivals are calculated.

proceeds of their sale in dried cowhides for export, found that the Anglo-French blockade of the river in 1839 made this barter exchange rather precarious, increasing the price of the dried hides at Goya from about 2 pesos fuertes each to 5.5. In the same blockade, ranchers in Entre Ríos who shipped wool to Buenos Aires had to pay boat charges of 10 pesos a day until the blockade was lifted.[36] Despite the occasional blockade and the ever-present drawbacks of wooden hulls and propulsion by sail, the riverboats of the Paraná River Basin effectively bound the riverine provinces to the staple economy of Buenos Aires. Even distant Paraguay, when not under the strictures of Francia's isolation policies, maintained commercial relations with the chief international port of southern South America (see Table 30).

### Saladeros and graserías

To a lesser extent than Buenos Aires, the provinces of the Interior were also influenced by the rise of the world economy, as both the Napoleonic conflicts and the industrial revolution in Europe set in motion certain price movements that gave the entire Río de la Plata a comparative advantage in producing pastoral raw materials. Foreign demand was so buoyant that Buenos Aires Province could not supply all the hides. Thus Mendoza, Tucumán, and Córdoba began shipping dried hides overland for embarkation at the port, where other pastoral products were arriving from the river provinces. Prices were important. A horsehide in Entre Ríos cost one shilling and, when shipped to England, brought seven or eight.[37] As in colonial days, goods for domestic consumption accompanied those export products that arrived in Buenos Aires from the Interior provinces. Porteño merchants received shipments of brandy, figs, and grapes from San Juan; cattlehides, goatskins, and raisins from Mendoza; hides, native textiles, and wool from Córdoba; hides and wool from San Luis; and hides, leather butts, and fur pelts from as far away as Salta and Tucuman. The river provinces shipped export products like hides, salted meat, and horsehair, and domestic goods like wheat, melons, and timber.[38] Approximately one-quarter of the value of all exports from the port of Buenos Aires came from the provinces, for provincial producers supplied half the horsehair exports, a third of the hides, and a fifth of the wool.[39] Yet these provinces also exported goods directly onto foreign ships at Rosario and

Table 30. *River traffic between Buenos Aires and the riverine provinces, 1810–60 (in percent)*

|                  | 1810 | 1820 | 1830 | 1840 | 1850 | 1860 |
|------------------|------|------|------|------|------|------|
| Banda Oriental   | 60.6 | 53.3 | 57.7 | 77.0 | 33.7 | 41.2 |
| Entre Ríos       | 24.7 | 16.7 | 23.6 | 11.5 | 35.4 | 20.8 |
| Santa Fe         | 8.4  | 10.0 | 8.8  | 8.3  | 24.1 | 16.8 |
| Corrientes       | 3.1  | 10.0 | 3.8  | 1.6  | 5.2  | 9.1  |
| Paraguay         | 1.6  | —    | —    | —    | —    | 6.0  |
| Others or unknown| 1.6  | 10.0 | 6.1  | 1.6  | 1.6  | 6.1  |

*Sources:* See various "Entradas y salidas de cabotaje," in Archivo General de la Nación, Buenos Aires, Sala 10, 36–8–9; Sala 10, 36–6–9; Sala 10, 37–1–1; Sala 10, 37–1–7; Sala 10, 37–3–7; Sala 10, 36–7–14, and Sala 10, 36–6–24. The percentages reflect the total number of arrivals and departures of rivercraft for the months of January and July only and exclude the riverboats that passed between Buenos Aires and river ports in Buenos Aires Province.

other river ports, and they shipped pastoral products to Montevideo for export. With the fall of the Potosí market shortly after 1810, the Interior provinces oriented themselves toward the Atlantic economy, stimulating growth both in pastoral production and in diversified domestic enterprise.

Because river transport effected a closer tie than overland trails to export markets at Buenos Aires and Montevideo, it is not surprising that the riverine provinces experienced a higher degree of staple development, commercial prosperity, and population growth than the other provinces of the Interior. For the most part, the ranching business was an ancient one in the Argentine mesopotamia, the region lying between the Uruguay and Paraná rivers. Jesuit missionaries taught cattle husbandry to the mission Indians of the region as early as 1600. At the time of the Revolution of 1810, several large estancias produced sizable herds of mules, horses, and cattle for the colonial market of Potosí. Enterriano ranchers suddenly found the Potosí market closed to them. Reorientation toward the Atlantic hide markets was not without colonial precedence, for Bajada de Paraná and other older river towns already had specialized in the slaughter of cattle for hides and tallow sold on international markets.[40]

Entre Ríos, Corrientes, and Santa Fe recovered rapidly from the revolutionary disturbances in the Litoral of Argentina. The Robertsons, English merchant brothers, organized the hide commerce in Entre Ríos and Corrientes, and thereafter, native traders assumed the collection and marketing of local goods for the export markets.[41] The provinces had been ravished by a series of confused civil wars among partisans of Gervasio Artigas, Portuguese and royalist troops, porteño armies, and followers of local caudillos. Ranchers and farmers began to return in the 1820s, and river commerce between Entre Ríos and Buenos Aires soon revived. Ranchers delivered hides and wood products to their agents in the port city and received rice, tobacco, sugar, and other goods on the return boats. Porteño capitalists were partly responsible for development of the ranching industry in the province, as they invested and owned many estancias in Entre Ríos.[42]

Enterrianos found ready outlets for their pastoral produce through the ports of Buenos Aires and Montevideo and eventually began their own processing industry. As early as 1834, riverboats brought the dried and salted meats and other products to Buenos Aires, where they were loaded onto ocean vessels bound for Brazilian markets at Bahía. Enterriano and *santafecino* merchants soon found an alternate port in Montevideo, especially when Buenos Aires was under foreign blockade. By midcentury, Entre Ríos annually was sending more than 250,000 dried and salted hides to Montevideo for export.[43] Although ranchers in 1840 still processed much of the cattle products on their estates, a few large saladeros, like the one owned by Justo José de Urquiza at Arroyo de Chino, slaughtered several hundred cattle a day and loaded the processed goods directly onto British ships for export. By 1850, Urquiza, governor of Entre Ríos and later president of Argentina, had developed his Santa Cándida saladero into a complex valued at 103,688 gold pesos and capable of processing 1,600 head of cattle and horses each month during the peak seasons.[44] Wheat growing and flour milling also had taken hold in Entre Ríos, as farmers and merchants in Gualiguay and Parana dispatched loads of flour aboard the rivercraft headed for Buenos Aires.[45] At midcentury, Entre Ríos boasted the existence of 4 million head of cattle and 2 million sheep, annual harvests of more than 1,600 metric tons of wheat, and a processing industry consisting of seventeen saladeros and graserías and thirty flour mills *(atahones)*.[46]

Like its neighboring river provinces, Corrientes also graduated from exporting dried hides to the rudimentary factory processing of cattle products for export. Already in 1811, the river port of Goyá had become the leading hide emporium in the provinces and foreign shoemakers, carpenters, and sailors had found a home in Corrientes, 1,200 kilometers up the Paraná River from the estuary. Local *correntino* merchants worried that English traders like the Robertsons might displace them in river commerce, but natives still retained their positions here and elsewhere in the provinces as retailers and hide collectors.[47] At midcentury, the processing techniques had also been adopted in Corrientes. One British estanciero maintained a steam vat capable of extracting 2,700 liters of grease from the bones of some 100 slaughtered bullocks, and several meat-salting plants appeared along the river, one of which had the capacity of processing the hides, meat, and bones of 200 animals a day.[48]

Santa Fe, meanwhile, developed not only as an important cattle-raising province, but also as the crucial commercial link between the northern and western provinces and the Atlantic shipping lanes. Provincial authorities promoted trade at the river port of Rosario in 1835 by eliminating most customs charges on goods from national and international ports. Soon a direct river trade between Montevideo and Rosario began to bypass Buenos Aires completely.[49] Rosario thrived modestly in the 1840s. Travelers reported watching stevedores moving cargoes over the forty-foot muddy embankment to eighteen or twenty vessels in the river beside the city. One could secure passage on a freight schooner from Buenos Aires to Rosario, dining on "tripe and maccaroni" provided by the Italian skipper. Rosario had become a major part of foreign trade on the Paraná River. In 1859, the weight of ocean ships departing the river port totaled 5,625 metric tons, while riverboats, which were far more numerous, totaled only some 2,030 tons. At the same time, oxcarts and packmules from the Interior provinces delivered 448 metric tons of cargo to the city.[50] In fact, the first railroad in the Interior was built between Córdoba and Rosario, entrepôt of overland freighting and the river trades.

### Wines tolerable but sweet

The other great entrepôt of the Interior's trade, through which passed the transit trade of Buenos Aires, Rosario, Mendoza, and Tucumán, was the city of Córdoba. But Córdoba also remained one of the principal producers of both export and domestic goods for the Buenos Aires marketplace. The province's governors fretted each time that civil war disrupted the vital trade to the Atlantic through Rosario and Buenos Aires because export products, by a three to one margin, formed a major portion of the province's trade. In 1820, Córdoba exported to Buenos Aires the following products (figures in silver pesos):[51]

| *manufactures* | | *export products* | |
|---|---|---|---|
| soap | 2,747 | cattlehides | 22,855 |
| ponchos | 6,669 | skins and pelts | 488 |
| blankets | 2,173 | horsehair | 428 |
| other | 673 | other | 13,076 |
| | 12,262 | | 36,847 |

Cordobes merchants never lost their markets in Buenos

Aires, Montevideo, and other provincial locales for their famous textile goods, *tejido del país*. In both 1829 and 1847, ponchos and blankets remained Córdoba's principal trade items, along with dried hides, raw wool, and leather butts.[52]

Whereas Buenos Aires and the Litoral had become the largest market for the province's domestic and export products, Córdoba carried on an important internal trade with other provinces. The cordobeses exported 36,847 silver pesos worth of freight to Buenos Aires in 1820 and another 18,296 pesos of goods to neighboring provinces. Manufactured textile goods were Córdoba's leading item of domestic trade, and merchants sold some 15,795 silver pesos worth of ponchos, blankets, and woven cloth to other provinces. Thus, Córdoba traded extensively with those provinces not having their own textile industry – Santa Fe and Buenos Aires. Córdoba also imported heavily from other provinces, up to 70,954 silver pesos in products and merchandise in 1820 – much of it in transit to Buenos Aires. Santa Fe sent yerba, and Catamarca traded in raw cotton, sandals, shoe leather, and tobacco. From Cuyo, Córdoba imported 9,890 pesos worth of wine and 7,165 pesos worth of brandy.[53]

Compared to the commercial bustle of Rosario and Córdoba, Mendoza's economic life in the nineteenth century appeared lethargic and depressed to many travelers. With its series of low mud fences enclosing farmers' fields outside the city, Mendoza remained an isolated agricultural oasis at the base of the Andes. Irrigation ditches conducted water runoff from melting Andean snow to orchards; vineyards; fields of corn, wheat, and tobacco; and pastures of clover. Wheat farmers packed their increasingly important crop of grain into bags made from sewn cowhides, and, by 1834, they had introduced waterwheels to grind wheat for domestic markets at San Luis and Buenos Aires.[54] Although Cuyo viticulture had a colonial heritage, the local wine was not yet comparable to European wines because the vines were little attended. Trade in brandy and raisins made from the grapes thus was more practical than wine. Foreign travelers judged the wine of Mendoza to be tolerable but rather sweet. Yet even the best domestic wines could not compete with foreign imports on the Buenos Aires marketplace, because the carriage over 1,600 kilometers of terrain lowered the quality of Cuyo wine and raised its price.[55]

Despite the loss of the porteño market for wine, the Cuyo provinces nevertheless carried on an active trade with the port city. In 1828, both Mendoza and San Juan provinces dispatched 784 metric tons of freight to Buenos Aires. Dried fruits, olives, and garlic composed most of the cargoes, but already a quarter of the freight consisted of wheat and flour, which thereafter continued to be Mendoza's chief sale items in Buenos Aires.[56] Although Mendoza sent the major portion of its brandy and dried fruit to Buenos Aires, the mendocinos traded actively with their provincial brethren, sending the largest shipments of wheat to San Luis and dispatching nearly all its hides to Chile. Córdoba and Santa Fe also received cargoes of Mendoza's wine and wheat. Cuyo was a staging area for the Chilean market across the cordilleras, and thousands of head of Argentine cattle, horses, and mules crossed the inhospitable Andes passes for sale in Santiago de Chile.[57] Landowners in San Luis had begun producing raw wool for export by midcentury, when local shopkeepers bought wool for about four reales per arroba (11.4 kilograms), paid about five reales freight charges to Buenos Aires, and sold it there for two pesos.[58] Cuyo trade thus was drawn to Buenos Aires, the leading export and domestic marketplace in the Río de la Plata region.

Consumers in other provinces also remained a crucial market for Mendoza's production. Mendocino merchants had found their way to Paraguay in 1811, where they sold wine and figs and bought tobacco and yerba in large volume. In the 1810–20 decade, Mendoza traded for leather butts from Córdoba, native textiles from Tucumán, and imported cotton goods from Buenos Aires. The wine and brandy of Cuyo found markets among the popular classes all over the Interior.[59] Political tensions with Chile ultimately caused a diminution of Mendoza's once-important trans-Andean commerce and a concurrent increase of trade with Buenos Aires. Mendoza's imports from Chile in 1833 dropped to just 6 percent of their 1826 level, while its trade with Buenos Aires nearly doubled.[60]

Tucumán, too, became inextricably connected to the rising domestic market, which needed the products of its timber and cart-building industry. A British traveler in 1825 reported that Tucumán's economy was recovering on the sale of lumber products to Buenos Aires, even though civil war and out-migration had drained the population by one-quarter. The leading labor sector in this locale consisted of the joiners, carpenters, smiths, and other handicraftsmen of the lumber industry.[61] Sugar milling in the 1830s came to employ several *trapiches,* or cane crushers, in which oxen powered the wooden grindstones that crushed cane for both sugar and brandy. Whereas the nascent sugar industry had yet to find a national market, tucumanos were able to sell their tobacco and other products in neighboring provinces.[62] By midcentury, Tucumán clearly had been incorporated into the Atlantic economy. Although imports from Buenos Aires rose from 88,067 gold pesos in 1850 to 99,144 in 1852, the Atlantic port was hardly the only customer of the tucumanos. A total of forty-eight oxcarts departed from Tucumán in 1850 with goods consigned to agents in Buenos Aires, and sixty-eight carts departed for other destinations.[63] Moreover, provincial customs records indicate that Tucumán's commerce did not profit from the naval blockades of Buenos Aires; in fact, trade fell off acutely during the blockades of 1826–7 and 1847–9, according to the following average annual customs receipts (in gold pesos) for the province of Tucumán:[64]

| | | | |
|---|---|---|---|
| 1816–20 | 38,864 | 1841–5 | 37,153 |
| 1821–5 | 22,429 | 1846–50 | 30,628 |
| 1826–30 | 19,678 | 1851–5 | 57,742 |
| 1831–5 | 19,093 | 1856–60 | 60,845 |
| 1836–40 | 22,020 | | |

Provincial economies suffered whenever the staple trade of Buenos Aires was disrupted.

Nineteenth-century commerce recovered slowly in those northern provinces, which had served the markets of Upper Peru in colonial times. Gone were the days when tucumano and salteño merchants commanded trade in foreign and domestic goods from Buenos Aires to Potosí and even to Peru and Chile. La Rioja and Catamarca in the Northwest appeared to have carried on little trade directly to the estuary, but their goods passed through Córdoba, the intermediary between the northern provinces and Buenos Aires. Catamarca's economy recovered with the advent of a strong provincial government in 1838 and the diminution of interprovincial conflict. Although its colonial export of raw cotton never recovered, Catamarca did increase its trade of tanned leather butts for the domestic market at Buenos Aires from

1,440 pieces in 1840 to 2,047 in 1850. La Rioja, outside the normal commercial channels, exchanged wine and oranges for cattle and foodstuffs from the surrounding provinces.[65]

In the Interior, economic recovery from the loss of Potosí's markets would not have occurred merely on the basis of interprovincial markets and independent of the growing domestic and export markets at Buenos Aires. Córdoba and Mendoza remained the principal overland trading partners of Buenos Aires throughout the first half of the nineteenth century. Although most provinces seemed to retain their share of the dwindling cart and mule commerce to the port city, much Interior trade at the same time was being diverted through the river entrepôt of Rosario (see Table 31).

Clearly, Buenos Aires became important to the Interior provinces not only as the emporium for the deposit of export products but also as the chief domestic consumer of a variety of artisan goods and articles of domestic supply. Moreover, the ability of the city to consume the Interior's products depended upon the health of the export trade. Porteños consumed no more of the Interior's artisan goods (ponchos, leather, carts) nor any more of its articles of supply (wheat, wine, charcoal) when the French blockade reduced foreign trade in 1839. Interruptions in the staple trade through the port affected the Interior as well, for fully 73 percent of the value of freight from the Interior consisted of export goods (see Table 32).

Table 31. *Origin of overland freight arriving at Buenos Aires, 1829*

| From (city) | Weight of freight (in metric tons) | Percent of total weight |
|---|---|---|
| Córdoba | 855 | 75.6 |
| Mendoza | 63 | 5.6 |
| San Juan | 61 | 5.4 |
| Tucumán | 133 | 11.8 |
| San Luis | 1 | 1.6 |
| Totals | 1,113 | 100.0 |

*Source:* Archivo General de la Nación, Buenos Aires, Sala 10, 42–8–5, "Censos" (1813–61), "Tablas generales de las tropas de carretas y arrias venidas del interior en 1829."

Table 32. *Content and value of the Interior's freight arriving at Buenos Aires,*
*1836–42 (in gold pesos)*

| Year | Export products | Artisan products | Domestic supply |
|---|---|---|---|
| 1836 2d half | 752,866 | 47,959 | 195,647 |
| 1837 1st half | 702,830 | 86,297 | 117,059 |
| 2d half | 678,524 | 55,990 | 228,918 |
| 1838 1st half | 461,453 | 69,187 | 144,386 |
| 1839 1st half | 48,570 | 27,055 | 49,065 |
| 2d half | 49,702 | 33,195 | 130,831 |
| 1841 1st half | 397,899 | 38,587 | 161,858 |
| 1842 1st half | 1,076,269 | 49,057 | 140,698 |
| Percentage of total Interior trade | 73 | 7 | 20 |

*Source:* Archivo General de la Nación, Buenos Aires, Sala 10, 42–10–11,
"Aduana, movimiento portuario" (1830–42). All figures, given in gold
pesos, have been corrected for inflation of paper currency. The year of the
French blockade of Buenos Aires was 1839.

## Hand looms and ponchos

Economic recovery of interprovincial trade meant the continued increase of the population of the Interior − a trend
inherited from the viceregal epoch. Argentina's populace
grew at a respectable rate of 2.47 percent per year, as the
estimated number of Argentines rose from 406,000 in 1809
to 1,304,000 in 1859. All the same, the region was relatively
underpopulated, for the size of its population at midcentury
was no greater than that of the island of Cuba.[66] Buenos
Aires and the riverine provinces, because they were the destinations of foreign immigration and domestic migration,
accounted for much of Argentina's population growth.
Travelers in the Interior noticed that some of the cart trains
carried up to 130 migrants (including women) bound for the
Litoral to find work.[67] Moreover, men from the provinces
who migrated often left their womenfolk behind, resulting in
skewed male−female ratios in the Interior. The population
of La Rioja in 1855 had only 88 men for every 100 women,
while in the Litoral provinces, the ratio was reversed. Buenos
Aires in 1869 had 124 men and Entre Ríos 114 men for
every 100 women.[68] Despite net out-migration, the pro-

vinces of the West and North increased their total population by an annual growth rate of 2.09 percent (see Table 33).

Population growth was an important factor in the development of a domestic market in Argentina and even enabled the native textile industry to survive an onslaught of cheap foreign cottons. Hand-woven textiles, a colonial manufacturing tradition in the Interior, continued to be produced in the first half of the nineteenth century because the popular classes persisted in wearing the traditional ponchos and *chiripás* (baggy cloth pants). In 1805, one of the principal artisan activities of Tucumán was the weaving of cotton and woolen ponchos, and the principal market for tucumano textiles was that great importer of foreign cloth, Buenos Aires.[69]

Compared to the mechanical production of textiles in Britain at the time, the manufacture of the colorful rugs and

Table 33. *Population growth of the Argentine provinces, 1809–69*

| Province | 1809 | 1869 | Annual population growth rate (in percent) |
|---|---|---|---|
| Buenos Aires | 92,000 | 495,107 | 3.15 |
| Santa Fe | 12,520 | 89,117 | 3.86 |
| Entre Ríos | 16,500 | 134,271 | 4.17 |
| Corrientes | 12,770 | 129,023 | 4.77 |
| Total Litoral | 133,790 | 847,518 | 3.63 |
| Mendoza | 21,492 | 65,413 | 1.95 |
| San Luis | 16,242 | 53,294 | 2.10 |
| San Juan | 22,220 | 60,319 | 1.74 |
| Total West | 59,954 | 179,026 | 1.91 |
| Córdoba | 60,000 | 210,508 | 2.23 |
| Santiago del Estero | 40,500 | 132,898 | 2.10 |
| Tucumán | 35,900 | 108,953 | 1.95 |
| Catamarca | 24,300 | 79,962 | 2.10 |
| La Rioja | 12,619 | 48,746 | 2.43 |
| Salta | 26,270 | 88,933 | 2.16 |
| Jujuy | 12,278 | 40,379 | 2.10 |
| Total North | 211,867 | 710,379 | 2.14 |

*Source: Jorge Ruiz Comandrán, Evolución demográfica argentina durante el período hispano (1535–1810)* (Buenos Aires, 1969), p. 115; and Ernesto J. A. Maeder, *Evolución demográfica argentina de 1810–1869* (Buenos Aires, 1969), p. 34 ff.

ponchos on Argentine hand looms appears rudimentary. In the 1820s, Córdoba's weavers still colored their yarn with vegetable dyes, soot, and dried cakes of cochineal. The handicraft industry depended entirely on individual women who slowly turned out coarse flannels on single-person hand looms after first spinning the yarn on hand spindles. Travelers commonly encountered individual female weavers at posthouses and farms along the trails. Santiago del Estero, another native textile center, lost some markets during the civil war decades of the 1810s and 1820s, but at midcentury the santiagueños still producted ponchos, saddle cloths, and blankets for sale in neighboring provinces. In addition, approximately 4,500 kilograms of cochineal from Santiago del Estero annually reached other handicraft weavers in Chile and Peru.[70] The traditional textile industry of other provinces also endured, although they may not have grown. In fact, Catamarca's famous textile weavers were insufficient in number to clothe their own population, so that the province's chief imports became not only foreign cloth from Buenos Aires but also the domestic cotton and woolen manufactures of Córdoba.[71] In the 1850s, Córdoba maintained its textile industry by marketing ponchos, blankets, and rugs in the other provinces of the Río de la Plata. The traditional manufacture of native textiles in the Interior did not grow much in the succeeding railroad age nor in the modern industrial age. But neither did the hand weavers in isolated country cottages of the Interior form the basis of the modern Argentine textile industry. Industrial spinning and weaving began after the dawn of the twentieth century at the heart of the staple export trade and in the chief international port, Buenos Aires.

During the first half of the nineteenth century, the Interior provinces underwent a reorientation of their economies away from Potosí and toward the rising staple trade at Buenos Aires and the estuary. Neither civil war, internal customs barriers, nor distance prevented integration with the Atlantic system — except that the connection was imperfect. The low technological level of the traditional modes of transportation placed a ceiling on the extent of actual consolidation of the national marketplace in Argentina. The river provinces experienced heady rates of expansion in terms of economic prosperity and population growth, while these provinces connected by overland transport to the Atlantic market participated in the staple trade to lesser degrees. For them, interprovincial exchange remained important and, without doubt, the sheer distance to Buenos Aires contributed to economic stagnation in Salta and Jujuy in the far Northwest, where trade with the mining regions of Upper Peru had diminished severely. Yet it is undeniable that the economies of the Interior provinces would not have recovered at all from the disruptions of the revolutionary and civil wars, had not the domestic consumers and export merchants of Buenos Aires offered alternate and growing markets for domestic manufactures, foodstuffs, and pastoral products. If the commercial connection was imperfect, then it remained for the railroad and steamship to promote a greater integration of the Interior of Argentina and the Atlantic economy. That occurred after 1860.

# Conclusion:
# the arrival of modern technology

The commercialization of Buenos Aires by 1860 had reached a technological plateau that limited the extension of economic growth on a national scale. Lack of modern port facilities meant a continued reliance on slow, hand-loading cargo procedures. Development of Buenos Aires as the regional trade center also met barriers in the form of congested marketplaces and expensive traditional modes of transportation. Only the riverine provinces, connected to the estuary by navigable waterways, participated fully in any increments to Atlantic shipping. Hampered by high transport costs, the Interior could hope to develop few new enterprises to serve either foreign trade or the major regional market at Buenos Aires. Frontier expansion, both socially and productively, had been impressive on the porteño pampa, yet no cattlemen had settled the far reaches of the province, let alone the vast stretches that lay south and west of Bahía Blanca. Without technological change, little opportunity existed for further diversification of the staple economy. Integration of a vigorous national market and additional settlement of virgin territory would have been slow.

The short rail line inaugurated at Buenos Aires in 1857 proved the harbinger of a new age for the entire Río de la Plata, and in the next half-century, modern technology transformed the economy. Soon railway traffic reached all portions of the porteño pampa, passing between the port and the Andean provinces in northern and western Argentina on nearly 16,100 kilometers of track in 1900 and on 34,500 kilometers by 1914.[1] Between the steam railroad on the prairies and steam navigation in the Paraná River Basin, new transport technology had far-reaching effects. Primarily, freight rates were radically reduced, encouraging greater domestic exchange. Steamboats plying the river trade in 1914 had undercut the freight rates of the old sailing barks by more than 600 percent. Railways effected comparable sav-

225

ings in overland freighting and actually reduced the physical distance between the provinces. Whereas the cart trail between Mendoza and Buenos Aires was 1,632 kilometers long, the rail line constructed between the two cities in 1895 was only 1,048. By 1910, Argentine railways carried 71 million passengers and 37 million tons of freight per year.[2]

Economical freight carriage broke through the spatial limits of rural production. Sheep raising moved west and especially south to the Patagonia, and cattle raising too had undergone transformation. Estancieros in Santa Fe and Córdoba provinces now specialized in breeding cattle, and those wealthy ranchers owning property in the lush pampa of Buenos Aires Province took to fattening yearlings for market.[3] Cattle drives to the stockyards had ceased, and livestock now arrived in rail cars. Farm production, also freed of its locational bounds, expanded readily. In the 1890s, Argentine producers from Santa Fe and Bahía Blanca began to send their wheat harvests to port on the railways. Cultivation of crops had expanded to some 20 million hectares of land by 1910, and Argentina was exporting nearly 2 million metric tons of wheat and an additional 111,000 tons of milled flour.[4] Once an importer of flour, Argentina now boomed on the export of wheat and a variety of staple grains.

Other technological advances followed the railroad to Argentina. Machinery and water pumps assisted farmers in increasing agricultural production and aided ranchers in ameliorating the effects of drought. Barbed wire fences enclosed fields and pastures and separated fine breeding stock. Construction of the harbor at Buenos Aires in the 1890s enabled the use of modern freight-handling equipment, so that foreign sea captains now tied up in their steam-powered vessels to berths at the very edge of the city. The Atlantic's new steam and steel ships plus the invention of refrigeration compressors made yet another staple-processing activity possible for the region — meat packing. Exports to meat-hungry Europeans of frozen and chilled mutton burgeoned and the popularity of Argentine beef in Europe encouraged estancieros to replace the native Longhorns with Shorthorn and Hereford stock. The obsolete saladeros were shut down by 1900. On the eve of the First World War, the new meat refrigeration plants were producing 368,986 metric tons of chilled beef and 58,688 tons of mutton for export.[5] Integration of the national market — final-demand linkage was strengthened by population increase and technological innovation — held out new economic possibilities for the Interior. Notably, Mendoza expanded wine manufacturing, and Tucumán developed its sugar industry to serve the national market. From 1860 to 1910, technological advance acted as the catalyst to further economic diversification, and the backward and forward linkages of new staple production broadened the prosperity of the Río de la Plata region.

One pattern of economic expansion remained from the era of traditional technology. Despite development of port facilities at Bahía Blanca and Rosario, economic and social life continued to focus on Greater Buenos Aires, an urban center whose population reached 1.5 million by 1910. It remained the major international entrepôt. Steam and sail navigation in the Paraná River Basin terminated at Buenos Aires and, to a lesser extent, at Montevideo. Rail trackage in 1910 connected every province in the nation to Buenos Aires — but not necessarily to the other provinces — and Buenos Aires remained the center of cattle processing, marketing, and warehousing. The arrival of 2.9 million immigrants between 1880 and 1914 merely reinforced the port city as the region's dominant domestic market.[6]

Whereas new technology permitted further expansion and diversification of production, its other characteristics added wholly new tendencies to the region's economic infrastructure. Prior to 1860, the traditional technology of domestic transportation, production, and processing was relatively cheap. In the Río de la Plata, creole and immigrant entrepreneurs were responsible for the development of production and marketing, whereas ranch production and cattle processing expanded because of native investment and management. Foreigners served only as the necessary — though hardly dominating — link to overseas markets for Argentine raw materials.

Modern technology, on the other hand, was foreign. Steam locomotives, rolling stock, and the iron rails over which the trains traveled came from abroad. At the turn of the century, Argentines were importing all their farm machinery, milling equipment, and steam engines. Natives neither manufactured modern equipment nor had the operating knowledge of the technological advances that stimulated their economy. Foreign technicians ran most of the railways and meat-packing plants. New technology also was costly, and importation of foreign capital, a rare phenomenon prior to 1860, became commonplace thereafter. British, French, and American financiers established themselves in Argentine banks with connections abroad. Fully 40 percent of all British prewar investment in Latin America was going to Argentina.[7] Foreign companies operated gasworks, electrical plants, urban tramways, and telegraph and telephone systems throughout the region. Economic expansion attracted massive immigration and promoted formation of a larger domestic market, yet Creole and immigrant entrepreneurs had relinquished control of much of the region's marketing and processing structure.

Native Argentines, however, did retain their dominance of agricultural and pastoral production. Rapid rural expansion following the Indian campaign of 1879 produced surpluses in Argentina's balance of trade.[8] Natives turned these profits back into the land and introduced livestock and plows to yet more virgin territory. Yet rising prices and wholesale speculation quickly put land out of reach of most rural residents. Wheat farming was accomplished on large ranches rather than exclusively on small farms. The resulting incidence of tenant farming seems to have dampened opportunity in some parts of the pampa, and the arrival of foreign laborers marginalized many native-born workers in the countryside.[9] Social opportunity seemed to be shifting to the cities.

Argentina's growing economy tended to absorb numbers of immigrants in the newer, expanding sectors. Many immigrants went into agricultural occupations (11.7 percent between 1895 and 1910) and into commercial trades (8.9 percent), but a greater number worked in manufacturing and crafts (17.3 percent).[10] Foreigners who crowded into Buenos Aires and other cities found opportunities as proprietors, managers, and workers in expanding shops and industries. Although foreigners shunned traditional native enterprises, 40.9 percent of all landowners in 1914 were still foreign born. More than three-quarters of the manufacturers and shopkeepers were aliens, and 62 percent of the wine producers were foreigners.[11] Furthermore, the immigrant found jobs, better wages, and possibilities of advancement as an urban worker. Although unemployment seemed rather high

(6.7 percent in 1913), real wages averaged about 25 percent more than those earned by workers in Paris. Suburban home ownership became a reality for many skilled workers, for an expert mechanic in Buenos Aires was able to buy a lot and built a house after saving regularly for a decade.[12]

Immigrants settled in the cities as well as on the prairies of Argentina. Buenos Aires city registered the greatest increases in population, and the national capital in 1914 contained more than 1.5 million persons. The next largest Argentina city, Rosario, had a population of only 222,592. Still, forty-seven other Argentine cities had more than 10,000 persons each. In fact, more than half Argentina's residents lived in urban settings by the second decade of the twentieth century.[13]

Do these socioeconomic trends beginning with the arrival of the railroad mean that Argentines suddenly discovered themselves in a "dependent" or "neocolonial" status? After all, foreign technology was found in nearly all sectors of the economy. Again, the historical analysis of dependency theory does not seem appropriate to La Plata's economic development. Modern technology, although foreign, did enlarge the domestic economic base, and new staple production caused linkage effects of wider intensity. At the outbreak of the First World War, Argentina added meat packing, wheat farming, wine making, and sugar refining to the existing hide and wool trade. All the economic indicators pointed to impressive growth rates (see Table 34). This export nation even enjoyed diversified markets despite close commercial ties to Great Britain, for nearly 76 percent of Argentine exports in 1909–13 were going to countries other than the United Kingdom.[14] Expanding staple exports ultimately induced industrialization.

The story of Argentine manufacturing was one of remarkable expansion throughout the staple era and of self-sustained industrialization in the 1930s. Scholars of Argentine history often provide a variety of explanations that emphasize the discrepancies and pathologies in industrial growth: control of capital and commercial assets by a landowning elite little interested in manufacturing, foreign investment only in the export and food-processing industries, government indifference toward industrial development, lack of political clout among immigrant manufacturers, and

Table 34. *Indicators of economic growth in Argentina, 1880–1914 (annual rate of growth in percent)*

| Indicator | Annual growth |
| --- | --- |
| Population [a] | 3.5 |
| Urbanization [b] | 5.4 |
| Railroad trackage [c] | 10.6 |
| Wheat exports [d] | 9.9 |
| Value of exports [e] | 15.2 |
| Value of imports [e] | 6.8 |
| Manufacturing product [f] | 9.3 |
| Gross Domestic Product [g] | 5.0 |

[a] From Comisión nacional de censos, *Tercer censo nacional 1914,* 10 vols. (Buenos Aires, 1916–19), Vol. 8, p. 16.

[b] Based on the Argentine census years of 1895 and 1914 in *Tercer censo,* Vol. 1, p. 119.

[c] From *Tercer censo,* Vol. 10, pp. 406–7.

[d] Based on average annual export, 1876–80 and 1910–14 in *Censo industrial y comercio,* boletín no. 17 (Buenos Aires, 1913), p. 9.

[e] Based on average annual values, 1876–80 and 1910–14, in *Tercer censo,* Vol. 8, p. 16.

[f] From Comisión directiva del censo, *Segundo Censo de la Repúblic Argentina 1895,* 3 vols. (Buenos Aires, 1898), Vol. 3, p. 271; and *Tercer censo,* Vol. 7, pp. 27–34.

[g] Estimate of Carlos F. Díaz Alejandro, *Essays on the Economic History of the Argentine Republic* (New Haven, Conn., 1970), p. 3.

competition from the import of foreign consumers goods.[15] Despite these handicaps, Argentine industry did make an impressive 276 percent gain in production between 1900–04 and 1925–30.[16]

Domestic processing of a variety of agricultural commodities introduced a pool of new technologies, whereas greater urbanization, improved communication, and the creation of investment capital stimulated nascent industry in Buenos Aires and the Litoral. In the 1890s, censuses show that tanneries, blacksmith shops, carpentry and metalworking plants, cigarette and match factories, burlap bag works, and shoe and shirt manufactories had developed to meet the needs of a wider domestic market. Immigration obviously was a boon in terms of labor and entrepreneurship, as ownership of domestic industries belonged principally to immigrants and foreign residents. In 1910, only 21 percent of all owners were Argentine born.[17] Although social conventions may not have conferred prestige upon those natives who chose careers in industry, immigrant entrepreneurship seems to have redressed the imbalance. Initially, Argentina's food processors gained overwhelming predominance in modern manufacturing. Flour milling, meat packing, wine pressing, and sugar refining had become the dynamic industries of the era. Together these four food-processing industries in 1914 commanded 10 percent of all industrial capital, 12 percent of the laborers, 18 percent of the motive power, and 35 percent of the production.[18] Although the flour and wine businesses were the provinces of native and immigrant entrepreneurs, much of the sugar-refining and especially the meat-packing industries remained under the control of foreign managers, who had little interest in spreading their technologies to other domestic industries.[19] Yet, industry benefited from a staple-induced growth in the domestic money market. By 1913, 143 banks operated in Argentina with capital assets of more than 552 million gold pesos. Of total capital investment, 28.3 percent was going into agriculture and cattle raising, 17.5 percent into railroads, and 8.4 percent into domestic industry.[20] Because capital formation was not sluggish at the time, industry appeared to receive its share of investment funds.

Argentina's consumer industries also grew impressively, despite obvious handicaps, as the national economy became integrated. Lacking both coal and iron ore deposits, the country had to import much of the raw materials and energy resources for its secondary industry. In 1910 alone, Argentine manufacturers utilized over 80 million gold pesos worth of foreign raw materials — nearly two-fifths of all the materials used in industry. In fact, the iron and steel manufacturers depended upon foreign sources for nearly 80 percent of their raw materials.[21] For the moment, Argentina's growth potential in consumer manufacturing appeared limited by the lack of domestic natural resources. Thus, the First World War temporarily set back industrial growth. The European war dried up traditional foreign sources of investment, machinery, and raw materials. Moreover, Argentina's staple economy suffered a severe contraction — including an unemployment rate of 19.4 percent in 1914.[22]

Following wartime setbacks, the Argentine economy resumed both its vigorous staple development and its industrial growth in the 1920s. Foreign capital inflows, railway building, immigration, and expansion of the domestic capital market continued their prewar trends. Little new territory was opened up to agricultural exploitation after the war, but rising capital investment in agricultural machinery and a developing regional specialization in breeding and fattening cattle for the meat packers improved rural productivity. Meat packing continued to expand in the 1920s with a new influx of U.S. investments. The arrival of the automobile industry added to the vigor of Argentina's light industries, also evidenced by the growth of the shoe and textile plant of Alpargatas, S.A., of the Frasers, a third generation Scot-Argentine family, and the expansion of Sociedad Industrial Americana de Maquinarías (SIAM) of the immigrant Torcuato di Tella. By 1930, Argentina had made progress toward alleviating its dependency on foreign sources of energy. The creation of the state-owned oil enterprise Yacimientos Petrolíferos Fiscales (YPF), helped the country to cut its per capita use of foreign coal and to supply more than half its petroleum requirement.[23] Argentina's economic growth in the 1920s even outstripped that of most "industrial" nations. The annual growth rate of the Gross Domestic Product of the country equaled 6.7 percent.[24]

Argentine industry ultimately overcame most of the weaknesses of its earlier dependence on foreign investment and raw material imports. For the worldwide depression of the 1930s provided the springboard for self-sustained industrial growth in Argentina. The share of manufacturing in national income had grown from 20 percent in 1910 to 45 percent in 1930. In the mid-1930s, total industrial product finally surpassed agricultural product, principally because of the performance of a host of consumer and light-engineering industries.[25] Meanwhile, the profusion of trucks and road building finally replaced the oxcart in the national transport system. Argentina, the former agrarian nation par excellence, entered the pantheon of industrial nations largely as a result of its prior staple export development.

The staple model of growth would seem more relevant to an analysis of Argentina's preindustrial economic development than the dependency model. Production for export after 1860 continued. to diversify and broaden the region's commercial and production infrastructure, a pattern of growth that had begun in the colonial period. Both the export of foodstuffs to Upper Peru and the silver trade out of Potosí provided the rationale for European settlement and commercial development in the Río de la Plata. Buenos Aires' connection with Atlantic shipping, established by the illegal silver trade, eventually fostered the pastoral industries of the Litoral. Then, the European and North American revolutions in manufacturing of the first half of the nineteenth century further stimulated rural production in the region, and exports of hides, wool, and a variety of pastoral goods more than replaced the deteriorating silver trade through the port. Ranching, marketing, and processing – despite the limitations of traditional technology – all expanded to support the export sector. Finally, the modern technology let loose by the industrial revolution reached the Río de la Plata in the years following 1860. Existing trends in population growth, settlement of virgin territories, and expansion of the domestic market quickened. New technology, even though controlled by foreigners, extended economic activity to the Interior and broadened Argentina's exports. It proved the catalyst for continuing growth and ultimately for industrialization.

Argentina's recent economic and social development has been obfuscated more by government policies and political conditions than at any time prior to the Second World War. More than anyone, the politician Juan Domingo Perón introduced the new age, for largely under his aegis the government has gained formal control of the economic apparatus. Bureaucrats determine export policies, monetary exchange, and domestic investment. In addition to the elaborate public welfare system, they manage the public utilities, domestic transport, and the state industries in electrical power, steel, and petroleum. The government has become the leading sector in the economy, and in a country that has had fourteen heads of state between 1955 and 1978, that fact has produced mixed results. The politicization of labor unions often saps the productivity of the individual worker, while uncontrollable inflation creates an ongoing crisis in falling real wages, flight of domestic capital, agricultural and industrial sluggishness, emigration of native technicians and professionals, and not a little political unrest. Meanwhile, multinational corporations – the most recent form of foreign capital investment – derive much strength from their immunity to domestic Argentine politics.[26] Formal staple theory can contribute little to the analysis of such political and economic complexities.

The task before Argentine planners is not a simple one: to balance continued industrial development with the country's considerable agricultural potential in an era of high political expectations. Having experienced industrial revolution and state intervention, the Argentines long since have lost their economic innocence.

# Appendix A: Conversion tables

## Money

The gold peso, equal to the colonial silver peso or *peso fuerte,* is the standard monetary unit used throughout this study. Paper money of Argentina printed in the national period is converted to the peso fuerte according to the tables of inflation in Juan Alvarez, *Temas de historia económica argentina* (Buenos Aires, 1914), pp. 99–101; and Jacinto Oddone, *La burguesía terrateniente argentina* (Madrid, 1935), p. 149.

| 1 gold peso | = | 1 silver peso | = | 1 peso fuerte |
|---|---|---|---|---|
| 1 gold peso | = | U.K. 4s sterling | = | U.S. $1   (1855) |
| 1 peso | = | 8 reales | | |

## Weights

| Argentine | English | Metric |
|---|---|---|
| 1 arroba | 25 lb. | 11.4 kg. |
| 1 quintal | 100 lbs. | 45.45 kg. |
| 1 tercio | 190 lb. | 86.4 kg. |
| 1 zurrón | 190 lb. | 86.4 kg. |
| 1 barrica (wheat) | 169.3 lb. | 76.9 kg. |
| 1 fanega (wheat) | 225 lb. | 102.3 kg. |
| 1 fardo | 1000 lb. | 454.5 kg. |
| 88 arrobas | 2202.4 | 1 metric ton |

## Capacity

| Argentine | English | Metric |
|---|---|---|
| 1 fanega | 3.9 bu. | 141.8 l. |
| 1 pipa (wine) | 120 gal. | 480 l. |
| 1 arroba | | 35.7 l. |

## Distance

| Argentine | English | Metric |
|---|---|---|
| 1 vara | 1 yd. | .84 m. |
| 1 legua | 3.23 mi. | 5.57 km. |

## Area

| Argentine | English | Metric |
|---|---|---|
| 1 legua cuadrada | 10.4 sq. mi. | 2693.6 ha. |
| 1 cuadra cuadrada | | 114.2 ha. |

235

# Appendix B: The districts of the province of Buenos Aires and the zones of production, 1838 and 1854

### Agricultural zone (more than 100 persons per square league)

| 1838 | 1854 | |
|---|---|---|
| Quilmes | Barracas al Sud | Las Conchas |
| San José de Flores | Quilmes | Dolores |
| San Antonio de Areco | Ranchos | Pergamino |
| San Isidro | San José de Flores | San Antonio de Giles |
| San Fernando | San Antonio de Areco | Villa Luján |
| Las Conchas | San Fernando | San Nicolás |
| Dolores | | |

### Mixed zone (from 41 to 99 persons per square league)

| 1838 | | 1854 | |
|---|---|---|---|
| Ranchos | Exaltación de la Cruz | Ensenada | Lobos |
| Morón | (Capilla del Señor) | Cañuelas | Pilar |
| Villa Luján | San Pedro | Morón | Exaltación de |
| Navarro | Pergamino | Fortín de Areco | la Cruz |
| San Antonio | San Nicolás | Mercedes | San Pedro |
| de Giles | | Chivilcoy | Zarate |
| | | Navarro | Baradero |

### Ranching zone (from 1 to 40 persons per square league)

| 1838 | | 1854 | |
|---|---|---|---|
| Ensenada | Matanzas | Magdalena | Bahía Blanca |
| Cañuelas | Fortín de Areco | Chascomús | Saladillo |
| Magdalena | Salto | San Vicente | Tapalqué |
| Chascomús | Lobos | Monte | Azul |
| San Vicente | Arrecifes | Pila | Tuyú |
| Monte | Pilar | Tordillo | Patagones |
| Tandil | Rojas | Ajó | Matanzas |
| Azul | Baradero | Mar Chiquita | Bragado |
| Bahía Blanca | Monsalvo | Lobería | Salto |
| Patagones | | Vecino | 25 de Mayo |
| | | Tandil | Junín (Federación) |
| | | Las Flores | Rojas |
| | | Monsalvo | Arrecifes |

Sources: For 1838, Archivo General de la Nación (AGN), Buenos Aires, Sala 10, 25-6-2, "Censo de habitantes. Capital y provincia de Buenos Aires" (1838). For 1854, *Registro estadístico de Buenos Aires, 1854,* p. 11; and AGN, Sala 10, 42-8-5, "Censos" (1813−61).

# Notes

The following abbreviations and short titles are used throughout the notes.

AGN                  Archivo General de la Nación, Buenos Aires. Manuscript documents are usually numbered according to the section (*sala*), the bundle (*legajo*; shown with three numbers, separated by hyphens), occasionally the file (*expediente*), and title (including, if applicable, collection and letter number), and place and date. Example: AGN, Sala 7, 16-4-8 (E. 1), Colección Ruiz Guiñazú (1541), Rosas to Terrero (Matanza, 2 Nov. 1813).

*Almanaque*        *Almanaque Político y de Comercio de la Ciudad de Buenos Aires.* Ed. by J. J. Blondel, Buenos Aires, 1826–36.

ANH, *Primer congreso*   Academia Nacional de la Historia, *Primer congreso de historia argentina y regional.* Buenos Aires, 1973.

"Annual Reports"     U.S. Treasury, "Annual Reports of Commerce and Navigation of the United States," in *Executive Documents* of the U.S. Senate and House of Representatives. Washington, D.C., 1822–62.

*Annual Statement*    Great Britain, Statistical Office. *Annual Statement of the Trade and Navigation of the United Kingdom with Foreign Countries and the British Possessions* (date of year covered in italics, year published in parentheses). London, 1855–63.

Archivo Anchorena    AGN, Sala 7, Archivo de Don Juan E. Anchorena y sucesores. 1810–19.

F.O. 6             Great Britain, Public Records Office, *General Correspondence; Argentine Republic* (F.O. 6). Microfilm.

MG                Manuel Gondra Manuscript Collection of the University of Texas Library. Manuscripts are given as "MG" with their numbers, such as MG 391.

*REBA*            *Registro Estadístico de Buenos Aires.* Buenos Aires, 1854–64.

## Introduction: Argentina in the era of traditional technology

1. The most recent works in economic "dependency" are Stanley J. and

237

Barbara H. Stein, *The Colonial Heritage of Latin America* (New York, 1970); Osvaldo Sunkel and Pedro Paz, *El subdesarrolo latinoamericano y la teoría del desarrollo* (México, 1970); and James D. Cockcroft, André Gunder Frank, and Dale L. Johnson, *Dependence and Underdevelopment* (Garden City, N.Y., 1972). For pioneer works on the theory, see Fernando Henrique Cardoso and Enzo Faletto, *Dependencia y desarrollo en America Latina* (Lima, 1967); and André Gunder Frank, *Capitalism and Underdevelopment in Latin America* (New York, 1967). On the application of the dependency model to Argentine history, see Liborio Justo, *Nuestra patria vasalla: De los Borbones a Baring Brothers* (Buenos Aires, 1968); Jose María Rosa, *Análisis histórico de la dependencia argentina* (Buenos Aires, 1974); Andrés M. Carretero, *Orígenes de la dependencia económica argentina* (Buenos Aires, 1974); and Juan Eugenio Corradi, "Argentina," in Ronald H. Chilcote and Joel C. Edelstein, eds., *Latin America: The Struggle with Dependency and Beyond* (Cambridge, Mass., 1974).

2. To be sure, the dependency "model" is not so well delineated. Within the dependency school, some theorists reject the notion that dependent growth everywhere promotes labor oppression, constriction of the domestic market, and a constant reproduction of underdevelopment. See Fernando Henrique Cardoso, "The Consumption of Dependency Theory in the United States," *Latin American Research Review,* vol. 23, no. 3 (1977), p. 19. For an excellent review of the current economic and political aspects of dependency theory, see C. Richard Bath and Dilmus D. James, "Dependency Analysis of Latin America: Some Criticisms, Some Suggestions," *Latin American Research Review,* vol. 11, no. 3 (1975), pp. 3—54.

3. Harold A. Innis, *The Fur Trade in Canada* (Toronto, 1930). Economist Melville H. Watkins had done more than anyone else to formalize staple theory in "A Staple Theory of Economic Growth," *Canadian Journal of Economics and Political Science,* vol. 29, no. 2 (May 1963), pp. 144—58. Also see Douglass C. North, *The Economic Growth of the United States, 1790—1860* (Englewood Cliffs, N.J., 1961); and Robert E. Baldwin, *Economic Development and Export Growth: A Study of Northern Rhodesia, 1920—1960* (Los Angeles, 1966).

4. Archibald R. M. Ritter, *The Economic Development of Revolutionary Cuba* (New York, 1974); and Michael Roemer, *Fishing for Growth: Export-led Development in Peru, 1950—1967* (Cambridge, Mass., 1970).

5. Roberto Cortés Conde, *The First Stages of Modernization in Spanish America* (New York, 1974); Ezequiel Gallo, "Agrarian Expansion and Industrial Development in Argentina, 1880—1930," in Raymond Carr, ed., *Latin American Affairs* (London, 1970), pp. 45—61; Guido di Tella and Manuel Zymelman, *Los etapas del desarrollo economico argentino* (Buenos Aires, 1967), pp. 4—12; and Carlos F. Díaz Alejandro, *Essays on the Economic History of the Argentine Republic* (New Haven, Conn., 1970), chap 1.

6. Albert O. Hirschman, *The Strategy of Economic Development* (New Haven, Conn., 1958), chap. 6.

1. Silver and contraband in the colonial Río de la Plata

1. Acarete du Biscay, *Account of a Voyage up the River de la Plata and Thence Overland to Peru* (London, 1698; reprinted, North Haven, Conn., 1968), pp. 43—5; and Gwendolin B. Cobb, "Supply and Transportation for the Potosi Mines, 1545—1640," *Hispanic American Historical Review,* vol. 24, no. 1 (February 1949), p. 26; and Lewis Hanke, *The Imperial City of Potosi* (The Hague, 1956), p. 1.

2. See calculations for the period 1556—1783 by Lamberto de Sierra, the treasurer of Potosí, in *Colleccíon de documentos inéditos para la historia de España* (Madrid, 1842—95), vol. 5, pp. 170—84; and Herbert S. Klein, "Structure and Profitability of Royal Finance in the Viceroyalty of the Rio de la Plata in 1790," *Hispanic American Historical Review,* vol. 52, no. 3 (August 1973), pp. 444—5. Both have created a series of official tax returns equal to a fifth and later a tenth of all production taxed by the royal authorities in Potosí.

3. Vicente Pazos, *Letters on the United Provinces of South America,* trans. by Platt H. Crosby (New York and London, 1819), pp. 136—8; Magnus Mörner, *The Political and Economic Activities of the Jesuits in the La Plata Region, Hapsburg Era,* trans. by Albert Read (Stockholm, 1953), p. 50; and Cobb, "Supply and Transportation," pp. 33, 40.

4. MG 791, Juan José de Priego y Caro, "Carta a S. M. dando noticias de probables invasiones portuguesas . . .," copy (Plata, 8 January 1775), p. 3.

5. Alberto Sánchez-Albornoz, *La saca de mulas de Salta al Perú, 1778—1808* (Rosario, 1965), p. 293. For description of the Salta mule fairs, see Concolorcorvo (Alfonso Carrió de la Bandera), *El Lazarillo: A Guide for Inexperienced Travelers between Buenos Aires and Lima — 1773,* trans. by Walter D. Kline (Bloomington, Ind., 1965), pp. 100—35. Also see Oscar Schmieder, "The Historic Geography of Tucumán," *University of California Publications in Geography,* vol. 2, no. 12 (Berkeley, 1928), p. 384; and Tulio Halperín-Donghi, *Revolución y guerra: formación de una élite dirigente en la argentina criolla* (Buenos Aires, 1972), p. 17.

6. Jorge Comandrán Ruiz, *Evolución demográfica argentina durante el período hispánico (1535—1810)* (Buenos Aires, 1969), pp. 80—1.

7. Du Biscay, *Account of a Voyage,* p. 29; MG 835, "Comercio de la Provincia del Paraguay," copy (1796?), p. 8; and Mörner, *Political and Economic Activities,* p. 189n.

8. Du Biscay, *Account of a Voyage,* p. 22; Concolorcorvo, *Lazarillo,* p. 77; Carlos Sempat Assadourian, *El tráfico de esclavos en Córdoba de Angola a Potosí, siglos XVI—XVII* (Córdoba, 1966); and Félix de Azara, "Viajes inéditos de Azara," *Revista de Derecho, Historia y Letras,* año 10, vol. 28, (Buenos Aires, November 1907), p. 368.

9. Concolorcorvo, *Lazarillo,* pp. 78, 110; and J. Campbell, *The Spanish Empire in America, By an English Merchant* (London, 1747), pp. 276—7. Campbell, a slave trader in Buenos Aires for the British South Seas Com-

pany, described Buenos Aires as a production subsector of Córdoba in provision of mules and cattle for the Potosí market in the 1740s. Acarete du Biscay mentioned that estancias around the port were sending cattle to Peruvian markets as early as the 1650s. See Du Biscay, *Account of a Voyage,* p. 31.

10. MG 781b, Ventura Santelice y Venet, "Carta a S.M. apuntando la importancia de establecer el comercio. . . .," copy (Potosí, 10 August 1756), p. 14; MG 541, Francisco de Barúa, "Manifiesto del terreno . . . llamado el Gran Chaco," copy (Potosí, 2 August 1756), p. 11; and MG 856, Joaquín Alós, "Relación del tiempo experimentado . . .," copy (Asunción, 30 June 1790), n.p. On early Paraguayan society see Elman R. Service, *Spanish–Guaraní Relations in Early Colonial Paraguay* (Westport, Conn., 1971).

11. Adapted from John Lynch, *Spanish Colonial Administration, 1782–1810: The Intendent System in the Viceroyalty of the Río de la Plata* (London, 1958), p. 146; MG 781b, Santelice y Venet, p. 13; and Félix de Azara, *Descripción e historia del Paraguay y del Río de la Plata,* trans. from the French (Madrid, 1847), vol. 1, p. 70.

12. Campbell, *Spanish Empire,* pp. 275–6; and Adalberto López, *The Revolt of the Comuneros, 1721–1735: A Study on the Colonial History of Paraguay* (Cambridge, Mass., 1976), pp. 25–7.

13. Martin Dobrizhoffer, *An Account of the Abipones, an Equestrian People of Paraguay,* trans. from the Latin (London, 1822), vol. 1, pp. 104–5; and MG 541, Barúa, p. 11.

14. Mörner, *Political and Economic Activities,* pp. 150–1, 158.

15. Azara, *Descripción e historia,* vol. 1, 313–14; and MG 2099, Felipe IV, "Real cedula de la audiencia que V. M. ha mandado fundar en las provincias del Río de la Plata . . .," copy (Madrid, 31 December 1662), p. 7.

16. Félix de Azara, *Memoria sobre el estado rural del Río de la Plata en 1801* (Madrid, 1847), pp. 131, 134; MG 451, Barúa, p. 11; and MG 16d, Antonio Pablo Marín, "Estado que manifiesta los efectos y caudales pertenecientes a la Real Renta del Tabaco . . .," copy (Buenos Aires, 24 April 1795), n.p.

17. MG 16d, Marín, n.p.; and MG 835, pp. 1–2.

18. MG 428, Santiago del Estero, "Informe sobre el valor de las mercancías que pasan por Santiago del Estero . . .," copy (3 November 1677), p. 4.

19. AGN Sala 9, 4-6-4, "Salvador de Alberdi al Consulado de Buenos Aires" (Tucumán, 10 Sept. 1805), as quoted by Halperín-Donghi, *Revolución y guerra,* p. 50; MG 791, Priego y Caro, pp. 1–2; and Pedro Santos Martínez, *Las industrias durante el virreinato, 1776–1810* (Buenos Aires, 1969), p. 143. On the carting trades, also see Concolorcorvo, *Lazarillo,* p. 90; and Schmieder, "Historical Geography of Tucumán," p. 384.

20. Du Biscay, *Account of a Voyage,* p. 36; and Concolorcorvo, *Lazarillo,* p. 137.

21. MG 421c, Bruno José de Urquiza, "Certificación de quelos gober-

nadores sacan los indios de los pueblos franciscanos . . .," copy (Buenos Aires, 20 July 1738), pp. 17—18; MG 541, Barúa, p. 2; Mörner, *Political and Economic Activities*, pp. 146—7; and Azara, *Descripción e historia*, vol. 1, p. 36.

22. Martínez, *Industrias*, pp. 55—8; Azara, *Descripción e historia*, p. 81; J. Campbell, *Spanish Empire*, p. 276; and Halperín-Donghi, *Revolución y guerra*, p. 25.

23. Concolorcorvo, *Lazarillo*, pp. 60, 74, 85; and Du Biscay, *Account of a Voyage*, pp. 32—4.

24. Azara, *Descripción e historia*, vol. 1, p. 82. John Lynch maintains that Spanish economic policies inhibited production, but he also suggests that long transportation lines and primitive technology were equally to blame for low production. See Lynch, *Spanish Colonial Administration*, pp. 164—5.

25. MG 428, Estero, p. 2; MG 781b, Santelice y Venet, p. 14; and MG 541, Barúa, p. 12.

26. Mörner, *Political and Economic Activities*, pp. 14, 52.

27. Concolorcorvo, *Lazarillo*, pp. 132. For official reports on tax evasion, see MG 1023, Pedro Castellana and Pedro Rodríguez de Cosío "Carta a S. M. sobre medidas que deben tomarse para impedir que la yerba . . . eludiendo el paso por Asunción . . .," copy (Buenos Aires, 28 November 1699), pp. 1—2; and MG 541, Barúa, p. 9. Although historians may fault Spanish officialdom for "unrealistic" internal duties, monopolies, and sales taxes, by the same token we ought to be thankful. Without their records, however incomplete, we would be hard put to ascertain what goods went from one place to another, let alone estimate their approximate amounts.

28. Concolorcorvo, *Lazarillo*, pp. 91—5; and David R. Ringrose, "Carting in the Hispanic World; An Example of Divergent Development," *Hispanic American Historical Review*, vol. 50, no. 1 (February 1970), pp. 30—51.

29. Concolorcorvo, *Lazarillo*, p. 93; and MG 835, pp. 6—7.

30. See MG 594, "Precios corrientes de los productos del Paraguay," copy (1796?), pp. 1—3; MG 835, pp. 1, 4.

31. AGN, Sala 7, 6-15-16, Gaspar de Santa Coloma, "Libro copiador de venta y remesas de efectos," (1792—1805). I have seen sections of these merchant accounts through the courtesy of Susan Migden Socolow.

32. For the early development of Buenos Aires, see MG 1828, Manuel de Frías, "Justificación del . . . procurador general del Río de la Plata y Paraguay . . .," copy (n.p., 1614?), p. 7; MG 1260, Pedro Sotelo Narváez, "Relación de las provincias de Tucumán . . .," copy (n.p., 1582), pp. 24—5; Enrique de Gandía, *Francisco de Alfaro y la condición social de los indios, Ríos de la Plata, Paraguay, Tucumán y Perú, siglos XVI y XVII* (Buenos Aires, 1939), p. 477; and especially Ricardo Zorraquin Becú, "Orígenes del comercio rioplatense (1580—1620)," *Anuario de Historia Argentina*, vol. 5 (1943—5), pp. 71—105.

33. Any textbook on colonial Latin American history will give the reader a description of this system. The basics were first outlined by C. H. Haring, *Trade and Navigation Between Spain and the Indies in the Time of the Hapsburgs* (Cambridge, 1918).
34. Zorraquín Becú, "Orígenes del comercio," p. 85n. For examples of contemporary correspondence, see MG 1262, Cabildo de Buenos Aires, "Memorial y instrucción para nuestro procurador general . . .," copy (Buenos Aires, 1614), pp. 3—6, 9; MG 549c, Manuel de Frías, "Carta a S.M. sobre que se prorrogue y amplíe la merced . . .," copy (n.p., 1618?), pp. 79—80; and MG 1205, Pedro Baygorri Irruez, "Informe extenso a S. M. sobre la provincia," copy (Buenos Aires, 6 December 1653), pp. 3—6.
35. MG 1828, Frías, pp. 14—15; and MG 32a, Frías "Viaje de Cádiz al Río de la Plata . . .," copy (Buenos Aires, 30 April 1621), p. 9.
36. For trade restrictions, see MG 1828, Frías, p. 4; MG 1410, Felipe III "Real Cédula deliberando y reglamentando el comercio . . .," copy (Madrid, 10 December 1618), pp. 1—3; MG 549e, Frías, pp. 75—78; and MG 318, Carlos II, "Resúmen de las consultas en que su magestad resolvió fundar y extinguir la Audiencia de Buenos Aires . . .," copy (n.p., 1672?), pp. 4—6.
37. Adapted from Comandrán Ruiz, *Evolución demográfica argentina*, pp. 43—4.
38. For the economic penetration of the Río de la Plata by Portuguese traders, see MG 32c, Manual de Frías, "Semillas introducidas en las provincias del Río de la Plata y Paraguay," copy (Buenos Aires, 21 May 1621), pp. 17—18; MG 1482, Martín Ignacio de Loyola, "Carta a S. M. sobre algunas cosas . . .," copy (Buenos Aires, 13 February 1602); MG 1205, Baygorri Irruez, p. 10; and MG 32a, Frías, pp. 4—5. Also see Alice Piffer Canabrava, *O comércio português no Rio da Prata, 1580—1640* (São Paulo, 1944); and Madaline W. Nichols, "Colonial Tucumán," *Hispanic American Historical Review*, vol. 18, no. 4 (November 1938), p. 480.
39. MG 1812g, Mateo Sánchez "Verdadero testimonio sacado de los libros Reales de los derechos . . .," copy (Buenos Aires, 18 May 1599), pp. 89—92; and MG 1812h, Sánchez, "Datos sobre artículos importados en Buenos Aires . . .," copy (Buenos Aires, 18 May 1599), pp. 94—100.
40. Mörner, *Political and Economic Activities*, p. 51; and Gandia, *Francisco de Alfaro*, pp. 478—9.
41. Gandía, *Francisco de Alfaro*, p. 478; Zorraquín Becú, "Orígenes del comercio," pp. 80—1; and Mario Rodríguez, "The Genesis of Economic Attitudes in the Río de la Plata," *Hispanic American Historical Review*, vol. 36, no. 2 (May 1956), p. 179n.
42. Zorraquín Becú, "Orígines del comercio," p. 95; and MG 1812h, Sánchez, p. 99.
43. Du Biscay, *Account of a Voyage*, pp. 13, 73—4; and Mörner, *Political and Economic Activities*, p. 167.
44. MG 318, Carlos II, pp. 1—4.
45. Du Biscay, *Account of a Voyage*, p. 3.
46. Ibid., pp. 68—9.

47. Arthur S. Aiton, "The Asiento Treaty as Reflected in the Papers of Lord Shelburne," *Hispanic American Historical Review*, vol. 8, no. 2 (May 1928), pp. 167−8.

48. Ibid., p. 171; Judith Blow Williams, "The Establishment of British Commerce with Argentina," *Hispanic American Historical Review*, vol. 15, no. 1 (February 1935), p. 44; George H. Nelson, "Contraband Trade under the Asiento, 1730−1739," *American Historical Review*, vol. 51, no. 1 (Oct. 1945), pp. 60−1; and Sergio R. Villalobos, *Comercio y contrabando en el Río de la Plata y Chile, 1700−1811* (Buenos Aires, 1965), p. 32.

49. Adapted from Rodríguez, "Genesis of Economic Attitudes," p. 179n; Emilio Ravignani, *Historia de la Nación Argentina*, 10 vols (n.p., n.d.), vol. 4, n.p.; and Aiton, "Asiento Treaty," p. 175.

50. J. Campbell, *Spanish Empire*, pp. 318−9; Jean Olivia McLachlan, *Trade and Peace with Old Spain, 1667−1750* (Cambridge, 1940), p. 82; and Vera Lee Brown, "The South Sea Company and Contraband Trade," *American Historical Review*, vol. 31, no. 4 (July 1926), pp. 666, 668, 672.

51. Nelson, "Contraband Trade," pp. 55, 63−4.

52. *An Account of Spanish Settlements in America* (Edinburgh, 1762), pp. 331−2; and Rodríguez, "Genesis of Economic Attitudes," pp. 188−9.

53. Villalobos, *Comercio y contrabando*, pp. 21−2; and H. E. S. Fisher, "Anglo-Portuguese Trade, 1700−1770," *Economic History Review*, 2d series (1963), p. 226. For the destruction of Colónia, see Dauril Alden, "The Undeclared War of 1773−1777: Climax of Luso-Spanish Platine Rivalry," *Hispanic American Historical Review*, vol. 41, no. 4 (February 1961), pp. 55−74.

54. J. Campbell, *Spanish Empire*, p. 280. Two historians who emphasize the significance of contraband are Sergio R. Villalobos and G. D. Ramsey. Villalobos says that smuggling in colonial Argentina and Chile was the solution for their economic needs. Ramsey concludes that the growth of European contraband all through the Americas resulted because of the inability of the Spanish bureaucracy to enforce laws so wildly out of touch with economic reality. See Villalobos, *Comercio y contrabando*, p. 17; and Ramsey, *English Overseas Trade During the Centuries of Emergencies* (London, 1957), pp. 199−206.

## 2. Buenos Aires in the Golden Age: the viceregal economy

1. Anthony Z. Helms, *Travels from Buenos Ayres, by Potosí, to Lima*, trans. from the German (London, 1807), p. 44.

2. Félix de Azara, *Descripción e historia del Paraguay y del Río de la Plata*, 2 vols. (Madrid, 1847), vol 1, p. 357: Azara's tables show that twenty-one Cádiz ships annually carried 631,615 pesos of Spanish goods and 923,313 pesos of foreign goods to Buenos Aires (ca. 1796).

3. One such New England merchant in the Latin American trades was William Gray. See Edward Gray, *William Gray of Salem, Merchant* (Boston, 1914), p. 51.

4. For information on early U.S. trading in the Río de la Plata, see

Charles Lyon Chandler, "United States Merchant Ships in the Río de la Plata (1801—1808), as Shown by Early Newspapers," *Hispanic American Historical Review,* vol 2, no. 1 (February 1919), pp. 27, 29; Chandler, "Documents: The River Plate Voyages, 1798—1800," *American Historical Review,* vol. 23, no. 4 (July 1918), p. 821; and Arthur P. Whitaker, "Early Commercial Relations Between the United States and Spanish America," in R. A. Humphreys and John Lynch, *The Origins of the Latin American Revolutions, 1808—1826* (New York, 1965), pp. 92—93.

5. See Azara, *Descripción e historia,* vol. 1, p. 357; Helms, *Travels from Buenos Aires,* p. 44; E. E. Vidal, *Picturesque Illustrations of Buenos Ayres and Montevideo* (London, 1820), p. xx; and Herbert S. Klein, "Las finanzas del Virreinato del Río de la Plata en 1790," *Desarrollo Económico, Revista de Ciencias Sociales,* vol. 13, no. 50 (Buenos Aires, July—Sept. 1973), p. 384. Klein's figure of 5,284,333 pesos of imports was derived from the revenue earned by the Buenos Aires' customshouse on import duties of 3 percent ad valorem. Another import estimate, this for 1802, is 4 million pesos. See Germán O. E. Tjarks, *El Consulado de Buenos Aires y sus proyecciones en la historia del Río de la Plata,* 2 vols. (Buenos Aires, 1962), vol. 2, p. 315.

6. John Lynch, *Spanish Colonial Administration, 1782—1810* (London, 1958), pp. 121—2.

7. John Lynch, *The Spanish American Revolutions, 1808—1826* (New York, 1973), pp. 45—6, lists the silver exports at 80 percent of total exports. Azara's annual figures were 2.1 million piastres in silver, 1.7 million in gold, and .9 million in pastoral goods. See Azara, *Descripción e historia,* vol. 1, p. 357.

8. Adapted from Sergio R. Villalobos, *Comercio y contrabando en el Río de la Plata y Chile, 1700—1811* (Buenos Aires, 1965), pp. 56, 97; Lynch, *Spanish Colonial Administration,* p. 169; and Helms, *Travels from Buenos Aires,* p. 44. I have purposely excluded the oft-quoted figures of Academia Nacional de la Historia [*Historia de la nación argentina,* 10 vols. (Buenos Aires, 1936—42), vol. 4, p. 265], because they seem unduly exaggerated. It lists annual exports of hides before 1783 at 800,000 and after 1873 at 1.4 million.

9. For the Cuban trade, see Alejandro Malaspina, *Viaje al Río de la Plata en el siglo XVIII* (Buenos Aires, 1938), p. 309; Azara, *Descripción e historia,* vol. 1, p. 357, and MG 16b, Pedro Melo de Portugal, "Carta a Diego de Gardogni dando cuenta del estado de la renta de S.M.," copy (Buenos Aires, 12 November 1795).

10. Manfred Kossok, *El Virreinato del Río de la Plata, su estructura económica-social,* trans. from the German (Buenos Aires, 1972), p. 76.

11. Susan Migden Socolow, "Economic Activities of the Porteño Merchants: The Viceregal Period," *Hispanic American Historical Review,* vol. 55, no. 1 (February 1975), pp. 1—24; and Socolow, "The Merchants of Viceregal Buenos Aires," Ph.D. diss. (Columbia University, 1973), pp. 245—6.

12. Lyman L. Johnson, "The Silversmiths of Buenos Aires: A Case Study

in the Failure of Corporate Organization," *Journal of Latin American Studies,* vol. 8, no. 2 (November 1976), pp. 187−8; Socolow, "Economic Activities," pp. 16−17; and Socolow, "Merchants of Viceregal Buenos Aires," pp. 245−6. Also see John Mawe, *Travels in the Interior of Brazil,* 2d ed. (London, 1823), pp. 49−51. Mawe was a British merchant who visited Buenos Aires in 1804.

13. Socolow, "Economic Activities," pp. 11−12.

14. Dorothy Burne Goebel, "British Trade to the Spanish Colonies, 1796−1823," *American Historical Review,* vol. 43, no. 2 (January 1938), p. 309. Also see Germán O. E. Tjarks and Alicia Viduarreta, *El comercio inglés y el contrabando: nuevos aspectos en el estudio de la política económica en el Río de la Plata, 1807−1810* (Buenos Aires, 1962), pp. 17−20; and Lynch, *Spanish Colonial Administration,* pp. 146−7.

15. AGN, Sala 9, 34-2-6 (E. 2515), "Contrabando sobre remate de los efectos aprehendios . . ." (1800). Tjarks and Viduarreta, *Comercio inglés,* p. 10, cites a similar case against merchant Antonio Obligado; and Socolow, "Economic Activities," p. 12n, cites another against Tomás Antonio Romero. On silver smuggling at Buenos Aires, see MG 2056, Marquez de Avilés, "Informe al Virrey Joaquín del Pino dando relación del gobierno de todas las provincias . . ." (Buenos Aires, 21 May 1801), pp. 14−15.

16. Pedro Santos Martínez, *Las industrias durante el virreinato, 1776−1810* (Buenos Aires, 1969), p. 65. For specific cases of tobacco contraband, see AGN, Sala 9, 33-5-2 (E. 1179), "Hacienda. Causa sobre la aprehensión echa en la campaña . . ." (1788); and Sala 9, 33-4-1 (E. 940), "Hacienda. Autos obrados con motivo de haver aprehendido . . ." (1786).

17. Félix de Azara, *Memoria sobre el estado rural del Río de la Plata en 1801* (Madrid, 1847), p. 33.

18. The best survey of industry in this era is Martínez, *Industrias,* pp. 42−7. His theme is the traditional one that colonial industry slumped because of competition from foreign imports. This cannot be the final word on the subject. Martínez himself notes growth in Salta's sugar industry and Cochabamba's cloth manufacturers. He shows, for instance, that Cochabamba employed 2,000 textile workers in 1788 and fully 80,000 a decade later. As for the colonial textile industries, I tend to agree with the observation of D. C. M. Platt that expensive European luxury goods hardly put cheap domestic cloth off the market. See D. C. M. Platt, *Latin American and British Trade, 1806−1914* (New York, 1973), p. 22.

19. MG 835, "Comercio de la Provincia del Paraguay," copy (n.p., 1796?), p. 8; and Mawe, *Travels in the Interior,* p. 26.

20. Azara, *Descripción e historia,* vol. 1, pp. 58−59. For various Paraguayan products on the porteño market, see MG 594, "Precios de los efectos de Castilla y de la tierra . . ." (Paraguay, 1796?).

21. Socolow, "Economic Activities," p. 17; Martínez, *Industrias,* pp. 122−40; and Horacio Juan Cuccorese and José Panettieri, *Argentina, manual de historia económica y social* (Buenos Aires, 1971), vol. 1, *Argentina criolla,* pp. 98−9.

22. MG 1055, Ignacio Flores, "Carta a José de Gálvez exponiendo su opinión sobre la erección de virreynatos . . .," copy (n.p., 15 March 1783), p. 5. The information about administrative expenditures comes from Klein, "Finanzas," p. 388.

23. MG 16c, Marín, p. 7.

24. Socolow, "Economic Activities," p. 5n; and Tjarks, *consulado,* vol. 1, p. 315.

25. Jorge Comandrán Ruiz, *Evolución demográfica argentina durante el período hispano (1535 – 1810)* (Buenos Aires, 1969), pp. 80, 115.

26. Lynch, *Spanish Colonial Administration,* p. 44.

27. Concolorcovo (Alfonso Carrío de la Bandera), *El Lazarillo: A Guide for Inexperienced Travelers between Buenos Aires and Lima – 1773,* trans. by Walter D. Kline (Bloomington, Ind., 1965), p. 97; Villalobos, *Comercio y contrabando,* p. 104; and MG 896, Joaquín del Pino, "Carta a Cayetano Soler sobre la exención de una tercera parte del cargamento . . .," copy (Buenos Aires, 11 December 1802), pp. 1 – 2.

28. Kossok, *Virreinato,* p. 79, uses *alcabala* (sales tax) receipts to demonstrate greater economic activity during the viceroyalty. His figures are:

| | |
|---|---|
| 1773 | 2,502 pesos |
| 1780 | 20,428 |
| 1790 | 28,137 |
| 1795 | 32,975 |
| 1800 | 46,390 |

29. Mawe, *Travels in the Interior,* pp. 11 – 14.

30. Concolorcorvo, *Lazarilla,* p. 56.

31. For descriptions of the vaquería, see the contemporary sources of Martin Dobritzhoffer, *An Account of the Abipones, an Equestrial People of Paraguay,* trans. from the Latin, 3 vols. (London, 1822), vol. 1, p. 221; and John Miller, *The Memoirs of General Miller in the Service of the Republic of Peru,* 2d ed., 2 vols. (London, 1829), vol. 1, p. 142. The seminal historical study remains Emilio Coni, *Historia de las vaquerías del Río de la Plata (1555 – 1750)* (Madrid, 1930).

32. Coni, *Historia de las vaquerías,* p. 25.

33. Dobritzhoffer, *Account of the Abigones,* vol. 1, p. 221; and John Contanse Davie, *Letters from Paraguay; Describing the Settlements of Montevideo and Buenos Aires* (London, 1805), p. 177.

34. Mawe, *Travels in the Interior,* pp. 28 – 30, 34; and Malaspina, *Viaje al Río de la Plata,* pp. 285 – 92.

35. Dobritzhoffer, *Account of the Abipones,* p. 220.

36. Azara, *Estado rural,* p. 8.

37. The observer was Malaspina, *Viaje al Río de la Plata,* p. 285. Also see Mawe, *Travels in the Interior,* p. 31. Both travelers were guilty of exaggeration, but overkill at times was a serious matter.

38. Dauril Alden, "The Undeclared War of 1773 – 1777: Climax of Luso-Spanish Platine Rivalry," *Hispanic American Historical Review,* vol. 41, no. 4 (Feb. 1961), pp. 55 – 8, 62.

39. Malaspina, *Viaje al Río de la Plata*, pp. 281–2; and Mawe, *Travels in the Interior*, p. 18.

40. Malaspina, *Viaje al Río de la Plata*, pp. 278–9; and AGN, Sala 9, 33-5-2 (E. 1177), "Hacienda. Sobre el asiento de la envernada de la Cavallada del Rey en la Estancia de Dn. Pedro García Posse . . ." (1788).

41. Juan Carlos Nicolau, *Antecedentes para la historia de la industria argentina* (Buenos Aires, 1968), pp. 38–9; and Cuccorese and Panettieri, *Argentina*, vol. 1, p. 96–8.

42. Comandrán Ruiz, *Evolución demográfica*, p. 99.

43. AGN, Sala 9, 33-4-1 (E. 941), Joaquín Antonio Camaño, "Sobre entrega de cueros en el pueblo de Paysandú" (1788); Sala 9, 37-5-4 (E. 4), "Solicita de D. Juan Jph. de Sagarti se le venda, o permita matar la Foxadr [?] dispersa . . ." (1799); and Sala 9, 33-5-2 (E. 1184, 1185), "Hacienda. Reconocimiento de los 941 cueros . . . [y de los 551 cueros . . .]" (1788).

44. For documental evidence on cattle and hide stealing, see AGN, Sala 9, 8-10-5 (E. 206), "Ganado. Para conservar elganado se prohiben las matanzas perjudiciales y faena clandestina de cueros" (9 March 1791); Sala 9, 37-5-4 (E. 3), Melchior Albín, "Sobre los perjuicios que se la siguen con motivo del Cassuíro [?] establecido en su estancia en el Partido de las Bacas" (1782); and Azara, *Estado rural*, p. 14.

45. The operations of the Estancia de las Vacas are detailed in the original account books preserved in the Archivo General de la Nación, Buenos Aires. Extant documentation, including 1789–99, when Florencio García, a meticulous bookkeeper, was the estate manager. See AGN, Sala 9, 37-5-4, "Cuentas de la Estancia de las Vacas en la Banda Oriental" (1790–1800).

46. AGN, Sala 9, 37-5-4 (E. 19), "Expediente sobre propuesta del administrador . . ." (1799); (E. 6), "Cuenta de cargos y data hecha por la administrador . . ." (1790); and Sala 9, 37-5-4 (E. 5), "Conocimientos de dichas mercaderías remitidas a dicho establecimiento . . ." (1790).

47. AGN, Sala 9, 37-5-4 (E. 6); Sala 9, 37-5-4 (E. 1), "Cuenta de cargo y data hecha por el administrador . . ." (1792); and Sala 9, 37-5-4 (E. 8), "Libro de cargo y data de entradas y salidas . . ." (1800).

48. See any of the estancia's pay books, such as AGN, Sala 9, 34-2-6 (E. 2526); and Sala 9, 37-5-4 (E. 7), "Cuentas de data hechas por el administrador . . ." (1791).

49. AGN, Sala 9, 37-5-4 (E. 19), p. 24. According to these accounts, a majority of the hides were sent to an orphanage run by the brotherhood in Buenos Aires. Presumably, the orphanage administrators resold the hides on the export market in order to support that institution.

50. See AGN, Sala 9, 37-5-4 (E. 1).

51. AGN, Sala 9, 37-5-4 (E. 19), p. 56.

52. See AGN, Sala 9, 37-5-4 (E. 6); and Sala 9, 37-5-4 (E. 19).

53. AGN, Sala 9, 37-5-4 (E. 12), "Libro de cargo y data de efectos y caudales" (1795).

54. AGN, Sala 9, 37-5-4 (E. 11), "Libro de entrada y salida de efectos y caudales" (1795). These figures are rounded off to the nearest peso. In

this table, I have taken the liberty to add receipts from the sale of estancia products already itemized in the text directly above the table. Unfortunately, we have no data on cost of transportation to market.

55. Klein, "Finanzas," p. 370; and Villalobos, *Comercio y contrabando,* pp. 56–7.

56. Lynch, *Spanish American Revolutions,* pp. 46–7.

57. Davie, *Letters from Paraguay,* p. 87. John Mawe, a British merchant, had been engaged in the legal trade between Cádiz and the Río de la Plata when the war broke out. He was seized in Montevideo in 1797. See Mawe, *Travels in the Interior.*

58. Whitaker, "Commercial Relations," pp. 88–9; and Villalobos, *Comercio y contrabando,* p. 85.

59. MG 2056, Aviles, pp. 15–16; Davie, *Letters from Paraguay,* p. 31; and MG 1689, Francisco de Saavedra, "Carta a Lázaro de Rivera en que informa sobre la conveniencia de contribuir una flota mercantil," copy (Asunción, 19 Nov. 1798), pp. 1–3.

60. Campbell, *Spanish Empire,* p. 304.

61. As quoted in R. A. Humphreys, *Liberation in South America, 1806–1827: The Career of James Paroissien* (London, 1952), p. 1.

62. For the text of Popham's letter, see W. B. Crump, *The Leeds Woollen Industry, 1780–1820* (Leeds, Eng., 1931), pp. 183–4.

63. Mawe, *Travels in the Interior,* pp. 14–15; Goebel, "British Trade," pp. 307–8; and Humphreys, *Liberation in South America,* pp. 5–9.

64. A figure of 1.2 million pounds sterling between 1 November 1808 and 1 November 1809 is most often quoted. See Lynch, *Spanish American Revolutions,* p. 47. Tjarks and Viduarreta, *Comercio inglés,* p. 21, put the figure as high as 1.6 million pounds sterling.

### 3. Industrial markets for Argentine raw materials

1. In the nineteenth century, the markets of other nations also became important to the Argentine economy — especially the Germanies, France, Spain, Sardinia, and to a lesser extent Brazil and Cuba. My intention in this chapter, however, is to study the impact of market changes in depth. Therefore, I chose Argentina's two leading customers, Great Britain and the United States, as a comparative case study.

2. James Bischoff, *A Comprehensive History of the Woollen and Worsted Manufactures,* 2 vols. (London, 1842), vol. 2, p. 89.

3. Peter C. Welsh, *Tanning in the United States to 1850* (Washington, D.C., 1964), pp. 64–5; and George Dodd, *Days at the Factories* (London, 1843), p. 176.

4. James Burnley, *The History of Wool and Woolcombing* (London, 1889), pp. 4–7.

5. David S. Landes provides a useful critique of technological change with his three hallmarks of modernization: (1) substitution of machines for human effort, (2) substitution of inanimate for animate sources of power,

and (3) substitution of the use of mineral for animal and vegetable materials. This framework provides a useful contrast between the leather industries, which underwent change, for the most part, in none of these categories, and the wool trades, which experienced transformations in all three. See Landes, *The Unbound Prometheus: Technological Change and Industrial Development in Western Europe from 1790 to the Present* (Cambridge, 1970).

6. For contemporary and modern estimates of industrial ranking, see Dodd, *Days at the Factories*, p. 184; *Reports of Proceedings at the Annual Dinner of the Hide and Leather Trade of the City of New York at the Metropolitan Hotel on Thursday, Feb. 10, 1859* (New York, 1859), p. 8; Arthur D. Gayer, W. W. Rostow, Anna Jacobson Schwartz, and Isaiah Frank, *The Growth and Fluctuation of the British Economy, 1750—1850*, 2 vols. (Oxford, 1953), vol. 2, p. 853; and Albert Fishlow, *American Railroads and the Transformation of the Antebellum Economy* (Cambridge, Mass., 1965), p. 257.

7. The literature abounds in descriptions of the traditional uses of leather. See Julia de Fontenelle, Jean Sebastian Eugene, and F. Malepeyre, *The Arts of Tanning, Currying, and Leather Dressing*, trans. from the French (Philadelphia, 1852), pp. 148—51; W. G. Rimmer, "Leeds Leather Industry in the Nineteenth Century," *Publications of the Thoresby Society*, vol. 4, misc. 13 (Leeds, Eng., 1960), pp. 121, 134; and George C. Burns, *The American Woolen Manufacturer; a Practical Treatise on the Manufacture of Woolens* (Central Falls, R.I., 1872), pp. 125—31.

8. Rimmer, "Leeds Leather Industry," p. 121.

9. R. A. Church, "Labour Supply and Innovation, 1800—1860; the Boot and Shoe Industry," *Business History*, vol. 12, no. 1 (Jan. 1970), p. 25.

10. Fisherlow, *American Railroads*, p. 257.

11. Blanche Evan Hazard, *The Organization of the Boot and Shoe Industry in Massachusetts before 1875* (New York, 1969), p. 68. On the British shoe trade, see P. Head, "Boots and Shoes," in Derek H. Alcroft, ed., *The Development of British Industry and Foreign Competition, 1874—1914* (London, 1968); and Church, "Labour Supply."

12. For the shoe export trade of one Boston wholesaling company, Mitchell and Bryant Co., see the reminiscences of Seth Bryant, *Shoe and Leather Trade of the Last One Hundred Years* (Boston, 1891), pp. 14, 26, 55. On the sewing machine in the footwear industry, consult Rimmer, "Leeds Leather Industry," p. 139; and Church, "Labour Supply," p. 31.

13. J. H. Clapham, *An Economic History of Modern Britain*, 2 vols. (Cambridge, 1930), vol. 1, p. 170; and Welsh, *Tanning in the United States*, pp. 37, 41.

14. The best descriptions of nineteenth-century tanning processes are to be found in the tanning manuals of the era. Several have been quoted at length by Harry B. and Grace M. Weiss, *Early Tanning and Currying in New Jersey* (Trenton, N.J., 1959), pp. 19—31. Also see Dodd, *Days at the Factories*, p. 163 ff.

15. Rimmer, "Leeds Leather Industry," p. 123; Dodd, *Days at the Factories,* p. 161; and Edgar Malone Hoover, *Location Theory and the Shoe and Leather Industries* (Cambridge, Mass., 1937), p. 125.

16. Rimmer, "Leeds Leather Industry," p. 141; and Weiss, *Early Tanning,* pp. 17, 19—23.

17. Hoover, *Location Theory,* p. 123—7, refers to colonial tanning, but small tanneries established later in Midwestern states operated on much the same scale.

18. Welsh, *Tanning in the United States,* p. 66; and Weiss, *Early Tanning,* p. 263.

19. For the use of French eggs in tanning, see Dodd, *Days at the Factories,* p. 170, 178—9. On chrome tanning, see R. A. Church, "The British Leather Industry and Foreign Competition, 1870—1914," *Economic History Review,* 2d series, vol. 24, no. 4 (Nov. 1971), p. 561.

20. *Report of Proceedings,* pp. 11—12; and de Fontenelle, et al., *Arts of Tanning,* p. 22.

21. Rimmer, "Leeds Leather Industry," pp. 122, 143; Dodd, *Days at the Factories,* pp. 164, 176—7; and Church, "British Leather Industry," p. 550.

22. Hoover, *Location Theory,* pp. 127—8; and Clark H. McDermott, ed., *A History of the Shoe and Leather Industries of the United States* (Boston, 1918), pp. 47—8.

23. *Reports of Proceedings,* pp. 4—6, 19—20; McDermott, *Shoe and Leather Industries,* p. 44; and Freeman Hunt, ed., *The Merchant's Magazine, and Commercial Review,* vol. 3 (New York, 1840), p. 146.

24. From census reports quoted by *Reports of Proceedings,* p. 10; McDermott, *Shoe and Leather Industries,* p. 47; and *Merchant's Magazine,* vol. 5 (1841), p. 96.

25. Rimmer, "Leeds Leather Industry," p. 14; and Dodd, *Days at the Factories,* p. 184.

26. Rimmer, "Leeds Leather Industry," pp. 124—5; and Church, "British Leather Industry," p. 551.

27. The problem of hide supply was already becoming critical by the mid-eighteenth century. See Joseph Massie, *Considerations on the Leather Trade of Great Britain* (London, 1757). By 1815, however, 40 million pounds of leather were produced from domestic hides and 20 million pounds from foreign hides. See Phyllis Deane and W. A. Cole, *British Economic Growth, 1688—1959: Trends and Structure* (Cambridge, 1962), p. 74.

28. Charles B. Kuhlman, "The Processing of Agricultural Products in the Pre-Railway Age," in Harold F. Williamson, ed., *The Growth of the American Economy* (New York, 1944), pp. 193—4. The New England and Delaware hide import estimates are from Fishlow, *American Railroads,* p. 246; and Welsh, *Tanning in the United States,* pp. 48—50.

29. McDermott, *Shoe and Leather Industries,* p. 42; Weiss, *Early Tanning,* pp. 13, 51; Hazard, *Boot and Shoe Industry,* p. 30; and Welsh, *Tanning in the United States,* pp. 9, 47—8, 64.

30. American hide factors usually advertised in newspapers, as did one Philadelphia merchant in 1837 who offered "4,200 La Plata hides, 3,000 Chile hides, 1,000 Rio Grande hides, 800 La Guyra [*sic*] hides, and 500 Pernambuco hides." See Weiss, *Early Tanning,* p. 51.

31. *Merchant's Magazine,* vol. 6 (1842), p. 474. Hides ranked third, behind coffee and sugar, among the major commodities in the Latin American trade of the United States. See Robert G. Albion, "Foreign Trade in the Era of Wooden Ships," in Williamson, *Growth of the American Economy,* p. 163. For British hide imports, see Rimmer, "Leeds Leather Industry," pp. 122, 131—2; and Thomas Baines, *History of the Commerce and Town of Liverpool, and of the Rise of Manufacturing Industry in the Adjoining Counties* (London, 1852), p. 804.

32. The British colonies proved keen competitors with Argentina for the British market. Cape Colony (South Africa), India, and Australasia together supplied one-third of Britain's hide imports and more than two-thirds of its imported wool. Werner Schlote, *British Overseas Trade from 1700 to the 1930's,* trans. by W. O. Henderson and W. H. Chaloner (Oxford, 1952), p. 164.

33. Masterful and readable accounts of the putting-out system in the woolen industry are found in T. S. Ashton, *An Economic History of England: the Eighteenth Century* (London, 1972), pp. 97—103; and Landes, *Unbound Prometheus,* pp. 57—60.

34. Arthur Harrison Cole, *The American Wool Manufacture,* 2 vols. (Cambridge, Mass., 1926), vol. 1, pp. 3—70.

35. John James, *History of the Worsted Manufacture in England, from the Earliest Times* (London, 1857), pp. 355—6, 384—5.

36. Eric Sigsworth, *Black Dyke Mills, A History* (Liverpool, 1958), p. 32; W. B. Crump and Gertrude Ghorbal, *History of the Huddersfield Woollen Industry* (Huddersfield, Eng., 1935), pp. 82, 118—9.

37. Crump and Ghorbal, *Huddersfield Woollen Industry,* pp. 84—5, 87.

38. Sigsworth, *Black Dyke Mills,* pp. 38—9; Landes, *Unbound Prometheus,* pp. 108—14; and Kenneth G. Ponting, *The Woollen Industry of South-west England* (Bath, Eng., 1971), pp. 45—6.

39. Cole, *American Wool Manufacture,* vol. 1, pp. 86—120; and Chester Whitney Wright, *Wool-Growing and the Tariff; a Study in the Economic History of the United States* (Cambridge, Mass., 1910), pp. 44, 53.

40. Wright, *Wool-Growing and the Tariff,* p. 115.

41. Sigsworth, *Black Dyke Mills,* pp. 12—27; Crump and Ghorbal, *Huddersfield Woollen Industry,* p. 116; and Clapham, *Economic History,* vol. 1, pp. 192—3.

42. James, *Worsted Manufacture,* pp. 511, 536.

43. Cole, *American Wool Manufacture,* vol. 1, p. 207.

44. Bischoff, *Comprehensive History,* vol. 2, p. 191.

45. On British blanket production and trade, see Frederick J. Glover, "The Rise of the Heavy Woollen Trade of the West Riding of Yorkshire in the Nineteenth Century," *Business History,* vol. 4, no. 1 (Dec. 1961), pp.

1—21; and Glover, "Philadelphia Merchants and the Yorkshire Blanket Trade, 1820—1860," *Pennsylvania History*, vol. 28, no. 2 (1961) pp. 121—141. For British blanket exports, see *Annual Statement 1853* (1855), p. 161.

46. Cole, *American Wool Manufacture*, vol. 1, p. 203.

47. Arthur H. Cole and Harold F. Williamson, *The American Carpet Manufacture, a History and Analysis* (Cambridge, Mass., 1941), pp. 12—21; and John S. Ewing and Nancy P. Norton, *Broadlooms and Businessmen: a History of the Bigelow-Sanford Carpet Company* (Cambridge, Mass., 1955), pp. 6—15.

48. Cole and Williamson, *American Carpet Manufacture*, pp. 57—65; and Ewing and Norton, *Broadlooms and Businessmen*, pp. 13—19.

49. *Annual Statement 1853* (1855), p. 161.

50. Cole and Williamson, *American Carpet Manufacture*, p. 44. Ewing and Norton, *Broadlooms and Businessmen*, p. 28, mentions the price decrease between the years 1842 and 1852.

51. Wright, *Wool-growing and the Tariff*, p. 75; and Gayer, et al., *Growth and Fluctuation*, vol. 2, p. 789.

52. Wright, *Wool-growing and the Tariff*, pp. 88, 95.

53. See parliamentary testimonies on domestic sheepbreeding in Bischoff, *Comprehensive History*, vol. 2, pp. 3, 8, 135, 150—1.

54. Bischoff, *Comprehensive History*, vol. 1, pp. 91—3.

55. Werner von Bergen and Herbert R. Mauersberger, *American Wool Handbook* (New York, 1938), p. 27.

56. Archibald Hamilton, "On Wool Supply," *Journal of the Statistical Society of London*, p. 495; vol. 33 (Dec. 1870), and Ewing and Norton, *Broadlooms and Businessmen*, p. 24. Apparently, the quality of Argentine wool later improved, for one historian notes that its "shrinkage rate" after cleaning was only 20 percent (Ewing and Norton, *Broadloom's and Businessmen*, p. 46).

57. Burnley, *Wool and Woolcombing*, pp. 96—101; and Wright, *Wool-growing and the Tariff*, pp. 104—5.

58. *Annual Statement 1853* (1855), p. 86; and Landes, *Unbound Prometheus*, p. 202.

59. Dodd, *Days at the Factories*, pp. 453, 163; and de Fontenelle, et al., *Arts of Tanning*, p. 21. For bone and horsehair import figures, see *Annual Statement 1853* (1855), pp. 43, 45.

60. For the use of bone and guano fertilizers, see F. M. L. Thompson, "The Second Agricultural Revolution, 1815—1880," *Economic History Review*, 2d series, vol. 21, no. 1 (April 1968), pp. 62—77. Bone import figures for 1853 may be found in *Annual Statement 1853* (1855), p. 25.

61. For a description of a London candle and soap factory, see Dodd, *Days at the Factories*, pp. 187—207.

62. R. A. Humphreys, ed., *British Consular Reports on the Trade and Politics of Latin America*, vol. 63, *1824—1826* (London, 1940), p. 63; Thomas Tooke and William Newmarch, *A History of Prices and the State of*

*the Circulation from 1792 to 1856,* 8 vols. (London, 1838–57) vol. 2, p. 415; and *Annual Statement 1853 (1855), p. 77.*

### 4. Buenos Aires as outpost of world trade

1. See Vera Blinn Reber, "British Mercantile Houses in Buenos Aires, 1810 to 1880," Ph.D. diss. (University of Wisconsin, 1972), p. 104; and George Fracker, *Voyage to South America* (Boston, 1826), pp. 8, 27.

2. Reber, "British Mercantile Houses," p. 86; *A Five Years' Residence in Buenos Aires* (London, 1825), p. 5; and W. H. B. Webster, *Narrative of a Voyage to the South Atlantic Ocean,* 2 vols. (London, 1834), vol. 1, pp. 85–6.

3. Isaac G. Strain, *Cordillera and Pampa, Mountain and Plain* (New York, 1853), p. 271. For descriptions of the city's vistas, also see *Five Years' Residence,* p. 66; E. E. Vidal, *Picturesque Illustrations of Buenos Ayres and Montevideo* (London, 1820), p. 8; and Charles Samuel Stewart, *Brazil and La Plata* (New York, 1856), pp. 177–80.

4. Strain, *Cordillera and Pampa,* p. 271; and *Five Years' Residence,* p. 11.

5. Reber, "British Mercantile Houses," pp. 95, 104. In 1835, it took forty-five lighters one month merely to unload the shipment of vermicelli, paper, and aguardiente from a Sardinian vessel. Obviously, much delay was caused by the fact that each box of freight had to be documented as it was loaded onto the boats. See AGN, Sala 10, 43–13–1, "Aduana. Registro de entradas y salidas de buques" (1828, 1834, 1835).

6. Reber, "British Mercantile Houses," pp. 105–6.

7. *Five Years' Residence,* p. 27, mentions that a pampero in 1820 blew sixty ships of various sizes off their moorings and destroyed the city pier. Also see Charles B. Mansfield, *Paraguay, Brazil, and the Plate* (Cambridge, 1856), p. 139; and the case of the overturned lighter in AGN. Registro No. 74 (Comercio 2), Antonio Fausto Gómez (1840), p. 39.

8. Mansfield, *Paraguay, Brazil and the Plate,* pp. 127, 150–1; Stewart, *Brazil and La Plata,* pp. 174–6; P. Campbell Scarlett, *South America and the Pacific,* 2 vols. (London, 1838), vol. 1, p. 73; and Vidal, *Picturesque Illustrations,* pp. 61–2.

9. J. A. B. Beaumont, *Travels in Buenos Ayres* (London, 1828), p. 77; Woodbine Parish, *Buenos Ayres and the Rio de la Plata* (London, 1839), p. 15; and Clifton B. Kroeber, *The Growth of the Shipping Industry in the Rio de la Plata Region, 1794–1860* (Madison, Wis., 1957), p. 35.

10. *Five Years' Residence,* p. 4; and the advertisement for the Pilotes Lemanes in *El Argos de Buenos Aires,* No. 75 (18 Sept. 1824), pp. 7–8.

11. For the port regulations, see F.O. 6, vol. 4, no. 3; F.O. 6, vol. 3, no. 6; and F.O. 6, vol. 5, no. 66.

12. For Montevideo and Colonia, see *Five Years' Residence,* pp. 159–62, 170–6; and Thomas Baines, *Observations on the Present State of the Affairs of the River Plate* (Liverpool, 1845).

13. See the correspondence of ship captains in La Plata to Philadelphia merchant Stephen Girard in 1810, in John Bach McMaster, *The Life and*

*Times of Stephen Girard, Mariner and Merchant* (Philadelphia, 1918), pp. 146–52.

14. Horacio William Bliss, *Del virreinato a Rosas; ensayo de historia económica argentina, 1779–1829* (Buenos Aires, 1959), pp. 95–105, contains a convenient résumé of revolutionary free trade reforms.

15. F.O. 6, vol. 4, no. 31; and Ignacio Benito Núñez, *An Account, Political, Historical, and Statistical of the United Provinces of the Río de la Plata* (London, 1825), p. 127. Customs and port revenues normally accounted for well over 80 percent of the income of the Buenos Aires provincial government. See Reber, "British Mercantile Houses," p. 316.

16. For the wheat ban, see F.O. 6, vol. 5, no. 64; and John M. Forbes to John Quincy Adams (25 November 1824), in U.S. Embassy, Republic of Argentina, *Despatches from United States Ministers to Argentina, 1817–1906,* microfilm.

17. For port charges and regulations, see Freeman Hunt, ed., *The Merchant's Magazine, and Commercial Review,* vol. 13 (New York, 1845), p. 294.

18. José María Mariluz Urquijo, *Estado e industria, 1810–1862* (Buenos Aires, 1969), pp. 113–9, has reproduced the text of the 1836 Ley de aduana. Nevertheless, one must see Juan Carlos Nicolau, "La ley de aduana de 1835," *Devenir Histórico,* año 1, no. 1 (Buenos Aires, 1970), pp. 5–14. Nicolau explains how Rosas later modified the protectionist law.

19. Baines, *Observations on the Present State,* pp. 11, 27–8.

20. Historians have done much work on tariff and other political-economic issues. See especially Miron Burgin, *The Economic Aspects of Argentine Federalism, 1820–1852* (Cambridge, Mass., 1946); Mariluz Urquijo, *Estado e industria;* and Juan Carlos Nicolau, "Liberalismo y proteccionismo económico en 1853," unpub. ms., 24 pp. (appearing in the newspaper *La Opinión,* 20 May 1973). For Alberdi's economic philosophy, see Juan Bautista Alberdi, *Sistema económico y rentístico de la Confederación Argentina según su Constitución de 1853* (Buenos Aires, 1954).

21. Kroeber, *Growth of the Shipping Industry,* pp. 73, 127; Juan Carlos Nicolau, "Comercio exterior por el puerto de Buenos Aires: movimiento marítimo (1810–1855)," unpub. ms., 11 pp., Table 2; *REBA,* 1857, vol. 2, p. 68; *REBA,* 1858, vol. 2, p. 81; and *REBA,* 1860, vol. 2, p. 105.

22. H. S. Ferns, *Britain and Argentina in the Nineteenth Century* (Oxford, 1960), p. 80. For specific listing of all British ships arriving at Buenos Aires, see reports by Woodbine Parish in F.O. 6, vol. 2, no. 17 (1826); F.O. 6, vol. 2, no. 382 (1826); F.O. 6, vol. 2, no. 34 (1826); F.O. 6, vol. 4, no. 37 (1825); and F.O. 6, vol. 8, no. 8 (1825).

23. *REBA,* 1857, vol. 2, p. 60; and *REBA,* 1860, vol. 2, pp. 105–6.

24. R. A. Humphreys, *Tradition and Revolt in Latin America and Other Essays* (New York, 1969), pp. 142–3. Philadelphia ships first found fine markets for their flour exports in the 1820s, but later New York and Boston vessels began to dominate the triangular trade that included

Buenos Aires and Havana. See S. W. Higginbotham, "Philadelphia Commerce with Latin America, 1820–1830," *Pennsylvania History,* vol. 9 (1942), pp. 252–66; and Robert G. Albion, *The Rise of New York Port, 1815–1860* (Hamden, Conn., 1961). For the Boston–Canton trade, see Samual Eliot Morison, *The Maritime History of Massachusetts, 1783–1860* (Boston and New York, 1921), p. 271; and Robert Bennet Forbes, *Personal Reminiscences,* 2d ed. (Boston, 1882), pp. 95–104.

25. Adapted from Nicolau, "Comercio exterior," table 4; and Woodbine Parish, *Buenos Ayres, and Provinces of the Rio de la Plata,* 2d ed. (London, 1852), p. 355. The first and second editions of Parish's book are substantially different.

26. Robert G. Albion, "British Shipping and Latin America, 1806–1914," *Journal of Economic History,* vol. 11 (Fall 1951), p. 364; and F.O. 6, vol. 2, no. 5 (1824).

27. Albion, "British Shipping," pp. 365–7; *Almanaque Comercial y Guía de Forasteros para el Estado de Buenos Aires* (Buenos Aires, 1855); and AGN, Sala 10, 42-3-10, "Salidas de Pasageros" (1854–6).

28. See D. C. M. Platt, *Latin America and British Trade, 1806–1914* (New York, 1973), pp. 9–10.

29. Parish, *Buenos Ayres,* 1st ed., pp. 338–9; and ibid., 2d ed., p. 362. Both Parish editions have excellent descriptions of Buenos Aires' foreign trade.

30. English trade figures are from Ferns, *Britain and Argentina,* pp. 132–3. Also see Ferns, "Beginnings of British Investments in Argentina," *Economic History Review,* 2d series, vol. 4, no. 3 (1952), p. 210; and Parish, *Buenos Ayres,* 2d ed., p. 362.

31. Parish, *Buenos Ayres,* 2d ed., p. 361. For an exceptional breakdown of Buenos Aires' imports and exports by country, see AGN, Sala 10, 42-10-11, "Aduana. Movimiento Portuario" (1830–42).

32. George Coggeshall, *Second Series of Voyages* (New York, 1852), p. 186.

33. Higginbotham, "Philadelphia Commerce"; and Frank R. Rutter, "South American Trade of Baltimore," in Johns Hopkins University, *Studies in Historical and Political Science,* vol. 15 (1897), pp. 383–4. For early U.S. flour trade at Buenos Aires, see Miller to Monroe (6 July 1812), in U.S. Consulate, *Buenos Aires Despatches, 1811–1852,* microfilm.

34. Collected from "Annual Reports."

35. *Five Years' Residence,* p. 50; and Karl Wilhelm Körner, *El Cónsul Zimmermann* (Buenos Aires, 1966), p. 130.

36. See Juan Carlos Nicolau, "Tabla del comercio del puerto de Buenos Aires, 1835–1842," unpub. ms., 3 p.; and AGN, Sala 10, 42-10-11, "Aduana." Also see Jacinto Oddone, *La burguesía terrateniente argentina,* 3d ed. (Buenos Aires, 1856), p. 149, for value of the paper peso in gold, 1826 to 1894, in order to compensate for inflation.

37. See Caesar A. Rodney and John Graham, *The Reports on the Present*

*State of the United Provinces* (London, 1819), pp. 127 – 8; and J. P. and W. P. Robertson, *Letters on South America,* 3 vols. (London, 1843), vol. 3, pp. 151 – 4.

38. Herbert Gibson, *The History and Present State of Sheep-Breeding in the Argentine Republic* (Buenos Aires, 1893), pp. 267 – 8.

39. Juan Carlos Nicolau, "Urquiza y su política económica en el período 1835 – 1851," unpub. ms., 31 pp.; and Manual Macchi, *Urquiza el saladerista* (Buenos Aires, 1972), pp. 209 – 10.

40. Parish, *Buenos Ayres,* 1st ed., pp. 353, 355.

41. See Reber, "British Mercantile Houses," pp. 35 – 40; and Ferns, *Great Britain and Argentina,* p. 214. Trade between Argentina and France was perfectly balanced, according to French figures for 1835 to 1840. See *Merchant's Magazine,* vol. 7 (1842), p. 233.

42. Núñez, *Account,* p. 172.

43. "Annual Reports" (1850 – 60).

44. A table on the numbers of British import – export firms in Buenos Aires can be found in Reber, "British Mercantile Houses," p. 319. Also see Kroeber, *Growth of the Shipping Industry,* p. 60; *Five Years' Residence,* pp. 37 – 9; and Forbes to Adams (25 Nov. 1824), U.S. Consulate, *Despatches.* For the conspicuous presence of British merchants throughout Latin America following the revolutions, see Tulio Halperín-Donghi, *Hispanoamérica después de la independencia: consecuencias sociales y económicas de la emancipación* (Buenos Aires, 1972), chap. 2.

45. Reber, "British Mercantile Houses," pp. 80 – 91.

46. Ibid., pp. 69, 319.

47. Kroeber, *Growth of the Shipping Industry,* pp. 61, 151n.

48. On numbers of American firms, see *Five Years' Residence,* p. 49; and Reber, "British Mercantile Houses," p. 122. For the supercargo system, see Dorothy Burne Goebel, "British – American Rivalry in the Chilean Trade, 1817 – 1820," *Journal of Economic History,* vol. 2, no. 2 (Nov. 1942), p. 191; Bruno Fritzsche, " 'On Liberal Terms': The Boston Hide Merchants in California," *Business History Review,* vol. 43, no. 4 (Winter 1968), p. 475; and Morison, *Maritime History,* p. 253.

49. Robertson, *Letters on South America,* vol. 3, pp. 215 – 16, 225; and Reber, "British Mercantile Houses," p. 67.

50. Reber, "British Mercantile Houses," pp. 138 – 40; and B. W. Clapp, *John Owens, Manchester Merchant* (Manchester, 1965), pp. 171 – 3.

51. On the DeForests, see Albion, *New York Port,* p. 188; and Benjamin Keene, *David Curtis DeForest and the Revolution of Buenos Aires* (New Haven, Conn., 1947). Also see Steward, *Brazil and La Plata,* p. 203; and Higginbotham, "Philadelphia Commerce," p. 263.

52. Reber, "British Mercantile Houses," pp. 84, 135. For the costs and procedures in landing cargo, see Andrés M. Carretero, *Los Anchorena: política y negocios en el siglo XIX* (Buenos Aires, 1970), p. 68.

53. Carretero, *Los Anchorena,* pp. 66 – 9. See AGN, Sala 7, 4-4-1, Archivo Anchorena, on correspondence and accounts with their agents upriver.

54. See the letterbook of an anonymous porteño merchant (he never signed copies of his letters) in AGN, Colección Biblioteca Nacional 381, "Libro de correspondencia comercial" (1847—49), especially his letters to Gex y Descosted and to J. J. M. de Mendia in Rio de Janeiro (Buenos Aires, 13 June 1842).

55. Körner, *El Consul Zimmermann,* p. 16; *La Gaceta Mercantil* (Buenos Aires, 23 April 1834); Parish, *Buenos Ayres,* 1st ed., p. 34; and *Five Years' Residence,* p. 33. For the public auction, see AGN, Sala 10, 37-1-9, "Entradas Terrestres" (1829—30).

56. Scarlett, *South America,* vol. 1, p. 186, mentions finding a French dry goods retailer in a Córdoba village. On British investments in shopkeeping, see *Five Years' Residence,* p. 35; and Ferns, "Beginnings of British Investment." Often, foreign merchants provided the capital that their countrymen needed to establish shops in Buenos Aires. See AGN, Registro No. 74, Gómez (1840), "Escritura de sociedad entre Dn. Nicolás Munck y Dn. Enrique Heffner"; and AGN, Registro No. 73 (Comercio 1), Manuel J. Saine de Cavia (1820), "Separación de companía Juan Luis Darbi y Tomás Barton."

57. Gibson, *History and Present State,* pp. 24—5.

58. Humphreys, *Tradition and Revolt,* p. 123; and Ralph W. Hidy, *The House of Baring in American Trade and Finance* (Cambridge, Mass., 1949), pp. 66, 559.

59. On the Bolivian enterprise, see R. A. Humphreys, *Liberation in South America, 1806—1827* (London, 1952), pp. 145—62. For La Famatina Company in La Rioja, consult the travelogue by its chief engineer, F. B. Head, *Rough Notes Taken During Some Rapid Journeys Across the Pampa and Among the Andes* (London, 1826); and AGN, Sala 10, 1-3-1 and -2, "Hullet Hermanos y Cía. Gran Bretaña. Correspondencia" (1825—37), which has accounts of the British mining enterprise.

60. *Five Years' Residence,* pp. 95—6; and especially Robertson, *Letters on South America,* vol. 3, p. 153.

61. Reber, "British Mercantile Houses," p. 46; and Clapp, *John Owens,* pp. 84—7. The latter implies that sales of hides on the British market did not always assure a profit.

62. Richard J. Cleveland, *In the Forecastle; or, Twenty-five Years a Sailor* (New York, 1840?), p. 9.

63. General information on nineteenth-century credit may be found in T. S. Ashton, "The Bill of Exchange and Private Banks in Lancashire, 1790—1830," *Economic History Review,* vol. 15, nos. 1 and 2 (1945), pp. 25—35; and Edwin J. Perkins, "Financing Antebellum Importers: The Role of Brown Bros. & Co. in Baltimore," *Business History Review,* vol. 45, no. 4 (Winter 1971), pp. 421—45. For specific use of credit in Buenos Aires, see Reber, "British Mercantile Houses," pp. 73—8; Clapp, *John Owens,* pp. 77, 83—4; and F.O. 6, vol. 9 (1825), p. 162.

64. Reber, "British Mercantile Houses," pp. 148—9; and Rodney and Graham, *Report on the Present State, p. 128.* For examples of libranzas

passing from foreign to native porteño merchants and from porteños to native merchants upriver, see AGN, Sala 7, 4-4-1, Archivo Anchorena. Reber's recent research on the letter of credit in Buenos Aires has filled a void in Argentine business history that was pointed out earlier by Tulio Halperín-Donghi, *El revisionismo histórico argentino* (Buenos Aires, 1970), pp. 74−5.

65. See Hidy, *The House of Baring;* and Perkins, "Financing Antebellum Importers," on Brown Bros. & Co.

66. A British naval vessel was stationed at Buenos Aires in order to protect English merchant ships, although the Foreign Office later decided to observe the Spanish blockade. Goebel, "British−American Rivalry," p. 190; and Charles K. Webster, ed., *Britain and the Independence of Latin America, 1812−1830: Select Documents from the Foreign Office Archives,* 2 vols. (London and New York, 1938), vol. 1, pp. 83, 96.

67. Charles Brand, *Journal of a Voyage to Peru* (London, 1828), p. 34. Also see F.O. 6, (1827), pp. 273−4; and John Murray Forbes, *Once años en Buenos Aires, 1820−1831; las crónicas diplomáticas de John Murray Forbes,* trans. by Felipe Espil (Buenos Aires, 1956), pp. 113−20.

68. Arthur Redford, *Manchester Merchants and Foreign Trade, 1794−1838* (Manchester, 1934), vol. 1, pp. 101−5.

69. See Anon. to J. M. Pieto de Acha in Burdeo (Buenos Aires, 4 July 1848), AGN, Colección Biblioteca Nacional 371, "Libro de correspondencia comercial."

70. McMaster, *The Life and Times,* p. 155; and F.O. 6, vol. 20 (1827), p. 275.

71. See "Annual Reports" for the years of blockade at Buenos Aires. Also see William R. Manning, ed., *Diplomatic Correspondence of the United States: Inter-American Affairs, 1831−1860,* vol. 1, *Argentina* (Washington, D.C., 1932), pp. 442−3; and Anon. to J. M. de Mendia in Rio de Janeiro (Buenos Aires, 17 Jan. 1848), AGN, Biblioteca Nacional 371, "Libro de correspondencia comercial."

72. Reber, "British Mercantile Houses," p. 185; F.O. 6, vol. 20 (1827), pp. 267−9.

73. Parish, *Buenos Ayres,* 1st ed., pp. 355−6.

74. The first break in commodity prices in Britain and the United States followed the conclusion of the Napoleonic Wars, when the cessation of trade disruptions eased the high cost of shipping. See explanations of continued price decline in Thomas Tooke and William Newmarch, *A History of Prices and the State of the Circulation from 1791 to 1856,* 5 vols. (London, 1838−57), vol. 2, pp. 348−9; and Landes, *Unbound Prometheus,* pp. 232−4.

75. Tooke and Newmarch, *History of Prices,* vol. 4, pp. 53, 64; Gayer et al., *Growth and Fluctuation,* vol. 2, p. 843; and Anne Bezanson, Robert D. Gray, and Miriam Hussey, *Wholesale Prices in Philadelphia, 1784−1861,* 2 vols. (Philadelphia, 1936−7), vol. 2, pp. 94, 264.

76. Julio Broide, *La evolución de los precios agropecuarios argentinos en el*

*período 1830–1850* (Buenos Aires, 1959). Broide's work shows that prices in paper pesos increased greatly due to inflation. In terms of gold or real prices, the trend at Buenos Aires was downward.

77. On the issue of economic imperialism, see Stanley J. Stein and Shane J. Hunt, "Principal Currents in the Economic Historiography of Latin America," *Journal of Economic History,* vol. 31 (March 1971), p. 251; Ferns, "British Informal Empire"; D. C. M. Platt, "The Imperialism of Free Trade: Some Reservations," *Economic History Review,* 2d series, vol. 21, no. 2 (Aug. 1968), pp. 299, 306; and W. M. Mathew, "The Imperialism of Free Trade: Peru, 1820–70," *Economic History Review,* 2d series, vol. 21, no. 3 (Dec. 1968), pp. 562–79.

### 5. Buenos Aires as emporium of regional trade and processing

1. J. P. and W. P. Robertson, *Letters on South America,* 3 vols. (London, 1843), vol. 2, pp. 34–41; E. E. Vidal, *Picturesque Illustrations of Buenos Ayres and Montevideo* (London, 1820), pp. 5–6; and P. Campbell Scarlett, *South America and the Pacific,* 2 vols. (London, 1838), vol. 1, p. 71.

2. See the personal, political, and commercial correspondence dispatches in 1855 via steam navigation in AGN, Colección Biblioteca Nacional 757, "Gelly y Obes" (15120–2). Also see Benjamín Vicuña Mackenna, *La Argentina en el año 1855* (Buenos Aires, 1936), pp. 106–7.

3. Juan Carlos Nicolau, "Tabla del comercio del puerto de Buenos Aires, 1835–1842," unpub. ms., 11 pp., p. 3; and *REBA,* 1858, vol. 2, no. 57, pp. 59–60.

4. Arrivals in 1860 are estimated on a two-to-three ratio to departures, consistent with ratios of previous years. My actual count of 1,287 seems too low. While researching, I tried to count the entry and departure of rivercraft at Buenos Aires between 1810 and 1860 from customs and marine documents in the AGN. The results were disappointing. Recording procedures varied considerably from year to year, and not all documents are extant. Furthermore, coastal vessels put into Boca del Riachuelo as well as other points along the coast. I wanted to reconstruct the data at five-year intervals but discovered records for particular years missing. Occasionally, two sources might yield conflicting figures. For 1840, "Marina" reported 739 departures, and "Aduana" recorded only 672. Both seem too low. Departures generally exceeded arrivals, because most cargoes of imported goods originated at Buenos Aires, whereas incoming coastal vessels unloaded goods at several points near the city. There remains little doubt, nevertheless, that traditional river traffic at Buenos Aires expanded considerably. See AGN, Sala 10, 36-8-9, "Marina, Entradas de buques de tráfico costero" (1809–14); Sala 10, 37-1-1, "Entradas de cabotaje" (1829–30); Sala 10, 36-7-14, "Marina, Salidas de cabotaje" (1859–60); and Sala 10, 36-6-24, "Marina, Entradas de cabotaje" (1858–60).

5. *REBA,* 1858, vol. 1, p. 143, shows 1,631 arrivals for Conchas, Tigre, and San Fernando and only 561 arrivals for Buenos Aires in 1828.

6. *REBA,* 1857, vol. 2, p. 62. The average size of rivercraft putting in at Buenos Aires was 44 tons each; at Boca, 18 tons; and at San Fernando, 5 tons.

7. Vidal, *Picturesque Illustrations,* p. 1; and *A Five Years' Residence in Buenos Ayres. During the Years 1820 to 1825* (London, 1825), p. 62.

8. For road conditions, see Robertson, *Letters on South America,* vol. 2, pp. 61—3; and Charles B. Mansfield, *Paraguay, Brazil and the Plate: Letters Written in 1852—1853* (Cambridge, 1856), p. 161. For overland freight traffic, see "Tabla general de las tropas de carretas y arrias que han salido al interior en 1829," in AGN, Sala 10, 42-8-5, "Censos" (1813—61); and Silvia Cristina Mallo, Amalia Latroubesse de Díaz, and María Concepción Orruma. "El comercio entre Buenos Aires y las provincias de 1830 a 1835," in ANH, *Primer congreso,* p. 269.

9. Many travelers described the unique carts of the era. See especially Charles Samuel Stewart, *Brazil and La Plata: The Personal Record of a Cruise* (New York, 1856), pp. 178—9; and Tom Bard Jones, *South American Re-discovered* (New York, 1968), which recapitulates the exploits of European travelers in nineteenth-century South America.

10. For descriptions of mule and cart trains at Buenos Aires in 1810, see Vidal, *Picturesque Illustrations,* pp. 89, 92. AGN, Sala 10, 37-3-5, "Hacienda-Aduana, Entradas y salidas marítimas y terrestres, tomas de razón" (1846—8), lists consignments of goods delivered to Buenos Aires by overland freight carriers.

11. See "Tabla general de las tropas de carretas y arrias venidas del interior en 1831," in AGN, Sala 10, 42-8-5, "Censos" (1813—61); and *REBA,* 1860, vol. 2, p. 83. Freight tonnage estimated on basis of 140 arrobas per cart and 8 arrobas per packmule, doubling the figures of the half year of 1831 in order to approximate the entire year's total.

12. Figures taken from Juan Carlos Nicolau, *Antecedentes para la historia de la industria argentina* (Buenos Aires, 1968), p. 154; *REBA,* 1858, vol. 1., p. 114; and *REBA,* 1860, vol. 2, p. 83. My own count of arrivals and departures of freight caravans at Buenos Aires was a good deal less satisfying than the count of river shipping. But fragmented data in archival sources, however unquantifiable, do point to a downturn in the Interior's overland freight traffic at Buenos Aires. For disparate sources, see various *entradas y salidas terrestres* in AGN, Sala 10, 37-2-17 (1826—8); Sala 10, 37-2-25 (1832—3); Sala 10, 37-3-5 (1846—8); Sala 10, 37-2-26 (1848—9); and Sala 10, 37-3-7 (1849—50).

13. Adapted from statistics in *REBA,* 1857, vol. 2, p. 62; and tables on cart and mule traffic in AGN, Sala 10, 42-8-5, "Censos" (1813—61). The idea that Buenos Aires' commercial prosperity, especially during the governorship of Juan Manuel de Rosas, did not extend to the Interior began with a contemporary, Juan Bautista Alberdi. Alberdi particularly detested internal customs duties that supposedly inhibited river navigation and overland transportation. See Alberdi, *Bases y puntos de partida para la organización política de la República Argentina* (Buenos Aires, 1914), pp.

87—8. Among recent historians, Miron Burgin contends that the economy of the Interior declined because of internal customs wars among the provincial governments, the end of silver production in Peru, and the inefficiency of traditional modes of transport. See Miron Burgin, *The Economic Aspects of Argentine Federalism, 1820—1852* (Cambridge, Mass., 1946), pp. 16, 118—21; and also James Scobie, *Argentina, A City and A Nation,* 2d ed. (New York, 1971), pp. 93—4; and Tulio Halperín-Donghi, *Revolución y guerra: formación de un élite dirigente en la Argentina criolla* (Buenos Aires, 1972), pp. 94—126.

14. AGN, Sala 10, 37-2-17, "Hacienda-Aduana, Entradas y salidas marímas y terrestres, tomas de razón" (1826—8).

15. See Oscar Luis Ensinck, "El puerto de Rosario, puerto de la Confederación Argentina, 1850—1860," in ANH, *Primer congreso,* pp. 319—33.

16. See the monthly market statistics for 1829 and 1861 in AGN, Sala 10, 42-8-5, "Censos" (1813—61).

17. *REBA,* 1859, vol. 2, p. 103; *REBA,* 1857, vol. 2, p. 165; and "Annual Reports" (1831). One fanega (2.5 bushels) of Argentine wheat weighed 9 arrobas or 102 kilograms and produced 6 arrobas or 68 kilograms of milled flour. One barrel of U.S. flour equaled 3.9 bushels and weighed approximately 95 kilograms or 8.4 arrobas.

18. For the Recova Vieja, see James Scobie, *Buenos Aires, Plaza to Suburb, 1870—1910* (New York, 1974), pp. 36—37; and police records on rental of retail stalls at the plaza in AGN, Sala 10, 36-1-1, "Policía, mercados y corrales" (1825—33). *Five Years' Residence,* p. 81, provides some detail on the central market.

19. From "Introdución de productos de industria rural durante el primer y segundo semestres de 1829," in AGN, Sala 10, 42-8-5, "Censos" (1813—61).

20. See various warehouse inventories listed in Nicolau, *Antecedentes para la historia,* p. 105; Diana Hernando, "Casa y Familia: Spatial Biographies in Nineteenth Century Buenos Aires," Ph.D. diss. (University of California at Los Angeles, 1973), p. 513; and AGN, Colección Biblioteca Nacional 226, "Manual Trelles, Autógrafos Donados" (3270/110), Miguel Otero to Juan Moreno (Buenos Aires, 20 Sept. 1849).

21. See the warehouse receipts from Andrés de la Peña Fernández to Juan José Cristobal de Anchorena in AGN: Sala 7, 4-3-6, Archivo Anchorena; and Andrés M. Carretero, *Los Anchorena: política y negocios en el siglo XIX* (Buenos Aires, 1970), p. 107.

22. See Woodbine Parish, *Buenos Ayres and the Rio de la Plata: Their Present State, Trade and Debt* (London, 1839), pp. 34—5; William MacCann, *Two Thousand Miles' Ride Through the Argentine Provinces,* 2 vols. (London, 1853), vol. 2, pp. 216—17; and Vicuña Mackenna, *Argentina,* p. 124.

23. In fact, the railways serving those markets were named for both the market terminals and the areas of service. The Northern Railroad terminated at North Market at Retiro Station; the Western Railroad in West

Market at Plaza Once; and the Southern Railroad in South Market at Plaza Constitución. See Scobie, *Buenos Aires,* pp. 40, 58, and 92–104; and V. Martin de Moussey, *Description géographique et statistique de la Confédération Argentine* (Paris, 1873), Planche 8. On the first rail terminal at West Market see "Relación de los frutos del país entrados en todo el presente mes por las vías terrestre y ferrea" in AGN, Sala 10, 42-8-5, "Censos" (1813–61).

24. Phillip Curtin, *The Atlantic Slave Trade: A Census* (Madison, Wis., 1969), p. 234, provides the following statistics on the importing of slaves into Brazil and Cuba:

|        | 1811–20 | 1821–30 | 1831–40 | 1841–50 | 1851–60 |
|--------|---------|---------|---------|---------|---------|
| Brazil | 266,800 | 325,000 | 212,000 | 338,300 | 3,300   |
| Cuba   | 79,900  | 112,500 | 126,100 | 47,600  | 123,300 |

25. Alfredo Montoya, *Historia de los saladeros argentinos* (Buenos Aires, 1956), pp. 33–6; Horacio William Bliss, *Del virreinato a Rosas: ensayo de historia económica argentina, 1776–1829* (Buenos Aires, 1959), p. 118; and for *graserías,* see AGN, Colección Biblioteca Nacional 226 (3270/167), Vicente Toruda to Juan Moreno (Buenos Aires, 11 Jan. 1851).

26. *REBA,* 1857, vol. 2, p. 46.

27. Mansfield, *Paraguay, Brazil and the Plate,* pp. 164–5. The italics are Mansfield's.

28. See the contract establishing the partnership and various accounting balances in AGN, Sala 7, 7-7-12 (20), "Libro de el establecimiento de carnes en el partido de los Quilmes" (1816).

29. Descriptions of salting operations abound in the travel literature of the period. See especially MacCann, *Two Thousand Miles' Ride,* vol. 1, pp. 211–5; Mansfield, *Paraguay, Brazil and the Plate,* pp. 164–5; Wilfred Latham, *The States of the River Plate: Their Industries and Commerce* (London, 1866), pp. 6–11, 113–25; and Francis Bond Head, *Reports Relating to the Failure of the Rio Plata Mining Association* (London, 1827), pp. 33–5.

30. On saladero efficiency, see Thomas J. Page, *La Plata, the Argentine Confederation and Paraguay* (New York, 1859), p. 323; Montoya, *Historia de los saladeros,* pp. 72–3; and Nicolau, *Antecedentes para la historia,* p. 103. Antoine (Antonio) Cambaceres settled permanently in Buenos Aires and established one of the socially elite families of the city. See Hernando, "Casa y Familia," pp. 716–46.

31. For production and work statistics, see *REBA,* 1854, p. 47; and "Datos estadísticos de los saladeros en el tercer y quarto trimestres de 1858 (Barracas al Sud, 8 January 1859)" in AGN, Sala 10, 42-8-5, "Censos" (1813–61). Several economic factors retarded the introduction of new breeds of cattle. The supposition was that the dominant saladero processing required the lean meat and thick hides provided by unimproved native longhorns. See Simon G. Hanson, *Argentine Meat and the British Market* (Palo Alto, Calif., 1938), p. 13; Burgin, *Economic Aspects,* p. 256;

and Scobie, *Argentina,* p. 81. In contracts with cattle ranchers, in fact, *saladeristas* required the delivery of well-fattened cattle. Steers were preferred over cows, because cows carried less weight in fat and had a thinner hide. Fat cattle simply furnished more tallow and grease, salable items in the export trade. The introduction of new strains of cattle awaited technological breakthroughs that allowed the chilling and transportation of quality meats and the economic use of barbed wire to separate the breeding stocks on the ranch.

32. MacCann, *Two Thousand Miles' Ride,* vol. 1, p. 211; and Montoya, *Historia de los saladeros,* pp. 73, 78.

33. For information on the corrals and beef provision, see Vidal, *Picturesque Illustrations,* pp. 35—6; *Five Years' Residence,* p. 83; Scarlett, *South America,* vol. 1, pp. 87—94; Latham, *States of the River Plate,* pp. 10—11; and H. M. Brackenridge, *Voyage to South America,* 2 vols. (London, 1820), vol. 1, pp. 255. Also see the corral administration papers in AGN, Sala 10, 36-1-1, "Policía"; Sala 10, 27-6-4, "Policía, reglamento para los corrales de abasto público" (1814—62); and Sala 10, 26-4-1, "Policía, corrales" (1833).

34. *REBA,* 1860, vol. 2, p. 101. See *REBA,* 1854, pp. 45—6, for Carlos Pelligrini's estimate on meat consumption. Although a porteño ate 227 kilograms or the beef of one steer per year, the country folk of the area each consumed 909 kilograms (four steers). By comparison, a Londoner of the era reportedly ate only 23 kilograms of meat a year.

35. See "Ganado introducido por las tabladas y movimiento de los corrales, 1861," in AGN, Sala 10, 42-8-5, "Censos" (1813—61). The figures do not include 12,035 mares and horses and 7,874 head of sheep also processed at the stockyards that month.

36. See Nicolau, *Antecedentes para la historia,* p. 99, for 1830 data; and *REBA,* 1857, vol. 2, p. 51. The latter year's statistics do not account for the wholesaling of 153,428 horses, 60,295 head of sheep, and 4,202 pigs.

37. See the advertisements in *El Argos de Buenos Aires,* 21 Aug. 1824, p. 6; and 23 June 1824, p. 4. John Lynch, *The Spanish-American Revolutions, 1808—1826* (New York, 1973), p. 86, maintains that the blacks and mulattoes made up 24.7 percent of Buenos Aires' population in 1822. Six of every ten blacks and three of every ten mulattoes were still held in bondage.

38. *Five Years' Residence,* pp. 67—8. Also see a draft copy of the 1824 British—Argentine treaty abolishing the international slave trade in the Río de la Plata in F.O. 6, vol. 5, no. 51, Parish to Canning (Buenos Aires, 3 Sept. 1824).

39. See a résumé of the 1822 census of Buenos Aires in *REBA,* 1858, vol. 1, p. 67; and *Almanaque Comercial y Guía de Forasteros para el Estado de Buenos Aires. Año de 1855* (Buenos Aires, 1855), p. 142.

40. Karl Frederick Graeber, "Buenos Aires: A Social and Economic History of a Traditional Spanish American City on the Verge of Change, 1810—1855," Ph.D. diss. (University of California at Los Angeles, 1977),

chap. 3. For an unusually good census giving occupation, origin, and family information on Buenos Aires' inhabitants, see AGN, Sala 10, 23-5-5, "Censo de la ciudad" (1827).

41. *REBA,* 1857, vol. 1, p. 124; and *REBA,* 1861, vol. 1, p. 94. The figures represent the number of passengers arriving subtracted by the total departing. In 1823–5, more were departing – thus the negative number.

42. For occupations of British residents at Buenos Aires, see F.O. 6, vol. 20, p. 314, James Brittain to Woodbine Parish (Buenos Aires, 7 Oct. 1827); and F.O. 6, vol. 9, p. 57. Parish to Canning (Buenos Aires, 6 Aug. 1825). For lists of riverboat crews, see AGN, Sala 10, 36-7-12, "Salidas de cabotaje, tripulación buques de cabotaje" (1855–7).

43. Ernesto J. A. Maeder, *Evolución demográfica argentina de 1810 a 1869* (Buenos Aires, 1969), pp. 30, 35.

44. *Five Years' Residence,* p. 69; and Vicuña Mackenna, *Argentina,* pp. 83–4. Apparently, unskilled blacks and mulattoes benefited less than others from the rising work opportunities in this export-led urban development. See Graeber, "Buenos Aires," chap. 4.

45. See correspondence of the Buenos Aires chief of police in AGN, Collección Biblioteca Nacional 226 (3270/5), Enrique Ochoa to Juan Moreno (Recoleta, 184?); and (3270/57), Pedro L. Echagüe to Juan Moreno (Barracas, 7 Feb. 1848).

46. *Five Years' Residence,* pp. 91–2. Other travelers noticed the rise of creoles back in the mid-1810s, when Spanish merchant dominance was declining in the face of new British trade. See Robertson, *Letters on South America,* vol. 2, pp. 67–8. Historians often discount the existence of an important middle level of creole merchants. See Roberto Cortés Conde, *The First Stage of Modernization in Spanish America* (New York, 1974), p. 124; Ferns, *Britain and Argentina in the Nineteenth Century* (Oxford, 1960), p. 144; and Aldo Ferrer, *La economía argentina: las etapas de su desarrollo y problemas actuales* (Buenos Aires, 1963), pp. 70–3.

47. *Almanaque, 1826,* lists 56 *negociantes* with foreign names and 29 with Spanish names. A count of merchants exporting goods in January 1850 reveals that 32 merchants with Anglo names, 21 Spanish, 11 Italian, and 8 French were actively engaged in exporting goods. See AGN, Sala 10, 37-3-7, "Aduana-Hacienda, Entradas y salidas marítimas, tomas de razón" (1849–50).

48. On the connections between foreign and native merchants, see Reber, "British Mercantile Houses," pp. 84, 135; Carretero, *Los Anchorena,* pp. 66–9; Karl Wilhelm Körner. *El Consul Zimmermann: su actuación en Buenos Aires, 1815–1847* (Buenos Aires, 1966), p. 16; and AGN, Sala 7, 4-4-1, Archivo Anchorena.

49. For merchants engaging in the river trades, see AGN, Sala 10, 37-3-7, "Aduana Hacienda"; Sala 10, 36-6-23, "Marina, Entradas de cabotaje" (1855–8); Sala 10, 37-1-4, "Aduana, Entradas de cabotaje" (1851); and Sala 7, 15-4-8, Colección de Félix Frías (93), Manuel Frías to Juan Frías (Montevideo, 18 July 1840).

50. For boat registeries at Buenos Aires, see AGN, Sala 10, 36-8-1, "Marina, Matrículas de zumacas, buques menores y balleneros"(1840—4); Sala 10, 26-8-4, "Matrículas del cabotaje nacional, libro segundo" (1844—57).

51. *El Argos de Buenos Aires* (29 May 1824), p. 4. For the merchants receiving freight from the Interior, see AGN, Sala 10, 37-2-17, "Aduana-Hacienda"; Sala 10, 37-2-25, "Aduana-Hacienda. Entradas y salidas marítimas y terrestres, tomas de razón" (1832—3); Sala 10, 37-2-26, "Aduana-Hacienda. Entradas marítimas" (1848—9); and Sala 10, 37-3-7, "Aduana-Hacienda."

52. See various "cuentas de venta y liquido de cueros" in AGN, Sala 7, 4-2-1 and 4-3-6, Archivo Anchorena.

53. The AGN has Larrea's letterbook containing his commercial correspondence. Although the author of the letterbook is anonymous, I have ascertained from the correspondence within that the book belonged to the Larrea brothers. See AGN, Colección Biblioteca Nacional 371, "Libro de correspondencia comercial" (1847—9).

54. See AGN, Sala 10, 37-2-1, "Aduana-Hacienda," and compare consignees with lists of porteño merchants in *Almanaque 1826*.

55. Kroeber, *Growth of the Shipping Industry,* p. 63; and Hernando, "Casa y familia," pp. 260, 273.

56. For proprietorship of warehouses and salting plants in Buenos Aires, see *Almanaque 1836*; AGN, Sala 3, 33-7-15, "Libro de patentes" (1836); and *REBA, 1857*, vol. 2, p. 46.

57. This information on capital and credit in the native merchant community is derived from various commercial contracts registered with public notaries of Buenos Aires. The AGN maintains these *registros comerciales* dating from the early colonial period up to the twentieth century. They register contracts for payment of debts, business partnerships, loans of money, commercial association, and authorizations of power-of-attorney. I have seen the following: AGN, Registro 73 (Comercio 1), Manuel J. Saine de Cavia (1819—20); Registro 74 (Comercio 2), Antonio Fausto Gómez (1840—9); and Registro 73 (Comercio 1), Pedro Callexa de Prieto (1860).

### 6. Expanding the frontiers of production on the pampa

1. Miron Burgin, *The Economic Aspects of Argentine Federalism. 1820—1852* (Cambridge, Mass., 1946); Tulio Halperín-Donghi, *Revolución y guerra: formación de una élite dirigente en la Argentina criolla* (Buenos Aires, 1972); James R. Scobie, *Argentina, a City and a Nation,* 2d ed. (New York, 1971); and Jacinto Oddone, *La burguesía terrateniente argentina,* 3d ed. (Buenos Aires, 1956).

2. For two fine monographs on pampa geography, see Oscar Schmieder, "Alteration of the Argentine Pampa in the Colonial Period," *University of California Publications in Geography,* vol. 2, no. 10 (1927); and Schmieder,

"The Pampa, a Natural or Culturally Induced Grassland?" *University of California Publications in Geography,* vol. 2, no. 8 (1927), pp. 255–70. Travel accounts also provide some description. See P. Campbell Scarlett, *South America and the Pacific,* 2 vols. (London, 1838), vol. 1, pp. 99–100; and Alcides d'Orbigny, *Viaje a la América Meridional,* trans. from the French, 4 vols. (Buenos Aires, 1844), vol. 1, p. 433.

3. Charles R. Darwin, *The Voyage of the Beagle* (New York, 1858), p. 101.

4. Ibid., p. 98; Wilfred Latham, *The States of the River Plate: Their Industries and Commerce* (London, 1866), p. 14; and Herbert Gibson, *The History and Present State of the Sheep-breeding Industry in the Argentine Republic* (Buenos Aires, 1893), pp. 20–1, 255–6.

5. For the delivery of rural products all year round, see the quarterly statistical tables of rural production for the district of Pila, 1858, in AGN, Sala 10, 42-8-5, "Censos" (1813–61).

6. Darwin, *Voyage of the Beagle,* p. 101; William MacCann, *Two Thousand Miles' Ride Through the Argentine Province,* 2 vols. (London, 1953), vol. 1, pp. 198–9; Latham, *States of the River Plate,* p. 15; and John Miller, *The Memoirs of John Miller in the Service of the Republic of Peru,* 2d ed., 2 vols. (London, 1829), vol. 1, p. 143.

7. MacCann, *Two Thousand Miles' Ride,* vol. 1, p. 273.

8. See the case of a Cañuelas estanciero, E. Costa, who was all but driven from his ten-year-old cattle ranch by the 1830 drought, in AGN, Sala 7, 16-4-10, Colección Ruiz Guiñazú (1722); E. Costa to J. M. de Rosas (Montevideo, 5 Sept. 1849).

9. Darwin, *Voyage of the Beagle,* p. 88. For other firsthand accounts of droughts, see *A Five Years' Residence in Buenos Aires, During the Years 1820 to 1825* (London, 1825), pp. 7, 83, 88–9; J. A. B. Beaumont, *Travels in Buenos Ayres, and the Adjacent Provinces of the Río de la Plata* (London, 1828), p. 21; and Alexander Caldcleugh, *Travels in South America During the Years 1819–20–21,* 2 vols. (London, 1825), vol. 1, p. 200.

10. Woodbine Parish, *Buenos Ayres and the Río de la Plata: Their Present State, Trade and Debt,* 1st ed. (London, 1839), p. 371; and "Annual Reports" (1830).

11. Gibson, *History and Present State,* pp. 260–1.

12. Parish, *Buenos Ayres,* 1st ed., p. 216. Also see Beaumont, *Travels in Buenos Ayres,* p. 43; and *Five Years' Residence,* p. 88.

13. *REBA,* 1857, vol. 2, p. 48.

14. For descriptions of farming, see Beaumont, *Travels in Buenos Ayres,* p. 31; Caldcleugh, *Travels in South America,* vol. 1, p. 152; *Francis Bond Head, Reports Relating to the Failure of the Río Plata Mining Association* (London, 1827), p. 31; Latham, *States of the River Plate,* p. 34; and Frederick Gerstaecker, *Narrative of a Journey Round the World* (New York, 1853), p. 39.

15. Latham, *States of the River Plate,* pp. 17, 179.

16. MacCann, *Two Thousand Miles' Ride,* vol. 1, p. 62, refers to the

situation in the ranching center of Chascomus. Agricultural historians recognize that location of rural production anywhere in the world was not determined so much by climate, soil, ethnic or political influences. "What farmers grow and where they grow it," writes one historian, "is determined primarily by the economic distance of the farm from the metropolis." John T. Schlebecker, "The World Metropolis and the History of American Agriculture," *Journal of Economic History,* vol. 20 (June 1960), pp. 187–208.

17. Juan Manuel de Rosas, *Instrucciones a los mayordomos de estancia* (Buenos Aires, 1951), pp. 16–17.

18. Descriptions of estancias may be found in Gibson, *History and Present State,* pp. 22–3, 288; E. E. Vidal, *Picturesque Illustrations of Buenos Ayres and Montevideo* (London, 1820), pp. 71–3; Head, *Reports Relating to the Failure,* pp. 15–19; Latham, *States of the River Plate,* p. 28; Beaumont, *Travels in Buenos Ayres,* pp. 63–4; and MacCann, *Two Thousand Miles' Ride,* vol. 1. For estancia inventories and layout, see Diana Hernando, "Casa y Familia: Spatial Biographies in Nineteenth Century Buenos Aires," Ph.D. diss. (University of California, Los Angeles, 1973), pp. 207–8, 611–14; and Pedro M. López Godoy, *Historia de la propiedad y primeros pobladores del Partido de Pergamino,* 2 vols. (Pergamino, Argentina, 1973), vol. 1, pp. 37, 217–18, 270–1.

19. Gerstaeker, *Narrative of a Journey,* p. 41.

20. Scarlett, *South America,* vol. 1, p. 106; and Vidal, *Picturesque Illustrations,* pp. 71–2.

21. Agustín Isaías de Elía, "Los Ramos Mexía; historia y tradiciones de viejas estancias argentinas," unpub ms. (Buenos Aires, n.d.), pp. 90, 122. This manuscript, which I perused through the courtesy of Eduardo Saguier, is a good historical and autobiographical account of nineteenth-century ranch life by a scion (born ca. 1890) of this famous Argentine ranching family.

22. Based upon the AGN, Colección Biblioteca National 739, "Libro diario de la Chacra San Francisco" (1864–70). Belonging to the Obligado family, this daily account book of the farm located in Matanza outside Buenos Aires is a rich source for the finances and operation of Argentine farming.

23. MacCann, *Two Thousand Miles' Ride,* vol. 1, p. 134; and Caldcleugh, *Travels in South America,* vol. 1, pp. 152, 171–2, 241.

24. Latham, *States of the River Plate,* p. 24. For wells on the pampa, see Noel S. Sbarra, *Historia de las aguadas y el molino* (La Plata, Argentina, 1961).

25. Gerstaeker, *Narrative of a Journey,* p. 34; and John Miers, *Travels in Chile and La Plata,* 2 vols. (London, 1826), vol. 1, p. 11.

26. William Henry Hudson, *Far Away and Long Ago; a History of My Early Life* (New York, 1924), p. 50. Hudson, author of the famous novel *Green Mansions,* was born on the Argentine estancia of his English parents.

27. For a historical account of early fencing and of the barbed wire that

replaced it see Noel Sbarra, *Historia del alambrado en la Argentina* (Buenos Aires, 1964).

28. Elía, "Los Ramos Mexía," p. 135; Francis Bond Head, *Rough Notes Taken During Some Rapid Journeys Across the Pampas and Among the Andes* (London, 1826), p. 32; and Latham, *States of the River Plate*, p. 34.

29. Latham, *States of the River Plate*, pp. 33–6; Simon G. Hanson, *Argentine Meat and the British Market* (Stanford, Calif., 1938), p. 12; and Prudencio de la C. Mendoza, *Historia de la ganadería argentina*, pp. 155–7. I am wary of the opinion of Mendoza, Hanson, and others that the estancia-saladero interests conspired against new breeding, when, in fact, there existed no economic impulse to breed fine beef stock. For more on the cattle industry, see Horacio C. E. Gilberti, *Historia económica de la ganadería* (Buenos Aires, 1954).

30. AGN, Sala 10, 36-1-1 (317), "Policía. Mercado corrales" (1825–33).

31. Elía, "Los Ramos Mexía," p. 135; Latham, *States of the River Plate*, pp. 29–32; and Rosas, *Instrucciones a los mayordomos*, p. 40.

32. Rosas, *Instrucciones a los mayordomos*, p. 19.

33. Derived from ranch account books in AGN, Sala 13, 15-4-3 (libro 3), "Estancia San Miguel del Monte de la familia Roca" (1809–12); and Museo Bartolomé Mitre, Buenos Aires, A1-C44-C71, no. 11, "Papeles referentes a la administración de la Estancia Las Palmas perteneciente a Doña Ana María Otarola" (1844–52).

34. Vidal, *Picturesque Illustrations*, p. 72. Also see *Five Years' Residence*, p. 82.

35. MacCann, *Two Thousand Miles' Ride*, vol. 1, pp. 277–9; and Gibson, *History and Present State*, pp. 24–5, 275–9.

36. Gibson, *History and Present State*, pp. 26, 269; and Latham, *States of the River Plate*, pp. 24–6.

37. Latham, *States of the River Plate*, pp. 23–4; MacCann, *Two Thousand Miles' Ride*, vol. 1, p. 279; and Gibson, *History and Present State*, pp. 254, 276–7.

38. Gibson, *History and Present State*, p. 277.

39. Ibid., p. 279. Also see Latham, *States of the River Plate*, pp. 42, 46–7.

40. Latham, *States of the River Plate*, p. 25; and Gibson, *History and Present State*, pp. 254, 270.

41. Gibson, *History and Present State*, pp. 31, 267–8.

42. Juan Álvarez, *Las guerras civiles argentinas* (Buenos Aires, 1972), p. 80.

43. Burgin, *Economic Aspects*, pp. 24, 31–2; and Scobie, *Argentina*, p. 79. Like Burgin, many historians have based their conclusions about farming on political sources. Burgin writes, "To judge by the debates in the provincial legislature and the annual reports to the Junta, agriculture hardly existed in Buenos Aires." Burgin, *Economic Aspects*, p. 262. He and others have not used market reports or rural production censuses.

44. On colonial farming, see John Mawe, *Travels in the Interior of Brazil,*

2d ed. (London, 1823), pp. 20, 30−2; Alejandro Malaspina, *Viaje al Río de la Plata en el siglo XVIII,* ed. by Hector R. Ratto (Buenos Aires, 1938), p. 287; Félix de Azara, *Descripción e historia del Paraguay y del Río de la Plata,* trans. from the French, 2 vols. (Madrid, 1847), vol. 1, pp. 79−80; and Azara, "Viajes inéditos de Azara," *Revista de Derecho, Historia y Letras,* año 10, vol. 28 (Buenos Aires, 1907), p. 209.

45. Caldcleugh, *Travels in South America,* vol. 1, p. 152; MacCann, *Two Thousand Miles' Ride,* vol. 1, p. 139; Latham, *States of the River Plate,* pp. 151−4; Gerstaeker, *Narrative of a Journey,* p. 58; and Charles Brand, *Journal of a Voyage to Peru* (London, 1828), p. 75.

46. *REBA,* 1854, Table 10.

47. See "Annual Reports"; and *Annual Statements* for lists of tool and machinery exports to Argentina. In another country, Great Britain, the use of improved hand tools like sickles, heavy hooks, and simple animal- and hand-powered machinery led to an incremental rise in farm productivity between 1790 and 1870 − a time when rural manpower was decreasing. See E. J. T. Collins, "Harvest Technology and Labour Supply in Britain, 1790−1870," *Economic History Review,* 2d series, vol. 22, no. 3 (Dec. 1969), pp. 453−73.

48. AGN, Colección Biblioteca Nacional 371, "Correspondencia comercial," Anon. to Gregorio Barragán of Talpalqué (Buenos Aires, 15 June 1848); Anon. to Ysidro Jurad of Talpalqué (Buenos Aires, 15 Jan. 1848); and Anon. to Juan José Fallino of Río Grande (Buenos Aires, 25 July 1848).

49. MacCann, *Two Thousand Miles' Ride,* vol. 1, p. 18; Hernando, "Casa y familia," pp. 611−14; and Schmieder, "Alteration of the Argentine Pampa," p. 317.

50. AGN, Colección Biblioteca Nacional 371, "Correspondencia comercial," Anon. to Pascual Gali of Chascomús (Buenos Aires, 18 Jan. 1848); and Anon. to Andrés Abascal of Tandil (Buenos Aires, 2 Jan. 1848).

51. AGN, Colección Biblioteca Nacional 226, "Manuel Trelles. Autógrafas donados" (3270/166), Miguel Rivera to Juan Moreno (Buenos Aires, 2 Dec. 1850).

52. AGN, Colección Biblioteca Nacional 371, "Correspondencia comercial," Anon. to Vicente Letamendi of Camarones (Buenos Aires, 4 Feb. 1949); Anon. to Letamendi (Buenos Aires, 28 Oct. 1848); and Anon. to Lorenzo Gatti of Fte. Azul (Buenos Aires, 1 Oct. 1848).

53. Ibid., Anon. to Gatti (Buenos Aires, 1 Oct. 1848); and Anon. to Juan María Larrea of Azul (Buenos Aires, 1 March 1848).

54. Ibid., Anon. to Larrea (Buenos Aires, 5 Feb. 1848).

55. See estanciero-saladerista contracts in AGN, Sala 7, 16-4-11, Colección Ruiz Guiñazú (1728), Contrato, Senillosa y Mancilla con Nicolás de Anchorena (Buenos Aires, 7 June 1850); and Sala 7, 16-4-7, Colección Ruiz Guiñazú (1346), Contrato Anchorena y Mariano Baudrix (Buenos Aires, 21 Jan. 1847).

56. MacCann, *Two Thousand Miles' Ride,* vol. 1, pp. 215−16; and

Latham, *States of the River Plate*, p. 32.
57. AGN, Colección Biblioteca Nacional 371, "Correspondencia comercial," Anon. to José Rafael Quintero of Estancia de Ponce (Buenos Aires, 26 Feb. 1849); and Anon. to Abascal (Buenos Aires, 4 Feb. 1849).
58. Ibid., Anon. to Abascal (Buenos Aires, 29 June 1849).
59. Ibid., Anon. to Abascal (Buenos Aires, 3 May 1848); and Anon. to Luis Olivera of Guardia del Monte (Buenos Aires, 18 June 1849).

## 7. Expansion of pastoral society on the pampa

1. For some representative historical judgments in this vein, see Miguel Angel Cárcano, *Evolución histórica del régimen de la tierra pública, 1810–1816* (Buenos Aires, 1972), p. 10; Ricardo Rodríguez Molas, *Historia social del gaucho* (Buenos Aires, 1968); and Juan Alvarez, *Las guerras civiles argentinas* (Buenos Aires, 1972), pp. 67–9.
2. The quotation is from A. F. Zimmerman, "The Land Policy of Argentina, with Particular Reference to the Conquest of the Southern Pampas," *Hispanic American Historical Review*, vol. 25, no. 1 (1945), p. 14. Also see James R. Scobie, *Argentina, A City and a Nation*, 2d. ed. (New York, 1971), pp. 98, 121; Miron Burgin, *The Economic Aspects of Argentine Federalism, 1820–1852* (Cambridge, Mass., 1946), p. 255; and Miguel Angel Cárcano, *Evolución histórica del régimen de la tierra pública, 1810–1916* (Buenos Aires, 1972). The issue of the Rosas era as one of economic stagnation no longer seems relevant in light of the most recent scholarship. "These years were not a hiatus in Argentine history," writes Diana Hernando, "but a period of estancia founding, of which Rosas was a part. When that period was over, Rosas' political life was over also." Diana Hernando, "Casa y familia: Spatial Biographies in Nineteenth Century Buenos Aires," Ph.D. diss. (University of California, Los Angeles, 1973), p. 160. Also see Tulio Halperín-Donghi, "La expansion ganadera en la campaña de Buenos Aires (1810–1852)," *Desarrollo Económico*, vol. 2, nos. 1–2 (1963), pp. 57–110.
3. Hernando, "Casa y Familia," pp. 22, 69–70; and Susan Migden Socolow, "The Merchants of Viceregal Buenos Aires," Ph.D. diss. (Columbia University, 1973), Appendix D.
4. Rural landowners living in the city is not a rare phenomenon elsewhere in Latin America. Since colonial days, big hacendados often lived in the city, effectively tying the city and countryside together socially and economically. See James Lockhart, "Ecomienda and Hacienda: The Evolution of the Great Estate in the Spanish Indies," *Hispanic American Historical Review*, vol. 29, no. 3 (Aug. 1969), pp. 411–29.
5. AGN, Sala 10, 25-6-2, "Censo de habitantes. Capital y provincia de Buenos Aires" (1838).
6. Susan Migden Socolow, "Economic Activities of the Porteño Merchants: The Viceregal Period," *Hispanic American Historical Review*, vol. 55, no. 1 (Feb. 1975), pp. 13, 15.

7. The quotation is from *A Five Years' Residence in Buenos Ayres, During the Years 1820 to 1825* (London, 1825), p. 74. Also see J. P. and W. P. Robertson, *Letters on Paraguay,* 2d ed., 3 vols. (London, 1839), vol. 1, pp. 55–8.

8. AGN, Colección Biblioteca Nacional 226, "Manuel Trelles. Autógrafos donados" (3720/118), Saturino Unzúe to Juan Moreno (Buenos Aires, 14 Aug. 1849).

9. See Hernando, "Casa y Familia," pp. 431–4, 469, 490.

10. Ibid., pp. 273, 400–1. Horizontally unified economic enterprise also had strong precedent in Latin America. See James Lockhart, "Encomienda and Hacienda: The Evolution of the Great Estate in the Spanish Indies," *Hispanic American Historical Review,* vol. 43, no. 3 (Aug. 1969), p. 425.

11. Cárcano, *Evolución histórica,* pp. 44–6; Jacinto Oddone, *La burguesía terrateniente argentina,* 3d ed. (Buenos Aires, 1956), p. 76 ff.; and Burgin, *Economic Aspects,* pp. 96–7.

12. See Horacio Juan Cuccorese and José Panettieri, *Argentina, manual de historia económica y social,* vol. 1, *Argentina criolla* (Buenos Aires, 1971), p. 384; Oddone, *La burguesía terrateniente,* p. 93; Zimmerman, "Land Policy," p. 14; and Andrés Carretero, *La propiedad de la tierra en la época de Rosas* (Buenos Aires, 1972), p. 30.

13. Hernando, "Casa y familia," p. 262.

14. AGN, Colección Biblioteca Nacional 187 (1800), "Los comandantes de Chascomús, y los Ranchos, no permitirán que Don Antonio Obligado haga establecimiento de corrales . . ." (Buenos Aires, 3 Nov. 1797).

15. For documents relating to farm rental, see AGN, Sala 7, 4-4-1, Archivo Anchorena, "Contrato, Anchorena y Feliciano Barrera" (Buenos Aires, 28 Sept. 1821); Colección Biblioteca Nacional 300, Archivo de Mariano Lozano (5435/285), Avelino Lerena to Mariano Lozano (Chacra, 23 May 1842); and Sala 7, 4-4-3, Archivo Anchorena, D. V. Morete to Felipe Senillosa (Lomas de Zamora, 18 May 1826).

16. Frederick Gerstaecker, *Narrative of a Journey Round the World* (New York, 1853), p. 42; and William Henry Hudson, *Far Away and Long Ago; a History of My Early Life* (New York, 1924), pp. 126–7.

17. Pedro M. López Godoy, *Historia de la propiedad y primeros pobladores del Partido de Pergamino,* 2 vols. (Pergamino, Argentina, 1973), vol. 2, pp. 449–50. The original figures are corrected for inflation.

18. Ibid., vol. 2, pp. 713–14.

19. See Andrés Carretero, *Orígenes de la dependencia económica argentina* (Buenos Aires, 1974), p. 128; Oddone, *La burguesía terrateniente,* pp. 70–1. On the rental of land, see AGN, Sala 7, 16-4-11, Colección Ruiz Guiñazú (177), D. Vélez Sarsfield to Justice of the Peace (Arrecifes, 21 Nov. 1855).

20. AGN, Sala 7, 16-4-11 (1736), "Testimonio de la escritura de venta de un establecimiento de estancia . . ." (Buenos Aires, 21 Jan. 1851). For another rural credit arrangement, see AGN, Registro 73 (Comercio 1),

Manuel J. Saine de Cavia, "Contrato Dn. Luis Dorrego y Dn. Julian Rodríguez," pp. 12 – 13.

21. Museo Bartolomé Mitre, Buenos Aires, A1-C44-C71, no. 11, Miguel Estanislao Soler, "Papeles referentes a la administración de la estancia 'Las Palmas' " (1844 – 1852).

22. Halperín-Donghi, "Expansión ganadera," pp. 69 – 70; Cuccorese and Panettieri, *Argentina,* p. 211; and Herbert Gibson, *The History and Present State of the Sheep-Breeding Industry in the Argentine Republic* (Buenos Aires, 1893), p. 202.

23. Ernesto J. A. Maeder, *Evolución demográfica argentina* (Buenos Aires, 1969), pp. 33 – 5.

24. P. H. Randle, *La ciudad pampeana; geografía urbana, geografía histórica* (Buenos Aires, 1969), p. 1.

25. AGN, Sala 10, 25-6-2, "Censo de habitantes. Capital y Provincia de Buenos Aires" (1838).

26. AGN, Sección Mapoteca, "Registro gráfico de los terrenos de propriedad pública y particular de la Provincia de Buenos Aires" (1852); and "Registro gráfico . . ." (1864).

27. The group includes the districts of Azul, Monsalvo, Cañuelas, Magdalena, Rojas, Lobos, Salto, and Baradero. See AGN, Sala 10, 25-6-2, "Censo de habitantes."

28. Ibid.

29. Ibid.

30. William MacCann, *Two Thousand Miles' Ride Through the Argentine Province,* 2 vols. (London, 1853), vol. 1, p. 227.

31. Augustín Isaías de Elía, "Los Ramos Mexía: historia y tradiciones de viejas estancias argentinas," unpub. ms. (Buenos Aires, n.d.), p. 125.

32. Carretero, *Orígenes de la dependencia,* p. 78; and Rodríguez Molas, *Historia social del gaucho.*

33. José Hernández produced *Martín Fierro* in 1872. Elía writes that he remembered the rural gaucho of his youth as a man of work, having little time to waste on guitars and drink. Elía, "Los Ramos Mexía," pp. 95 – 102.

34. AGN, Colección Biblioteca Nacional 226 (3270/31), Simón Pereyra to Juan Moreno (Buenos Aires, n.d.).

35. *Registero Oficial de la Provincia de Buenos Aires* (Buenos Aires, 1823), pp. 134 – 6.

36. AGN, Sala 9, 3-10-4 (E. 249), "Bando publicado prohibiendo el uso de las carretas grandes . . .," (Buenos Aires, 23 Dec. 1783).

37. AGN, Sala 10, 25-6-2, "Censo de habitantes."

38. Elía, "Los Ramos Mexía," pp. 95 – 7; and AGN, Colección Biblioteca Nacional 226 (3270/33 and 34), Simón Pereyra to Mayordomo Castro (Buenos Aires, n.d.).

39. AGN, Sala 7, 16-15-4, Colección Ruiz Guiñazú (2236), "Contrato, Lazala y Sanders" (Buenos Aires, 1849).

40. Alvarez, *Guerras civiles,* p. 41; and my own research into estancia account books.

41. AGN, Colección Biblioteca Nacional 800–1, "Libros de cuentas corrientes de Pastor Obligado desde 1848."

42. AGN, Colección Biblioteca Nacional 739, "Libro diario de la chacra San Francisco" (1864–70).

43. On the Pampa Indian, see Charles Redmon Berry, "The Conquest of the Desert: A Study of the Argentine Indian Wars, 1810–1885," M.A. thesis (University of Texas, 1963); Alfred J. Tapson, "Indian Warfare on the Pampa During the Colonial Period," *Hispanic American Historical Review*, vol. 42, no. 1 (Feb. 1962), pp. 1–28; and Oscar Schmieder, "Alteration of the Argentine Pampa in the Colonial Period," *University of California Publications in Geography*, vol. 2, no. 10 (1927), pp. 303–21. Travel descriptions include J. P. and W. P. Robertson, *Letters on South America*, 3 vols. (London, 1843), vol. 2, pp. 274–5; John Constanse Davie, *Letters from Paraguay; Describing the Settlements of Montevideo and Buenos Aires* (London, 1805), p. 49; J. A. B. Beaumont, *Travels in Buenos Ayres, and the Adjacent Provinces of the Río de la Plata* (London, 1828), p. 55; MacCann, *Two Thousand Miles' Ride*, vol. 1, p. 134; Charles R. Darwin, *The Voyage of the Beagle* (New York, 1958), p. 103; and Gibson, *History and Present State*, pp. 153–4.

44. Darwin, *Voyage of the Beagle*, p. 88.

### 8. Formation of the Anchorena cattle business

1. Juan José Sebreli, *Apogeo y ocaso de los Anchorena* (Buenos Aires, 1972), pp. 37–40; Andres M. Carretero, *Los Anchorena: política y negocios en el siglo XIX* (Buenos Aires, 1970), p. 10; and Susan Migden Socolow, "The Merchants of Viceregal Buenos Aires," Ph.D. diss. (Columbia University, 1973), appendix.

2. Sebreli, *Apogeo y ocaso*, pp. 52–7.

3. Ibid., pp. 70–1; Carretero, *Los Anchorena*, p. 16; and Hugo Raúl Galmarini, *Negocios y política en la época de Rivadavia* (Buenos Aires, 1974), p. 27.

4. Juan José de Anchorena, *Dictámen sobre el establecimiento de una Compañía General de Comercio* (Buenos Aires, 1818).

5. Sebreli, *Apogeo y ocaso*, pp. 106–10; and Carretero, *Los Anchorena*, pp. 18–50. Also see Julio Irazusta, *Tomás M. de Anchorena, o la emancipación americana a la luz de la circunstancia histórica* (Buenos Aires, 1962); and Juan Carlos Nicolau, *Dorrego Gobernador: economía y finanzas, 1826–1827* (Buenos Aires, 1977), for the Anchorena family in the politics of the era.

6. *Almanaque 1826.*

7. Galmarini, *Negocios y política*, pp. 27, 75, 108.

8. AGN, Sala 7, 4-1-7, Archivo Anchorena, "Libro de cuentas de J. J. de Anchorena."

9. Ibid., "S. O. Francisco Alzogaray por suma de la cuenta."

10. Ibid., "Mi hermano Tomás según cuenta desde su salida a Montevideo."

11. Ibid., "Desembolsos en varios objectos de campaña."

12. *Almanaque 1836.*

13. AGN, Sala 7, 16-4-8, Colección Ruiz Guiñazú (1541), Rosas to Terrero (Matanza, 2 Nov. 1834); and Sala 7, 16-4-7, Colleción Ruiz Guiñazú (1285), Declaration of Rosas, Terrero y Cía (Camarones, 17 Jan. 1819).

14. AGN, Sala 7, 16-4-11, Colección Ruiz Guiñazú (1796), Rosas to Estanislada Arana de Anchorena (Southampton, Eng., 31 May 1864).

15. AGN, Sala 7, 16-4-7, Colección Ruiz Guiñazú (1297), Venta de Terreno a Rosas (Buenos Aires, 21 May 1824); and (1301), Rosas a Sr. Juez de la Primera Ynstancia (n.p., 1824).

16. AGN, Sala 7, 16-5-7, Colección Ruiz Guiñazú (1293), Rosas a Juez de la Primera Ynstancia (n.p., 1824).

17. AGN, Sala 7, 16-4-8, Colección Ruiz Guiñazú (1473), Rosas to N. Anchorena (Río Colorado, 14 June 1833).

18. AGN, Sala 7, 4-1-6, Archivo Anchorena, López a J. Anchorena, (n.p., 1821); and Sala 7, 16-4-8, Colección Ruiz Guiñazú (1522), N. Anchorena to Nemecio López (Buenos Aires, 25 Jan. 1834).

19. Jacinto Oddone, *La burguesía terrateniente argentina,* 3d ed. (Buenos Aires, 1956), p. 101.

20. Pedro M. López Godoy, *Historia de la propiedad y primeros pobladores del Partido de Pergamino,* 2 vols. (Pergamino, Argentina, 1973), vol. 2, pp. 430–1, 444–5. Today, the original Estancia Fortezuelas is divided into eighty-four large properties and several smaller units.

21. AGN, Sala 7, 4-4-3, Archivo Anchorena, Sosa to J. Anchorena, (Amistad, 3 June 1823); and Sala 7, 4-4-3, Arista to J. Anchorena (Averías, 7 Aug. 1830).

22. Andrés M. Carretero, *La propiedad de la tierra en la época de Rosas* (Buenos Aires, 1972), pp. 12–13; Sebreli, *Apogeo y ocaso,* p. 216; and Benjamín Vicuña Mackenna, *La Argentina en el año 1855* (Buenos Aires, 1936), p. 118.

23. AGN, Sala 7, 4-4-3, Archivo Anchorena, Sosa to J. Anchorena (Matanza, 26 June 1821, 18 Mar. 1822, 22 April 1822, 9 July 1822, 15 May 1823, 29 May 1823, and 2 May 1829).

24. AGN, Sala 7, 16-4-7, Colección Ruiz Guiñazú (1328), Rosas to Morillo (Cerrillos, 8 Jan. 1826); and Sala 7, 4-1-7, Archivo Anchorena, Puddicomb and Gallardo to Celis (Buenos Aires, 19 Mar. 1830).

25. AGN, Sala 7, 4-4-3, Archivo Anchorena, Belar to J. Anchorena (San Martín, 4 Sept. 1825).

26. AGN, Sala 7, 16-4-7, Colección Ruiz Guiñazú (1318), Receipt for 1,000 head of cattle (Buenos Aires, 9 April 1825).

27. Ibid., J. Anchorena a Rosas (Buenos Aires, 19 Feb. 1828).

28. AGN, Sala 7, 16-4-7, Colección Ruiz Guiñazú (1341), Rosas to Morillo (Poronquitos, 30 Nov. 1826); and AGN, Sala 7, 16-4-9, Colección Ruiz Guiñazú (1546), N. Anchorena to Morillo (Buenos Aires, 8 July 1835).

29. AGN, Sala 7, 16-4-7, Colección Ruiz Guiñazú (1334), Morillo to Rosas (Tala de Anchorena, 19 Oct. 1826); and (1320), Rosas to Francisco Romero (Buenos Aires, 1 July 1825).
30. AGN, Sala 7, 16-4-8, Colección Ruiz Guiñazú (1400), Morillo to Rosas (Camerones, 13 Jan. 1830); Sala 7, 16-4-9, Colección Ruiz Guiñazú (1560), N. Anchorena to Décima (Buenos Aires, 6 April 1836).
31. AGN, Sala 7, 16-4-9, Colección Ruiz Guiñazú (1561), N. Anchorena to Décima (Buenos Aires, 6 April 1836).
32. AGN, Sala 7, 16-4-7, Colección Ruiz Guiñazú (1276), Rosas to J. Anchorena (San Martín, 18 March, 1822).
33. AGN, Sala 7, 16-4-8, Colección Ruiz Guiñazú (1413), Rosas to Morillo (Chacarita, 24 Jan. 1831).
34. Ibid. (1400); and Sala 7, 4-2-1, Archivo Anchorena, Saavedra to N. Anchorena (Del Tala, 14 Jan. 1833).
35. AGN, Sala 7, 16-4-7, Colección Ruiz Guiñazú (1320); and Sala 7, 16-4-7, Colección Ruiz Guiñazú (1337), Rosas to Morillo (n.p., 6 Nov. 1826).
36. AGN, Sala 7, 16-4-8, Colección Ruiz Guiñazú (1542), N. Anchorena to Morillo (Buenos Aires, 28 Dec. 1834); and AGN, 4-4-2, Archivo Anchorena, J. Anchorena to N. Anchorena (Buenos Aires, 22 Dec. 1828).
37. AGN, Sala 7, 16-4-8, Colección Ruiz Guiñazú (1406, 1542).
38. Ibid. (1404), Morillo to Rosas (Camarones, 13 Jan. 1830); Sala 7, 16-4-9, Colección Ruiz Guiñazú (1546); and Sala 7, 4-4-2, Archivo Anchorena, N. Anchorena to Rosas (Buenos Aires, 16 Nov. 1830).
39. AGN, Sala 7, 4-4-2, Archivo Anchorena, Morillo to J. Anchorena (Chascomús, 22 Oct. 1830 and 17 Dec. 1830); Sala 7, 4-4-3, Archivo Anchorena, Morillo to J. Anchorena (Chascomús, 20 June 1830, 23 July 1830, and 23 Nov. 1830), and Arista to J. Anchorena (Chascomús, 3 Sept. 1830); Sala 7, 4-1-6, Archivo Anchorena, Morillo to J. Anchorena (Chascomús, 23 March, 1831, 25 April 1831, and 26 April 1831).
40. AGN, Sala 7, 4-4-3, Archivo Anchorena, Sosa to J. Anchorena (Matanza, 11 Jan. 1827).
41. Ibid., Décima to J. Anchorena (Camarones, 26 April 1830).
42. See Anchorena's account books in AGN, Sala 7, 4-1-7, "Libro de cuentas de Juan José Anchorena."
43. AGN, Sala 7, 16-4-7; Colección Ruiz Guiñazú (1312), "Filiación de los esclavos del Sr. Dn. Juan Manuel de Rosas" (Cerrillos, 24 Feb. 1825), and (1317), "Filiación de los esclavos de Estancia Camarones de Anchorena" (4 April 1825).
44. Ibid. (1338), Rosas to Angel Salvadores (San Martín, 12 Nov. 1826), and (1335), Rosas to Morillo (n.p., 24 Oct. 1826).
45. AGN, Sala 10, 25-6-2, "Censo de habitantes: Capital y Provincia de Buenos Aires" (1838).
46. AGN, Sala 7, 16-4-7, Colección Ruiz Guiñazú (1335).
47. Ibid. (1345), Rosas to Morillo (Guardia del Monte, 24 Dec. 1826).

48. AGN, Sala 7, 4-1-6, Archivo Anchorena, Sosa to J. Anchorena (n.p., 22 Jan. 1818).

49. Ibid., Morillo to J. Anchorena (Villaneuva, 15 Feb. 1831).

50. AGN, Sala 7, 16-4-7, Colección Ruiz Guiñazú (1340), Rosas to Décima (San Martín, 13 Nov. 1826).

51. Ibid. (1354), Morillo to Saavedra (Camarones, 25 July 1827).

52. AGN, Sala 7, 4-4-2, Archivo Anchorena, Morillo to J. Anchorena (Camarones, 22 Oct. 1830 and 24 Oct. 1830), and N. Anchorena to Arista (Buenos Aires, 30 Oct. 1830, and 23 Nov. 1830).

53. AGN, Sala 7, 16-4-7, Colección Ruiz Guiñazú (1354).

54. AGN, Sala 7, 4-4-2, Archivo Anchorena, "Cuenta de gastos en la obra" (28 July 1827).

55. AGN, Sala 7, 4-4-1, Archivo Anchorena, Morillo to J. Anchorena (Camarones, 17 May 1831); Sala 7, 16-4-9, Colección Ruiz Guiñazú (1555), Contract, Morillo and Gilgen; and Ibid. (1836).

56. AGN, Sala 7, 4-4-1, Archivo Anchorena, Morillo to J. Anchorena (14 Sept. 1830); Sosa to J. Anchorena (Navarro, 11 March 1831, 23 Feb. 1831, and 25 Feb. 1831).

57. AGN, Sala 7, 16-4-7, Colección Ruiz Guiñazú (1347), Rosas to Morillo (Cerrillos, 31 Jan. 1827); and (1325).

58. Ibid. (1302), "Protesta de Rosas por saca de hacienda" (n.p., 14 July 1824).

59. Ibid. (1344), Rosas to Morillo (Guardia del Monte, 24 Dec. 1826).

60. Ibid. (1324); AGN, Sala 7, 16-4-10, Colección Ruiz Guiñazú (1724), Prudencio de Rosas to N. Anchorena (Chascomús, 26 Oct. 1849).

61. AGN, Sala 7, 16-4-7, Colección Ruiz Guiñazú (1347); Sala 7, 16-4-8, Colección Ruiz Guiñazú (1406), Rosas to Décima (Buenos Aires, 25 March 1830); Sala 7, 4-4-3, Archivo Anchorena, Sosa to J. Anchorena (Matanza, 13 June 1825); Sala 7, 4-1-6, Archivo Anchorena, Morillo to J. Anchorena (Camarones, 26 April 1831 and 2 March 1832).

62. AGN, Sala 7, 4-4-2, Archivo Anchorena, N. Anchorena to Saavedra (Buenos Aires, 26 June 1830); and *Colección de marcas de ganados de la Provincia de Buenos Aires* (Buenos Aires, 1830).

63. AGN, Sala 7, 16-4-7, Colección Ruiz Guiñazú (1324) and (1339), Rosa to Federico Raus (San Martín, 12 Nov. 1826).

64. AGN, Sala 7, 16-4-9, Colección Ruiz Guiñazú (1552), N. Anchorena to Rosas (Buenos Aires, 13 Oct. 1835); Sala 7, 4-1-6, Archivo Anchorena, Morillo to J. Anchorena (Camarones, 2 March 1832); Sala 7, 4-4-3, Archivo Anchorena, Décima to J. Anchorena (Camarones, 14 Sept. 1830); and Sala 7, Archivo Anchorena, Sosa to Anchorena (Dulce, 5 Aug. 1831).

65. AGN, Sala 7, 16-4-7, Colección Ruiz Guiñazú (1278), Rosas to Sr. Juez de la Primera Ynstancia (Buenos Aires, 14 Aug. 1822); and (1321), Report of Rosas (n.p., 1825).

66. AGN, Sala 7, 4-4-3, Archivo Anchorena, Arista to J. Anchorena

(Averías, 7 Aug. 1830); and Sala 16-4-8, Colección Ruiz Guiñazú (1423), Prudencio de Rosas to Morillo (Buenos Aires, 30 July 1831).
67. AGN, Sala 7, 4-1-6, Archivo Anchorena, Morillo to J. Anchorena (Camarones, 26 April 1831, 2 March 1832).
68. AGN, Sala 7, 4-4-3, Archivo Anchorena, Morillo to J. Anchorena (Chascomús, 20 June 1830).
69. AGN, Sala 4-4-2, Archivo Anchorena, N. Anchorena to Saavedra (Buenos Aires, 26 June 1830); N. Anchorena to Arista (Buenos Aires, 7 Aug. 1830); and N. Anchorena to Sosa (Buenos Aires, 14 Aug. 1830).
70. Ibid., Archivo Anchorena, N. Anchorena to Saavedra (Buenos Aires, 26 June 1830); AGN, Sala 7, 4-1-6, Archivo Anchorena, Morillo to J. Anchorena (Camarones, 2 March 1832); and Arista to J. Anchorena (Averías, 8 Aug. 1830).
71. AGN, Sala 7, 4-2-1, Archivo Anchorena, Saavedra to N. Anchorena (Del Tala, n.d., 1830); N. Anchorena to Saavedra (Buenos Aires, 20 Aug. 1830); Sala 7, Colección Ruiz Guiñazú (1452), Rosas to Décima (Buenos Aires, 20 March 1832); and Sala 7, 4-4-2, Archivo Anchorena, Morillo to J. Anchorena (Camarones, 31 Jan. 1832).
72. AGN, Sala 7, 4-4-2, Archivo Anchorena, N. Anchorena to Décima (Buenos Aires, 7 Aug. 1830); AGN, Sala 7, 4-1-6, Archivo Anchorena, Morillo to J. Anchorena (Camarones, 16 March 1832); and Sala 7, 4-4-3, Archivo Anchorena, Décima to J. Anchorena (Camarones, 14 Sept. 1830 and 6 June 1830).
73. AGN, Sala 7, 4-4-3, Archivo Anchorena, Décima to J. Anchorena (Camarones, 26 April 1830); and AGN, Sala 7, 4-4-2, Archivo Anchorena, N. Anchorena to Saavedra (Buenos Aires, 26 June 1830); and Sala 7, 16-4-8, Colección Ruiz Guiñazú (1406).
74. AGN, Sala 7, 4-1-6, Archivo Anchorena, Morillo to J. Anchorena (Camarones, 16 March 1832).
75. AGN, Sala 7, 4-4-3, Archivo Anchorena, Sosa to J. Anchorena (Matanza, 28 Aug. 1821).
76. Ibid., Arista to J. Anchorena (Chascomús, 5 May 1830); and AGN, Sala 7, 4-4-2, Archivo Anchorena, N. Anchorena to Arista (Buenos Aires, 8 June 1830).
77. AGN, Sala 7, 16-4-7, Colección Ruiz Guiñazú (1334).
78. AGN, Sala 7, 16-4-9, Colección Ruiz Guiñazú (1630), Contract, N. Anchorena and Vicente Letamendi (Buenos Aires, 17 Aug. 1839).
79. AGN, Colección Biblioteca Nacional 371, "Correspondencia comercial," Anon. to Letamendi (Buenos Aires, 28 Oct. 1848).
80. Ibid. (1 May 1849, 18 June 1849, 21 May 1849, 26 May 1849, and 8 June 1849).
81. Ibid. (5 Aug. 1848, 8 June 1849, and 8 Dec. 1848). Larrea's clean wool brought the equivalent of U.S. 6.6¢ per pound.
82. Ibid. (13 Feb. 1849, 1 Dec. 1848, and 28 Oct. 1848).
83. Ibid. (11 Oct. 1848).

84. Ibid. (1 May 1849, 9 June 1849).
85. AGN, Sala 7, 4-1-7, Archivo Anchorena, Sosa to J. Anchorena (Laguna Dulce, 24 May 1831, 13 Feb. 1831, and 29 April 1831); and receipt of Mariano Cejas (Laguna Dulce, 20 May 1831).
86. AGN, Sala 7, 16-4-8, Colección Ruiz Guiñazú (1400); and Sala 7, 4-4-2, Archivo Anchorena, receipt of Tte. Crol. Ignación Ibarra (Guardia de Ranchos, 14 Nov. 1827).
87. AGN, Sala 7, 16-4-8, Colección Ruiz Guiñazú (1525), "Créditos que se reclamen contra el Tesoro" (n.p., 8 Jan. 1834).
88. AGN, Sala 7, 16-4-9, Colección Ruiz Guiñazú (1552) and (1554), N. Anchorena to Rosas (Buenos Aires, 4 Dec. 1835).
89. Ibid. (1400); and AGN, Sala 7, 16-4-8, Colección Ruiz Guiñazú (1542).
90. AGN, Sala 7, 16-4-7, Colección Ruiz Guiñazú (1325).
91. AGN, Sala 7, 16-4-9, Colección Ruiz Guiñazú (1547), "N. Anchorena propone reces para Bahía Blanca" (Buenos Aires, 1 Sept. 1835); (1551), N. Anchorena to Rosas (Buenos Aires, 5 Oct. 1835); and (1549), Contract, N. Anchorena and Minister of Hacienda (Buenos Aires, 27 Aug. 1835).
92. Ibid. (1563), N. Anchorena to Morillo and Décima (Buenos Aires, 6 May 1836); (1565), N. Anchorena to Morillo and Décima (Buenos Aires, 11 July 1836); and (1572), N. Anchorena to Rosas (Buenos Aires, 6 Jan. 1837).
93. AGN, Sala 7, 16-4-10, Colección Ruiz Guiñazú (1716), Contract, N. Anchorena and A. C. Santamaría Llambí y Cambaceres (Buenos Aires, 21 Jan. 1849).
94. Ibid. (1714), Contract, N. Anchorena and Medrano y Soler (Buenos Aires, 20 Jan. 1849); (1575), Contract, N. Anchorena and Tomás Rousse (Buenos Aires, 8 May 1837); AGN, Sala 7, 16-4-11, Colección Ruiz Guiñazú (1729), Contract: N. Anchorena and Anderson Welles (Buenos Aires, 1850); Sala 7, 4-4-3, Archivo Anchorena, Morillo to J. Anchorena (Camarones, 20 Nov. 1830); and Sala 7, 4-1-6, Archivo Anchorena, Morillo to J. Anchorena (Villaneuva, 15 Feb. 1830).
95. AGN, Sala 7, 16-4-11, Colección Ruiz Guiñazú (1746), Contract, N. Anchorena and Santamaria Llambí (Buenos Aires, 28 April 1852).
96. AGN, Sala 7, 16-4-7, Colección Ruiz Guiñazú (1336), Rosas to Morillo (n.p., 24 Nov. 1826); Sala 7, 16-4-2, Colección Ruiz Guiñazú (831), "Orden del Sr. Dn. N. Anchorena" (n.p., n.d.); Sala 7, 16-4-9, Colección Ruiz Guiñazú (1560); and Sala 7, 4-4-3, Archivo Anchorena, Sosa to J. Anchorena (Matanza, 8 June 1827).
97. AGN, Sala 7, 16-4-10, Colección Ruiz Guiñazú (1715), Contract, N. Anchorena and Mariano Haedo (Buenos Aires, 22 Jan. 1849), and (1714), Contract, Medrano y Soler and N. Anchorena (Buenos Aires, 20 Jan. 1849); Sala 7, 16-4-11, Colección Ruiz Guiñazú (1729) and (1728); Sala 7, 16-4-9, Colección Ruiz Guiñazú (1576), Contract N. Anchorena and Tomás Rousse (Buenos Aires, 8 May 1837).

98. AGN, Sala 7, 4-4-2, Archivo Anchorena, receipt from Barando from Ruperto Villarreal (Buenos Aires, 4 Nov. 1831).

99. AGN, Sala 7, 4-1-6, Archivo Anchorena, receipt of Rodríguez from Juan Arista (Achiras, 15 Dec. 1830); and Sala 7, 16-4-7, Colección Ruiz Guiñazú (1347).

100. AGN, Sala 7, 4-4-2, Archivo Anchorena, Morillo to J. Anchorena (Camarones, 22 Oct. 1830); Baranda to J. Anchorena (Buenos Aires, 15 Jan. 1831); and receipt of Baranda from Ruperto Villarreal (Buenos Aires, 4 Nov. 1831).

101. Ibid., N. Anchorena to Saavedra (Buenos Aires, 11 Sept. 1830); Sala 10, 37-2-25, p. 97.

102. AGN, Sala 7, 4-4-2, Archivo Anchorena, "Cuenta de venta de varios frutos" (Buenos Aires, 11 Oct. 1831).

103. Ibid., Baranda to J. Anchorena (Buenos Aires, 15 Jan. 1831), and various "Gastos de peones y barracage de los cueros."

## 9. Depression and renaissance of commerce in the Interior provinces

1. For the effect of foreign trade on the Interior's economy in the colonial period, see Pedro Santos Martínez, *Las industrias durante el virreinato, 1776–1810* (Buenos Aires, 1969), pp. 148–50; and John Lynch, *Spanish Colonial Administration, 1782–1810* (London, 1958), pp. 169–71. For the national period, see Miron Burgin, *The Economic Aspects of Argentine Federalism* (Cambridge, Mass., 1946), p. 15; Horacio William Bliss, *Del virreinato a Rosas; ensayo de historia económica argentina, 1776–1829* (Buenos Aires, 1959), p. 148; John Lynch, *The Spanish American Revolutions, 1808–1826* (New York, 1973), p. 65; and Clifton B. Kroeber, *The Growth of the Shipping Industry in the Río de la Plata Region, 1794–1860* (Madison, Wis., 1957), p. 110.

2. Juan Eugenio Corradi, "Argentina," in Ronald H. Chilcote and Joel C. Edelstein, eds., *Latin America: The Struggle with Dependency and Beyond* (Cambridge, Mass., 1974), pp. 320–2; and André Gunder Frank, *Capitalism and Underdevelopment in Latin America* (New York, 1967), p. 28.

3. AGN, Sala 10, 42-10-11, "Estado general que manifiesta los buques que en el 2 semestre de 1838 han entrado al puerto de Buenos Ayres."

4. Joseph Andrews, *Journey from Buenos Aires Through the Provinces of Cordova, Tucuman, and Salta to Potosi*, 2 vols. (London, 1827) vol. 1, p. 303, vol. 2, p. 4; and Hebe Judith Blasi, "Las relaciones comerciales entre las provincias y Buenos Aires (1835–1839)," in ANH, *Primer congreso*, p. 284.

5. ANH, *Primer congreso*, pp. 281, 284; and AGN, Sala 10, 43-3-1, "Aduana Registro de entrades y salidas de buques," 1828–35.

6. AGN, Colección Biblioteca National 679, Colección Félix Frias (9939), "Copia de un acapite de carta escrita de Tucumán circa 1839 o 1840."

7. Lynch, *Spanish American Revolutions*, pp. 121–2; and Tulio

Halperín-Donghi, *Revolución y guerra: formación de una élite dirigente en la Argentina criolla* (Buenos Aires, 1972), pp. 264—7.

8. AGN, Sala 7, 4-2-3, *Archivo Anchorena,* Francisco Gabriel del Portal to J. J. de Anchorena (Jujuy, 10 Sept. 1815).

9. AGN, Sala 3, 21-5-10, "Aduana, documentos terrestres de pago y de contratos" (1817).

10. For traveler's accounts of conditions in the Interior, see Andrews, *Journey from Buenos Ayres,* vol. 1, pp. 184—5, 188—9; and Edmond Temple, *Travels in Various Parts of Peru, Including a Year's Residence in Potosí,* 2 vols. (London, 1830), vol. 1, pp. 145—52, 200—18.

11. Martínez, *Industrias,* pp. 106—7.

12. Temple, *Travels in Various Parts,* vol. 1, pp. 308—9.

13. Ibid., vol. 2, pp. 466—7; and Andrews, *Journey from Buenos Aires,* vol. 1, pp. 304.

14. J. P. and W. P. Robertson, *Letters on South America,* 3 vols. (London, 1843), vol. 1, pp. 208—18.

15. Charles Brand, *Journal of a Voyage to Peru* (London, 1828), p. 21; and R. A. Humphreys, ed., *British Consular Reports on the Trade and Politics of Latin America,* vol. 63, *1824—1826* (London, 1940), p. 40.

16. Robertson, *Letters on South America,* vol. 1, pp. 23—5; 252—6; and Rengger and Longchamps, *The Reign of Doctor Joseph Gaspard Roderick de Francia in Paraguay* (London, 1827), pp. 37—8.

17. On effects of the civil wars, see Peter Schmidtmeyer, *Travels into Chile, over the Andes, in the Years 1820 and 1821* (London, 1824), pp. 175—96; Edward Hibbert, *Narrative of a Journey from Santiago de Chile to Buenos Ayres* (London, 1824), pp. 122—3; and Félix Converso, Jorge Grossi Belaunde, and Beatriz Rosario Solviera, "Contribución al estudio del comercio entre Catamarca y Córdoba, 1815—1831," in ANH, *Primer congreso,* p. 227.

18. Hibbert, *Narrative of a Journey,* pp. 65—6.

19. For descriptions of roadhouses, see Temple, *Travels in Various Parts,* vol. 1, p. 78; and Isaac G. Strain, *Cordillera and Pampa, Mountain and Plain* (New York, 1853), pp. 255, 259, 263—4.

20. For the customs regulations of Tucumán, see Alfredo Bousquet, *Estudio sobre el sistema rentístico de la provincia de Tucumán de 1820 a 1876* (Tucumán, 1878), pp. 10—29.

21. Silvia Cristina Mallo, Amalia Latroubesse de Díaz, and María Concepción Orruma, "El Comercio entre Buenos Aires y las provincias de 1830 a 1835," in ANH, *Primer congreso,* pp. 265—6; and Karín Larsson de Reinhold, "Notas para el estudio del comercio entre Córdoba y las demás provincias en 1820," *Anuario del Departamento de Historia* (Universidad de Córdoba), vol. 1, no. 1 (1963), pp. 158—9.

22. AGN, Sala 3, 21-5-10, "Aduana."

23. MG 1387b, Provincia de Buenos Aires, "Minuta de decreto que establece las contribuciones . . . en la aduana . . .," copy (Buenos Aires, 1823), p. 4. For further information on the customs duties, see Luis Marcos

Bonano, "La legislación comercial de Alejandro Heredia en Tucumán (1832—1838)," in ANH, *Primer congreso, p. 184; Maria Celia Cano et al., "Comercio interprovincial, 1840—1850*," in ANH, *Primer congreso,* p. 288; and Beatriz Rosario Solveira, "La aduana de la Provincia de Córdoba," in *Ateno de Historia Argentina,* no. 2 (Córdoba, 1973), mimeo, pp. 8—9.

24. See AGN, Sala 10, 42-10-11, "Estado general . . . en el 2do semestre de 1838"; and Sala 3, 21-5-10, "Aduana."

25. Manuel Macchi, *Urquiza, el saladerista* (Buenos Aires, 1971), p. 195; and Burgin, *Economic Aspects,* p. 148. One of those politicians opposed to Rosas on the question of free navigation was Pedro Ferré, governor of Corrientes province. See his *Memoria del Brigadier General Pedro Ferré* (Buenos Aires, 1921), pp. 54—6, 365; and also Bousquet, *Estudio sobre el sistema,* pp. 41—2, 51—6.

26. H. M. Brackenridge, *Voyage to South America,* 2 vols. (London, 1820), vol. 1, p. 251; and Archibald MacRae, "Report of Journeys Across the Andes and Pampas of the Argentine Provinces," in vol. 2 of *The U.S. Naval Astronomical Expedition to the Southern Hemisphere During the Years 1849—50—51—52* (Washington, D.C., 1855), p. 18.

27. Woodbine Parish, *Buenos Ayres, and Provinces of the Rio de la Plata,* 2d ed. (London, 1852), p. 276.

28. For descriptions of the caravans, see MacRae, "Report of Journeys," p. 18; and AGN, Sala 10, 8-4-2, "Hacienda, Informe sobre el establecimiento de las postas de bueyes" (1814).

29. Burgin, *Economic Aspects,* p. 118.

30. Allen F. Gardiner, *A Visit to the Indians on the Frontiers of Chile* (London, 1841), pp. 26, 30—1; Francis Bond Head, *Rough Notes Taken During Some Rapid Journeys Across the Pampas and Among the Andes* (London, 1826), pp. 42—3; and MacRae, "Report of Journeys," p. 18.

31. Isaac G. Strain, *Cordillera and Pampa, Mountain and Plain* (New York, 1853), p. 268.

32. For descriptions of services along the trails, see ibid., pp. 232—4; Schmidtmeyer, *Travels into Chile,* pp. 174—5; MacRae, "Report of Journeys," pp. 21—3; and Temple, *Travels in Various Parts,* vol. 1, p. 157.

33. On the improvement of cart trails, see AGN, Sala 10, 8-4-2, "Hacienda"; and Converso et al., "Contribución al estudio," in ANH, *Primer congreso,* p. 232.

34. Sixteenth-century Peru presents another example of economic and social development during a period of political civil war. See James Lockhart, *Spanish Peru, 1535—1600* (Madison, Wis., 1968), p. 221.

35. For a description of riverboating on the Paraná River, see J. P. and W. P. Robertson, *Letters on Paraguay,* 3 vols. (London, 1939), vol. 1, pp. 182—5, 224—5, 343—4, 350.

36. AGN, Sala 7, 15-4-8, Colección Félix Frias (93), M. Frías to J. Frías (Montevideo, 18 July 1840); and (83) J. Frías to F. Frías (Punta Gorda, 22 January 1840).

37. Humphries, *British Consular Reports,* vol. 63, p. 41; and Robertson,

*Letters on South America,* vol. 1, pp. 257—8.

38. AGN, Sala 10, 37-2-25, "Aduana-Hacienda. Entradas y salidas marítimas y terrestres, Tomas de razón" (1832—3); Sala 10, 37-2-26, "Aduana-Hacienda. Entradas marítimas" (1848—9); and Sala 10, 37-3-5, "Hacienda-Aduana. Entradas y salidas marítimas y terrestres, tomas de razón" (1846—8).

39. *REBA,* 1857, vol. 2, pp. 29—30.

40. Robertson, *Letters on Paraguay,* vol. 1, pp. 226—31.

41. Robertson, *Letters on South America,* vol. 1, pp. 174—83.

42. Parish, *Buenos Ayres,* 2d ed., pp. 248—9; and Robertson, *Letters on South America,* vol. 1, pp. 205—6. On those ranchers who returned to Entre Ríos in the 1820s, see the letters of Isabel de Alzaga to Juan Ballestero y Patiño (Gualiguaychú, 1823) in Augustín Isaías de Elía, *Los Ramos Mexía: historia y tradiciones de viejas estancias argentinas,* unpub. ms. (Buenos Aires, n.d.), pp. 208—13.

43. Juan Carlos Nicolau, "Urquiza y su política económica in le período 1835—1851," unpub. ms. (Buenos Aires, n.d.), pp. 9—11.

44. Thomas J. Page, *La Plata, The Argentine Confederation and Paraguay* (New York, 1859), pp. 321—3; and Macchi, *Urquiza, el saladerista,* p. 7. Macchi's work, based on Urquiza's private papers and accounts, is an excellent survey of the economic empire of Urquiza in Entre Ríos.

45. AGN, Sala 10, 37-3-6, "Aduana-Hacienda. Entradas maritimas" (1849).

46. Nicolau, "Urquiza y su política," pp. 1, 6.

47. Robertson, *Letters on Paraguay,* vol. 1, pp. 247—8; and Robertson, *Letters on South America,* vol. 3, pp. 58—9, 82—7.

48. Comdr. Mackinnon, *Steam Warfare on the Parana,* 2 vols. (London, 1848), vol. 1, pp. 251—6.

49. Mallo et al., "El comercio entre Buenos Aires y las provincias," in ANH, *Primer congreso,* p. 266.

50. MacRae, "Report of Journeys," pp. 41—2; and Oscar Luis Ensinck, "El puerto de Rosario, puerto de la Confederación Argentina, 1850—1860," in ANH, *Primer congreso,* pp. 329—30.

51. Larsson de Reinhold, "Notas para el estudio," pp. 154, 161—2. For other information on Córdoba, see Parish, *Buenos Ayres,* 2d ed., p. 282; and María Cristina Vera de Flachs, "Algunas aspectos de la educación y del comercio durante el gobierno de Alejo Carmen Guzmán (1852—1855)," in ANH, *Primer congreso,* pp. 377—85.

52. AGN, Sala 10, 42-11-2 "Colecturía general de aduana" (1830—4); and Sala 10, 37-3-6, "Aduana-Hacienda."

53. Larsson de Reinhold, "Notas para el estudio," pp. 140—1, 147—9.

54. Robert Procter, *Narrative of a Journey Across the Cordillera of the Andes* (London, 1825), p. 47; Schmidtmeyer, *Travels into Chile,* p. 168; Strain, *Cordillera and Pampa,* pp. 201—3; Gardiner, *A Visit to the Indians,* pp. 41—3; P. Campbell Scarlett, *South America and the Pacific,* 2 vols.

(London, 1838), vol. 1, pp. 248–50; and Hibbert, *Narrative of a Journey*, pp. 62–3, 72.

55. Hibbert, *Narrative of a Journey*, pp. 70, 83–5; Schmidtmeyer, *Travels into Chile*, p. 182–3; Procter, *Narrative of a Journey*, p. 41.

56. *REBA*, 1858, vol. 1, p. 47. The tonnage represents eleven months of 1828. Mendoza sent 488 metric tons overland directly to Buenos Aires and San Juan added 296 tons.

57. MacRae, "Report of Journeys," pp. 16–17; and Parish, *Buenos Ayres*, 2d ed., p. 330.

58. Strain, *Cordillera and Pampa*, p. 289.

59. On Mendoza's interprovincial trade, see Robertson, *Letters on Paraguay*, vol. 1, pp. 277–8, vol. 2, pp. 287–9; Parish, *Buenos Ayres*, 2d ed., p. 337; and AGN, Sala 10, 42-3-2, "Aduana. Buques matriculados" (1811–54).

60. Mallo et al., "El comercio entre Buenos Aires y las provincias," in ANH, *Primer congreso*, p. 267; and Blasi, "Las relaciones comerciales," in ANH, *Primer congreso*, pp. 277–8.

61. Andrews, *Journeys from Buenos Ayres*, vol. 1, pp. 203–4, 240–2.

62. Parish, *Buenos Ayres*, 2d ed., pp. 298–9; and Juan Carlos Nicolau, *Antecedentes para la historia de la industria argentina* (Buenos Aires, 1968), pp. 144–5.

63. Nélida Beatriz Robledo, "Introducción al estudio del comercio tucumano, 1848–1852," in ANH, *Primer congreso*, p. 191.

64. Horacio William Bliss, "Algunas consideraciones sobre los ingresos públicos de Tucumán en el periodo 1816–1860," in ANH, *Primer congreso*, p. 387.

65. On Catamarca and La Rioja, see Andrews, *Journey from Buenos Ayres*, vol. 1, p. 48; Blasi, "Las relaciones comerciales," in ANH, *Primer congreso*, p. 281; Luis Eugenio Zolla, "Catamarca: Economía y relaciones comerciales (1838–1852)," in ANH, *Primer congreso*, pp. 343–4; and Graciela Giordano de Rocca, Robert Luis Nanzer, and Elsa Ester Pavón, "Contribución al estudio del comercio entre Catamarca y Córdoba, 1828–1852," in ANH, *Primer congreso*, p. 241.

66. Ernesto J. A. Maeder, *Evolución demográfica argentina de 1810 a 1869* (Buenos Aires, 1969), p. 21. Nicolás Sánchez-Albornoz estimates that Argentina in 1850 had a population of 1.1 million and that Cuba had 1.186 million. See Sánchez-Albornoz, *La población de América Latina, desde los tiempos precolombinos al año 2000* (Madrid, 1973), p. 193.

67. Andrews, *Journey from Buenos Ayres*, vol. 1, p. 38.

68. Maeder, *Evolución demográfica*, pp. 36, 40, 49.

69. D. C. M. Platt, *Latin America and British Trade, 1806–1914* (New York, 1973), pp. 11, 20–2; and María Amalia Duarte, "Contribuciones y empréstitos de San Miguel de Tucumán," in ANH, *Primer congreso*, pp. 151–2.

70. For travelers' descriptions of native textile manufacture, see

Schmidtmeyer, *Travels into Chile,* p. 149; Procter, *Narrative of a Journey,* p. 42; Temple, *Travels in Various Parts,* vol. 1, p. 132; Andrews, *Journey from Buenos Ayres,* vol. 1, pp. 144–5, 151–2, 159–60; and Parish, *Buenos Ayres,* 2d ed., pp. 290–1.

71. Zolla, "Catamarca," in ANH, *Primer congreso,* p. 247. For a good summary of manufacturing in the Interior, see Juan Carlos Nicolau, *Industria argentina y aduana, 1835–1854* (Buenos Aires, 1975), pp. 79–100.

## Conclusion: the arrival of modern technology

1. For railway expansion, see R. Winthrop Wright, *British-Owned Railways in Argentina* (Austin, Tex., 1974), p. 31; Horacio Juan Cuccorese, *Historia de los ferrocarriles en la Argentina* (Córdoba, 1969), and Paul B. Goodwin, Jr., "The Central Argentine Railway and the Economic Development of Argentina, 1854–1881," *Hispanic American Historical Review,* vol. 57, no. 4 (Nov. 1977), pp. 613–32; and Alejandro E. Bunge, *Ferrocarriles argentinos* (Buenos Aires, 1918), pp. 129–31.

2. Juan Alvarez, *Las guerras civiles argentinas* (Buenos Aires, 1972), pp. 36–7; Comisión Directiva del Censo, *Segundo censo de la República Argentina 1895,* 3 vols. (Buenos Aires, 1898) vol. 3, p. 462; and Comisión General de Censos, *Tercer censo nacional 1914,* 10 vols. (Buenos Aires, 1916–19) vol. 10, pp. 406–7.

3. Carl C. Taylor, *Rural Life in Argentina* (Baton Rouge, La., 1948); and Peter H. Smith, *Politics and Beef in Argentina* (New York, 1969).

4. James R. Scobie, *Revolution on the Pampa* (Austin, Tex., 1964); Ernesto Tornquist & Co., *The Economic Development of the Argentine Republic in the Last Fifty Years* (Buenos Aires, 1919); and Dirección General de Estadística de la Nación, *Extracto estadístico de la República Argentina 1915* (Buenos Aires, 1916), pp. 66, 72–3.

5. Comisión General de Censos, *Tercer censo,* vol. 7, p. 517. Also see Scobie, *Buenos Aires,* pp. 70–91; and Simon G. Hanson, *Argentine Meat and the British Market* (Stanford, Calif., 1938).

6. Dirección General de Estadística de la Nación, *Extracto estadístico,* pp. xxx–xxxi.

7. Irving Stone, "British Direct and Portfolio Investment in Latin America Before 1914," *Journal of Economic History,* vol. 37, no. 3 (Sept. 1977), p. 706.

8. Roberto Cortés Conde, *Corrientes inmigratorias y surgimiento de industrias en Argentina, 1870–1914* (Buenos Aires, 1964), appendix.

9. Scobie, *Revolution on the Pampa,* pp. 47, 50; and Carl Solberg, "Farm Workers and the Myth of Export-led Developments in Argentina," *The Americas,* vol. 31, no. 2 (July 1974), pp. 121–38.

10. Comisión General de Censos, *Tercer censo,* vol. 4, pp. 396–7.

11. *Censo industrial y de comercio,* boletín no. 9 (Buenos Aires, 1910), pp. 6–7; and Ibid., boletín no. 13 (1910), p. 14.

12. Tornquist, *Economic Development,* p. 21; Scobie, *Buenos Aires,* p. 178;

and Carlos F. Díaz Alejandro, *Essays on the Economic History of the Argentine Republic* (New Haven, Conn., 1970), p. 41.

13. The figures represent the number of persons living in urban centers of more than 2,000 persons. Comisión General de Censos, *Tercer censo,* vol. 4, pp. 469–75.

14. Dirección General de Estadística de la Nación, *Resúmenes estadísticos retrospectivos* (Buenos Aires, 1914), p. 98.

15. Aldo Ferrer, *La economía argentina: las etapas de su desarrollo y problemas actuales* (Buenos Aires, 1963), p. 115; Roberto Cortés Conde, "Problemas del crecimiento industrial (1870–1914)," in Torcuato di Tella, Gino Germani, and Jorge Graciarena, eds., *Argentina, sociedad de masas* (Buenos Aires, 1965), p. 65; Eduardo F. Jorge, *Industria y concentración económica* (Buenos Aires, 1971), pp. 132–3; A. G. Ford, "British Investment and Argentine Economic Development, 1880–1914," in David Rock, ed., *Argentina in the Twentieth Century* (Pittsburgh, 1975), p. 13. For a perceptive review of the literature on exports and industrialization, see Ezequiel Gallo, "Agrarian Expansion and Industrial Development in Argentina, 1880–1930," in Raymond Carr, ed., *Latin American Affairs* (London, 1970), pp. 45–61.

16. Roger Gravil, "The Anglo-Argentine Connection and the War of 1914–1918," *Journal of Latin American Studies,* vol. 9, no. 1 (May 1977), p. 87.

17. *Censo industrial y de comercio,* boletin no. 13, pp. 14, 18–19; and Comisión Directiva del Censo, *Segundo censo,* vol. 3, pp. 270–1.

18. Comisión General de Censos, *Tercer censo,* vol. 7, pp. 27, 34.

19. Ibid., vol. 8, p. 446, states that 64.5 percent of all industrial investments originated from foreign-born entrepreneurs, but the census does not distinguish between immigrant capital and true foreign capital.

20. The percentage-of-investment figures are for 1900. See Díaz Alejandro, *Essays on Economic History,* p. 7; H. S. Ferns, *Britain and Argentina in the Nineteenth Century* (Oxford, 1960), p. 337; *Censo industrial y de comercio,* boletín no. 18 (1914), p. 11; M. G. and E. T. Mulhall, *Handbook of the River Plate,* 2 vols. (Buenos Aires, 1869; 6th ed., London, 1892), vol. 2, p. 49; and Cortés Conde, *Corrientes immigratorias,* pp. 54–5.

21. *Censo industrial y de comercio,* boletín no. 13, p. 15; and Comisión General de Censos, *Tercer censo,* vol. 7, p. 118.

22. Tornquist, *Economic Development,* p. 21; and Gravil, "Anglo-Argentine Connection," pp. 88–9. Between 1910 and 1914, Argentina imported more than 3.5 million metric tons of coal per year, principally from England. After the war began, coal imports dropped to a low of 700,000 tons in 1917. See Comisión General de Censos, *Tercer censo,* vol. 8, p. 20; and Tornquist, *Economic Development,* p. 98.

23. For the postwar economy, see Guido di Tella and Manuel Zymelman, *Las etapas del desarrollo económico argentino* (Buenos Aires, 1967), chap. 5; Díaz Alejandro, *Essays on Economic History,* chap. 1; H. S. Ferns, *The Argentine Republic, 1560–1971* (New York, 1973), chap. 6;

Smith, *Politics and Beef,* chap. 2; and Adolfo Dorfman, *Historia de la industria argentina,* 3d ed. (Buenos Aires, 1970), chap. 11.

24. Díaz Alejandro, *Essays on Economic History,* p. 52.

25. Di Tella and Zymelman contend that Argentine take-off came in 1933, and Díaz Alejandro notes a significant spurt of industrial production after 1930. Di Tella and Zymelman, *Las etapas del desarrollo,* p. 104; and Díaz Alejandro, *Essays on Economic History,* p. 209.

26. For recent developments in the political economics of Argentina, see Laura Randall, *An Economic History of Argentina in the Twentieth Century* (New York, 1978); and Ferns, *Argentine Republic.* On recent political unrest, see Donald C. Hodges, *Argentina, 1843−1976: The National Revolution and Resistance* (Albuquerque, N.M., 1976).

# Selected bibliography

## Manuscript collections in archives

Archivo General de la Nación, Buenos Aires.
Colección de Manuscritos. Biblioteca Nacional.
  Archivo de Angel Justiniano Carranza.
  Archivo de Mariano Lozano.
  Colección de Manuscritos Relativos a América.
Sala 3. División Nacional. Contaduría.
  "Aduana." 1817–28.
  "Contribución Directa. Entradas Terrestres." 1848–51.
  "Libro de Patentes." 1836
  "Receptoría General. Entradas Terrestres." 1848–51.
Sala 7. Documentación Donada y Adquirida.
  Archivo de Justo José de Urquiza. Sección Mercantil. 1846–58.
  Archivo Dr. Juan E. Anchorena y Sucesores. 1721–1832.
  Colección de Félix Frias.
  Colección de los López. 1807–1922.
  Colección Dr. Ernesto Celesia.
  Colección Dr. Ruiz Guiñazú. 1511–1960.
  Colección Gaspar de Santa Coloma. 1792–1805.
Sala 9. División Colonia. Sección Gobierno.
  "Bando." 1795.
  "Cabildo de Buenos Aires. Correspondencia con el Virrey."
    1797–1816.
  "Comerciales." 1785.
  "Hacienda." 1740–1813.
  "Interior." 1809.
  "Justicia." 1791–9.
  "Licencias y Pasaportes." 1789.
  "Padrones de Buenos Aires." 1812–17.
  "Tribunales." 1791–1802.
Sala 10. División Nacional. Sección Gobierno.
  "Aduana." 1809–60.
  "Capitanía del Puerto." 1844–63.
  "Censos." 1813–64.
  "Estadísticas inéditas." 1828–46.
  "Guerra. Padrones de Campaña." 1815.
  "Hacienda." 1814–53.
  "Hullet Hermanos. Correspondencia." 1816–37.

288 *Selected bibliography*

"Marina." 1809–60.
"Policía." 1814–62.
"Puerto. Movimiento del." 1830–42.
"Staples, Roberto. Gran Bretaña." 1812–18.
Sala 13. División Colonia. Contraduría.
  "Hermandad de Caridad." 1778–1812.
  "Particulares." 1789–1813.
Sección Mapoteca.
  Colleción del Archivo.
  Colleción Biedma-Pillado.
  Colección Senillosa.
Sección Tribunales. Protocolos de Registros Públicos.
  Registro 73 (Comercio 1). 1812–63.
  Registro 74 (Comercio 2). 1824–49.
Latin American Collection of the University of Texas, Austin.
  Great Britain. Public Record Office. Foreign Office 6 (F.O. 6). "General
    Correspondence: Argentine Republic," 1823–52. Microfilm.
  Manuel E. Gondra Manuscript Collection.
  United States Consulate. Buenos Aires. "Despatches from United States
    Consuls in Buenos Aires." 1811–1906. Microfilm.
  United States Embassy. Republic of Argentina. "Despatches from
    United States Ministers to Argentina." 1817–1906. Microfilm.
Museo Bartolomé Mitre. Buenos Aires.
  Soler, Miguel Estanislao, "Papeles." 1844–52.

Published and unpublished works

Academia Nacional de la Historia. *Primer congreso de historia argentina y regional, celebrado en San Miguel de Tucumán, del 14 al 16 de agosto de 1971.* Buenos Aires, 1973.
Aiton, Arthur S. "The Asiento Treaty as Reflected in the Papers of Lord Shelburne." *Hispanic American Historical Review,* vol. 8, no. 2 (May 1928), pp. 167–77.
Alberdi, Juan Bautista. *Bases y puntos de partida para la organización política de la República Argentina.* Buenos Aires, 1914.
  *Organizacion política y económica de la Confederación Argentina.* Paris, 1856.
  *Sistema económico y rentístico de la Confederación Argentina según su Constitución de 1853.* Buenos Aires, 1954.
Albion, Robert G. "British Shipping and Latin America, 1806–1914." *Journal of Economic History,* vol. 11 (Fall 1951), pp. 361–74.
Albion, Robert G., *The Rise of New York Port, 1815–1860.* Hamden, Conn., 1961.
Alden, Dauril. "The Undeclared War of 1773–1777: Climax of Luso-Spanish Platine Rivalry." *Hispanic American Historical Review,* vol. 41, no. 4 (Feb. 1961), pp. 55–74.

*Almanaque Comercial y Guía de Forasteros para el Estado de Buenos Aires. Año de 1855.* Buenos Aires, 1855.

*Almanaque Federal para el Año de Señor 1851.* Buenos Aires, 1851.

*Almanaque Político y de Comercio de la Ciudad de Buenos Aires 1826–1836.* Ed. by J. J. Blondel. Buenos Aires, 1826–36.

*Almanaque Político y de Comercio para 1826.* Prologue by Enrique M. Barba. Buenos Aires, 1969.

Alvarez, Juan. *Las guerras civilies argentinas.* Buenos Aires, 1972.

Andrews, Joseph. *Journey from Buenos Ayres Through the Provinces of Cordova, Tucuman, and Salta to Potsi.* 2 vols. London, 1827.

Azara, Félix de. *Descripción e historia del Paraguay y del Río de la Plata.* Trans. from the French. 2 vols. Madrid, 1847.

*Memoria sobre el estado rural de Río de la Plata en 1801.* Madrid, 1847.

"Viajes inéditos de Azara." *Revista de Derecho, Historia y Letras.* Año X, vol. 28 (Buenos Aires, 1907), pp. 193–212, 363–85, 509–31.

Barth, Richard C., and Dilmus D. James. "Dependency Analysis of Latin America: Some Criticisms, Some Suggestions." *Latin American Research Review,* vol. 11, no. 3 (1975), pp. 3–54.

Beaumont, J. A. B. *Travels in Buenos Ayres, and the Adjacent Provinces of the Río de la Plata.* London, 1828.

Bischoff, James. *A Comprehensive History of the Woollen and Worsted Manufactures.* 2 vols. London, 1842.

Bliss, Horacio William. *Del virreinato a Rosas; ensayo de historia económica argentina, 1776–1829.* Buenos Aires, 1959.

Bousquet, Alfredo. *Estudio sobre el sistema rentístico de la Provincia de Tucumán de 1820 a 1876.* Tucumán, 1878.

Brackenridge, H. M. *Voyage to South America.* 2 vols. London, 1820.

Brand, Charles. *Journal of a Voyage to Peru: A Passage Across the Cordillera of the Andes, in the Winter of 1827.* London, 1828.

Broide, Julio. *La evolución de los precios agropecuarios argentinos en el período 1830–1850.* Buenos Aires, 1951.

Burgin, Miron. *The Economic Aspects of Argentine Federalism, 1820–1852.* Cambridge, Mass., 1946.

Burnley, James. *The History of Wool and Woolcombing.* London, 1889.

Burns, George C. *The American Woolen Manufacturer; a Practical Treatise on the Manufacture of Woolens.* Central Falls, R.I., 1872.

Caldcleugh, Alexander. *Travels in South America During the Years 1819–20–21.* London, 1825.

Campbell, J. *The Spanish Empire in America, by an English Merchant.* London, 1747.

Canabrava, Alice Piffer. *O comércio português no Rio da Prata (1580–1640).* São Paulo, 1944.

Cárcano, Miguel Angel. *Evolución histórica del régimen de la tierra pública, 1810–1916.* Buenos Aires, 1972.

Cardoso, Fernando Enrique, and Enzo Faletto. *Dependencia y desarrollo en América Latina.* Lima, 1967.

290     *Selected bibliography*

Carretero, Andrés M. *Los Anchorena: política y negocios en el siglo XIX.* Buenos Aires, 1970.

*Orígenes de la dependencia económica argentina.* Buenos Aires, 1974.

*La propiedad de la tierra en la época de Rosas.* Buenos Aires, 1972.

*Censo industrial y de comercio.* Buenos Aires, 1910–14.

Church, R. A. "The British Leather Industry and Foreign Competition, 1870–1914." *Economic History Review,* vol. 24, no. 4 (Nov. 1971), pp. 543–70.

"Labour Supply and Innovation, 1800–1860; the Boot and Shoe Industry." *Business History,* vol. 12, no. 1 (Jan. 1970), pp. 25–45.

Cobb, Gwendolin B. "Supply and Transportation for the Potosi Mines, 1545–1640." *Hispanic American Historical Review,* vol. 29, no. 1 (Feb. 1949), 25–45.

Cockroft, James D., André Gunder Frank, and Dale L. Johnson. *Dependence and Underdevelopment: Latin America's Political Economy.* Garden City, N.Y., 1972.

Cole, Arthur H. *The American Wool Manufacture.* 2 vols. Cambridge, Mass., 1926.

and Harold F. Williamson. *The American Carpet Manufacture: A History and Analysis.* Cambridge, Mass., 1941.

Comandrán Ruiz, Jorge. *Evolución demográfica argentina durante el período hispano (1535–1810).* Buenos Aires, 1969.

Comisión Directiva del Censo. *Segundo censo de la República Argentina 1895.* 3 vols. Buenos Aires, 1898.

Comisión General de Censos. *Tercer censo nacional 1914.* 10 vols. Buenos Aires, 1916–19.

Concolorcorvo (Carrió de la Bandera, Alonso). *El Lazarillo: A Guide for Inexperienced Travelers Between Buenos Aires and Lima, 1773.* Trans. by Walter D. Kline. Bloomington, Ind., 1965.

Coni, Emilio. *Historia de las vaquerías de Río de la Plata (1555–1750).* Madrid, 1930.

Cortés Conde, Roberto. *Corrientes inmigratorias y surgimiento de industrias en Argentina, 1870–1914.* Buenos Aires, 1964.

*The First Stage of Modernization in Spanish America.* New York, 1974.

Crump, W. B. *The Leeds Woollen Industry, 1780–1820.* Leeds, Eng., 1931.

and Gertrude Ghorbal. *History of the Huddersfield Woollen Industry.* Huddersfield, Eng., 1935.

Cuccorese, Horacio Juan. *Historia de los ferrocarriles en la Argentina.* Córdoba, 1969.

and José Panettieri. *Argentina, manual de historia económica y social,* vol. 1, *Argentina criolla.* Buenos Aires, 1971.

Darwin, Charles R. *The Voyage of the Beagle.* New York, 1958.

Davis, Ralph. *The Rise of the English Shipping Industry in the 17th and 18th Centuries.* New York, 1962.

Di Tella, Guido, and Manuel Zymelman. *Las etapas del desarrollo económico argentino.* Buenos Aires, 1967.

Di Tella, Torcuato, Gino Germani, and Jorge Graciarena, eds. *Argentina, sociedad de masas.* Buenos Aires, 1965.

Díaz Alejandro, Carlos F. *Essays on the Economic History of the Argentine Republic.* New Haven, Conn., 1970.

Dirección General de Estadísticas de la Nación, *Extracto estadístico de la República Argentina 1915.* Buenos Aires, 1916.

Dirección General de Estadísticas de la Nación, *Resúmenes estadísticos retrospectivos.* Buenos Aires, 1914.

Dobritzhoffer, Martin. *An Account of the Abipones, an Equestria People of Paraguay.* Trans. from the Latin. 3 vols. London, 1822.

Dodd, George. *Days at the Factories.* London, 1843.

Dorfman, Adolfo. *Historia de la industria argentina.* 3d ed. Buenos Aires, 1970.

Elía, Augustín Isaías de. "Los Ramos Mexía: historia y tradiciones de viejas estancias argentinas." Unpub. ms. 321 pp.

Ewing, John S., and Nancy P. Norton. *Broadlooms and Businessmen: a History of the Bigelow-Sanford Carpet Company.* Cambridge, Mass., 1955.

Ferns, H. S. *Argentina.* New York, 1969.

*The Argentine Republic, 1560–1971.* New York, 1973.

*Britain and Argentina in the Nineteenth Century,* Oxford, 1960.

Ferrer, Aldo. *La economía argentina: las etapas de su desarrollo y problemas actuales.* Buenos Aires, 1963.

Fishlow, Albert. *American Railroads and the Transformation of the Antebellum Economy.* Cambridge, Mass., 1965.

*A Five Years' Residence in Buenos Ayres, During the Years 1820 to 1825.* London, 1825.

Frank, André Gunder. *Capitalism and Underdevelopment in Latin America; Historical Studies of Chile and Brazil.* New York, 1969.

Gallo, Ezequiel. "Agrarian Expansion and Industrial Development in Argentina, 1880–1930." In Raymond Carr, ed., *Latin American Affairs,* pp. 45–61. London, 1970.

Gayer, Arthur D., W. W. Rostow, Anna Jacobson Schwartz, and Isaiah Frank. *The Growth and Fluctuation of the British Economy, 1750–1850.* 2 vols. Oxford, 1953.

Gibson, Herbert. *The History and Present State of the Sheep-Breeding Industry in the Argentine Republic.* Buenos Aires, 1893.

Gilberti, Horacio C. E. *Historia económica de la ganadería argentina.* 2d ed. Buenos Aires, 1966.

Glade, William P. *The Latin American Economies; a Study of Their Institutional Evolution.* New York, 1969.

Graeber, Karl Frederick. "Buenos Aires: A Social and Economic History of a Traditional Spanish American City on the Verge of Change, 1810–1855." Ph.D. diss., University of California, Los Angeles, 1972. 307 pp.

Great Britain, Statistical Office. *Annual Statement of the Trade and*

*Navigation of the United Kingdom with Foreign Countries and the British Possessions.* London, 1855—63.

Hadfield. William. *Brazil, the River Plate, and the Falkland Islands.* London, 1854.

Halperín-Donghi, Tulio. *The Aftermath of Revolution in Latin America.* Trans. by Josephine de Bunsen. New York, 1973.

"La expansión ganadera en la campaña de Buenos Aires (1810—1852)." *Desarrollo Económico,* vol. 3, nos. 1—2. (April—Sept. 1963), pp. 57—110.

*Hispanoamérica después de la independencia: consecuencias sociales y económicas de la emancipación.* Buenos Aires, 1972.

*Politics, Economics and Society in Argentina in the Revolutionary Period.* Trans. by Richard Southern. Cambridge, 1975.

*El revisionismo histórico argentino.* Buenos Aires, 1970.

*Revolución y guerra; formación de una élite dirigente en la Argentina criolla.* Buenos Aires, 1972.

Haring. C. H. *Trade and Navigation Between Spain and the Indies in the Time of the Hapsburgs.* Cambridge, Mass., 1918.

Hazard, Blanche Evans. *The Organization of the Boot and Shoe Industry in Massachusetts Before 1875.* New York, 1969.

Head, Francis Bond. *Reports Relating to the Failure of the Rio Plata Mining Association.* London, 1827.

*Rough Notes Taken During Some Rapid Journeys Across the Pampas and Among the Andes.* London, 1826.

Hernando, Diana. "Casa y Familia: Spatial Biographies in Nineteenth Century Buenos Aires," Ph.D. diss., University of California, Los Angeles, 1973. 746 pp.

Hidy, Ralph W. *The House of Baring in American Trade and Finance: English Merchant Bankers at Work, 1763—1861.* Cambridge, Mass., 1949.

Higginbotham, S. W. "Philadelphia Commerce with Latin America, 1820—1830." *Pennsylvania History,* vol. 9 (1942), 252—66.

Humphreys, R. A., ed. *British Consular Reports on the Trade and Politics of Latin America,* vol. 63, *1824—1826,* London, 1940.

*Tradition and Revolt in Latin America and Other Essays,* New York, 1969.

and John Lynch. *The Origins of the Latin American Revolutions, 1808—1826.* New York, 1965.

Innis, Harold A. *The Fur Trade in Canada.* Toronto, 1930.

James, John. *History of the Worsted Manufacture in England, from the Earliest Times.* London, 1857.

Jorge, Eduardo F. *Industria y concentración económica.* Buenos Aires, 1971.

Klein, Herbert S. "Las finanzas del Virreinato del Río de la Plata en 1790." *Desarrollo Económico,* vol. 13, (July 1973), pp. 369—400.

"Structure and Profitability of Royal Finance in the Viceroyalty of the Río de la Plata in 1790." *Hispanic American Historical Review,* vol. 53, no. 3 (Aug. 1973), pp. 440—69.

Kossock, Manfred. *El Virreinato del Río de la Plata; su estructura económica-social.* Trans. from the German. Buenos Aires, 1972.

Kroeber, Clifton, B. *The Growth of the Shipping Industry in the Río de la Plata Region, 1794–1860.* Madison, Wis., 1957.

Landes, David S. *The Unbound Prometheus: Technological Change and Industrial Development in Western Europe from 1750 to the Present.* Cambridge, 1970.

Latham, Wilfred. *The States of the River Plate: Their Industries and Commerce.* London, 1866.

Levin, Jonathan. *The Export Economies: Their Pattern of Development in Historical Perspective.* Cambridge, Mass., 1960.

Lipson, Ephraim. *History of the Woollen and Worsted Industry.* London, 1921.

López Godoy, Pedro M. *Historia de la propiedad y primeros pobladores del Partido de Pergamino.* 2 vols. Pergamino, Argentina, 1973.

Lynch, John. *The Spanish American Revolutions, 1808–1826.* New York, 1973.

   *Spanish Colonial Administration, 1782–1810; the Intendent System in the Viceroyalty of the Río de la Plata.* London, 1958.

MacCann, William. *Two Thousand Miles' Ride Through the Argentine Province.* 2 vols. London, 1853.

Macchi, Manuel. *Urquiza el saladerista.* Buenos Aires, 1971.

McDermott, Charles H., ed. *A History of the Shoe and Leather Industries of the United States.* Boston, 1918.

Maeder, Ernesto J. A. *Evolución demográfica argentina de 1810 a 1869.* Buenos Aires, 1969.

Malaspina, Alejandro. *Viaje al Río de la Plata en el siglo XVIII.* Ed. by Hector R. Ratto. Buenos Aires, 1938.

Manning, William R. *Diplomatic Correspondence of the United States: Inter-American Affairs, 1831–1860,* vol. 1, *Argentina.* Washington, D. C., 1932.

Mansfield, Charles B. *Paraguay, Brazil and the Plate: Letters Written in 1852–1853.* Cambridge, 1856.

Mariluz Urquijo, José María. "La comercialización de la producción sombrera porteña (1810–1835)." *Investigaciones y Ensayos,* vol. 5 (1968), pp. 1–27.

   *Estado e industria, 1810–1862.* Buenos Aires, 1969.

Martínez, Pedro Santos. *Las industrias durante el virreinato, 1776–1810.* Buenos Aires, 1969.

Mendoza, Prudencio de la Cruz. *Historia de la ganadería argentina.* Buenos Aires, 1928.

Miers, John. *Travels in Chile and La Plata.* 2 vols. London, 1826.

Montoya, Alfredo. *Historia de los saladeros argentinos.* Buenos Aires, 1956.

Morison, Samuel Eliot. *The Maritime History of Massachusetts, 1783–1860.* Boston and New York, 1921.

Mörner, Magnus. *The Political and Economic Activities of the Jesuits in the La Plata Region, Hapsburg Era.* Trans. by Albert Read. Stockholm, 1953.

"The Spanish American Hacienda: A Survey of Recent Research and Debate." *Hispanic American Historical Review,* vol. 53, no. 2 (May 1973), pp. 183–216.

Mulhall, M. G. and E. T. *Handbook of the River Plate.* 2 vols. Buenos Aires, 1869.

Nelson, George H. "Contraband Trade Under the Asiento, 1730–1739." *American Historical Review,* vol. 51, no. 1 (Oct. 1945), pp. 55–67.

Nicolau, Juan Carlos. *Antecedentes para la historia de la industria argentina: la industria durante la colonia; la industria argentina de 1810 a 1835.* Buenos Aires, 1968.

*Dorrego Gobernador: economía y finanzas (1826–27).* Buenos Aires, 1977.

*Industria Argentina y aduana, 1835–1854.* Buenos Aires, 1975.

Oddone, Jacinto. *La burguesía terrateniente argentina.* 3d ed. Buenos Aires, 1956.

Parish, Woodbine. *Buenos Ayres, and Provinces of the Río de la Plata.* 2d ed. London, 1852.

*Buenos Ayres and the Río de la Plata: Their Present State, Trade and Debt.* London, 1839.

Perkins, Edwin J. "Financing Antebellum Importers: The Role of Brown Bros. & Co. in Baltimore." *Business History Review,* vol. 45, no. 4 (Winter 1971), pp. 421–51.

Platt, D. C. M. "The Imperialism of Free Trade: Some Reservations." *Economic History Review,* 2d series, vol. 21, no. 2 (Aug. 1968), pp. 296–306.

*Latin America and British Trade, 1806–1914.* New York, 1973.

Puiggrós, Rodolfo. *Historia económica del Río de la Plata.* 4th ed. Buenos Aires, 1974.

Randall, Laura. *An Economic History of Argentina in the Twentieth Century.* New York, 1978.

Randle, P. H. *La ciudad pampeana; geografía urbana, geografía histórica.* Buenos Aires, 1969.

Reber, Vera Blinn. "British Mercantile Houses in Buenos Aires, 1810 to 1880." Ph.D. diss., University of Wisconsin, 1972. 346 pp.

*Registro Estadístico de la Provincia de Buenos Aires.* Buenos Aires, 1854–1862.

*Registro Oficial de la Provincia de Buenos Aires.* Buenos Aires, 1823.

Rimmer, W. G. "Leeds Leather Industry in the Nineteenth Century." *Publications of the Thoresby Society,* vol. 46, misc. 13. Leeds, Eng., 1960.

Ringrose, David R. "Carting in the Hispanic World: An Example of Divergent Development." *Hispanic American Historical Review,* vol. 50, no. 1 (Feb. 1970), pp. 30–51.

Robertson, J. P. and W. P. *Letters on Paraguay; Comprising an Account of a Four Years' Residence in that Republic Under the Government of the Dictator Francia.* 2d ed. 3 vols. London, 1839.

*Letters on South America; Comprising Travels on the Banks of the Parana and Río de la Plata.* 3 vols. London, 1843.

Rodney, Caesar A., and John Graham. *Report on the Present State of the United Provinces.* London, 1819.

Rodríguez, Mario. "The Genesis of Economic Attitudes in the Río de la Plata." *Hispanic American Historical Review,* vol. 36, no. 2 (May 1956), pp. 171–89.

Rodríguez Molas, Ricardo. *Historia social del gaucho.* Buenos Aires, 1968.

Rosas, Juan Manuel de. *Instrucciones a los mayordomos de estancia.* Buenos Aires, 1951.

Rostow, W. W. *British Economy of the Nineteenth Century.* Oxford, 1948.

Sánchez-Albornoz, Nicolás. *La población de América Latina, desde los tiempos pre-colombinos al año 2000.* Madrid, 1973.

*La saca de mulas de Salta al Perú, 1778–1809.* Rosario, 1965.

Sbarra, Noel H. *Historia del alambrado en la Argentina.* Buenos Aires, 1964.

*Historia de las aguadas y el molino.* La Plata, Argentina, 1961.

Scarlett, P. Campbell. *South America and the Pacific; Comprising a Journey Across the Pampas and the Andes, from Buenos Ayres to Valparaiso, Lima, and Panama.* 2 vols. London, 1838.

Schmieder, Oscar. "Alteration of the Argentine Pampa in the Colonial Period." *University of California Publications in Geography,* vol. 2, no. 10 (1927), pp. 303–21.

"The Historic Geography of Tucumán." *University of California Publications in Geography,* vol. 2, no. 12 (1928), pp. 359–86.

"The Pampa, a Natural or Culturally Induced Grassland?" *University of California Publications in Geography,* vol. 2, no. 8 (1927), pp. 255–70.

Scobie, James R. *Argentina, a City and a Nation.* 2d ed. New York, 1971.

*Buenos Aires: Plaza to Suburb, 1870–1910.* New York, 1974.

*Revolution on the Pampa: a Social History of Argentine Wheat, 1860–1910.* Austin, Tex., 1964.

Sempat Assadourian, Carlos. *El tráfico de esclavos en Córdoba de Angola a Potosí, siglos XVI–XVII.* Córdoba, 1960.

Shaw, Joseph J. *The Wool Trade of the United States, History of a Great Industry.* Washington, D.C., 1909.

Sigsworth, Eric. *Black Dyke Mills, a History.* Liverpool, 1958.

Smith, Peter H. *Politics and Beef in Argentina: Patterns of Conflict and Change.* New York, 1969.

Smith, W. B., and A. H. Cole. *Fluctuations in American Business, 1790–1860.* Cambridge, Mass., 1935.

Socolow, Susan Migden. "Economic Activities of the Porteño Merchants: The Viceregal Period." *Hispanic American Historical Review,* vol. 45, no. 1 (Feb. 1975), pp. 1–24.

"The Merchants of Viceregal Buenos Aires." Ph.D. diss., Columbia University, 1973. 337 pp.

Southey, Thomas. *The Rise, Progress and Present State of Colonial Wools.* London, 1848.

Stein, Stanley J. and Barbara H. *The Colonial Heritage of Latin America;*

*Essays on Economic Dependence in Perspective.* New York, 1970.

Strain, Isaac G. *Cordillera and Pampa, Mountain and Plain. Sketches of a Journey to Chile, and the Argentine Provinces in 1849.* New York, 1853.

Sunkel, Osvaldo, and Pedro Paz. *El subdesarrollo latinoamericano y la teoría del desarrollo.* México, 1970.

Tapson, Alfred J. "Indian Warfare on the Pampa During the Colonial Period." *Hispanic American Historical Review,* vol. 42, no. 1 (Feb. 1962), pp. 1−28.

Taullard, A. *Los planos mas antiguos de Buenos Aires, 1580−1880.* Buenos Aires, 1940.

Taylor, Carl C. *Rural Life in Argentina.* Baton Rouge, La., 1948.

Temple, Edmond. *Travels in Various Parts of Peru, Including a Year's Residence in Potosí.* 2 vols. London, 1830.

Tjarks, German O. E. *El Consulado de Buenos Aires y sus proyecciones en la historia del Río de la Plata.* 2 vols. Buenos Aires, 1962.

and Alicia Vidaurreta. *El comercio inglés y el contrabando: neuvos aspectos en el estudio de la política económica en el Río de la Plata, 1807−1810.* Buenos Aires, 1962.

Tooke, Thomas, and William Newmarch. *A History of Prices and the State of the Circulation from 1792 to 1856.* 5 vols. London, 1838−57.

Tornquist & Co., Ernesto. *The Economic Development of the Argentine Republic in the Last Fifty Years.* Buenos Aires, 1919.

U.S. Treasury. "Annual Reports of Commerce and Navigation of the United States," in *Executive Documents* of the U.S. Senate and House of Representatives. Washington, D.C., 1822−62.

Vicuña Mackenna, Benjamín. *La Argentina en el año 1855.* Buenos Aires, 1936.

Vidal, E. E. *Picturesque Illustrations of Buenos Ayres and Montevideo.* London, 1820.

Villalobos, Sergio R. *Comercio y contrabando en el Río de la Plata y Chile, 1700−1811.* Buenos Aires, 1965.

Watkins, Melville H. "A Staple Theory of Economic Growth." *Canadian Journal of Economics and Political Science,* vol. 29, no. 2 (May 1963), pp. 144−58.

Webster, Charles K., ed. *Britain and the Independence of Latin America, 1812−1830: Select Documents from the Foreign Office Archives.* 2 vols. London and New York, 1938.

Wedovoy, Enrique. *La evolución económica rioplatense a fines del siglo XVIII y principios del siglo XIX a la luz de la historia del seguro.* La Plata, Argentina, 1967.

Williams, Judith Blow. "The Establishment of British Commerce with Argentina." *Hispanic American Historical Review,* vol. 15, no. 1 (Feb. 1935), pp. 43−64.

Williamson, Harold F., ed. *The Growth of the American Economy, an Introduction to the Economic History of the United States.* New York, 1944.

Wright, Chester Whitney. *Wool-Growing and the Tariff; a Study in the Economic History of the United States.* Cambridge, Mass., 1910.
Wright, Winthrop R. *British-Owned Railways in Argentina.* Austin, Tex., 1974.
Zimmerman, A. F. "The Land Policy of Argentina, with Particular Reference to the Conquest of the Southern Pampas." *Hispanic American Historical Review,* vol. 25, no. 1 (1945), pp. 3–26.
Zorraquín Becú, Ricardo. "Orígenes de comercio rioplatense (1580–1620)." *Anuario de Historia Argentina,* vol. 5 (1943–5), pp. 71–105.

# Index

agriculture, *see* production, agricultural
Anchorena family
  as landowners, 151, 158, 174–5, 200
  Nicolás de Anchorena as landowner, 186–7
  as merchants, 86, 108, 119, 176–8
  in politics, 176–7

Buenos Aires
  as colonial commercial town, 21
  costs of imports, 22
  domestic trade of, 34
  the port of, 8–9, 70–2, *see also* shipping
  as viceregal capital, 28–9

Carlos II, King of Spain, 24
carting, *see* transportation, oxcarting
cattle raising, *see* production, cattle raising
*chacras, see* production, agricultural
Colônia do Sacramento, 26
commerce, *see* trade
communications on the pampa, 185
contraband, 23–6, 31–2
  extent of, 9, 10, 26
  interpretation of, 26, 32
Córdoba
  as colonial administrative capital, 14
  trade of, 14, 216–17
Corrientes, production in, 215
customs duties, *see* taxes and customs

drought, *see* production, effect of drought on

emphyteusis, *see* policies, economic
Entre Ríos, production in, 214–15

*estancia, see* production: cattle raising; sheep raising
estancieros, *see* landowners

family, rural, 157–9
farming, *see* production, agricultural
fleet system, *see* shipping, foreign
free trade, *see* policies, economic

growth
  Argentine economic, 230
  export-led, 1, 8, 48–9
  interpretation of, 6
  limits on Argentine economic, 225

hides, trade in, 24–5, 30, 40
  *see also* production, cattle processing

immigration
  to Buenos Aires, 115–16
  and economic development, 228
  on the pampa, 157, 160–1, 163
imperialism, economic,
  interpretation of, 69–70, 94–6
income, distribution of, 7
Indians
  Guaraní, 14
  on the pampa, 170, 172–3, 192
  as threat to transport, 12, 206
industrialization
  Argentine, 229–32
  North Atlantic, impact on Argentina, 50–1
industry
  Argentine textile, 222–3
  boatbuilding, 100–1
  candle and soap, 66–7
  carpets and blankets, 62–3
  cart building, 17
  cattle processing, 109–14, 120

industry *(cont.)*
  leather, 51−4
  supply of raw materials, 47,
    57−8, 63−6, 69
  tanning, 24−7
  woolen, 51−2, 58−61
Interior provinces
  depression, interpretation of,
    201−2
  economy of, 103
  trade of, 34−5
investment
  by the Anchorenas, 181
  Argentine, 88, 110, 121
  of colonial merchants, 31
  foreign, 87−8, 92, 227−8
  in land, 153−4
  rural, 166−7

labor, rural, 38, 133, 137, 161−4
  in agriculture, 169−70
  of the Anchorenas, 187−90
  the gaucho, 165
  interpretation of, 161
  occupations, 155−6
  in sheep raising, 139−40, 168
  slaves, 42, 163
  slaves of the Anchorenas, 187−8
  in Uruguay, 42
  wages, 43, 164
  wages of the Anchorena's,
    189−90
labor, urban, 31, 114−16
  slaves in Buenos Aires, 114
land, acquisition of, 149−52
  by the Anchorenas, 179, 181−3
  in frontier expansion, 123−4,
    126
  interpretation of, 3
land
  rental of, 151−2
  value of, 152−3
landholding, family, 164
  interpretation of, 146−7, 123
  Obligado family, 166−71
  reduction in size of, 162
  size of, 3, 125−6, 147, 150,
    158−60
  *see also* Anchorena family
landowners, 147−9, 160, 180,
  200
landownership, 8, 159

manufacturing, *see* industry
marketing, retail
  of the Anchorenas, 194−6
  rural, 43, 142−3
marketing, wholesale
  of the Anchorenas, 196−8
  cattle drives, 143−4
  marketplaces, 105−9
  rural, 119−20
  warehouses, 107−8, 199
markets
  domestic of Buenos Aires, 99,
    105−7
  foreign, 2−3, 20
  for local provision, 33
  and production, 1
Mendoza, trade of, 17, 217−18
mercantilism and monopoly,
    Spanish, 18
merchants
  Argentine, 86−7, 108, 117−21
  British, 85
  of Buenos Aires, 17
  colonial wholesale, 31
  foreign, 84−7, 88−90, 92, 109,
    117−18
  immigrant, 117−18
  interpretation of Argentine,
    116−17
  North American, 85−7, 91
  rural Argentine, 142−4, 194−6
mines, silver, *see* Potosi
Montevideo, trade of, 35
mules, Salta fair, 12
  trade in, 12, 14, 16
  *see also* transportation, packmules

northern provinces, trade of, 219

opportunity, social, 7−8
oxen, *see* production, breeding of
  oxen

pampa
  economy of, 123, 144−5
  physical description, 124−5, 126
Paraguay
  as production center, 14
  production of yerba, 15
  trade of, 16
policies, economic
  Bourbon reforms, 27, 29, 32
  emphyteusis, 149−50

of Perón, 233
trade regulations, 73−4
during wartime, 47−8
population
of Argentina, 221−2
of Argentine cities, 229
of Buenos Aires city, 22, 34, 116, 227
of Córdoba, 14
of the Interior provinces, 35−6
of Potosí, 10
ratios of women to men, 221−2
rural, 39, 155
Potosí
commerce of, 34
decline of mining, 204
labor in, 10
as a market, 2, 9, 11, 20
silver mining complex of, 9−11
prices of raw materials, 92−4
production
agricultural, 129−31, 134−6, 141−2, 168−71
in Argentina, 2−3
breeding of oxen, 17
cattle processing, 110−12
cattle raising, 2−3, 37, 40, 129, 132−3, 136−8
cattle raising by the Anchorenas, 184−7, 190−4
effect of drought on, 127−8, 135
effect of drought on the Anchorenas, 192−4
interpretation of agricultural, 140
on the pampa, 123−4, 125, 144−5
sheep raising, 129, 136, 138−40, 167
structure of ranching, 131−4
vaquerías, 36−7
zones of, 131−2
profits
in agriculture, 170
in cattle raising, 45, 110, 154−5, 167−8
in river trade, 178
pulpería, *see* marketing, retail

ranching, *see* production: cattle raising; sheep raising
raw materials, *see* industry; prices of raw materials

retailing, *see* marketing, retail
revolution, industrial, *see* industrialization
Rosas, Juan Manuel de
as cattle processor, 110
interpretation of historical role, 146−7
as landowner, 179
political policies, 150
as politician, 127
as ranch administrator, 137, 179, 185−6

*saladeros, see* industry, cattle processing
Salta
as commercial town, 17
mule fair of, 12
Santa Fe as center of yerba trade, 15
river trade at, 17, 216
Santiago del Estero, as commercial town, 16
settlement
of colonial Argentina, 11−12
of the frontier, 39
shipping, foreign
at Buenos Aires, 99
fleet system, 21
permission ships, 22
in the Río de la Plata, 70−2, 75−7
*see also* transportation
silver, *see* trade; Potosí
slaughterhouses, *see* industry, cattle processing
slaves
British trade in, 25−6
import of, 25
trade and contraband in, 23
*see also* labor, rural; labor, urban
smuggling, *see* contraband
sources for Argentine economic history, 5
Spain, products of, 22
stockyards, *see* marketing, wholesale

taxes and customs
provincial rivalry, 206−7
Spanish, 18
technology
agricultural, 134−6, 141−2
arrival of modern, 1, 225−6

technology *(cont.)*
  of cattle processing, 111–12
  and depression of the Interior,
    202
  in manufacturing, 50
  of shipping, 77, 98
  of tanning, 54–7
  traditional technology and
    growth, 1, 208
  of transportation, 225–6
  in woolen industry, 59–61
theory
  dependency, 4, 5, 229
  staple theory of economic
    growth, 5–7, 97–8, 233–4
tobacco, royal monopoly of, 16
trade
  balance of, 30, 77–8, 80–4
  disruptions of, 46–9, 90–2,
    203–6
  domestic, 9, 11, 102, 119–20,
    212–14, 220–1
  domestic and foreign
    competition, 202–3
trade, domestic
  of the river provinces, 40,
    98–100, 177–8
  routes, 13, 18
trade, foreign
  at Buenos Aires, 18, 29–30,
    75–7, 78–9
  credit in, 88–90
  export products, 24, 30, 79–80,
    81–3, 109
  exports of silver, 23, 30

  import products, 24, 30, 78–9,
    82–3
  imports of wheat and flour, 73,
    79
  with Spain, 21, 29
  with the United Kingdom, 83
  with the United States, 83
transportation
  cost of, 11
  cost of oxcarting, 19, 20, 143
  cost of river shipping, 19, 20
  immigrants in river shipping,
    115–16
  oxcarting, 16, 19, 101–5, 107,
    208–12
  packmules, 11, 102–3, 104
  railways, 108
  river shipping, 98–101, 118,
    178, 210–13
  technology of, 20
  traditional modes of, 9, 11
Tucumán
  cart trades of, 16
  trade of, 218–19

Uruguay
  cattle production in, 38–9, 41–6
  hide production in, 38–9, 43–4

vaquerías, *see* production, vaquerías
villages, rural, 155–6

wine of Mendoza, 17–18, 218
women on the pampa, 157

yerba, *see* Paraguay

# Cambridge Latin American Studies

1  Simon Collier. *Ideas and Politics of Chilean Independence, 1808–1833*
2  Michael P. Costeloe. *Church Welath in Mexico: A study of the Juzgado de Campellanias in the Archbishopric of Mexico, 1800–1856*
3  Peter Calvert. *The Mexican Revolution 1910–1914: The Diplomacy of Anglo-American Conflict*
4  Richard Graham. *Britain and the Onset of Modernization in Brazil, 1850–1914*
5  Herbert S. Klein. *Parties and Political Change in Bolivia, 1880–1952*
6  Leslie Bethell. *The Abolition of the Brazilian Slave Trade: Britain, Brazil and the Slave Trade Question, 1807–1869*
7  David Barkin and Timothy King. *Regional Economic Development: The River Basin Approach in Mexico*
8  Celso Furtado. *Economic Development of Latin America: Historical Background and Contemporary Problems:* (second edition)
9  William Paul McGreevey. *An Economic History of Colombia, 1845–1930*
10  D. A. Brading. *Miners and Merchants in Bourbon Mexico, 1763–1810*
11  Jan Bazant. *Alienation of Church Wealth in Mexico: Social and Economic Aspects of the Liberal Revolution, 1856–1875*
12  Brian R. Hamnett. *Politics and Trade in Southern Mexico, 1750–1821*
13  J. Valerie Fifer. *Bolivia: Land, Location, and Politics since 1825*
14  Peter Gerhard. *A Guide to the Historical Geography of New Spain*
15  P. J. Bakewell. *Silver Mining and Society in Colonial Mexico, Zacatecas 1564–1700*
16  Kenneth R. Maxwell. *Conflicts and Conspiracies: Brazil and Portugal, 1750–1808*
17  Verena Martinez-Alier. *Marriage, Class and Colour in Nineteenth-Century Cuba: A Study of Racial Attitudes and Sexual Values in a Slave Society*
18  Tulio Halperin-Donghi. *Politics, Economics and Society in Argentina in the Revolutionary Period*
19  David Rock. *Politics in Argentina 1890–1930: the Rise and Fall of Radicalism*
20  Mario Gongora. *Studies in the Colonial History of Spanish America*
21  Arnold J. Bauer. *Chilean Rural Society from the Spanish Conquest to 1930*
22  James Lockhart and Enrique Otte. *Letters and People of the Spanish Indies: The Sixteenth Century*
23  Leslie B. Rout, Jr. *The African Experience in Spanish America: 1502 to the Present Day*
24  Jean A. Meyer. *The Cristero Rebellion: The Mexican People between Church and State, 1926–1929*
25  Stefan De Vylder. *Allende's Chile: The Political Economy of the Rise and Fall of the Unidad Popular*

26    Kenneth Duncan and Ian Rutledge, with the collaboration of Colin Harding. *Land and Labour in Latin America: Essays on the Development of Agrarian Capitalism in the Nineteenth and Twentieth Centuries*

27    Guillermo Lora, edited by Laurence Whitehead. *A History of the Bolivian Labour Movement, 1848–1971*

28    Victor Nunes Leal, translated by June Henfrey. *Coronelismo: The Municipality and Representative Government in Brazil*

29    Anthony Hall. *Drought and Irrigation in North-east Brazil*

30    S. M. Socolow. *The Merchants of Buenos Aires 1778–1810: Family and Commerce*

31    Charles F. Nunn. *Foreign Immigrants in Early Bourbon Mexico, 1700–1760*

32    D. A. Brading. *Haciendas and Ranchos in the Mexican Bajio*

33    Billie R. DeWalt. *Modernization in a Mexican Ejido: A Study in Economic Adaptation*

34    David Nicholls. *From Dessalines to Duvalier: Race, Colour and National Independence in Haiti*

35    Jonathan C. Brown. *A Socioeconomic History of Argentina, 1776–1860*